LEARN TO READ GREEK

LEARN TO READ
GREEK
PART 1

Andrew Keller
Collegiate School

Stephanie Russell
Collegiate School

Yale
UNIVERSITY PRESS
New Haven & London

Yale University Press books may be purchased in quantity for educational, business, or promotional use. For information, please e-mail sales. press@yale.edu (U.S. office) or sales@yaleup.co.uk (U.K. office).

PUBLISHER: Mary Jane Peluso
EDITORIAL ASSISTANT: Elise Panza
PROJECT EDITOR: Timothy Shea
PRODUCTION CONTROLLER: Aldo Cupo

Designed by James J. Johnson.
Set in Arno Roman type by Integrated Composition Systems.
Printed in the United States of America.

Library of Congress Cataloging-in-Publication Data

Keller, Andrew, 1960–
    Learn to read Greek / Andrew Keller, Stephanie Russell.
        p. cm.
    Text in English and Greek.
    Includes index.
    ISBN 978-0-300-11589-5 (part 1) — ISBN 978-0-300-11590-1 (part 2)   1. Greek language—Grammar.
2. Greek language—Grammar—Problems, exercises, etc.   3. Greek language—Readers.   I. Russell,
Stephanie, 1946– II. Title.
    PA258.K435 2011
    488.2'421—dc22   2011003149

A catalogue record for this book is available from the British Library.

This paper meets the requirements of ANSI/NISO Z39.48-1992 (Permanence of Paper).

10 9 8 7 6 5

Cover illustration: Rembrandt van Rijn, *Aristotle with a Bust of Homer,* 1653. The Metropolitan Museum of Art, New York. Purchase, special contributions and funds given or bequeathed by friends of the Museum, 1961 (61.198). Image copyright © The Metropolitan Museum of Art.

CONTENTS

CHAPTER 2

CHAPTER 4

PREFACE

Learn to Read Greek is closely modeled on *Learn to Read Latin,* our textbook published by Yale University Press in 2003. *LTRG* is both an introductory grammar and a first reader for the Attic dialect of ancient Greek. The book aims to help students acquire as quickly as possible an ability to read and appreciate the great works of ancient Greek literature. Learning the language of ancient Greece is a lifelong challenge and an abiding pleasure for the curious intellect. Many factors combine to make ancient Greek a difficult language to master: a large, nuanced vocabulary (more than three times the number of words in extant Latin); extensive and inconstant morphology for nouns, adjectives, and verbs; and a wide variety of dialects offering many variants in spelling, syntax, and word usage. In addition, various authors have their own specially developed vocabularies, syntactic habits, and writing styles. One must, in effect, learn the Greek of Thucydides, the Greek of Sophocles, the Greek of Homer. If the task is difficult, however, the rewards for the devoted effort of serious students are great: what is to be gained is nothing less than direct access to the words and thoughts of Plato, Euripides, Aristophanes, and many others.

LTRG differs from many other beginning Greek books in offering students interesting and rewarding samples of real Greek texts for reading practice from the third chapter on. These readings quickly become substantial and challenging, and, in our view, are a far better means for studying the language than fabricated stories in Greek such as often appear in other textbooks. While *LTRG* is an Attic Greek text, we include readings containing forms from other dialects (with appropriate explanatory notes) in order to expose students to a wider range of authors and to accustom them to non-Attic forms that they will encounter in Attic Greek texts. We also include readings from Greek writers of the Roman period who wrote in Attic Greek, which by then was recognized as an important literary language and used by a select number of educated writers.

Our Latin and Greek texts both drew inspiration from books written by our former colleagues at the Brooklyn College of CUNY Latin/Greek Institute: *Latin: An Intensive Course,* by Floyd L. Moreland and Rita M. Fleischer, and *Greek: An Intensive Course,* by Hardy Hansen and Gerald M. Quinn. Floyd Moreland, founder of the Latin/Greek Institute, provided us with our most important guiding principles for teaching Latin and Greek: first, if clearly and completely presented, no element of these languages is more difficult for students to learn than any other; and second, excessive simplification and omission are harmful, not helpful. Summer after summer at the LGI and for many years in our own teaching, these principles have been tested and vindicated, and we have used them to guide our decision making throughout the writing of *LTRG.*

We could not have produced *LTRG* in its present form without the aid of the digital version of the *Thesaurus Linguae Graecae.* This excellent online resource made it possible to choose vocabulary for each chapter based on each word's frequency in a selected list of major authors and texts. In this way we could be sure that students using this textbook will learn words that they will encounter regularly when reading classical Greek. Special effort was made to include in the early chapters the words that occur most often in Attic Greek. Searching the *TLG* also helped us find for each chapter appropriate readings drawn from a wide range of prose and poetry. These are the authors that we used most frequently in our searches not only to find passages for inclusion but also to answer questions of meaning and usage:

Aeschines	Isocrates
Aeschylus	Lysias
Aristophanes	Plato
Demosthenes	Sophocles
Euripides	Thucydides
Herodotus	Xenophon

To resolve broader questions of usage, word frequency, or morphology, or to confirm impressions we had formed from our initial searches, we often searched the works of every *TLG* author from the eighth to the fourth centuries B.C.E. In some instances, particularly to confirm the rarity of Greek forms, we searched the works of every *TLG* author from the eighth century B.C.E. to the first century C.E. These searches allowed us to include information in the textbook about the rarity of particular words, the occurrence of verbs in certain moods and voices, and the existence or nonexistence of certain forms. They also informed our decisions about the order of presentation in the textbook and led us to exclude forms and words that we discovered were uncommon in Attic Greek. Statements in the textbook about the frequency of certain forms or about the most common meanings of Greek words are based on our examination of evidence gathered from the *TLG*.

ACKNOWLEDGMENTS

Andrew Keller wishes to thank Collegiate School for its generous support of the work on this textbook through Curriculum Grants awarded for the summers of 2006–2009. Professors Naomi Rood, William Stull, and Joshua Reynolds of Colgate University used the textbook and workbook in manuscript form. All found many errors, raised many astute questions, and offered excellent advice. Their participation in this project is greatly appreciated. Professor Maria Pantelia of the University of California, Irvine, the Director of the *Thesaurus Linguae Graecae,* was prompt, friendly, and helpful whenever questions or problems arose. Special mention and thanks are owed to Felipe Gurascier, who contributed greatly with his diligent survey of vocabulary frequency in each chapter of the textbook, and to Hunter Ford, the Collegiate student who created the excellent map of Greek dialects included in the Introduction.

Stephanie Russell is most grateful to Collegiate School for a one-semester sabbatical in 2006 that provided time for writing this textbook. Sincere thanks are also due to the members of the Collegiate Foreign Language Department for their patience, generous support, and encouragement. Professor Jonathan Ready of the Classics Department at Indiana University at Bloomington used an incomplete version of this textbook in a Greek Prose Composition class. His comments and encouragement were most helpful. Thanks also go to Stanislav Dikiy, who organized all vocabulary files with intelligence, patience, and fortitude.

We extend our warm thanks to the Greek students at Colgate University and at Collegiate School who used early versions of our book, caught countless errors, and offered many helpful suggestions. No contributions to this book are more valued than theirs.

We are sincerely grateful to the classicists who reviewed the manuscript of this book for Yale University Press: Kasia Allen (University of Wisconsin-Madison), Richard P. Martin (Stanford University), Kirk Ormand (Oberlin College), Louise Pratt (Emory University), Philip E. Schwartz (Friends Seminary), and Pavlos Sfyroeras (Middlebury College).

After she saw the Latin book through to publication, Mary Jane Peluso at Yale University Press encouraged us to write a Greek book. Tim Shea, the Projects Editor for Languages, ably took over from Mary Jane and carried this book through to completion, handling a variety of thorny issues along the way. Susan Laity, our manuscript editor, helped us see many inconsistencies and infelicities. We are grateful to them all.

HOW TO USE
LEARN TO READ GREEK

The following is a detailed description of the components of *Learn to Read Greek,* accompanied by suggestions for their most effective use by students and teachers. Only if the textbook is used in partnership with the workbook can the best results be achieved.

Overview: Components and Organization

The main text of *LTRG* comprises sixteen chapters, divided into two parts, that present all the basic morphology and syntax for an elementary course in Attic Greek. Depending on the amount of time available for one's course (meetings per week, minutes per meeting), these sixteen chapters can be studied in two or three college semesters or in two or three years in high school.[1]

The actual teaching and learning units of this book are the sections, and there are approximately ten sections in each chapter. Two or three weeks in college (perhaps twice as much in high school) should be devoted to the study of each chapter. Substantial vocabulary lists and complex Greek sentences (both synthetic and authentic) allow students to significantly advance their knowledge of syntax and to practice and refine their reading skills. The book as a whole, as well as each of the chapters taken individually, aims not at hasty coverage of material but at thorough understanding and engagement as soon as possible with Greek literary texts.

Vocabulary Lists

Each chapter begins with a list of new words to be memorized, placed first for ready reference. The vocabulary has been chosen to provide students with words that appear commonly in a wide variety of Greek authors. In many chapters certain pieces of morphology and syntax must be presented before new vocabulary is learned, but the vocabulary list is given prominence to emphasize its importance and to encourage its acquisition by students as early as possible in the study of each chapter. As the book progresses and chapters are devoted to more advanced syntax, words that are commonly found with the constructions to be learned in those chapters are included in the vocabulary.

At the back of both the textbook and the workbook are complete Greek–English and English–Greek

---

1. An ideal arrangement for a three-semester course would be to begin in the spring term or semester and cover six chapters, then complete the book over the two semesters of the following year. This would allow ample time for readings.

vocabulary lists containing all the words that appear in the chapter vocabularies. Some additional meanings and idioms that appear only in the vocabulary notes or elsewhere in the textbook are included. These lists also include the names of the gods and cardinal and ordinal numbers.

Vocabulary Notes

Vocabulary notes follow the word list in each chapter. Since essential information about the forms, meanings, and usage of new vocabulary words is contained in these notes, students should always read them, and the teacher should emphasize the most important points. Particularly in the early chapters, important information about the forms of vocabulary entries (adjectives, principal parts of verbs, etc.) and new morphology is included in the vocabulary notes. This information should be presented in conjunction with the new material in the chapters. It is included in the vocabulary notes for ease of reference, and students should consult these notes frequently while mastering the material in the chapter. (For those who would like to learn more about the development of the Greek language, information has also been included about word formation and Indo-European linguistic features.) Immediately following the vocabulary notes in each chapter are lists of English **derivatives** and **cognates** for many of the new words in the chapter. Although by no means exhaustive, the lists allow students to see how Greek words are related to English words.

Summaries and Synopsis Blanks

When beginning each new chapter, students should tear out from the back of the workbook all the **summaries** for that chapter. These summaries include a copy of the vocabulary list, a list of the new verbs with information about the voices in which they occur and their meanings in different voices, and—most important—one or two pages of compact summaries of the new morphology and syntax introduced in the chapter. These summaries should be consulted when drills on new material are being done in class, and they can serve as valuable learning aids as students work toward mastery of the material presented in each chapter. Included after the summaries for all the chapters are verb **synopsis blanks** that can be torn out and used to make multiple copies for drills.

Sections and Drills

The **sections** that present new morphology and syntax are numbered consecutively from Part 1 through Part 2 of the textbook, as in a reference grammar. Frequently throughout these sections (as well as in the vocabulary notes), brief instructions appear in capital letters (for example, "MEMORIZE THIS IRREGULAR FORM"). These instructions are addressed directly to students and are intended to ensure that no essential point is overlooked.

Following many of the morphology and syntax sections are sentences pointing to appropriate **drills** in the workbook for individual sections or groups of sections. The drills are designed to reinforce new material as it is presented. The sentences pointing to appropriate drills indicate the natural breaks within chapters, and they can be used to determine how much material to introduce in a class period.

Drills on new forms and syntax include only vocabulary from earlier chapters, unless new morphology or syntax requires the use of new vocabulary. For example, when the morphology of a particular type of third-declension noun is introduced, it is necessary to include new nouns in the corresponding drills to reinforce the new morphology. Also, additional drills on new verbs are added in appropriate places in order to provide more complete coverage of the morphology of new verbs.

Drills are provided in such sufficiently large numbers that some can be done at sight in class, others assigned for homework, and still others used for individual work or quizzes.

Exercises

Following the drills in each chapter in the workbook, **exercises** are provided that allow comprehensive practice of all new vocabulary, morphology, and syntax introduced in a chapter, while reinforcing material presented in earlier chapters. The exercises, consisting of synthetic sentences, are divided into three sections. After the first two chapters, the first section contains Greek sentences *without* accents, and correct accents must be added before the sentences are translated; the second section offers Greek sentences for translation; and the third section provides sentences in English to be translated into Greek. This last section gives students practice in writing clear, correct Greek in plausible Greek word order. The exercises should not be assigned until all new material in a chapter has been introduced, unless a teacher selects only those exercise sentences that contain material already presented.

In the synthetic Greek sentences (drills, exercises, and examples used in the textbook), we have tried to include only usages found in extant Attic Greek; often exact phrases from Greek texts have been included in these sentences.

In our experience, *LTRG* works best when translations of some exercise sentences are assigned as written homework, while class time is devoted to the reading of other exercise sentences at sight. As many as sixty such sentences are provided in the early chapters, but this number is gradually reduced as it becomes possible to reinforce new material through unabridged Greek passages.

Readings

Beginning in Chapter 3, the introduction of new material is followed by a section of **short readings**, unabridged Greek passages drawn from a wide range of ancient authors. Each short reading is preceded by a brief introduction to establish context.[2] Beneath each reading are vocabulary glosses for words that do not appear in the chapter vocabulary lists.[3] The inclusion of these short readings, which steadily increase in number and length, reflects our belief that the best way to learn to read Greek is to study specimens of authentic Greek as soon as possible. The short readings have been chosen to reinforce the vocabulary, morphology, and syntax of the chapters in which they appear and to provide examples of various word orders from Greek prose and poetry. Many of these short readings can be read at sight in class, and some

---

2. Introductions are usually *not* provided for short readings that are identified as fragments.
3. Vocabulary glosses for each reading are listed in the order in which the words appear in the passage for ease of use by the student. A dagger (†) indicates a word requiring a special note.

may be read before all the new material of a chapter has been introduced, provided that they not contain material that has not yet been presented.

Beginning in Chapter 6, each section of short readings is followed by a section of **longer readings**, also unabridged Greek passages.[4] In addition to introductions and vocabulary glosses, at the first appearance of an author or a work we have included brief biographies of the authors and descriptions of the works from which the readings are taken. A list of authors and passages allows students and teachers to refer to this material when authors or works appear again in subsequent longer readings or to investigate further when short readings feature these authors or works.

To help give students a basic knowledge of the history and development of Greek literature and to foster their interest in further study, we have organized all readings from ancient authors in each chapter in chronological order by author. (Works by the same author are arranged alphabetically.) Since the texts of Greek literature that survive contain examples of the language as each writer in each period chose to style it, this chronological arrangement helps students observe the evolution of various styles of both prose and poetry. Through the short and longer readings, *LTRG* is meant to become in part a literary venture, and there are many opportunities for consideration of rhetoric and style as well as of forms and syntax.

Names and Meter

A section on the names of the Greek gods and one on basic meters of Greek poetry are included after chapters 5 and 6, respectively. Information presented in these sections is incorporated in subsequent readings in the textbook, and students may either learn the material in these sections or look back at them when necessary, knowledge of which will enhance their reading and appreciation of the authentic Greek passages in the readings.

---

4. As a general rule, longer readings are those that have ten or more vocabulary glosses.

ABBREVIATIONS

¨	diaeresis
*	indicates that a form is hypothetical
< >	enclose an element added by editors
[ ]	when referring to authors, indicates that, contrary to the tradition, an author is *not* considered the writer of a work
<	(derived) from
>	becomes
§	section
a, p, u	antepenult, penult, ultima
acc.	accusative
act.	active
adj.	adjective
adv.	adverb
aor.	aorist
B.C.E	Before the Common Era
C.E.	The Common Era
cf.	*confer*, compare
conj.	conjunction
d.a.	direct address
d.o.	direct object
dat.	dative
demonstr.	demonstrative
DH	dactylic hexameter
EC	elegiac couplet
e.g.	*exempli gratia*, for example
etc.	*et cetera*, and the remaining things
exclam.	exclamatory
f.	feminine
fem.	feminine
frag.	fragment
fut.	future
gen.	genitive
i.e.	*id est*, that is
i.o.	indirect object
IE	Indo-European
imperf.	imperfect
indef.	indefinite
indic.	indicative
infin.	infinitive
interj.	interjection
interrog.	interrogative
intrans.	intransitive
m.	masculine
masc.	masculine
mid.	middle
n.	neuter
neut.	neuter
nom.	nominative
obj.	object
part.	participle
pass.	passive
perf.	perfect
PIE	Proto-Indo-European
pl.	plural
pluperf.	pluperfect
poss.	possessive
pred.	predicate
prep.	preposition
prep. phrase	prepositional phrase
pres.	present
pron.	pronoun
rel.	relative
sing.	singular
subj.	subject
suppl.	supplementary
subst.	substantive
trans.	transitive
voc.	vocative

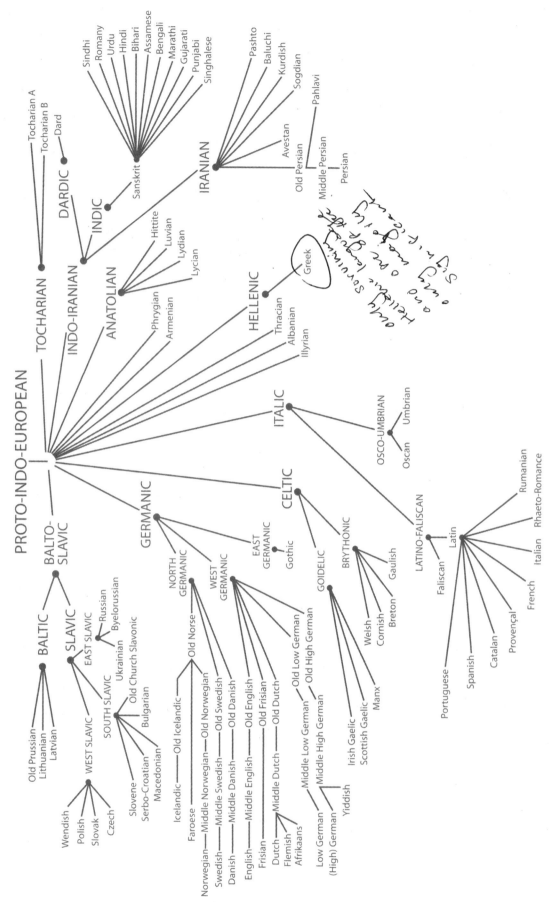

Figure 1. This chart shows the principal languages of the Indo-European family, arranged in a diagrammatic form that displays their genetic relations and loosely suggests their geographic distribution. Copyright © 1981 by Houghton Mifflin Harcourt Publishing Company. Adapted and reproduced by permission from *The American Heritage Dictionary of the English Language*.

INTRODUCTION

§1. The Greek Language and Its Dialects

The Greek language belongs to the Indo-European family of languages. The name "Indo-European" indicates the geographic area where these languages were originally spoken. The family includes most of the languages spoken in Europe, as well as those spoken as far east as ancient Persia, Afghanistan, and India. By the careful comparison of vocabulary, morphology, and syntax, scholars have shown that all these languages descended from a common ancestor that is called either **Indo-European (IE)** or **Proto-Indo-European (PIE)**, which was probably spoken some time in the fifth millennium B.C.E. (see figure 1). The people who spoke this original language are supposed to have gradually dispersed throughout Europe, Asia, and India, and the language over time changed differently in different places until the variety of languages belonging to this family gradually appeared.

No direct evidence, written or archaeological, survives either for PIE or for the people who spoke it. What is known of the language comes from the comparative study of the languages that descended from it. The study of these languages began at the end of the eighteenth century when Sir William Jones, a lawyer and student of eastern languages, first asserted publicly that Greek, Latin, and Sanskrit, the language of ancient India, were descended from a common source. The scientific study of the Indo-European languages began in the early part of the nineteenth century when Franz Bopp compared the forms of the verb in Latin, Greek, Sanskrit, ancient Persian, and the Germanic languages, of which English is one.

The Indo-European languages have been analyzed and divided into various subgroups, and Greek belongs to the subgroup called **Hellenic**. Hellenic comprises many varieties of ancient Greek, which are called *dialects,* for which written evidence has survived. The earliest Greek dialect for which there is surviving written evidence is **Mycenean**, which was written in a script called **Linear B**. Evidence for this language and this script has been found in several sites in mainland Greece and on Crete and dates from as early as the late fifteenth century B.C.E. For reasons that are still uncertain, Mycenean culture had experienced a sharp decline by the end of the thirteenth century B.C.E., and the Linear B script in which the Mycenean dialect was written ceased to be used.

No Greek writing survives from the next several centuries, but by the beginning of the eighth century B.C.E. a new alphabet was being used, and various forms of writing from this period onward are extant. Linguists now identify about two dozen dialects of Greek (see figure 2 for their geographical distribution), which are known from the thousands of inscriptions that survive, and al-

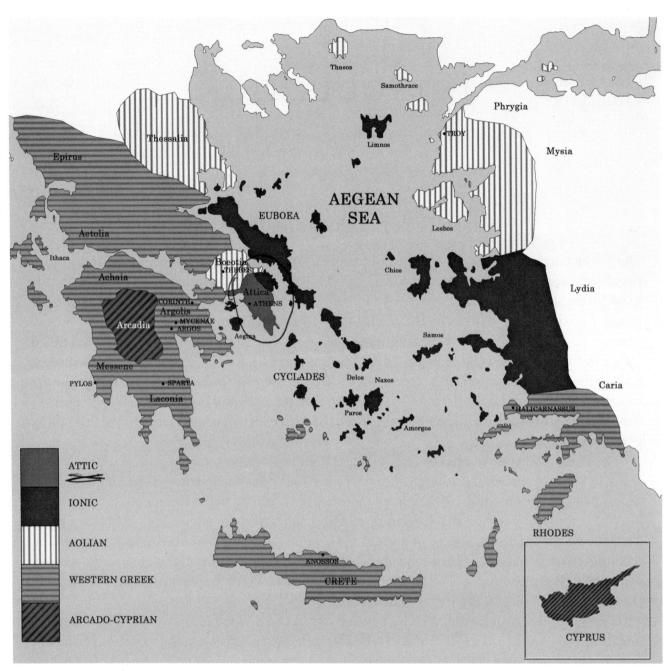

Figure 2. Map of Greek Dialects

though these share basically the same alphabet and many of the same linguistic features, they also exhibit marked differences in spelling, pronunciation, vocabulary, and morphology. Although it is likely that speakers of different dialects could have understood one another to some extent, there must have been many moments of confusion. Most dialects of Greek may be organized under the following four headings:

Arcado-Cyprian (two old dialects that seem to have developed from Mycenean)
Western Greek or **Doric** (a large group of dialects that includes Laconian, the language of ancient Sparta)
Aeolic (Boeotian, Thessalian, and Lesbian)
Attic-Ionic (two dialects of great literary importance, Attic and Ionic)

OBSERVATIONS

1. Ionic was spoken and written by Greeks living along the western and southwestern coast of Asia Minor, on many of the islands close to this coast, and in Euboea in mainland Greece. Many of the earliest writers of prose wrote in this dialect, among whom are the philosophers Thales, Anaximander, and Anaxagoras; the medical writer Hippocrates; and the historian Herodotus.

2. The Attic dialect, closely related to Ionic, was spoken and written in Athens and in Attica, the area around Athens. It is the language of, among others, the tragedians Aeschylus, Sophocles, and Euripides; the comic poet Aristophanes; the historians Thucydides and Xenophon; the philosophers Plato and Aristotle; and the orators Lysias, Isocrates, and Demosthenes. Because of the prominence given to this dialect by these and other great writers, after the fifth century B.C.E. Attic became the predominant literary language throughout the Greek-speaking world.

3. From Attic Greek a common dialect eventually developed called **Koine** (< κοινὴ διάλεκτος, "common language"), which became the standard language throughout much of the Greek-speaking world, and from which modern Greek developed. The New Testament was written in Koine Greek.

As the names of the dialects and the map in figure 2 suggest, different forms of Greek were initially spoken and used in particular localities in the Greek-speaking world. However, many were also shaped by different writers into *literary languages,* and the importance of their compositions established *literary* versions of these languages with strict rules of vocabulary and syntax. Different literary languages often crossed dialectal borders and once established for a particular type of poetry or writing were used by writers regardless of their native dialects. The language of the *Iliad* and the *Odyssey,* for example, shows features of Ionic with a substantial admixture of Aeolic elements. This mixed dialect became associated with poetry written in hexameters (the Homeric meter), and the poet Hesiod, although a Boeotian, used this mixed dialect in his hexameter poetry.[1] The early Ionic prose writers influenced later prose writers to adopt that dialect for their works. In a similar way, a literary version of Doric became the standard language for choral lyric poetry, and it was used by

---

1. The Greek of the *Iliad* and the *Odyssey* cannot, however, be considered a true literary language because these poems were composed over several centuries by preliterate bards, that is, poets of a culture that lacked the art of writing. This is known as the **oral tradition**.

Athenian tragedians in the choral portions of their tragedies, while the language of the rest of the plays remained Attic.

This textbook provides an introduction to Attic Greek. Differences in usage between poetry and prose are pointed out, but for the most part the rules of Attic Greek presented here may be presumed to hold true for the literature of the fifth and fourth centuries B.C.E. Readings from later writers such as Plutarch and Diogenes Laertius are also included because they wrote in deliberate imitation of the Attic Greek of an earlier time. Readings from writers in other dialects are included as well, along with brief notes about their dialectal differences from Attic.

§2. Pronunciation and Orthography of Attic Greek

There were variations in the pronunciation of Attic Greek over the course of the centuries in which it was spoken and written, but there is considerable evidence for a standard in pronunciation, and rules approximating that standard are presented here.[2]

The rules for pronouncing Attic Greek have been reconstructed from several types of evidence:

1. The statements of Greek grammarians and Greek authors on specific points of pronunciation. Many of these grammarians were contemporaries or near-contemporaries of the ancient authors.
2. The orthography, or writing—particularly spelling—of Greek words in inscriptions and manuscripts. Ancient spelling, both in Greek and in other ancient languages, was considerably less standardized than modern spelling. Variations in spelling usually indicate differences in pronunciation.
3. The representation or transliteration of Greek words in other languages and the representation or transliteration of foreign words in Greek. The transliteration of names, in particular, provides valuable information about pronunciation.
4. The grammatical and poetic structure of Greek. This includes the evidence available from the meters of Greek poetry.
5. The etymology of Greek words and the development of Greek words in other languages.
6. Greek wordplay and onomatopoeia (the formation of words to imitate sounds).

Alphabet

The Greek alphabet used in modern printed texts has twenty-four letters. The following chart presents them in their Greek order along with their conventional names and guidelines for pronunciation with English equivalents.

---

2. For the presentation of pronunciation the authors are indebted to W. S. Allen's *Vox Graeca* (Cambridge, 3rd ed., 1987), although they have not followed it in all particulars.

Uppercase	Lowercase	Name	Pronunciation
A	α	alpha	α (short) as the *first* **a** of **a**wait (or as the **u** of **cup**)
			ā (long) as the **a** of **father**
B	β	beta	as **b**
Γ	γ	gamma	as the **g** of **get**
			as the **n** of ba**n**k before γ, κ, ξ, or χ
Δ	δ	delta	as **d**
E	ε	epsilon	as the **e** of p**e**t
Z	ζ	zeta	as the **sd** of wi**sd**om
H	η	eta	as the **a** of l**a**te
Θ	θ	theta	as the **t** of **t**op or as the **th** of **th**eater
I	ι	iota	ι (short) as the **i** of b**i**t
			ī (long) as the **ee** of f**ee**t
K	κ	kappa	as **k**
Λ	λ	la(m)bda	as **l**
M	μ	mu	as **m**
N	ν	nu	as **n**
Ξ	ξ	xi	as the **x** of a**x**
O	o	omicron	as the **o** of s**o**ft
Π	π	pi	as the **p** of to**p**
P	ρ	rho	as a rolled **r**
Σ, C	σ, ς, c	sigma	as the **s** of **s**oft
			as **z** before β, γ, or μ
T	τ	tau	as the **t** of **c**oat
Υ	υ	upsilon	υ (short) as the **u** of p**u**t
			ū (long) as the **oo** of f**oo**l
Φ	φ	phi	as the **p** of **p**eople or as the **f** of **f**eel
X	χ	chi	as the **c** of **c**at or as the **ch** of lo**ch**
Ψ	ψ	psi	as the **ps** of a**ps**e
Ω	ω	omega	as the **aw** of s**aw** or as the **o** of h**o**pe

[Handwritten annotation in margin: in old printed greek text you wouldn't see σ lunate (c, c) σ used when this letter occurs in the middle or beginning of text ~ ς end of text]

OBSERVATIONS

1. Although in the most ancient manuscripts only the uppercase letters were used, modern editions of ancient works use the lowercase letters developed in the Middle Ages. Capital letters are used, however, for the first letters of proper names, the first letters of direct quotations with the exception of drama, and sometimes for the first letters of paragraphs.

2. Most of the Greek alphabet was derived from the Phoenician alphabet, and many of the names given to the Greek letters are derived from the Phoenician names for their letters. The names *epsilon, omicron, upsilon,* and *omega* were developed in the Middle Ages as the sounds they represented changed.[3]

3. The name for λ in common use today is *lambda,* but the classical name appears to have been *labda.*

4. The pronunciations given for long and short upsilon do *not* represent the sound of original At-

3. *Epsilon* and *upsilon* mean, respectively, "ε written simply" and "υ written simply" (< ε or υ + ψῑλόν, "simple"). By the Byzantine period certain diphthongs (see below) were pronounced in the same way as these vowels, and *epsilon* and *upsilon* were developed to refer to the simple vowels. *Omicron* means "little o" (< o + μῑκρόν), and *omega* means "big o" (< o + μέγα). These terms also arose in the Byzantine period.

tic Greek but are common substitutes used by English speakers. An upsilon in Attic Greek represented a sound between English **u** and English **i**.

5. The alternate pronunciation given for the vowel omega does *not* represent the sound of original Attic Greek but is a common substitute used by English speakers because it makes a clearer distinction between the sounds of omicron and omega.

6. The alternate pronunciations given for theta, phi, and chi are the pronunciations that these letters had at a later period in the development of Greek. They are often used as common substitutes for the sounds these letters had in Attic Greek because they allow English speakers to distinguish clearly the sounds of different Greek letters. For example, the difference between theta and tau is strictly the difference between an aspirated **t** (a **t** with a puff of air after it, as most English speakers pronounce every **t**) and one without aspiration (as may occur when a **t** is pronounced at the end of a word in English).

7. The letter ζ is a double consonant and represents the sound **zd**. It is possible that it was also used to represent the sound **dz**.

8. The letters ξ and ψ are double consonants and represent, respectively, **ks** and **ps**.

9. Of the three different lowercase symbols for sigma used in modern printed texts of ancient Greek, σ is used *only* when the letter appears at the beginning or in the middle of a word; ς is used *only* at the *end* of a word and is sometimes called **final sigma**. The third symbol, c, called **lunate sigma**, may be used anywhere in a word. For example: στάσις or ϲτάϲιϲ. The lunate sigma was commonly used in ancient Greek manuscripts from the third century B.C.E. on, and its adoption in modern printed texts reflects a desire to imitate more closely the ancient written tradition. In this textbook, the short and longer readings in even-numbered chapters use lunate sigmas, while those in odd-numbered chapters employ the more conventional sigmas in order to familiarize students with all forms.

10. One letter that occurs in many Greek dialects but is not found in Attic-Ionic is the digamma (Ϝ), which represents the English "w" sound.

☛ DRILL 2 A–D MAY NOW BE DONE.

Consonants

Nine Greek consonants are called **mutes** or **stops** because when they are pronounced the breathing passage must be closed or *stopped*. These consonants are further distinguished in the following chart:

	Voiceless	Voiced	Aspirated	+ σ
Labials	π	β	φ	ψ
Dentals	τ	δ	θ	
Palatals	κ	γ	χ	ξ

OBSERVATIONS

1. **Voiceless** consonants are made with no vibration of the vocal chords and no aspiration. **Voiced** consonants are made with some vibration of the vocal chords and no aspiration. **Aspirated** consonants (or **Aspirates**) are consonants followed by a puff of air.

2. A **labial** ("relating to the lips") is a sound that is produced using the lips. A **dental** ("relat-

ing to the teeth") is a sound that is produced (when properly made) by placing the tongue against the teeth. A **palatal** ("relating to the palate") is a sound that is produced using the soft palate.[4]

3. When *any labial* is followed by a σ in a Greek word (e.g., φσ), the two consonants are replaced by a ψ. When *any palatal* is followed by a σ in a Greek word (e.g., γσ), the two consonants are replaced by a ξ.

Greek also has two consonants called **liquids** (λ, ρ), sounds that may be prolonged; two consonants called **nasals** (μ, ν), sounds that are produced with vibration in the nasal passage; and one **sibilant** (σ), a hissing sound that may be pronounced without a break.

It is necessary to be familiar with these terms for Greek consonants. Understanding the relations among consonants is often important in the formation of Greek words and in the changes that many Greek words undergo.

Vowels, Diphthongs, and Iota Subscripts and Adscripts

Greek has two sets of five vowels:

Short	Long
α	ᾱ
ε	η
ι	ῑ
ο	ω
υ	ῡ

OBSERVATIONS

1. Vowels have both *quantity* and *quality*. **Quantity** refers to the *length* of a vowel. A long vowel takes approximately twice as long to pronounce as a short vowel. In this text, when an α, ι, or υ is long, it is marked with a long mark or **macron**(ˉ). The letters η and ω are *always* long vowels and do not require macrons. The letters ε and ο are *always* short vowels. **Quality** refers to the *sound* of the vowel. In most cases a long vowel differs in *both* quantity *and* quality from its related short vowel.

2. Each vowel in a Greek word is either long or short *by nature*. α and ᾱ, for example, are two different vowels, even if they are closely related.

3. Differences in vowel length often convey significant differences in meaning. For example, ἱστάμεθα means "we *are* standing"; ἱστάμεθα means "we *were* standing."

A MACRON ON A LONG VOWEL SHOULD BE CONSIDERED PART OF THE SPELLING OF A GREEK WORD. WHEN LEARNING NEW VOCABULARY, MEMORIZE ALL MACRONS AND ALWAYS WRITE THEM ON LONG ALPHAS, IOTAS, AND UPSILONS.

A **diphthong** (δίφθογγος, "double sound") is a single sound made from pronouncing two

4. The palate is the roof of the mouth and is divided into the front, hard portion and the back, softer portion. Palatals are made with the soft palate at the back of the mouth. Palatals may also be called **velars**, "relating to the velum," because the velum is another name for the soft palate.

vowels together. The quantity of a diphthong is equivalent to that of a long vowel. The eight diphthongs of Greek are αι, ει, οι, υι, αυ, ευ, ου, and ηυ. They are pronounced as follows:

αι as the **i** of h**i**gh
ει as the **a** of l**a**te
οι as the **oy** of b**oy**
υι as a combination of **u** and **i** (uwi) or as the **wi** of t**wi**n
αυ as the **ow** of h**ow**
ευ as a combination of **e** and **u**
ου as the **oo** of f**oo**l
ηυ hardly different from ευ

OBSERVATIONS

1. There is no English sound corresponding to the Greek diphthong υι. As its spelling indicates, it
is a combination of the short vowels υ and ι pronounced as one sound. The sound is approximated
in the swift pronunciation of the vowels in *Bedouin* (pronounced as if spelled "Bédowin").
2. There is no English sound corresponding to the Greek diphthong ευ. As its spelling indicates,
it is a combination of the short vowels ε and υ pronounced as one sound. If Elmer Fudd pronounced *very* (ve**w**y), the **ew** would closely resemble the Greek sound.

In Attic Greek there are three additional diphthongs, which combine a long vowel (ᾱ, η, or ω) with
an ι: ᾱι, ηι, and ωι. In Attic Greek the ι in these diphthongs was very lightly pronounced, and by the
second century B.C.E. it was not pronounced at all. Eventually, the ι was not even written, but since
it was important for spelling and distinguishing words, the scholars of the Middle Ages began to
write it *under* the appropriate long vowel. This ι is called an **iota subscript**. When the ι is written
next to the long vowel, it is called an **iota adscript**.

Iota *subscript*	Iota *adscript*
ᾳ	ᾱι
ῃ	ηι
ῳ	ωι

When the first letter of such a diphthong is capitalized, the ι is *always* written as an adscript.

Iota adscript
Αι
Ηι
Ωι

OBSERVATIONS

1. When a long **alpha** with an iota subscript or adscript appears in this text, the macron over the
alpha is regularly omitted.
2. For a long time, only the iota subscript was used in representing the lowercase versions of
these diphthongs in modern editions of ancient texts, but in recent years iota adscripts have

become more common. This text uses iota subscripts. NEITHER AN IOTA SUBSCRIPT NOR AN IOTA ADSCRIPT SHOULD BE PRONOUNCED.

Rough and Smooth Breathings

Whenever a vowel or diphthong begins a word, it *must be accompanied by* a **rough breathing** (‘) or a **smooth breathing** (’) mark. A rough breathing indicates that an *h*-sound (the blowing out of air called aspiration) should be pronounced at the beginning of the word. A smooth breathing indicates that there is *no h*-sound at the beginning of the word. A rough or a smooth breathing is placed *above* a lowercase vowel. It is placed *before* an uppercase vowel. It is placed on the *second* vowel of a diphthong. For example:

ὁδός	(rough breathing *above* lowercase vowel)
Ὁδός	(rough breathing *before* uppercase vowel)
αἱρέω	(rough breathing *above second* vowel of a diphthong)
Αἱρέω	(rough breathing *above second* vowel of a diphthong with uppercase first letter)
ἀγορά	(smooth breathing *above* lowercase vowel)
Ἀγορά	(smooth breathing *before* uppercase vowel)
οἰκίᾱ	(smooth breathing above *second* vowel of a diphthong)
Οἰκίᾱ	(smooth breathing *above second* vowel of a diphthong with uppercase first letter)

If a word begins with the consonant ρ (rho), the consonant *always* receives a rough breathing mark. For example: ῥήτωρ (Ῥήτωρ). This aspiration is not usually pronounced by English speakers.

Punctuation

Although the earliest Greek writings had no breaks between words and almost no punctuation, ancient Greek texts are now printed with words divided and punctuation marks added, some of which are identical to those used in English.

The punctuation marks in common use are the following:

	Punctuation Mark	*Example*
Period	. (as in English)	ἀγαθόν.
Comma	, (as in English)	ἀγαθόν,
Semicolon	· (a raised dot)	ἀγαθόν·
Colon	· (a raised dot)	ἀγαθόν·
Question mark	; (an English semicolon)	ἀγαθόν;

No exclamation point is used. When editors of modern printed Greek texts wish to indicate direct speech, some use quotation marks, as in English (" "), others capitalize the first letter of the quotation, and others do both.

Syllabification

A Greek word has as many syllables as it has vowels and diphthongs. When a word is divided into syllables, each syllable should begin with a consonant whenever possible. For example:

θά/να/τος   (3 syllables)
θε/οῖς   (2 syllables)
ἐ/τε/θύ/κε/σαν   (5 syllables)

If there are two or more consonants in a row, the *last* consonant goes with the following syllable:

συμφορά̄   συμ/φο/ρά̄
ἔργον   ἔρ/γον
πολλάκις   πολ/λά/κις

If, however, the combination of two consonants is a *mute* (π, β, φ, τ, δ, θ, κ, γ, χ) followed by a *liquid* (λ, ρ), the two consonants are kept together:

αἰσχρός   αἰσ/χρός
ὅπλον   ὅ/πλον
Ἀλέξανδρος   Ἀ/λέ/ξαν/δρος

The last three syllables of a Greek word are known as the *antepenult, penult,* and *ultima:*

last syllable = **ultima** ("last")
second to last syllable = **penult** ("almost last")
third to last syllable = **antepenult** ("before almost last")

θά/   να/   τος
antepenult   penult   ultima

☛   DRILL 2 E–K MAY NOW BE DONE.

§3. Accentuation 1: The Possibilities of Accent

Almost every Greek word has one of three kinds of accent marks over the vowel or diphthong in one particular syllable.[5] These accent marks originally indicated various changes in tone or pitch as follows:

acute accent (´)   raised tone
grave accent (`)   no change in tone or tone raised less than for an acute
circumflex (^)[6]   raised and lowered tone

Although changes in tone also occur when English words are pronounced, more prominent is a *stress accent,* by which one syllable of an English word is pronounced more loudly or with greater

---

5. There are some words that have no accents, and in certain situations some words might have two accented syllables.
6. The circumflex can be written ˆ, ̑, or ˜.

emphasis than the others.[7] The accented syllables in Greek words usually receive a stress accent (rather than a change of tone) when pronounced by speakers of English. This stress accent sounds the same no matter what kind of accent mark appears. For example:

ἄνθρωπον (antepenult is stressed)
τοιοῦτος (penult is stressed)
ἀγαθά (ultima is stressed)

An accent is placed *above* a vowel or above the *second* vowel of a diphthong. If a syllable with a rough or smooth breathing is accented, an acute or grave accent is placed *to the right* of the breathing, and a circumflex is placed *above* the breathing:

τεκμήριον (acute accent above a vowel)
ἑταῖρος (circumflex above the second vowel of a diphthong)
ἂν (grave accent above a vowel to the right of a smooth breathing)
ὅλον (acute accent above a vowel to the right of a rough breathing)
οἶκος (circumflex above a smooth breathing above the second vowel of a diphthong)

An accent for a *capitalized* vowel is placed *before* the vowel rather than above it. When the first vowel of a *diphthong* is capitalized, the accent is placed above the *second* vowel. However, *when a diphthong contains an iota adscript,* the accent is placed *before* the vowel:

Ἕκτωρ (acute accent to the right of a rough breathing before an uppercase vowel)
Αἴσων (acute accent to the right of a smooth breathing above the second vowel of a diphthong with an uppercase first letter)
Ἅιδης (acute accent to the right of a rough breathing before an uppercase letter followed by an iota adscript)

No matter how long a Greek word is, its accent may appear only on the ultima, the penult, or the antepenult—that is, on one of the last three syllables. Each accent should be considered part of the spelling of each Greek word and should be learned with care and precision. As a word changes its form (e.g., as a noun becomes plural or a verb changes tense), or as it appears in a particular place in a sentence, the accent on a word may *change* either in the type of accent or in the syllable over which the accent appears or both. Changes in accent, however, are limited according to six unchanging rules for the possibilities of accent.

1.	a	p	ù	(if ultima is followed by another word)
2.	a	p	ú	(if ultima is followed by a punctuation mark that signals a pause)
3.	a	ṕ	u	(*not* possible if penult is long and ultima is short)
4.	á	p	ŭ	(ultima *must be short*)
5.	a	p	û	(ultima *must be long*)
6.	a	p̂	ŭ	(if penult is long and is accented and if ultima is short)

---

7. Sometimes more than one of the syllables in an English word is stressed.

1. In the rules pictured above, **a**, **p**, and **u** represent the last three syllables of any Greek word. A **breve** (˘) represents a short vowel. A syllable having *neither* of these marks may contain a short vowel, a long vowel, or a diphthong.

2. The grave accent (rule 1) appears only over the ultima. Whenever a word having an acute accent on the ultima is followed by another word with no intervening punctuation, the accent changes from an acute to a grave. Thus, every grave accent was originally an acute accent that was forced to change to a grave because of the flow of the words in a sentence. When an ultima has a grave accent, it need not be stressed.

3. The acute accent may appear over the ultima (rule 2) *if* a pause indicated by some sort of punctuation (period, comma, semi-colon, question mark) follows immediately. The ultima may be long or short.

4. The acute accent may appear over the penult (rule 3) *except* when the penult contains a long vowel or diphthong *and* the ultima contains a short vowel. If the penult must be accented under these conditions, it is accented with a circumflex (rule 6).

5. The acute accent may appear over the antepenult (rule 4) *only if* the ultima contains a short vowel.

6. The circumflex may appear over the ultima (rule 5) *only if* the ultima contains a long vowel or diphthong. A circumflex *never* appears over a short vowel. *Macrons are regularly omitted from a syllable that has a circumflex* because the accent mark itself indicates that the vowel is long.

7. The circumflex may appear over the penult (rule 6) *only if* the penult contains a long vowel or diphthong *and* the ultima is short. A circumflex *never* appears over a short vowel. If the penult of a word containing a long vowel or diphthong (a so-called *long penult*) is to be accented, and the ultima contains a short vowel (a so-called *short ultima*), the accent on that penult *must* be a circumflex.

MEMORIZE AND BE ABLE TO WRITE FROM MEMORY THE SIX RULES FOR THE POSSIBILITIES OF ACCENT.

☛   DRILL 3 MAY NOW BE DONE.

§4. Vocabulary, Morphology, and Syntax

Elementary language study may be divided into three parts: vocabulary, morphology, and syntax.

Vocabulary

Vocabulary refers first to the acquisition of the English meanings of words in another language. Thus, the Greek word σοφίᾱ means "wisdom"; the word λέγω means "say, tell." In addition to English meanings vocabulary encompasses certain other important elements that give crucial information about gender (for nouns), stems, and parts of speech. A *full vocabulary entry* (the way the word appears in the dictionary) includes all these pieces of information. ALWAYS MEMORIZE THE FULL

VOCABULARY ENTRY FOR EACH NEW WORD TO BE LEARNED. The English meaning alone will never be enough.

Morphology

Morphology is the study of the *different forms* words take in a given language. In English, for example, various pieces of verb morphology must be learned:

1. the third-person singular present tense form of most English verbs is formed by the addition of **-s** or **-es**:

   laugh → laugh**s**   go → go**es**

2. the past tense of many English verbs is formed by the addition of **-ed**:

   laugh → laugh**ed**

Morphology extends as well to nouns, adjectives, and certain other parts of speech that have multiple forms. *The changing of form to convey changed meaning* is called **inflection**.

   Some languages are more inflected (have more forms) than others. Thus, the English noun regularly appears in only four forms:

   dog (singular)   dogs (plural)
   dog's (singular possessive)   dogs' (plural possessive)

The Greek noun, by contrast, regularly appears in ten or more forms. *Since Greek is a more inflected language than English, Greek morphology is considerably more extensive than English morphology, and mastery of Greek's many forms is essential.*

Syntax

The grammatical function of a word in a sentence is the **syntax** of that word. In the English sentence "Dan gave his mother a gift," "Dan," "mother," and "gift" all have different grammatical functions that help convey the complete meaning of the sentence:

   Dan   subject
   mother   indirect object
   gift   direct object

The terms **subject**, **indirect object**, and **direct object** are examples of English syntax, and these and several other terms of English syntax are also used in Greek syntax. Accurate translation of a Greek sentence requires the identification of the syntax of the words in that sentence. Throughout this textbook, new Greek syntactical terms are introduced and defined. These terms are always boldfaced at their first appearance. LEARN ALL BOLDFACED SYNTACTICAL TERMS.

CHAPTER 1

Vocabulary

→ ἀγορά, ἀγορᾶς, ἡ agora, marketplace[1]
οἰκίᾱ, οἰκίᾱς, ἡ house
→ σοφίᾱ, σοφίᾱς, ἡ wisdom
→ συμφορά, συμφορᾶς, ἡ circumstance; misfortune, disaster
χώρᾱ, χώρᾱς, ἡ land; country

→ βουλή, βουλῆς, ἡ will; plan; council; advice
→ γνώμη, γνώμης, ἡ judgment; spirit, inclination; opinion
→ δίκη, δίκης, ἡ justice
εἰρήνη, εἰρήνης, ἡ peace
→ Ἑλένη, Ἑλένης, ἡ Helen
μάχη, μάχης, ἡ battle
→ ψῡχή, ψῡχῆς, ἡ soul; life force

→ Ἀλέξανδρος, Ἀλεξάνδρου, ὁ Alexander
ἄνθρωπος, ἀνθρώπου, ὁ or ἡ human being, man
ἑταῖρος, ἑταίρου, ὁ companion
θεός, θεοῦ, ὁ or ἡ god; goddess
→ λόγος, λόγου, ὁ word; speech; argument
νῆσος, νήσου, ἡ island
→ νόμος, νόμου, ὁ custom; law

→ ὁδός, ὁδοῦ, ἡ road, path; journey; way
πόλεμος, πολέμου, ὁ war
→ Πρίαμος, Πριάμου, ὁ Priam

→ ἔργον, ἔργου, τό task, work; deed
ζῷον, ζῴου, τό living being; animal
→ ὅπλον, ὅπλου, τό tool; *pl.*, arms, weapons
τέκνον, τέκνου, τό child

→ εἰς, ἐς (prep. + acc.) to, toward; into; against; with a view to, regarding
→ ἐκ, ἐξ (prep. + gen.) (out) from, out of; resulting from, in accordance with
→ ἐν (prep. + dat.) in, on; among, in the presence of
→ καί (conj.) and; καί . . . καί . . . both . . . and . . .
(adv.) even, also
ὁ, ἡ, τό (article) the
→ περί (prep. + gen.) concerning, about
(prep. + dat.) around
(prep. + acc.) around; concerning, about
→ σύν/ξύν (prep. + dat.) (along) with; with the aid of; in accordance with
ὦ (interj.) O

---

1. An arrow next to a vocabulary word indicates that there is important additional information about the word in the vocabulary notes.

Vocabulary Notes

→ The basic meaning of ἀγορά, ἀγορᾶς, ἡ is "assembly." In Homer it refers to an assembly of the people (as distinct from a meeting of the chiefs in council) and is spelled ἀγορή. It also has the more general meaning of "public meeting place" or "market." The ἀγορά in fifth-century Athens was situated between the Acropolis (hilltop fortress) and the Dipylon (city gate) and contained the temples and public buildings used for the work of the Athenian democracy. Because there is no exact English equivalent for the Greek ἀγορά, it is often translated "agora."

→ Although σοφίᾱ, σοφίᾱς, ἡ may mean "wisdom" in the sense of broad learning and deep understanding, it more often refers to a certain cunning, cleverness, or practical skill in some specific area. The art or craft of gods such as Athena or Hephaestus may be called σοφίᾱ, as may skill in, for example, music, medicine, and divination. Particularly (but not exclusively) in Plato, two other ideas are associated with σοφίᾱ: sound "judgment" or intelligence in matters of moral life and "knowledge" as opposed to ignorance.

→ συμφορά, συμφορᾶς, ἡ refers to a *bringing together* or conjunction of elements. Thus the word has neutral meanings such as "event" or "circumstance." More often, however, συμφορά means "misfortune" or "disaster." With an appropriate adjective, συμφορά may also refer to *good* "fortune." Because the first syllable of συμφορά is related to the preposition σύν, it also has an older Attic spelling, ξυμφορά, in the tragedians and Thucydides. Be prepared to recognize both forms of this noun.

→ βουλή, βουλῆς, ἡ is the "will" of a person or god. It is also the name of the smaller deliberative body of the Athenian democracy, the "boule" or "council." After the reforms of Cleisthenes in 508/507 B.C.E., the βουλή was made up of five hundred Athenian citizens whose job was to carry on the day-to-day business of the democracy. Members were chosen by lot to serve one-year terms.

→ γνώμη, γνώμης, ἡ is related to a verb meaning "know" and is used to refer to several different aspects of the intellect. It means "judgment" or "reason" and may be contrasted with "anger," "passion," or "chance." γνώμη often expresses ideas close to the English "mind" or "spirit," as well as the "will" or "inclination" of one's mind or spirit. Finally, γνώμη may refer to a particular "opinion" or "plan."

→ The original meaning of δίκη, δίκης, ἡ was "custom" or "usage," and δίκη characterized behavior consistent with one's place in society. It soon came to mean "*right* conduct" or "justice." In poetry, Δίκη is sometimes a goddess, the close ally of Zeus. In addition to its abstract meaning of "justice," δίκη has the concrete meaning of "lawsuit."

→ Ἑλένη, Ἑλένης, ἡ, "Helen," is the wife of Menelaus, king of Sparta. After being carried away to Troy, Helen is also referred to as the "wife" of Paris, her abductor and consort.

→ ψῡχή, ψῡχῆς, ἡ means "soul" in two important senses. First, it is the *animating element,* the "life force" that departs from the body at the time of death and travels under the earth to the house of Hades. This soul is said to be both immaterial (ghostly) and immortal. Second, ψῡχή is the unseen *moral, emotional, and intellectual center* of the self or individual. This soul (equivalent to many uses of the English words *heart* and *mind*) can be good or bad and is often the seat of emotions, desires, and rational thought.

→ Ἀλέξανδρος, Ἀλεξάνδρου, ὁ, "Alexander," is the Greek name of Paris, son of the Trojan king Priam and consort of Helen. From Homer onward, both names, Πάρις and Ἀλέξανδρος, appear in Greek texts, but the latter is more common. Ἀλέξανδρος is also the name of Philip of Macedon's son, often known as "Alexander the Great" (356–323 B.C.E.), who conquered and united all of Greece, as well as most of the lands surrounding the Mediterranean. The philosopher Aristotle was his tutor.

→ λόγος, λόγου, ὁ is a noun related to the verb λέγω, "speak," and its many meanings are derived from a general idea of verbal expression. When it refers simply to what is *said,* λόγος means "speech," "story," "discussion," or "word." When λόγος refers to the account of a person, it can be translated "repute" or "report."

    λόγος is also used to refer to any rational expression, written or spoken, that is an "explanation" (of a theory, of a cause), an "account" (of financial transactions, of an occurrence, of an idea), or an "argument" in a legal or philosophical context. By extension from these meanings λόγος is used in a more abstract sense to mean "reason" or "reasoning."

    Sometimes the meaning of λόγος is clarified by its use in contrast with other words. When λόγος is opposed to ideas such as actuality, fact, or truth, it means "theory" or, more negatively, "pretence." When it is opposed to "myth," however, it means "(rational) account."

→ νόμος, νόμου, ὁ is used of any habitual practice, usage, or "custom." From this develops its second meaning, "law," either a formal statute (the laws of Solon) or a more general guiding principle (the laws of gods and men). Human behavior is often characterized as *according to* or *contrary to* νόμος.

→ ὁδός, ὁδοῦ, ἡ is used for any actual or figurative "road," "path," "street," or "course" (the road to the agora, the path of—that is, to—truth). It may also refer to a voyage or "journey" on either land or sea. Finally, ὁδός means "way" in a broadly metaphorical sense (a *way* of doing something, a *way* of speaking).

→ Πρίαμος, Πριάμου, ὁ, "Priam," is the king of Troy, husband of Hecuba, and father of many children, including Hector, Alexander, and Cassandra.

→ ἔργον, ἔργου, τό means "work" in the sense of "toil" or "labor" in general, but it may also refer to specific occupations or activities, particularly when qualified by a noun in the genitive case (the works of war, of feasting, of marriage). ἔργον may also be used of the *products* of labor. In Homer, for example, the phrase ἔργα ἀνθρώπων refers to tilled land. Frequently contrasted with λόγος, ἔργον in such contexts means either "deed" or "fact."

→ ὅπλον, ὅπλου, τό in the singular means any kind of "tool" or implement. The plural most often refers to the implements of war, "arms," "weapons."

→ The preposition εἰς/ἐς is a proclitic and is followed by the *accusative case only.* A **proclitic** (< προκλίνω, "lean forward") is a word that has no accent of its own but is pronounced closely with the word that *follows* it. The form commonly used in Attic prose is εἰς, *except* by the historian Thucydides, who uses ἐς exclusively. In Attic tragedy, ἐς is more common than εἰς, but both forms are used.

    εἰς/ἐς expresses direction "to," "toward," or "into" a place.

ἡ ἐς ἀγορὰν ὁδός	the road (subj.) *to* the agora
εἰς τὴν οἰκίᾶν	*into* the house

εἰς/ἐς may also mean "with a view to" or "regarding."

τὰς συμφορὰς εἰς τὰ τέκνα	the misfortunes (d.o.) *regarding* the children

In contexts suggesting hostility, εἰς/ἐς means "against."

πόλεμον εἰς τοὺς θεούς	war (d.o.) *against* the gods

➡ The preposition ἐκ is spelled ἐξ when it is followed by a *word beginning with a vowel*. A proclitic, ἐκ/ἐξ is followed by the *genitive case only*. ἐκ/ἐξ expresses direction "from" or "out from" a place, usually with the article, to indicate *origin*. It may also appear with a Genitive of Separation (§6).

ἐξ ἀγορᾶς	*out from* the marketplace
ἐκ τῆς οἰκίας	*out from* the house
οἱ ἐκ τῶν νήσων ἄνθρωποι	the men (subj.) *from* the islands

ἐκ/ἐξ also may convey an idea of *cause* with the meanings "resulting from" or "in accordance with."

ἐκ τοῦ τῆς Ἑλένης ἔργου	*resulting from* (caused by) the deed of Helen
ἐκ τῶν νόμων	*in accordance with* the laws

➡ The preposition ἐν is a proclitic and is followed by the *dative case only*. It expresses location "in" a place, condition, or position.

ἐν τῇ ἀγορᾷ	*in* the marketplace
ἐν ὅπλοις	*in* arms
ἐν πολέμῳ	*in* war

ἐν may also mean "in the number of," "among," or "in the presence of," "in the power of."

ἐν ἀνθρώποις	*among* men
ἐν τοῖς θεοῖς	*in the power of* the gods

➡ καί is a *coordinating conjunction*. A **coordinating conjunction** connects only *parallel* or *grammatically balanced* words, phrases, or clauses. When two or more nouns are connected, they must be in the same case: for example, τοῦ Πριάμου καὶ τῆς Ἑλένης (of Priam and of Helen). Grammatical elements other than nouns (verbs, adjectives, prepositional phrases, etc.) may also be connected by καί: for example, ἐκ τῆς οἰκίας καὶ εἰς τὴν ὁδόν (out of the house and into the road).

To create an even greater balance of elements that are to be joined in Greek, καί is often used to mark *each* element. Thus, καὶ τῷ Πριάμῳ καὶ τῷ τέκνῳ. It is convenient to translate the first καί with the English word "both": "both for Priam and for his child." When such a parallel series contains more than two elements (καὶ οἱ θεοὶ καὶ οἱ ἄνθρωποι καὶ τὰ ζῷα), one may omit translation of the first καί and translate the others "and": "gods and men and animals (subj.)."

καί is also an *adverb* that qualifies any single element in a sentence: καὶ ταῖς θεοῖς ("even for the goddesses"), καὶ ἐν πολέμῳ ("also in war").

➡ The preposition περί generally means "around" or "about" in both physical and figurative senses. When followed by the genitive case, περί means "concerning" or "about." The word in the genitive case expresses the *thing about which* one is speaking, writing, or thinking.

When followed by the dative case (rare in both prose and poetry), περί means "around" and *locates* something *around* a place.

When followed by the accusative case, περί means "concerning" or "about." It may also report *motion* or position around a place or *connection* with a person ("around," "about," "connected with").

Sometimes περί is written *after* the noun or pronoun it governs, and *its accent shifts to the penult:* δίκης πέρι, "about justice." This reverse order of a preposition and its object is called **anastrophe** (ἀναστροφή, "turning back"). Anastrophe may occur with many other **disyllabic** (two-syllable) prepositions and is always indicated by the shift of the accent to the penult.

→ The preposition σύν (more common in poetry than in prose) is always followed by a noun in the *dative* case. It expresses a general idea of *accompaniment* and means "with" in these senses: "along with," "with the aid of," "in accordance with." These common phrases serve as models for the uses of σύν:

σὺν ὅπλοις	"along with arms" (= "armed" or "bearing arms")
σὺν (τοῖς) θεοῖς	"with the aid of the gods"
σὺν δίκῃ	"in accordance with justice" (= "justly")

The older Attic form ξύν is favored by Thucydides and the tragedians.

Flash Cards

The mastery of vocabulary is an essential part of learning Greek, and the creation and use of flash cards help students memorize and retain words as their vocabulary increases. To make a flash card for a noun, one should write the full vocabulary entry in Greek—nominative singular, genitive singular, and article indicating gender—on one side of a card and the English meaning(s) on the other. Additional meanings or other important information given in the Vocabulary Notes can be included as well. Flash cards are most effective when the Greek entry and meanings are *said aloud*.

βουλή, βουλῆς, ἡ	will; plan; council; advice

For a preposition, adverb, or conjunction write the Greek word on one side of a flash card and all other information—including such things as part of speech, cases taken, and English meanings—on the other.

<table>
<tr><td>περί</td><td>(prep. + gen.) concerning, about
(prep. + dat.) around
(prep. + acc.) around; concerning, about</td></tr>
</table>

MAKE A FLASH CARD FOR *EVERY* NEW VOCABULARY ITEM AND INCLUDE *ALL* INFORMATION FROM THE VOCABULARY ENTRY ON THE VOCABULARY PAGE ABOUT EACH WORD.

Derivatives and Cognates

Many English words are *derived from* Greek words; that is, they descend *directly* from words in Greek. Such words are called **derivatives**. The English word *polemic,* for example, is a derivative of the Greek word πόλεμος. In many instances, the differences in sound and spelling between a Greek word and its English derivative are not significant enough to obscure the fact that the two words are related. Some English words are derived from the *roots* of one or more than one Greek word. A **root** is the basic element or stem of a word that carries its meaning and from which many other words are made. The English word *economics,* for example, is derived from the roots of two Greek words, οἰκίᾱ (οἰκο-) and νόμος (νομ-).

An English word and a Greek word can also be related if they both descend (are derived) from a common Proto-Indo-European word or root, even if the English word is *not* derived from Greek but from another ancient language (such as Latin). Such words are called **cognates** because they are *related* to each other, but one is *not* derived from the other. It is often impossible to tell that an English word and a Greek word are cognates because the PIE root from which they descend has undergone radically different changes in pronunciation and spelling as it has developed in each language family. The English word *parliament* is cognate with the Greek word βουλή, for example, but the words do not appear to be related. As words developed and changed from one language to the next, their meanings often changed *radically,* and therefore the *meanings* of words do not help to identify cognates. Cognates are identified by first tracing a word or root in a language back to a word or root in an older language (often PIE) and then applying what is known about how the individual sounds in that root changed in different languages.

In each chapter a list of some English derivatives and cognates of the new Greek vocabulary appears at the end of the vocabulary notes. This list is intended in part to help students remember the meanings of new vocabulary words by associating them with certain English words. It may also help students expand their English vocabulary and stimulate further interest in learning about the relations among words. The cognates are provided to show how the same root or word in PIE has given rise to a wide variety of seemingly unrelated words in English. Sometimes only the *root* of an English word is related to the corresponding Greek word. Where possible, the portion of the English word that descends from that root is set in boldface.[2]

2. For further information on these and other derivatives and cognates, students may consult the Indo-European Roots Appendix of the *American Heritage Dictionary of the English Language,* 4th ed. (Houghton-Mifflin, 2000).

	Derivatives	*Cognates*
ἀγορά	**agora**phobia, all**egory**	a**ggreg**ate, cram
ἄνθρωπος	**anthrop**ology, mis**anthrope**	
βουλή	abulia	ball, ballistic, de**vil**, para**ble**, parliament
γνώμη	gnomic	know, can, **no**tice, dia**gno**sis
δίκη	**dic**ast, theo**dicy**	toe, ad**dict**, in**dict**
ἔργον	erg, en**erg**y, Ge**org**e	work, irk, organ, orgy
ζῷον	**zo**diac, **zo**ology	**qu**ick, **vi**vid, **whis**key, **bio**logy
θεός	a**the**ism, en**thu**siasm, **ti**ffany	feast, pro**fa**ne
λόγος	**log**ic, apo**logy**, epi**logue**	**leg**al, dia**lect**, inte**llig**ent
μάχη	theo**machy**	might, may
νόμος	auto**nom**ous, eco**nom**y	**nom**ad, **nim**ble
ὁδός	**odo**meter, ex**odus**	
ὅπλον	**hopl**ite	
οἰκίᾱ	**ec**onomy, **ec**ology	village, villain
πόλεμος	polemic	
σοφίᾱ	philo**sophy**	
τέκνον		thane, **toc**ology
ψῡχή	Psyche, psychic	

§5. Accentuation 2: Persistent Accent

The accent on each Greek *noun* is given by the first form of the word as it appears in vocabulary lists and dictionaries. One could say that each Greek noun has a given accent on a given syllable "by nature." When the form of a noun is changed (by the addition of different endings), the given accent is usually *persistent*. A **persistent accent** ideally *remains the same kind of accent (acute or circumflex) on the same syllable*. Sometimes, however, the rules for the possibilities of accent require a noun's persistent accent to change to a different kind of accent or move to a different syllable (§3). For example:

First Form with Given Accent	Changed Forms
δίκη	δίκης, δίκᾱς
πόλεμος	πόλεμον, πολέμου
ψεῦδος	ψεύδους, ψεύδη
σῶμα	σώματος, σωμάτων
ἐλπίς	ἐλπίδος, ἐλπίσιν

OBSERVATIONS

1. When the ending -η of the noun δίκη is changed to –ης or –ᾱς, *no change of accent* is required. The persistent accent given in δίκη, an acute on the penult, remains unchanged.

2. When the ending -ος of the noun πόλεμος is changed to -ον, no change of accent is required. Since the ultima remains *short,* the given accent (acute on the antepenult) does not change. When the ending is changed to -ου, the ultima is no longer short, and no accent may appear on the antepenult. The persistent accent remains acute but moves to the penult.

3. When the ending -ος of the noun ψεῦδος is changed to -ους or -η, the ultima is no longer short. The persistent accent remains on the same syllable, but it changes to an acute.

4. When the noun σῶμα is changed to σώματος or σωμάτων, the syllable bearing the given accent (σω-) becomes the antepenult instead of the penult. In the form σώματος the persistent accent may remain over the same syllable (σω-), but it must change to an acute since only an acute accent may appear on the antepenult. In the form σωμάτων, no accent is possible on the syllable σω- in the antepenult because the ultima is long. The persistent accent is forced both to move to the penult and to change to an acute.

5. When the noun ἐλπίς adds a syllable in its changed forms, the given accent is no longer on the ultima, but it may remain the same accent on the syllable -πι- when that syllable is the penult.

If a noun's given accent is an acute on the ultima, this acute almost always changes to a grave when the noun is followed by another word with no intervening punctuation.

First Form with Given Accent	First Form with Word Following
ποιητής	ποιητὴς νέος
θεός	θεὸς πολέμου

☛ DRILL 5 MAY NOW BE DONE.

§6. The Greek Noun and Its Properties: Gender, Number, and Case

A noun is the name of a person, place, or thing.[3] Every noun in Greek has three properties: **gender**, **number**, and **case**.

GENDER—Greek nouns have the genders **masculine** or **feminine**. Nouns that are neither masculine nor feminine are called **neuter**. In the vocabulary entry for each noun, the gender is indicated by a particular form of the article "the": ὁ = masculine, ἡ = feminine, τό = neuter (§10). The gender for each noun must be memorized.

NUMBER—Greek nouns appear in the **singular** when referring to one and in the **plural** when referring to more than one. The **dual** refers to *pairs* of things (e.g., hands, feet, the sons of Atreus), but dual forms are fairly uncommon. Forms of the dual are given in the Morphology Appendix along with singular and plural forms.

CASE—Greek nouns occur in a variety of different forms in both the singular and the plural. Each different form, or **case**, is indicated by an **ending** attached to a stem that remains the same. Each case ending indicates a noun's syntax, the grammatical function that it has in a sentence. When a Greek noun functions as the subject of a sentence, for example, it has one case ending, but when it functions as the direct object, it usually has a different case ending.

The parent language of Greek, Indo-European, had eight cases for nouns, each case with its own grammatical function or functions. Greek has only five cases, which nevertheless express all the functions of the original eight. This is possible because certain cases in Greek perform more than one grammatical function. In order to clarify the functions of cases in particular instances, prepositions are often used. The names of the Greek cases and their basic functions are:

Nominative Case

—used for the *subject* of a sentence
—used for the *predicate nominative*

The two essential elements of every sentence are the *subject* and the *predicate*. The **subject** is that which is spoken about, and the **predicate** is all that is said about the subject.

Helen wept.
The man will send a letter to his brother.

In these sentences, "Helen" and the "the man" are subjects; "wept" and "will send a letter to his brother" are predicates. Both "Helen" and "the man" would be in the nominative case in Greek, and the syntax of each would be **Nominative, Subject**.[4]

---

3. There are, in fact, several kinds of nouns:
   common nouns: woman, song, town, pancake
   proper nouns: Maisie, Greece, Castor, Beatles
   collective nouns: crowd, tribe, senate, army
   abstract nouns: friendship, beauty, freedom, excellence
   verbal nouns: walking (gerund), to walk (infinitive)
4. The syntax of any noun includes the *case* of the noun and its *grammatical function*.

Certain verbs, such as "be," "become," and "seem," are called **copulative** or **linking** verbs. A linking verb is followed *not* by a direct object but rather by *an element that is equivalent to the subject*, and this element is called a **Predicate Nominative**.

Helen is a queen.
The man will become a god.

In these sentences "Helen" and "the man" are subjects, while "a queen" and "a god" are Predicate Nominatives. Both the subjects and the Predicate Nominatives would be in the nominative case in Greek, and the syntax of a "a queen" or "a god" would be **Predicate Nominative**.

Genitive Case

—used to *qualify* or *limit* another noun in a variety of ways
—often corresponds to a translation using the English preposition "of"
—also expresses *separation* and in this usage corresponds to a translation using the English preposition "from"

In the phrases "the beauty of Helen," "a fear of death," "the brave ones of the soldiers," the phrases "of Helen," "of death," and "of the soldiers" qualify or limit in various ways the nouns on which they depend. These phrases would be expressed in Greek by "Helen," "death," and "soldiers" in the genitive case *with no separate Greek word* corresponding to the English word "of." That is, the genitive case ending *contains within it the idea of* "of."

One idea commonly expressed by the genitive case is that of ownership or possession. In the phrase "the house of the man" (= the house belonging to the man), "of the man" would be expressed in Greek by the word "man" in the genitive case, and the syntax of that word would be **Genitive of Possession**.

In the sentence "We departed from the land," the phrase "from the land" indicates that "we" were *separated* "from the land." In the sentence "They will remove the general from office," "the general" will be *separated* "from office." These two examples begin to illustrate the genitive's *separative* or "from" function. "From the land" and "from office" would be expressed in Greek by "the land" and "office" in the genitive case, and the syntax of each of those words would be **Genitive of Separation**. Sometimes a preposition meaning "from" accompanies a Genitive of Separation in order to clarify this function of the genitive case and distinguish it from other functions of the same case.

Dative Case

—used to express the *person* or *thing interested in or affected by* the action of a verb and in this usage corresponds to a translation using the English prepositions "(with reference) to" or "for"
—also expresses *means* or *instrument* and in this usage corresponds to a translation using the English prepositions "with" or "by (means of)"
—also expresses *location* (in space or time) and in this usage corresponds to a translation using the English prepositions "in," "on," or "at"

In the sentence "To the Corinthians war is inevitable," the phrase "to the Corinthians" expresses the persons *with reference to whom* or *in whose opinion* "war is inevitable." "To the Corinthians" would be expressed in Greek by the word "Corinthians" in the dative case, and the syntax of that word would be **Dative of Reference**. *No separate Greek word* corresponding to the English preposition "to" would be used; such an idea *is contained within* the dative case ending.

In the sentence "She struck him with a sword," the phrase "with a sword" indicates what "she" *used* to strike "him," the *instrument by means of which* "she struck him." "With a sword" would be expressed in Greek by the word "sword" in the dative case, and the syntax of that word would be **Dative of Means** (or **Dative of Instrument**). *No separate Greek word* corresponding to the English preposition "with" would be used; such an idea *is contained within* the dative case ending.

In the sentence "In the house he is safe," the phrase "in the house" expresses an idea of *location*. It answers the question "*Where* is he safe?" The prepositional phrase "in the house" would be expressed in Greek by the word "house" in the dative case *preceded by* a preposition meaning "in."

Accusative Case

—used to express the direct object of a verb
—used following certain prepositions

In the sentence "The poet composes a song," the noun "song" is the *direct object* of the verb "composes" because the action of the verb "composes" is directly exerted on the object "song." "Song" would be expressed in Greek in the accusative case, and the syntax of that word would be **Accusative, Direct Object**.

In the sentence "The army was moving toward the city," the words "the city" express the place *toward which* the "army was moving." "Toward the city" would be expressed in Greek by the word "city" in the accusative case *preceded* by a preposition meaning "toward." Many ideas of motion *toward, into,* or *against* are expressed in Greek by a noun in the accusative case preceded by a preposition.

Vocative Case

—used for *addressing* someone *directly*

In the sentence "Tell me, friend, why you are here," the word "friend" expresses the person being addressed directly by the speaker of the sentence. The word "friend" would be expressed in Greek in the vocative case, usually preceded by a Greek word similar to the English interjection "O."

Summary of Cases and Their Basic Functions

Case Name	Used to Express
Nominative	1. subject
	2. predicate nominative
Genitive	1. "of"
	2. "from"
Dative	1. "to," "for"
	2. "with," "by (means of)"
	3. "in," "on" (with preps.)
Accusative	1. direct object
	2. "toward," "(in)to," "against" (with preps.)
Vocative	direct address

☞ DRILL 6 MAY NOW BE DONE.

§7. The Three Declensions

Greek nouns are grouped in three families called **declensions**. Each noun belongs to *one declension only,* and each declension has its own distinctive sets of case endings.

A full vocabulary entry for a Greek noun contains, in the following order, the *nominative singular,* the *genitive singular,* one of the three *nominative singular* forms of the article "the" to indicate gender,[5] and the English meaning(s). For example:

First Declension	σοφίᾱ, σοφίᾱς, ἡ	wisdom
	γνώμη, γνώμης, ἡ	judgment
Second Declension	λόγος, λόγου, ὁ	word
	ὅπλον, ὅπλου, τό	tool
Third Declension	δαίμων, δαίμονος, ὁ or ἡ	divinity
	σῶμα, σώματος, τό	body

OBSERVATIONS

1. Nouns ending in -ᾱ or -η in the nominative singular and -ᾱς or -ης in the genitive singular belong to the *first* declension.

2. Nouns ending in -ος or -ον in the nominative singular and -ου in the genitive singular belong to the *second* declension.

3. Nouns of the third declension have a great variety of nominative singular forms. Their genitive singular forms usually end in -ος.

5. For a complete presentation of the Greek article, see §10.

4. The masculine singular nominative of the article (ὁ) indicates that a noun is masculine in gender. The feminine singular nominative of the article (ἡ) indicates that a noun is feminine in gender. The neuter singular nominative of the article (τό) indicates that a noun is neuter.

Finding the Stem

The genitive singular given in the vocabulary entry for each noun helps indicate the declension to which the noun belongs. The genitive singular is also the form from which a **stem** is derived for use in making all other forms of the noun.

To find the stem of most nouns, *remove the ending from the genitive singular* (the second element given in the vocabulary entry). What remains is the stem.

σοφίᾱ, σοφίᾱς, ἡ wisdom	stem = σοφι-
γνώμη, γνώμης, ἡ judgment	stem = γνωμ-
λόγος, λόγου, ὁ word	stem = λογ-
ὅπλον, ὅπλου, τό tool	stem = ὁπλ-
δαίμων, δαίμονος, ὁ or ἡ divinity	stem = δαιμον-
σῶμα, σώματος, τό body	stem = σωματ-

All the forms of a noun are created by taking the stem of that noun and adding the case endings that belong to its particular declension. When one generates a complete set of forms for a noun in Greek, one is said to decline the noun, and the resulting set of forms is called a declension of the noun.[6]

§8. Noun Morphology: First Declension 1

Most nouns of the first declension are feminine; some are masculine. There are no neuter first-declension nouns.

The two most common kinds of first-declension nouns are those whose nominative singular forms end in -ᾱ, which are called **long-alpha nouns**, and those whose nominative singular forms end in -η, which are called **eta nouns**. Long-alpha nouns use the set of endings on the left below; eta nouns use the set of endings on the right. *The plural endings of both sets are identical.*

	Case Endings of the First Declension			
	Singular	*Plural*	*Singular*	*Plural*
Nominative/Vocative	-ᾱ	-αι	-η	-αι
Genitive	-ᾱς	-ῶν	-ης	-ῶν
Dative	-ᾳ	-αις	-ῃ	-αις
Accusative	-ᾱν	-ᾱς	-ην	-ᾱς

MEMORIZE EACH SET OF ENDINGS, PROCEEDING DOWN THE SINGULAR COLUMN AND THEN DOWN THE PLURAL COLUMN. BE PREPARED TO RECITE THE ENDINGS QUICKLY.

---

6. *Declension* thus has two meanings: it is both the name for each of the three families of nouns (first declension, second declension, third declension) and the name for a complete set of forms for an individual noun.

To decline a long-alpha noun of the first declension, add the appropriate endings to the stem. For example:

oἰκίᾱ, οἰκίᾱς, ἡ house
stem = οἰκι-

Singular

Nom./Voc.	οἰκίᾱ	a house (subject or predicate nominative)
		house (direct address)
Gen.	οἰκίᾱς	of a house; from a house
Dat.	οἰκίᾳ	to a house/for a house; by a house/with a house; in a house
Acc.	οἰκίᾱν	house (direct object)

Plural

Nom./Voc.	οἰκίαι	houses (subj. or pred. nom.)
		houses (d.a.)
Gen.	οἰκιῶν	of houses; from houses
Dat.	οἰκίαις	to houses/for houses; by houses/with houses; in houses
Acc.	οἰκίᾱς	houses (d.o.)

OBSERVATIONS

1. The abbreviations for the case names used in the model declension above are standard and appear frequently in this textbook. The abbreviations *subj.* (subject), *pred. nom.* (predicate nominative), *d.a.* (direct address), and *d.o.* (direct object) are also standard and used throughout.

2. In both long-alpha and eta first-declension nouns, the nominative and vocative endings are identical in both singular and plural and are therefore listed together. In long-alpha first-declension nouns, -ᾱς is the ending of both the genitive singular and accusative plural.

3. There is no indefinite article in Greek, but the English indefinite article (*a, an*) may be freely supplied in translations of Greek nouns.

4. The accent on nouns is *persistent* and is given by the nominative singular. The rules for the possibilities of accent allow the acute accent on the penult in the word οἰκίᾱ to remain persistent throughout the declension (§3). One accent rule, however, applies to *all* first-declension nouns: the genitive plural ending -ων *always* has a circumflex *no matter where the persistent accent falls*. MEMORIZE THIS ADDITIONAL RULE OF ACCENT.[7]

5. All first-declension nouns have an alternate dative plural ending, -αισι(ν), which appears in Attic poetry and in other dialects. This alternate ending has a nu in parentheses, which is called a **nu movable** or a **movable nu**. It usually appears as part of the dative plural when the word to which it is attached is followed by a word beginning with a vowel *or* when the word to which it is attached is the last word in a clause or sentence. BE PREPARED TO RECOGNIZE THIS ALTERNATE ENDING WHEN IT OCCURS IN READINGS.

6. Although the English translation "from" is given for a word in the genitive case, a genitive is sometimes also preceded by a Greek preposition meaning "from." The English translation

7. In earlier Greek, the genitive plural ending of first-declension nouns was -άων. In Attic Greek the two vowels contracted and resulted in the ending and accent -ῶν.

"in" for the dative is usually used *only* when the noun is preceded by a Greek preposition meaning "in."

To the declension of **οἰκίᾱ** one may compare the declensions of several other first-declension nouns:

	χώρᾱ, χώρᾱς, ἡ land Stem = χωρ-	ἀγορά, ἀγορᾶς, ἡ marketplace Stem = ἀγορ-	δίκη, δίκης, ἡ justice Stem = δικ-	βουλή, βουλῆς, ἡ will Stem = βουλ-
Singular				
Nom./Voc.	χώρᾱ	ἀγορά	δίκη	βουλή
Gen.	χώρᾱς	ἀγορᾶς	δίκης	βουλῆς
Dat.	χώρᾳ	ἀγορᾷ	δίκῃ	βουλῇ
Acc.	χώρᾱν	ἀγοράν	δίκην	βουλήν
Plural				
Nom./Voc.	χῶραι	ἀγοραί	δίκαι	βουλαί
Gen.	χωρῶν	ἀγορῶν	δικῶν	βουλῶν
Dat.	χώραις	ἀγοραῖς	δίκαις	βουλαῖς
Acc.	χώρᾱς	ἀγοράς	δίκᾱς	βουλάς

OBSERVATIONS

1. Although long alpha was the original distinguishing vowel of first-declension nouns, in Attic Greek this long alpha remained only in nouns whose stems end in epsilon, iota, or rho (e.g., **οἰκίᾱ, χώρᾱ, ἀγορά**). In all other nouns, the long alpha changed to an eta (e.g., **δίκη, βουλή**). The vocabulary entry for each noun makes clear whether a noun is a long-alpha noun or an eta noun. Both groups have the same endings in the plural.

2. For the noun **χώρᾱ**, the persistent accent on the penult in the nominative/vocative plural is a circumflex because the ultima is short. For *all* first-declension nouns, the final diphthong -αι in the nominative/vocative plural counts as *short* for purposes of accent. MEMORIZE THIS ADDITIONAL RULE OF ACCENT.

3. If the persistent accent on any first-declension noun is an acute on the ultima (as in **ἀγορά** and **βουλή**), the acute becomes a circumflex in the genitive and dative singular and plural. MEMORIZE THIS ADDITIONAL RULE OF ACCENT.

Summary of Accent Rules for First-Declension Nouns
1. The nominative/vocative plural ending -αι counts as *short* for purposes of accent.
2. The genitive plural ending -ων has a circumflex in *all* first-declension nouns regardless of persistent accent.
3. If the nominative singular has an acute on the ultima, the genitive and dative singular and plural have a circumflex on the ultima.

☞ DRILL 7–8 MAY NOW BE DONE.

§9. Noun Morphology: Second Declension

Nouns of the second declension ending in **-ος** in the nominative singular are either masculine or feminine. Those ending in **-ον** are neuter.

Case Endings of the Second Declension: Masculine/Feminine		
	Singular	*Plural*
Nominative	**-ος**	**-οι**
Genitive	**-ου**	**-ων**
Dative	**-ῳ**	**-οις**
Accusative	**-ον**	**-ους**
Vocative	**-ε**	**-οι**

MEMORIZE THESE ENDINGS, DOWN THE SINGULAR AND THEN DOWN THE PLURAL, AND BE PREPARED TO RECITE THEM QUICKLY.

To decline a masculine/feminine noun of the second declension, add these endings to the stem. For example:

νόμος, νόμου, ὁ custom; law
stem = **νομ-**

Singular
Nom.	νόμος	custom (subj. or pred. nom.)
Gen.	νόμου	of custom; from custom
Dat.	νόμῳ	to/for, by/with, in custom
Acc.	νόμον	custom (d.o.)
Voc.	νόμε	custom (d.a.)

Plural
Nom.	νόμοι	customs (subj. or pred. nom.)
Gen.	νόμων	of customs; from customs
Dat.	νόμοις	to/for, by/with, in customs
Acc.	νόμους	customs (d.o.)
Voc.	νόμοι	customs (d.a.)

OBSERVATIONS

---

1. The vocative singular of masculine/feminine nouns of the second declension has an ending (**-ε**) that is *different from* the nominative singular ending (**-ος**). In *all* declensions *all* vocative plural endings are identical with nominative plural endings.

2. The persistent accent on **νόμος** (given by the nominative singular) remains unchanged throughout the declension. Unlike first-declension nouns, second-declension nouns do not all have **-ῶν** in the genitive plural.

3. All second-declension nouns have an alternate dative plural ending, **-οισι(ν)**, which appears in Attic poetry and in other dialects. This alternate ending has a nu movable. BE PREPARED TO RECOGNIZE THIS ALTERNATE ENDING WHEN IT OCCURS IN READINGS.

	Case Endings of the Second Declension: Neuter	
	Singular	*Plural*
Nominative/Vocative	-ον	-α
Genitive	-ου	-ων
Dative	-ῳ	-οις
Accusative	-ον	-α

MEMORIZE THESE ENDINGS, DOWN THE SINGULAR AND THEN DOWN THE PLURAL, AND BE PREPARED TO RECITE THEM QUICKLY.

To decline a neuter noun of the second declension, add these endings to the stem. For example:

τέκνον, τέκνου, τό child
stem = **τεκν-**

Singular		
Nom./Voc.	τέκνον	child (subj. or pred. nom.)
		child (d.a.)
Gen.	τέκνου	of a child; from a child
Dat.	τέκνῳ	to/for, by/with, in a child
Acc.	τέκνον	child (d.o.)
Plural		
Nom./Voc.	τέκνα	children (subj. or pred. nom.)
		children (d.a.)
Gen.	τέκνων	of children; from children
Dat.	τέκνοις	to/for, by/with, in children
Acc.	τέκνα	children (d.o.)

OBSERVATIONS

1. Neuter nouns of the second declension are distinguished from the masculine/feminine nouns by the ending **-ον** in the nominative/vocative *and* accusative singular and by the ending **-α** in the nominative/vocative and accusative plural. *In all neuter nouns in Greek the accusative ending is identical with the nominative/vocative ending, both in the singular and in the plural.*

2. The persistent accent on **τέκνον** (given by the nominative singular) remains unchanged throughout the declension.

3. All second-declension nouns have an alternate dative plural ending, **-οισι(ν)**, which appears in Attic poetry and in other dialects. This alternate ending has a nu movable. BE PREPARED TO RECOGNIZE THIS ALTERNATE ENDING WHEN IT OCCURS IN READINGS.

To the declensions of **νόμος** and **τέκνον** one may compare the declensions of several other second-declension nouns:

	θεός, θεοῦ, ὁ or ἡ god; goddess Stem = θε-	ἄνθρωπος, ἀνθρώπου, ὁ or ἡ human being Stem = ἀνθρωπ-	ζῷον, ζῴου, τό animal Stem = ζῳ-
Singular			
Nom.	θεός	ἄνθρωπος	ζῷον
Gen.	θεοῦ	ἀνθρώπου	ζῴου
Dat.	θεῷ	ἀνθρώπῳ	ζῴῳ
Acc.	θεόν	ἄνθρωπον	ζῷον
Voc.	—[8]	ἄνθρωπε	ζῷον
Plural			
Nom./Voc.	θεοί	ἄνθρωποι	ζῷα
Gen.	θεῶν	ἀνθρώπων	ζῴων
Dat.	θεοῖς	ἀνθρώποις	ζῴοις
Acc.	θεούς	ἀνθρώπους	ζῷα

OBSERVATIONS

1. If the given accent on any second-declension noun is an acute on the ultima (as in θεός), the acute becomes a circumflex in the genitive and dative singular and plural (cf. ἀγορά, ἀγορᾶς). MEMORIZE THIS ADDITIONAL RULE OF ACCENT.

2. In accordance with the rules for the possibilities of accent, the persistent accent on ἄνθρωπος (acute on the antepenult) must move to the penult in the genitive and dative singular and the genitive, dative, and accusative plural (§3, rules 3 and 4).

3. For the noun ἄνθρωπος, the persistent accent remains on the antepenult in the nominative/vocative plural because the ultima counts as short. For *all* second-declension nouns, the final diphthong -οι in the nominative/vocative plural counts as *short* for purposes of accent (cf. -αι in the first declension). MEMORIZE THIS ADDITIONAL RULE OF ACCENT.

4. In accordance with the rules for the possibilities of accent, the persistent accent on ζῷον (circumflex on a long penult with a short ultima) must change to an acute in the genitive and dative singular and plural because the ultima in these forms is long (§3, rule 3).

Summary of Accent Rules for Second-Declension Nouns
1. Nominative/vocative plural ending -οι counts as *short* for purposes of accent.
2. If nominative singular has acute on ultima, genitive and dative singular and plural have circumflex on ultima.

☞ DRILL 9 MAY NOW BE DONE.

§10. The Article

The Greek word that most closely corresponds to the English definite article, *the,* has separate forms for masculine, feminine, and neuter.[9] MEMORIZE THE DECLENSION OF THE ARTICLE ACROSS THE SINGULAR AND ACROSS THE PLURAL.

8. The vocative singular of this noun (θεέ) does not appear in Attic Greek.
9. There is no Greek word that exactly corresponds to the English indefinite article, *a, an.* A Greek noun *without an article,* however, may be translated using "a" or "an."

	M.	F.	N.
Singular			
Nom.	ὁ	ἡ	τό
Gen.	τοῦ	τῆς	τοῦ
Dat.	τῷ	τῇ	τῷ
Acc.	τόν	τήν	τό
Plural			
Nom.	οἱ	αἱ	τά
Gen.	τῶν	τῶν	τῶν
Dat.	τοῖς	ταῖς	τοῖς
Acc.	τούς	τάς	τά

OBSERVATIONS

1. The masculine and feminine nominative singular and nominative plural of the article (ὁ, ἡ, οἱ, αἱ) have rough breathings and *do not have accents*. Words such as these are called **proclitics** (< προκλίνω, "lean forward") because they are pronounced closely with the words that follow them. These articles are *proclitics*.

2. In all genders the genitive and dative singular and plural of the article have circumflexes. The acute accents on the remaining forms of the article regularly change to *grave* accents because the article is always followed by another word. For example: τὴν βουλήν, τὰ ἔργα.

3. As for all first- and second-declension nouns, all dative plural forms of the article have alternate forms, τοῖσι(ν) (masc., neut.) and ταῖσι(ν) (fem.), which appear in Attic poetry and in other dialects. This alternate ending has a nu movable. BE PREPARED TO RECOGNIZE THESE FORMS WHEN THEY OCCUR IN READINGS.

4. There is no vocative case for the article. When generating a full declension of an article and a noun, however, it is convenient to include the vocative case forms of the noun in the singular and plural, each preceded by the interjection ὦ, "O." This is the usual, unemphatic form of direct address in Greek. For example: ὦ ἑταῖρε, "(O) companion."

5. Many forms of the article resemble the endings of first- and second-declension nouns with the addition of an initial tau.

Agreement of Article and Noun

The article always agrees with its noun in *gender, number, and case*.

ἡ ὁδός	(both article and noun are feminine singular nominative)
τοὺς ἀνθρώπους	(both article and noun are masculine plural accusative)

☛ DRILL 10 MAY NOW BE DONE.

§11. Uses of the Article; The Attributive Position

1. The article may be used to refer to *specific* people or things.

οἱ νόμοι	the (specific) customs (subj.), the customs (subj.)
τὴν γνώμην	the (specific) judgment (d.o.), the judgment (d.o.)

2. The article is often used with the names of famous people and of people previously named. The English word "the" is *not* regularly used when translating proper names.

ὁ Πρίαμος	Priam (subj.) (famous or previously named)
τῇ Ἑλένῃ	for Helen (famous or previously named)

3. The article is used to indicate that a noun *belongs to* someone in a sentence, often the subject. An article so used is translated by forms of the English possessive adjectives ("my," "your," "his," "her," "its," "our," "their").

(She sees) τὰ τέκνα.	(She sees) *her* children.

4. The article is used to refer to *generic* people or things. The English word "the" is *not* regularly used when translating a generic use of the article in Greek.

οἱ ἄνθρωποι	(the class of) human beings (subj.), human beings (subj.)
τὰ ἔργα	deeds (generally) (subj. or d.o.); deeds (subj. or d.o.)

5. The article is *regularly* used with abstract nouns. The English word "the" is *not* regularly used when translating an abstract noun.

ἡ σοφίᾱ	wisdom (subj.)
ἡ δίκη	justice (subj.)

OBSERVATIONS

1. In each of the first three uses, the article indicates that the noun with which it agrees refers to a *specific* person, thing, or group.

2. When a name has *not* been previously mentioned, the article is usually *omitted*.

3. Although in uses 4 and 5 the English word "the" is omitted in translation, the article still serves to *identify* the noun with which it agrees, either as a class or as an abstract concept.

In many expressions of time and place and in many prepositional phrases, the article can be omitted in Greek but should be supplied in English.

εἰς ἀγορᾱ́ν	to the marketplace

The Attributive Position

A word or phrase that describes or limits a noun (e.g., a Genitive of Possession or a prepositional phrase) may be placed *directly after an article* agreeing with that noun. Such a placement is called the **attributive position.**

ἡ τῆς Ἑλένης οἰκίᾱ	the *of Helen* house (subj.)
	the house (subj.) *of Helen*
τὰ ἐν τῇ χώρᾳ ζῷα	the *in the land* animals (subj. or d.o.)
	the animals (subj. or d.o.) *in the land*
ἡ οἰκίᾱ ἡ τῆς Ἑλένης	the house (subj.), the one *of Helen*
	the house (subj.) *of Helen*
τὰ ζῷα τὰ ἐν τῇ χώρᾳ	the animals (subj. or d.o.), the ones *in the land*
	the animals (subj. or d.o.) *in the land*

OBSERVATIONS

1. In the first two examples, the words in the attributive position (τῆς Ἑλένης, ἐν τῇ χώρᾳ) appear *between* the article and the noun. In such an arrangement, there is a slight emphasis on the elements placed in the attributive position.

2. In the second two examples, the words in the attributive position appear *directly after a repeated article*. This arrangement is somewhat less common than the first, and there is a slight emphasis on the *noun* rather than on the elements in the attributive position.

3. Sometimes a noun without an article is followed by an attributive phrase.

οἰκίᾱ ἡ τῆς Ἑλένης   a house (subj.), the one of Helen

In this least-common arrangement, the attributive is added as an afterthought or explanation to a word that otherwise would *not* have a definite article ("a house—I mean the one of Helen").

4. Elements are placed in the attributive position in order to express the *close descriptive or adjectival relation* of these words to the nouns with which they appear.

5. Certain words and certain noun syntax *must* appear in the attributive position. The Genitive of Possession and prepositional phrases *may* appear in the attributive position but do not always do so.

☛   DRILL 11 MAY NOW BE DONE.

CHAPTER 2

Vocabulary

→ αἰτίᾱ, αἰτίᾱς, ἡ cause; responsibility

→ ἀρχή, ἀρχῆς, ἡ beginning;
(supreme) power, rule; empire

→ δόξα, δόξης, ἡ opinion, belief;
reputation; glory; expectation

→ θάλαττα, θαλάττης, ἡ sea

→ ἀλήθεια, ἀληθείᾱς, ἡ truth

→ μοῖρα, μοίρᾱς, ἡ fate

→ Γοργίᾱς, Γοργίου, ὁ Gorgias
νεᾱνίᾱς, νεᾱνίου, ὁ young man

→ Ἅιδης, Ἅιδου, ὁ Hades

→ Ἀτρείδης, Ἀτρείδου, ὁ Atreides,
son of Atreus

→ Εὐρῑπίδης, Εὐρῑπίδου, ὁ Euripides
ποιητής, ποιητοῦ, ὁ maker; poet
πολίτης, πολίτου, ὁ citizen

→ δῆμος, δήμου, ὁ (the) people
φόβος, φόβου, ὁ fear

οὗτος, αὕτη, τοῦτο (demonstr. adj./
pron.) this; pl., these (§20)

ἀγαθός, ἀγαθή, ἀγαθόν good
Ἀθηναῖος, Ἀθηναίᾱ, Ἀθηναῖον
Athenian; masc. pl. subst., Athenians

→ δεινός, δεινή, δεινόν fearsome, terrible;
marvelous, strange; clever

δίκαιος, δικαίᾱ, δίκαιον right, just

→ ἐχθρός, ἐχθρά, ἐχθρόν hated, hateful;
hostile; masc. subst., enemy
κακός, κακή, κακόν bad, evil
καλός, καλή, καλόν beautiful; noble;
fine
Λακεδαιμόνιος, Λακεδαιμονίᾱ,
Λακεδαιμόνιον Lacedaemonian,
Spartan; masc. pl. subst.,
Lacedaemonians, Spartans

→ μόνος, μόνη, μόνον only, alone
σοφός, σοφή, σοφόν wise

→ φίλος, φίλη, φίλον (be)loved, dear;
loving, friendly; masc./fem. subst.,
friend; loved one

→ ἄδικος, ἄδικον unjust

→ ἀθάνατος, ἀθάνατον deathless,
immortal

→ ἀλλά (conj.) but

→ ἀπό (prep. + gen.) (away) from

→ διά (prep. + gen.) through
(prep. + acc.) on account of,
because of
ἤ (conj.) or; ἤ . . . ἤ . . . either . . . or . . .
μή (adv.) not
μόνον (adv.) only

→ οὐ, οὐκ, οὐχ (adv.) not
οὐ/μὴ μόνον . . . ἀλλὰ καί . . .
not only . . . but also . . .

Vocabulary Notes

→ αἰτίᾱ, αἰτίᾱς, ἡ means "cause" or "responsibility," most often in the negative sense of "guilt" or "blame." It often appears with an Objective Genitive (§17).

> τὴν αἰτίᾱν τούτων τῶν κακῶν   the responsibility (d.o.) for these evils
> ἡ τῆς συμφορᾶς αἰτίᾱ   the cause (subj.) of misfortune

→ ἀρχή, ἀρχῆς, ἡ expresses an idea of *being first* and means "beginning," particularly in phrases such as ἐξ ἀρχῆς, "from the beginning," and ἐν ἀρχῇ, "in the beginning." When ἀρχή means "rule," it may be accompanied by a Subjective Genitive (§16) or an Objective Genitive (§17) or both.

> τὴν τῶν Ἀθηναίων ἀρχὴν τὴν τῆς θαλάττης
> the rule (d.o.) of the Athenians (Subj. Gen.) of the sea (Obj. Gen.)

→ δόξα, δόξης, ἡ is related to the verb δοκέω, meaning "think"; "seem." δόξα refers either to how things seem to a person ("belief," "[mere] opinion") or to how a person seems to others ("reputation"; "glory"). When δόξα means "belief" or "opinion," it may be contrasted with words for "truth" or "knowledge," but a δόξα itself may be true or false.

    When δόξα refers to the estimation of others and is not modified by any adjective, it usually suggests a *good* reputation, but one's δόξα may also be expressly identified as good or bad. What one has a reputation *for* is in the genitive case.

> δόξαν σοφίᾱς   a reputation (d.o.) for wisdom

In contexts that look to the past or the future, δόξα means "expectation." Events are often said to have taken place "contrary to expectation" or "according to expectation."

→ θάλαττα, θαλάττης, ἡ, "sea," has an alternate spelling, θάλασσα, θαλάσσης, which originated in the Ionic dialect and was brought over into Attic by Thucydides and the tragedians. Other Attic writers used the later Attic spelling with -ττ- rather than -σσ-. Be prepared to recognize both forms of this noun.

→ ἀλήθεια, ἀληθείᾱς, ἡ is composed of the prefix ἀ-, "not," "without" (called the **alpha privative**) and a root that means "escaping notice." Thus, "truth" is understood as what is "not escaping notice." The word refers both to *truth* as opposed to lies or false things and to *reality* as opposed to mere appearance. The dative singular form (almost always with the article and sometimes with the preposition ἐν) often functions as a Dative of Respect (§18) and is translated "in truth" or "truly."

> ἄνθρωπος τῇ ἀληθείᾳ σοφός   a man (subj.) truly wise

→ The first meaning of μοῖρα, μοίρᾱς, ἡ is "part" or "portion," and one's "fate" or "destiny" is understood as one's allotted portion. When capitalized, **Μοῖρα** refers in the singular to the goddess Fate and in the plural to the three daughters of Zeus and Themis known as the Fates.

→ Γοργίᾱς, Γοργίου, ὁ is the name of Gorgias of Leontini in Sicily, who visited Athens in 427 B.C.E. He was an orator, and, as is indicated in the Platonic dialogue that bears his name, he also taught rhetoric, the art of persuasion in speech.

→ Ἄιδης, Ἄιδου, ὁ (the "Unseen one") is a son of the Titans Kronos and Rhea and a brother of Zeus and Poseidon. He is lord of the underworld, and his consort for two-thirds of the year is Persephone, daughter of Zeus and Demeter. Because Hades is the name of a god and *not* the name of a place, the name appears as a Genitive of Possession in certain common prepositional phrases, in which a noun meaning "house" or "abode" is to be supplied.

ἐξ Ἅιδου	(out) from (the house of) Hades
ἐν Ἅιδου	in (the house of) Hades
εἰς/ἐς Ἅιδου	to (the house of) Hades

One may compare abbreviated English expressions such as "to Tom's" (i.e., to Tom's *house*).

→ When it appears in the singular, Ἀτρείδης, Ἀτρείδου, ὁ, "son of Atreus," usually refers to Agamemnon rather than to his younger brother, Menelaus. Agamemnon is said by Homer to have brought the largest contingent of ships on the expedition to Troy, and he is portrayed in the *Iliad* as the leader of all the Greek forces there. When Ἀτρείδης appears in the plural (or in the dual), both brothers, Agamemnon and Menelaus, are meant.

→ Εὐρῑπίδης, Εὐρῑπίδου, ὁ "Euripides," is one of the Attic tragedians whose plays were performed in Athens during the fifth century B.C.E. Euripides was born in 480 and died in 406, having left Athens in 408 to reside in Macedonia. Nineteen of his more than ninety plays survive.

→ The first meaning of δῆμος, δήμου, ὁ is a piece of land, "district," or "deme." It can also mean "the people" inhabiting such a district or deme. Later δῆμος came to refer collectively to "the common people" as opposed to the aristocracy and then in a political sense to the free citizens, or "the people," in the Athenian democracy.

→ δεινός, δεινή, δεινόν means "fearsome" or "terrible" and can be applied, for example, to deeds, weapons, and gods. A second meaning is "marvelous" or "strange," and with this meaning δεινός describes, for example, human beings, love, and the act of giving birth. δεινός may also mean "clever," and a particular ability or skill is usually specified: δεινὸς περὶ λόγους "(a man, subj.) clever about speeches."

Neuter substantives of δεινός, both in the singular (usually with the article) and in the plural (usually *without* the article) are common. In the plural (δεινά), it is most often the object of verbs meaning "do" or "suffer," and the substantive, "terrible things," signifies illegal, arbitrary conduct or treatment.

→ ἐχθρός, ἐχθρά, ἐχθρόν has the passive meanings "hated," "hateful" and the active meaning "hostile." A Dative of Reference may indicate *to whom* a person or thing is hateful or hostile.

ἔργα τῷ δικαίῳ ἐχθρά	deeds (subj. or d.o.) *hateful* to the just man
Λακεδαιμόνιαι Ἑλένῃ ἐχθραί	Spartan women (subj.) *hostile* to Helen

→ μόνος, μόνη, μόνον most often appears in a nonattributive position. It may appear with a Genitive of Separation, and it is sometimes repeated in the same phrase for emphasis.

μόνοι οἱ θεοί	*only* the gods (subj.)/the gods *alone* (subj.)
Ἑλένης μόνος	(a man, subj.) *alone* from (i.e., apart from) Helen
σὺν τέκνοις μόνη μόνοις	(a woman, subj.) *alone* with her children *alone*

➡ In addition to the common passive meanings "(be)loved," "dear," **φίλος, φίλη, φίλον** may have the active meanings "loving" or "friendly." A Dative of Reference often indicates *to whom* someone or something is dear or friendly.

> **ἄνθρωπον τοῖς θεοῖς φίλον**   a man (d.o.) *dear to the gods*
> **οἱ θεοὶ οἱ ἀνθρώποις φίλοι**   the gods (subj.) *friendly to men*

➡ Adjectives such as **ἄδικος, ἄδικον** and **ἀθάνατος, ἀθάνατον** have only *two* sets of endings because one set of second-declension endings is used for both masculine and feminine. Two-ending adjectives are often *compound adjectives*. A **compound adjective** is composed of a *root* adjective and one or more than one *prefix* or *suffix*.[1] The adjectives **ἄδικος** and **ἀθάνατος** both have the prefix ἀ-, "not," "without" (called the alpha privative). **ἄδικος** means "not just," "unjust"; **ἀθάνατος** means "not mortal," "immortal."

➡ The coordinating conjunction **ἀλλά**, "but," is called an **adversative conjunction** because it introduces an *opposition* or *contrast* to what precedes. After negatives, **ἀλλά** has the force of "but rather." Any two elements of a sentence may be pointedly balanced by the phrase **οὐ/μὴ μόνον . . . ἀλλὰ (καὶ) . . .**, "not only . . . but (also) . . ."

> **οὐ μόνον ἀνθρώποις, ἀλλὰ καὶ θεοῖς**   *not only* for men *but also* for gods

In narrative transitions and responses in dialogue **ἀλλά** may be translated "but yet" or "well, . . ."

➡ **ἀπό** is a preposition meaning "from" or "away from" and is followed by the genitive case only. Although both **ἐκ** and **ἀπό** reinforce the basic separative function of the genitive case, **ἀπό** differs from **ἐκ** in expressing *more remote* ideas of distance and descent.

> **χώρᾱ ἀπὸ θαλάσσης**   a land (subj.) *(at a distance) away from* the sea
> **τοὺς ἀπὸ τῶν θεῶν ἀνθρώπους**   men (d.o.) *(remotely) descended from* the gods

ἀπό can also express departure or *motion away from* a place and in many contexts indicates the starting point, source, or cause of an action.

➡ When **διά** is followed by the genitive case, it expresses the idea of movement "through" a place or a thing.

> **διὰ τῆς χώρᾱς**   *through* the land

With the genitive **διά** may also express *agency* with persons and *means* with things.

> **διὰ τῶν Ἀθηναίων**   *through (the agency of)* the Athenians
> **διὰ καλῶν λόγων**   *through (i.e., with)* fine words

When **διά** is followed by the accusative case, it means "on account of," "because of."

---

1. A **prefix** is a unit of meaning added to the *beginning* of a root word to produce another word. A **suffix** is a unit of meaning added to the *end* of a root word to produce another word.

διὰ τὴν τῶν θεῶν βουλήν	*on account of* the will of the gods
διὰ τὸν πόλεμον	*because of* the war

➙ The proclitic adverb **οὐ**, "not," has three spellings. When it is followed by a word beginning with a consonant, it is spelled **οὐ**. When it is followed by a word beginning with a vowel or diphthong with a smooth breathing, it is spelled **οὐκ**. When it is followed by a word beginning with a vowel or diphthong with a rough breathing, it is spelled **οὐχ**. When **οὐ** is the last word in a clause or sentence, it receives an acute accent. For its use with substantive adjectives, see §15.

τὸ τέκνον τὸ οὐ κακόν	the *not* bad child (subj. or d.o.)
οὐκ ἐν τῇ οἰκίᾳ	*not* in the house
οὐχ ὅπλοις	*not* with weapons

Flash Cards

To make a flash card for an adjective, write out *in full* the nominative singular forms of the adjective on one side and the English meaning(s) on the other side.

καλός, καλή, καλόν	beautiful; noble; fine

Derivatives and Cognates

	Derivatives	*Cognates*
ἀγαθός	Agatha	
αἰτίᾱ	**eti**ology	
ἀλήθεια		**leth**argy, Lethe
ἀπό	**apo**gee	of, off, after, **post**-
δεινός	**dino**saur	
δῆμος	**demo**cracy, epi**dem**ic	tide, time
δόξα	ortho**doxy**, para**dox**	**dog**ma, **doc**trine
θάλαττα	**thalass**ocracy	
κακός	**caco**phany	poppy**cock**
καλός	**cali**sthenics	
	kaleidoscope	
μοῖρα		poly**mer**, **mer**it
μόνος	**mono**logue, monk	**min**now
νεᾱνίᾱς		**ani**mal, **ani**mate
οὐ		no, aught, ever, aye, nay
ποιητής	poet	
φίλος	**phil**ology	
φόβος	agora**phob**ia, **phob**ic	

§12. Noun Morphology: First Declension 2

Short-Alpha Nouns

Some feminine nouns of the first declension have the nominative and genitive singular endings -α, -ᾱς or -α, -ης. These nouns, called **short-alpha nouns**, have only two endings that differ from long-alpha and eta nouns.

	Case Endings of Short-Alpha Nouns			
	Singular	*Plural*	*Singular*	*Plural*
Nominative/Vocative	-α	-αι	-α	-αι
Genitive	-ᾱς	-ῶν	-ης	-ῶν
Dative	-ᾳ	-αις	-ῃ	-αις
Accusative	-αν	-ᾱς	-αν	-ᾱς

Memorize these endings, down the singular and then down the plural, and be prepared to recite them quickly.

To decline a short-alpha noun of the first declension, add the appropriate endings to the stem. For example:

	μοῖρα, μοίρᾱς, ἡ fate stem = μοιρ-		δόξα, δόξης, ἡ opinion stem = δοξ-	
	Singular	*Plural*	*Singular*	*Plural*
Nom./Voc.	μοῖρα	μοῖραι	δόξα	δόξαι
Gen.	μοίρᾱς	μοιρῶν	δόξης	δοξῶν
Dat.	μοίρᾳ	μοίραις	δόξῃ	δόξαις
Acc.	μοῖραν	μοίρᾱς	δόξαν	δόξᾱς

OBSERVATIONS

1. The *short* alpha that is the nominative/vocative singular ending also appears in the accusative singular ending (-αν). *In these two endings only,* short-alpha nouns differ in declension from long-alpha and eta nouns.

2. Like long-alpha and eta nouns, short-alpha nouns have vocative endings identical with nominative endings, both in the singular and in the plural.

3. When the stem of a short-alpha noun ends in epsilon, iota, or rho, the genitive and dative singular endings are -ᾱς and -ᾳ. Otherwise, the genitive and dative singular endings are -ης and -ῃ.

4. The plural endings for short-alpha nouns are identical with the plural endings for all other first-declension nouns.

5. Regular rules for persistent accent apply to short-alpha nouns. As for all other first-declension nouns, the -αι ending of the nominative/vocative plural counts as *short* for purposes of accent, and the ending -ῶν of the genitive plural receives a circumflex.

Masculine Nouns Ending in -ᾱς, -ου; -ης, -ου

Some names of men and other *masculine* nouns of the first declension have the nominative and genitive singular endings -ᾱς, -ου and -ης, -ου and have vocative singular endings that differ from the nominative singular. In all other forms these nouns have endings identical with those of long-alpha and eta nouns.

Case Endings of Masculine First-Declension Nouns

	Singular	Plural	Singular	Plural
Nominative	-ᾱς	-αι	-ης	-αι
Genitive	-ου	-ῶν	-ου	-ῶν
Dative	-ᾳ	-αις	-ῃ	-αις
Accusative	-ᾱν	-ᾱς	-ην	-ᾱς
Vocative	-ᾱ	-αι	-η/-α	-αι

MEMORIZE THESE ENDINGS, DOWN THE SINGULAR AND THEN DOWN THE PLURAL, AND BE PREPARED TO RECITE THEM QUICKLY.

To decline a masculine noun of the first declension, add the appropriate endings to the stem. For example:

	νεᾱνίᾱς, νεᾱνίου, ὁ young man stem = νεᾱνι-		πολίτης, πολίτου, ὁ citizen stem = πολῑτ-	
	Singular	Plural	Singular	Plural
Nom.	νεᾱνίᾱς	νεᾱνίαι	πολίτης	πολῖται
Gen.	νεᾱνίου	νεᾱνιῶν	πολίτου	πολῑτῶν
Dat.	νεᾱνίᾳ	νεᾱνίαις	πολίτῃ	πολίταις
Acc.	νεᾱνίᾱν	νεᾱνίᾱς	πολίτην	πολίτᾱς
Voc.	νεᾱνίᾱ	νεᾱνίαι	πολῖτα	πολῖται

OBSERVATIONS

1. The genitive singular ending -ου is borrowed from the masculine genitive singular ending of the second declension. *Only in this ending and in the nominative and vocative singular endings* do masculine first-declension nouns differ from long-alpha and eta nouns.

2. When the stem of a first-declension masculine noun ends in epsilon, iota, or rho, the dative and accusative singular endings are -ᾳ and -ᾱν. Otherwise, the dative and accusative singular endings are -ῃ and -ην.

3. When the stem of a first-declension masculine noun ends in epsilon, iota, or rho, the vocative singular ending is -ᾱ. Otherwise, the vocative singular ending is -η, but if the nominative singular ends in -της, the vocative singular ending is -α. Thus, the vocative singular of Εὐρῑπίδης, Εὐρῑπίδου, ὁ, "Euripides," is Εὐρῑπίδη, but the vocative singular of πολίτης, πολίτου, ὁ, "citizen," is πολῖτα.

4. The plural endings for first-declension masculine nouns are identical with the plural endings for all other first-declension nouns.

5. Regular rules for persistent accent apply to masculine first-declension nouns. As for all other first-declension nouns, the -αι ending of the nominative/vocative plural counts as *short* for purposes of accent, and the ending -ῶν of the genitive plural receives a circumflex. If a masculine first-declension noun has an acute accent on the ultima in the nominative singular, this accent becomes a circumflex in the genitive and dative singular and plural. For example: ποιητής, ποιητοῦ, ὁ.

☞   DRILL 12 MAY NOW BE DONE.

§13. First-Second-Declension Adjectives

An adjective describes or modifies a noun. Examples of adjectives in English are *just, important, blue, graceful.*

Greek nouns generally have one gender and belong to one declension. Adjectives, however, have *all genders.* The vocabulary entry for a first-second-declension adjective contains either three forms (masculine, feminine, neuter nominative singular) or two forms (masculine/feminine, neuter nominative singular), followed by the meaning(s).

καλός, καλή, καλόν	beautiful; noble; fine
ἄδικος, ἄδικον	unjust

First-second-declension adjectives with three forms in the vocabulary entry (such as **καλός, καλή, καλόν**) use endings borrowed from the first declension when modifying feminine nouns and from the second declension when modifying masculine and neuter nouns. First-second-declension adjectives with two forms in the vocabulary entry (such as **ἄδικος, ἄδικον**) use endings borrowed from the second declension only.

Like nouns, adjectives are declined. To decline a first-second-declension adjective, TAKE THE STEM FROM THE NEUTER SINGULAR NOMINATIVE FORM BY DROPPING THE ENDING -ον AND ADD ENDINGS FROM THE FIRST AND SECOND DECLENSIONS OF NOUNS. For example:

καλός, καλή, καλόν beautiful; noble; fine
stem = καλ-

	Singular			Plural		
	M.	*F.*	*N.*	*M.*	*F.*	*N.*
Nom.	καλός	καλή	καλόν	καλοί	καλαί	καλά
Gen.	καλοῦ	καλῆς	καλοῦ	καλῶν	καλῶν	καλῶν
Dat.	καλῷ	καλῇ	καλῷ	καλοῖς	καλαῖς	καλοῖς
Acc.	καλόν	καλήν	καλόν	καλούς	καλάς	καλά
Voc.	καλέ	καλή	καλόν	καλοί	καλαί	καλά

OBSERVATIONS

1. All the endings in the declension of **καλός, καλή, καλόν** are identical with the endings used for eta first-declension and second-declension nouns.

2. The accent on *all* adjectives is *persistent*, given by the *neuter* singular nominative form. Like nouns similarly accented, first-second-declension adjectives with an acute accent on the ultima in the nominative singular have a circumflex in the genitive and dative singular and plural.

ἄδικος, ἄδικον unjust
stem = ἀδικ-

	Singular		*Plural*	
	M./F.	N.	M./F.	N.
Nom.	ἄδικος	ἄδικον	ἄδικοι	ἄδικα
Gen.	ἀδίκου	ἀδίκου	ἀδίκων	ἀδίκων
Dat.	ἀδίκῳ	ἀδίκῳ	ἀδίκοις	ἀδίκοις
Acc.	ἄδικον	ἄδικον	ἀδίκους	ἄδικα
Voc.	ἄδικε	ἄδικον	ἄδικοι	ἄδικα

OBSERVATIONS

---

1. All the endings in the declension of ἄδικος, ἄδικον are identical with the endings used for second-declension nouns.

2. In adjectives with two forms in the nominative singular, *one* set of endings (-ος, -ον, etc.) is used for *both* masculine and feminine.

3. The accent on *all* adjectives is *persistent*, given by the *neuter* singular nominative form. Final -οι counts as *short* for purposes of accent.

Some first-second-declension adjectives with three forms in the nominative singular have stems ending in epsilon, iota, or rho. For such adjectives, the feminine singular uses the endings of long-alpha first-declension nouns rather than eta first-declension nouns. For example:

Ἀθηναῖος, Ἀθηναίᾱ, Ἀθηναῖον Athenian
stem = Ἀθηναι-

	Singular			*Plural*		
	M.	F.	N.	M.	F.	N.
Nom.	Ἀθηναῖος	Ἀθηναίᾱ	Ἀθηναῖον	Ἀθηναῖοι	Ἀθηναῖαι	Ἀθηναῖα
Gen.	Ἀθηναίου	Ἀθηναίᾱς	Ἀθηναίου	Ἀθηναίων	Ἀθηναίων	Ἀθηναίων
Dat.	Ἀθηναίῳ	Ἀθηναίᾳ	Ἀθηναίῳ	Ἀθηναίοις	Ἀθηναίαις	Ἀθηναίοις
Acc.	Ἀθηναῖον	Ἀθηναίᾱν	Ἀθηναῖον	Ἀθηναίους	Ἀθηναίᾱς	Ἀθηναῖα
Voc.	Ἀθηναῖε	Ἀθηναίᾱ	Ἀθηναῖον	Ἀθηναῖοι	Ἀθηναῖαι	Ἀθηναῖα

OBSERVATIONS

---

1. All the endings in the declension of Ἀθηναῖος, Ἀθηναίᾱ, Ἀθηναῖον are identical with the endings used for long-alpha first-declension and second-declension nouns.

2. The accent on *all* adjectives is *persistent*, given by the *neuter* singular nominative form. *Unlike* first-declension nouns, however, the accent does *not* shift to the ultima in the feminine plural genitive form. Final -οι and -αι count as *short* for purposes of accent.

§14. Noun-Adjective Agreement; Placement of Adjectives

Every adjective must agree with the noun it modifies in gender, number, and case. When an adjective is used to give a quality or attribute of a noun, it may precede or follow a noun when there is no article. When an article is used, the adjective is placed in the *attributive position.*

ὁδὸς ἀγαθή	a good road (subj.)	(ἀγαθή = fem. sing. nom.)
ὁ καλὸς λόγος	the beautiful speech (subj.)	(καλὸς = masc. sing. nom.)
τὴν ἄδικον ψῡχήν	the unjust soul (d.o.)	(ἄδικον = fem. sing. acc.)
τοῖς ποιηταῖς τοῖς καλοῖς	for the noble poets	(καλοῖς = masc. pl. dat.)

Although they may not always have endings identical with the endings of the nouns they modify, the adjectives in the examples above have the same *gender, number,* and *case* as the nouns they modify.

☛ DRILL 13–14 MAY NOW BE DONE.

§15. Substantive Use of the Adjective

In English an adjective modifying no noun but preceded by the definite article "the" functions as a noun. For example:

> Lonely are *the brave.*
> Your donation will help *the poor.*

In these sentences the phrases "the brave" (subject of the verb "are") and "the poor" (direct object of the verb "will help") are virtual nouns, and words such as "ones" or "people" may be easily understood after the adjectives "brave" and "poor."[2]

In Greek, an adjective *with or without* the article may stand alone and function as a noun. An adjective so used is called a **substantive**, and one may refer to the **substantive use** of an adjective or to an adjective **used substantively.**

When a Greek substantive is translated into English, it is convenient to reflect the gender and number by supplying a word such as "man," "woman," or "thing" (sing.) or "men," "women," "people," "ones," or "things" (pl.).

καλά	beautiful *things* (subj. or d.o.)
τῇ ἀγαθῇ	for the good *woman*
τὸν κακόν	the bad *man* (d.o.)
τὸ κακόν	the bad *thing* (subj. or d.o.)

Adjectives used as substantives may be negated by two different adverbs, **οὐ**, which is a proclitic, and **μή**. Both mean "not," but **οὐ** negates *specific* substantives, and **μή** negates *generic* substantives.

---

2. Many English adjectives have also become nouns in their own right and are frequently used as such. For example: "Do *good* whenever you can." "The love of money is the root of all *evil.*"

οἱ καλοί	the (specific) noble men (subj.)
	(the class of) noble men (subj.)
οἱ οὐ καλοί	the (specific) not noble men (subj.)
οἱ μὴ καλοί	(the class of) not noble men (subj.)

OBSERVATION

A substantive adjective with *no negation* may be either specific or generic, as the two translations of the first example indicate. However, when a substantive is negated, the particular negative indicates whether the substantive refers to someone or something specific or to someone or something generic.

Some Greek adjectives are commonly used as substantives, and substantive meanings are given in their vocabulary entries. These substantive meanings should be learned along with the given meanings. Four such adjectives are:

Ἀθηναῖος, Ἀθηναίᾱ, Ἀθηναῖον Athenian; *masc. pl. subst.,* Athenians
ἐχθρός, ἐχθρά, ἐχθρόν hated, hateful; hostile; *masc. subst.,* enemy
Λακεδαιμόνιος, Λακεδαιμονίᾱ, Λακεδαιμόνιον Lacedaemonian, Spartan; *masc. pl. subst.,*
  Lacedaemonians, Spartans
φίλος, φίλη, φίλον (be)loved, dear; loving, friendly; *masc./fem. subst.,* friend; loved one

☛ DRILL 15 MAY NOW BE DONE.

§16. Subjective Genitive

When a noun in the genitive case expresses the person or thing *performing a verbal action implied in another noun,* it is called a **Subjective Genitive**. For example:

> τῇ τοῦ θεοῦ βουλῇ   by the will of the *god*

The syntax of the italicized word (θεοῦ) is **Subjective Genitive**.

OBSERVATIONS

1. In the phrase above, the noun βουλῇ implies a verbal action (willing) that is *performed by* the noun θεοῦ in the genitive case: *the god wills* something. Because θεοῦ is understood to be *performing* an implied verbal action (willing), its syntax is Subjective Genitive.

2. In prose the Subjective Genitive is often placed in the *attributive* position.

§17. Objective Genitive

When a noun in the genitive case expresses the person or thing *receiving a verbal action implied in another noun,* it is called an **Objective Genitive**. For example:

> τὸν λόγων ποιητήν   (ποιητής, ποιητοῦ, ὁ maker)
> the maker (d.o.) *of speeches*

The syntax of the italicized word (λόγων) is **Objective Genitive**.

OBSERVATION

> In the phrase above, the noun ποιητήν implies a verbal action (making) that is *performed on* the noun in the genitive case (λόγων): someone *makes speeches.* Because λόγων is understood to be *receiving* the implied verbal action, its syntax is Objective Genitive.

Distinguishing Subjective and Objective Genitives

Sometimes a noun may be construed as *either* a Subjective *or* an Objective Genitive, and context usually makes clear the precise syntax. For example:

> τὸν τῶν Ἀθηναίων φόβον   (φόβος, φόβου, ὁ fear)
> the fear (d.o.) *of the Athenians*

This phrase may mean that the Athenians *are fearing* something, and the syntax of Ἀθηναίων would be Subjective Genitive. However, it may also mean that someone *fears* the Athenians, and the syntax of Ἀθηναίων would be Objective Genitive.

Occasionally a Subjective and Objective Genitive appear together. For example:

> τὸν τῶν Ἀθηναίων φόβον τὸν τοῦ πολέμου
> the fear (d.o.) *of the Athenians of war*

This phrase implies that the Athenians fear war. Ἀθηναίων is a Subjective Genitive, and πολέμου is an Objective Genitive.

For greater clarity or to accommodate English usage, alternate translations of Subjective and Objective Genitives can be used. For example:

> τὸν τῶν Ἀθηναίων φόβον τὸν τοῦ πολέμου
> the fear (d.o.) *of war on the part of the Athenians*
> (Subjective Gen. translated with "on the part of")

> περὶ τῆς τῶν Λακεδαιμονίων αἰτίας τῆς τοῦ πολέμου   (αἰτίᾱ, αἰτίᾱς, ἡ responsibility)
> concerning *the Spartans'* responsibility *for the war*
> (Subjective Gen. translated as possessive; Objective Gen. translated with "for")

§18. Dative of Respect

A noun in the dative case may limit the meaning of an adjective, a verb, or a clause or sentence by specifying the *respect in which* the adjective (verb, clause, sentence) is to be understood. Such a noun is called a **Dative of Respect**. For example:

> **λόγῳ φίλοι, ἀλλὰ ἔργῳ οὔ**   (φίλος, φίλη, φίλον [be]loved, dear; *masc./fem. subst.*, friend)
> *in (respect to) word* friends, but *in (respect to) deed* (in fact) not
>
> **ἄνθρωπον τῇ ἀληθείᾳ ἀγαθόν**   (ἀλήθεια, ἀληθείᾱς, ἡ truth; ἀγαθός, ἀγαθή, ἀγαθόν good)
> a man (d.o.) good *in (respect to) truth*
> a man (d.o.) *truly* good

The syntax of each italicized word (λόγῳ, ἔργῳ, ἀληθείᾳ) is **Dative of Respect**.

OBSERVATIONS

---

1. The Dative of Respect may have developed from the Dative of Means (§ 6), and it is sometimes difficult to distinguish between the two.
2. The article may appear with a Dative of Respect.
3. When τῇ ἀληθείᾳ functions as a Dative of Respect, it may be translated with the English adverb "truly."

§19. Accusative of Respect

A noun in the accusative case may limit the meaning of an adjective, a verb, or a clause or sentence by specifying the *respect in which* the adjective (verb, clause, sentence) is to be understood. Such a noun is called an **Accusative of Respect**.[3] For example:

> **τῷ ψῡχὴν καλῷ**   (καλός, καλή, καλόν beautiful; noble)
> for the man noble *in (respect to) soul*
>
> **αἱ γνώμην σοφαί**   (σοφός, σοφή, σοφόν wise)
> women (subj.) wise *in (respect to) judgment*

The syntax of each italicized word (ψῡχήν, γνώμην) is **Accusative of Respect**.

---

3. The Accusative of Respect is sometimes called the **Accusative of Specification**.

1. While the Dative of Respect may have developed from the instrumental function of the dative case, the Accusative of Respect reflects the capacity of the accusative case to express *extent*: "noble *to the extent (of)* soul," "noble *as far as soul goes*."

2. The Accusative of Respect is often used for parts of the body, both literal (arm, leg, etc.) and figurative (soul).

3. The article may appear with an Accusative of Respect.

☞ DRILL 16–19 MAY NOW BE DONE.

§20. The Demonstrative Adjective and Pronoun οὗτος, αὕτη, τοῦτο

A **demonstrative adjective** or **pronoun** is used to *point out* or *refer specifically* to someone or something. A demonstrative *adjective agrees with or modifies an expressed noun*. A demonstrative *pronoun stands alone*.

This book is interesting. (*This* is a demonstrative *adjective* modifying the noun *book*.)
This is interesting. (*This* is a demonstrative *pronoun*, standing alone and referring to something nearby in context.)

Like the article ὁ, ἡ, τό (which is also essentially an adjective), οὗτος, αὕτη, τοῦτο, "this" (sing.), "these" (pl.), has forms for all three genders, singular and plural.

		Singular			*Plural*	
	M.	F.	N.	M.	F.	N.
Nom.	οὗτος	αὕτη	τοῦτο	οὗτοι	αὗται	ταῦτα
Gen.	τούτου	ταύτης	τούτου	τούτων	τούτων	τούτων
Dat.	τούτῳ	ταύτῃ	τούτῳ	τούτοις	ταύταις	τούτοις
Acc.	τοῦτον	ταύτην	τοῦτο	τούτους	ταύτας	ταῦτα

MEMORIZE THIS DECLENSION ACROSS THE SINGULAR AND ACROSS THE PLURAL.

1. There are no vocative case forms for οὗτος, αὕτη, τοῦτο.

2. With the exception of the neuter singular nominative and accusative, the endings of οὗτος, αὕτη, τοῦτο are identical with endings of the first and second declensions.

3. The forms of οὗτος, αὕτη, τοῦτο that begin with a rough breathing (masculine and feminine singular and plural nominative) are the same as the forms of the article that begin with a rough breathing (ὁ, ἡ, οἱ, αἱ). *All* forms of οὗτος, αὕτη, τοῦτο have accents, and *all* are accented on the penult.

4. In all feminine forms *except* the genitive plural the stem contains the diphthong -αυ-. This diphthong also appears in the neuter plural nominative and accusative forms.

5. In the masculine and feminine plural nominative forms, final -**οι** and -**αι** count as *short* for purposes of accent.

When **οὗτος, αὕτη, τοῦτο** functions as an adjective modifying a noun, it agrees with that noun in gender, number, and case. In prose the noun has an article, and the demonstrative adjective is placed *not* in the attributive position but *before* or *after* the article-noun phrase.[4] The article in such phrases is *omitted* in English translations.

οὗτοι οἱ νόμοι	these laws (subj.)
ἐν ταύτῃ τῇ ὁδῷ	on this road
τὰ ὅπλα ταῦτα	these weapons (subj. or d.o.)

When **οὗτος, αὕτη, τοῦτο** stands alone and functions as a pronoun referring to someone or something already mentioned, it is convenient to reflect the gender and number in English translations by supplying the words "man," "woman," or "thing" (sing.) or "men," "women," or "things" (pl.).

τούτους	these men (d.o.)
περὶ τούτων	concerning these things (men, women)
ταύτῃ	for this woman
ἡ τούτου σοφία	the wisdom (subj.) of this man

OBSERVATION

When the pronoun **οὗτος, αὕτη, τοῦτο** is used as a Genitive of Possession, it regularly appears in the *attributive position* in prose. This Genitive of Possession always refers to someone or something already mentioned.

In addition to pointing out people and things, **οὗτος, αὕτη, τοῦτο** may be used to refer to someone famous or notorious. When **οὗτος** is so used, it is regularly placed *after* the noun it modifies, and the definite article is regularly omitted. The word "famous" or "notorious" is added to the translation of the demonstrative adjective.

Ἀλέξανδρος οὗτος	this famous/notorious Alexander (subj.)

☞ DRILL 20 MAY NOW BE DONE.

§21. Apposition

Sometimes a noun or pronoun receives further definition or limitation from another noun placed next to it, often set off in commas. The second noun is called an **appositive** or is said to be **in apposition to** the noun before it. A NOUN IN APPOSITION MUST BE IN THE SAME CASE AS THE WORD THAT IT DEFINES OR LIMITS. For example:

---

4. In poetry the article is often omitted.

τῷ Ἀλεξάνδρῳ, τέκνῳ Πριάμου
for Alexander, a child of Priam

τὴν εἰρήνην, τοῖς ἀνθρώποις καλόν   (καλός, καλή, καλόν beautiful)
peace (d.o.), a beautiful thing for men

In the first phrase, the syntax of τέκνῳ is dative, in apposition to Ἀλεξάνδρῳ. In the second phrase, the syntax of καλόν is accusative, in apposition to εἰρήνην.

CHAPTER 3

Vocabulary

→ γαῖα, γαίᾱς, ἡ earth; land

→ γῆ, γῆς, ἡ earth; land

→ ξένος, ξένου, ὁ host, guest, guest-friend;
stranger, foreigner
οὐρανός, οὐρανοῦ, ὁ sky, heaven
πόνος, πόνου, ὁ labor, toil; distress,
suffering

→ σύμμαχος, συμμάχου, ὁ ally

→ ἄρχω, ἄρξω, ἦρξα, ἦρχα, ἦργμαι,
ἤρχθην rule (+ gen.); middle, begin
(+ gen.)

→ διδάσκω, διδάξω, ἐδίδαξα, δεδίδαχα,
δεδίδαγμαι, ἐδιδάχθην teach; explain;
middle, cause (someone) to be taught

→ ἐθέλω/θέλω, ἐθελήσω, ἠθέλησα,
ἠθέληκα, ――, ―― be willing, wish

→ λέγω, λέξω, ἔλεξα/εἶπον, ――,
λέλεγμαι, ἐλέχθην say; speak (of), tell
(of), recount

→ μέλλω, μελλήσω, ἐμέλλησα, ――,
――, ―― intend, be about, be likely (+
inf.)

→ παύω, παύσω, ἔπαυσα, πέπαυκα,
πέπαυμαι, ἐπαύθην stop (trans.);
middle, stop (intrans.), cease

→ πείθω, πείσω, ἔπεισα, πέπεικα,
πέπεισμαι, ἐπείσθην persuade; middle,
obey; heed; believe (+ dat.)

→ πέμπω, πέμψω, ἔπεμψα, πέπομφα,
πέπεμμαι, ἐπέμφθην send

→ αἰσχρός, αἰσχρά, αἰσχρόν disgraceful,
shameful; ugly

→ κοινός, κοινή, κοινόν common (to),
shared (with); (+ gen. or dat.)
public

→ ἆρα (interrog. particle) introduces a
question

→ γάρ (postpositive conj.)
explanatory, for
confirming, indeed, in fact

→ δέ (postpositive conj.)
adversative, but
connective, and
εὖ (adv.) well

→ μέν (postpositive particle) on the one
hand; μέν..., δέ... on the one hand...,
on the other hand...; ..., but...
νῦν (adv.) now
πολλάκις (adv.) many times, often
πότε (interrog. adv.) when

→ πρός (prep. + gen.) from; by;
in the name of
(prep. + dat.) near; in addition to
(prep. + acc.) toward; against;
in reply to, in the face of, in
relation to

→ πῶς (interrog. adv.) how

→ ὑπό (prep. + gen.) (from) under; by;
at the hands of
(prep. + dat.) under; under the
power of
(prep. + acc.) under; during

Vocabulary Notes

→ γαῖα, γαίᾱς, ἡ means "earth" or "land," and although it does appear in prose, it is essentially the po-etic equivalent of γῆ, γῆς, ἡ. When capitalized, **Γαῖα** is the primal procreative Earth, who generates and then unites with **Οὐρανός**, Sky, to produce many offspring, including the Titans.

→ γῆ, γῆς, ἡ has a circumflex on all singular forms. Plural forms do not occur in Attic Greek and are rare elsewhere. In Attic prose γῆ is the word for the "earth" as opposed to the heavens and the sea. It is also used as a general word for "land," and it frequently appears even in tragedy with this meaning.

→ The earliest meaning of ξένος, ξένου, ὁ is "host," "guest," or "guest-friend," and it is used for either of two people (or states) who are joined by an exchange of gifts in a pact of friendship. In Attic Greek ξένος more often refers to the guest than to the host. The words ξένος and φίλος are not mutually exclusive, but ξένος suggests a more formal bond between two people. By extension of the meaning of "guest," ξένος is also used of a "stranger" and is a common term of address in both Attic tragedy and Plato. It may also be used of any "foreigner" from the perspective of the writer of a work.

→ Because the first syllable of σύμμαχος, συμμάχου, ὁ, "ally," is related to the preposition σύν, it also has an older Attic spelling, ξύμμαχος, which appears frequently. Be prepared to recognize both forms of this noun.

Flash Cards for Verbs

Since all the stems for all the forms of each Greek verb are found in the principal parts, the first step in learning a verb is the memorization of those principal parts. It is efficient to learn at one time all the principal parts for each verb. The second step is memorizing particular meanings for both the *active* and (if any) *middle* voices (§23). (Except in special instances discussed in the vocabulary notes, the passive may be assumed to mean the passive of the active. Thus, for example, the meaning of ἄρχω in the passive voice is "be ruled.")[1] To make a flash card for a verb, write out all principal parts on one side—use a blank when a verb *lacks* a principal part—and write the English meaning(s) on the other side. Each blank should be *memorized* as part of the principal parts of a verb. Flash cards are most effective when the principal parts or meanings are *said aloud*.

ἄρχω, ἄρξω, ἦρξα, ἦρχα, ἦργμαι, ἤρχθην

Active Meaning(s)	Middle Meaning(s)
rule (+ gen.)	begin (+ gen.)

The following chart may be used to make flash cards for the verbs in Chapter 3. The first meanings given in a vocabulary entry are always those for the *active* voice. A verb with *no* meaning given for the middle voice either has *no* middle voice forms or appears in the middle voice rarely—and when it does, its meaning in the middle voice is hardly distinguishable from its meaning in the active voice. Four of the verbs given below have special middle meanings.

---

1. For meanings of verbs in all three voices, students may consult the Principal Parts of Verbs list at the back of the textbook.

ἄρχω, ἄρξω, ἦρξα, ἦρχα, ἦργμαι, ἤρχθην rule (+ gen.); *middle*, begin (+ gen.)

διδάσκω, διδάξω, ἐδίδαξα, δεδίδαχα, δεδίδαγμαι, ἐδιδάχθην teach, explain;
middle, cause (someone) to be taught

ἐθέλω/θέλω, ἐθελήσω, ἠθέλησα, ἠθέληκα, ——, —— be willing, wish

λέγω, λέξω, ἔλεξα/εἶπον, ——, λέλεγμαι, ἐλέχθην say; speak (of), tell (of), recount

μέλλω, μελλήσω, ἐμέλλησα, ——, ——, —— intend, be about, be likely

παύω, παύσω, ἔπαυσα, πέπαυκα, πέπαυμαι, ἐπαύθην stop (trans.);
middle, stop (intrans.), cease

πείθω, πείσω, ἔπεισα, πέπεικα, πέπεισμαι, ἐπείσθην persuade;
middle, obey; heed; believe (+ dat.)

πέμπω, πέμψω, ἔπεμψα, πέπομφα, πέπεμμαι, ἐπέμφθην send

In the fourth and fifth principal parts of most Greek verbs beginning with a *consonant,* the first consonant is *doubled* with the addition of an epsilon: for example, π̄έμπω: fourth principal part, π̄έπομφα; fifth principal part, π̄έπεμμαι. In the fourth and fifth principal parts of most Greek verbs beginning with a *vowel,* the doubling of the initial vowel produces a *lengthened* vowel: for example, ἄ̄ρχω: fourth principal part, ῆ̄ρχα, fifth principal part, ῆ̄ργμαι. Both types of doubling are called **reduplication.**

→ ἄρχω, ἄρξω, ἦρξα, ἦρχα, ἦργμαι, ἤρχθην in the active voice may sometimes mean "initiate" or "be the first to start" (a war, a conversation), but much more common is the meaning "rule." Whom or what one rules is in the genitive case. This use of the genitive case arises from the idea of ruler implied in the verb and may be considered an Objective Genitive.

οἱ Ἀθηναῖοι τῶν νήσων ἦρχον.   The Athenians were ruling (i.e., were the rulers of) *the islands.*

ἄρχω in the middle voice means "begin" and is usually accompanied by an Objective Genitive or an Object Infinitive (§36), but it may also be used absolutely; that is, it may occur without an expressed direct object.

οἱ Λακεδαιμόνιοι τοῦ πολέμου ἄρχονται. (Objective Gen.)
The Spartans are beginning *the war.*

ὁ Γοργίᾱς λέγειν ἄρχεται. (Object Infin.)
Gorgias is beginning *to speak.*

ἄρχεται ὁ πόλεμος ἐκ τῶν ἀδίκων ἔργων. (used absolutely)
The war *is beginning* resulting from unjust deeds.

→ διδάσκω, διδάξω, ἐδίδαξα, δεδίδαχα, δεδίδαγμαι, ἐδιδάχθην is formed from the IE root *dek-,* "be fitting," and exhibits reduplication with iota in *all* its principal parts. In the fourth and fifth principal parts, ordinary reduplication of the initial consonant (with epsilon) *also* occurs.
    διδάσκω in the active voice is transitive and takes an Accusative, Direct Object of the *person*

taught, and it may take an Object Infinitive (§36) or a *second* Accusative, Direct Object to express the *thing taught.* These two direct objects are sometimes referred to as a **Double Accusative**.

> τὸ τέκνον εὖ λέγειν διδάσκω. (Acc., D.O., Object Infin.)
> I am teaching *my child to speak* well.
>
> τὸ τέκνον τὴν τῶν ποιητῶν σοφίᾱν διδάσκω. (Double Acc.)
> I am teaching *my child the wisdom* of the poets.

The thing taught may also be expressed in a prepositional phrase.

> τὸ τέκνον περὶ τοῦ πολέμου διδάσκω.   I am teaching my child *about war.*

διδάσκω in the middle voice means "cause (someone) to be taught." The thing taught may be expressed in the same variety of ways as in the active voice.

> τὸ τέκνον εὖ λέγειν διδάσκομαι.   I am causing my child to be taught to speak well.

διδάσκω in the passive voice means "be taught." Even in the passive voice διδάσκω may be accompanied by an accusative to express the *thing taught* or by an Object Infinitive. The accusative that appears with a passive form of διδάσκω is called a **Retained Accusative** because it is as if the accusative has been retained from a statement of the same idea in the active voice.

> ὁ ἀγαθὸς τὴν τῶν ποιητῶν σοφίᾱν τὸν νεᾱνίᾱν διδάσκει.
> The good man is teaching the young man *the wisdom* of the poets.
>
> ὁ νεᾱνίᾱς ὑπὸ τοῦ ἀγαθοῦ διδάσκεται τὴν τῶν ποιητῶν σοφίᾱν.
> The young man is being taught *the wisdom* of the poets by the good man.
> (τὴν . . . σοφίᾱν = Retained Accusative)

➙ ἐθέλω/θέλω, ἐθελήσω, ἠθέλησα, ἠθέληκα, ——, —— has *active voice forms only.* For present tense forms the alternate present stem θελ- is regularly used in tragedy and appears in prose authors as well, particularly (but not only) when the preceding word ends in a vowel. The imperfect tense is always formed with the stem ἐθελ-, and the augmented stem is ἠθελ-.

The first meaning of ἐθέλω, "be willing," refers to the consent rather than to the desire of the subject, but the word may also mean "wish." When ἐθέλω is negated by οὐ or μή, the adverb and the verb together may be translated by the English verb "refuse." ἐθέλω frequently takes an Object Infinitive (§36), and in certain contexts this infinitive may be implied but not expressed.

> λέγειν ἐθέλεις;   Are you willing *to speak?*
> οὐκ ἐθέλω.   I refuse (to speak).

➙ In Homer the most common meaning of λέγω, λέξω, ἔλεξα/εἶπον, ——, λέλεγμαι, ἐλέχθην is "pick," "gather," but in Attic prose and poetry it usually means "say"; "speak (of)," "tell (of)," "recount." λέγω is related to the noun λόγος. The form εἶπον in the third principal part is not derived from the same root as the other forms of λέγω, but it is a common alternate of ἔλεξα. λέγω appears commonly in the active and passive voices. Middle voice forms are rare.

λέγω regularly takes an Accusative, Direct Object, a Dative of Indirect Object (§38), or both, and it may also appear with a variety of prepositional phrases.

τὰς συμφορὰς Ἑλένης ἔλεγεν.	He was recounting *the misfortunes* of Helen. (Acc., D.O.)
Ἑλένῃ ἔλεγεν.	He was speaking *to Helen*. (Dat., I.O.)
ταῦτα τῷ τέκνῳ λέγω.	I am telling *my child these things*. (Acc., D.O. and Dat., I.O.)
ὁ Γοργίας περὶ τῆς δίκης λέγει.	Gorgias is speaking *about justice*. (prepositional phrase)

When λέγω means "call," it takes an Accusative, Direct Object and a *second* word in the accusative case called a **Predicate Accusative**.

συμμάχους τοὺς ξένους λέγομεν.	We call the foreigners *allies*. (συμμάχους = Pred. Acc.)

λέγω sometimes has the noun λόγος as a direct object.

λόγον περὶ εἰρήνης ἔλεγον.	I was speaking a speech about peace.

When the direct object of a verb is a noun derived from the same root as that of the verb, it is called a **Cognate Accusative**. One may compare English expressions such as "dream a dream," "sing a song."

When λέγω means "tell" in the sense of "command" it takes a Dative of Indirect Object (§38) and an Object Infinitive (§36).

τῷ τέκνῳ λόγου ἄρχεσθαι ἔλεγον.	I was telling (commanding) *my child to begin* a speech.

λέγω may also have the meaning "mean."

πῶς τοῦτο λέγεις, ὦ Γοργία;	How do you mean this, Gorgias?

→ When μέλλω, μελλήσω, ἐμέλλησα, ——, ——, —— means "intend," "be about," or "be likely," it takes a present or future infinitive, both of which are translated as present.

μέλλουσι λέγειν/λέξειν.	They are about *to speak*.

μέλλω almost always appears in the active voice.

→ παύω, παύσω, ἔπαυσα, πέπαυκα, πέπαυμαι, ἐπαύθην is transitive in the active voice and means "make (someone or something) stop." In addition to an Accusative, Direct Object, a Genitive of Separation may appear.

λόγον νῦν παύω.	I am now stopping *(my)* speech.
Εὐρῑπίδην τοῦ λόγου ἐπαύομεν.	We were making *Euripides* stop *(from)* his speech.

In the middle voice παύω is an *intransitive* verb meaning "stop (oneself)," "cease."

> οὐ παύεται ὁ πόλεμος.   The war is not stopping.
> ἔργων κακῶν παύσομαι.   I shall cease from evil deeds.

παύω in the passive voice means "be stopped."

→ πείθω, πείσω, ἔπεισα, πέπεικα, πέπεισμαι, ἐπείσθην, "persuade," is transitive in the active voice. It takes an Accusative, Direct Object of the *person persuaded,* and it may take an Object Infinitive (§36) or a prepositional phrase as well.

> οἱ τῶν ἀνθρώπων λόγοι τοὺς θεοὺς οὐ πείθουσιν.
> The words of men do not persuade *the gods.*
>
> περὶ τούτων τὰ τέκνα ἔπειθον.
> *Concerning these things* I was persuading *my children.*
>
> τοὺς Λακεδαιμονίους παύεσθαι πολέμου πείθει.
> He is persuading *the Spartans to cease* from war.

Particularly in the present and imperfect tenses, πείθω often has a *conative* significance. If a verb is understood as **conative**, its action is only *attempted* or *intended* and is not actually accomplished. Thus, ἔπειθον in the second sentence above and πείθει in the third sentence may be translated "I was *trying to persuade*" and "he is *trying to persuade.*"[2]

πείθω in the middle voice is intransitive and means "obey," "heed," "believe." The person or thing one obeys or believes is expressed as a Dative of Reference.

> τοῖς νόμοις πειθόμεθα.   We are obeying *the laws.*
> εὖ λέγει, ἀλλὰ τούτῳ οὐ πείθομαι.   He is speaking well, but I do not believe *this man.*

πείθω in the passive voice means "be persuaded."

→ πέμπω, πέμψω, ἔπεμψα, πέπομφα, πέπεμμαι, ἐπέμφθην, "send," is *transitive* in the active voice and takes an Accusative, Direct Object. It may also appear with an *implied but not expressed* direct object such as "a messenger" or "ambassadors."

> Ἑλένην ἐκ τῆς χώρᾱς πέμψει.
> He will send Helen out from the land.
>
> περὶ εἰρήνης εἰς τὰς νήσους ἔπεμπον.
> They were sending (ambassadors) to the islands concerning peace.

πέμπω may be used with an Accusative, Direct Object and a Dative of Indirect Object (§38).

> ὅπλα τοῖς Ἀθηναίοις οὐκ ἐπέμπομεν.   We were not sending weapons *to the Athenians.*

---

2. Although *any* verb in the present or imperfect tense *may* have conative significance, only verbs for which this force is common are identified as such in the vocabulary notes.

πέμπω appears in the passive voice but is rare in the middle voice.

→ αἰσχρός, αἰσχρά, αἰσχρόν is related to a noun meaning "disgrace" or "shame" (αἶσχος) and so means "disgraceful" or "shameful." It is also used of a person's physical appearance with the meaning "ugly." In either of these senses it is used as the opposite of καλός.

→ κοινός, κοινή, κοινόν means "common" or "shared" when describing something held or experienced in common with others (rule, the sea, laws, dangers). In this sense κοινός may be accompanied by a genitive *or* dative of the person or people to or with whom something is common or shared.

> τὸν κοινὸν νόμον
> the common law (d.o.)
>
> ἡ ἀρχὴ ἡ κοινὴ τῶν Ἀθηναίων καὶ Λακεδαιμονίων
> the rule (subj.) shared with the Athenians and Spartans
>
> αἱ συμφοραὶ αἱ ἀνθρώποις κοιναί
> the misfortunes (subj.) common to human beings

κοινός also means "public" (as opposed to private), and it may modify such things as a speech, a constitution, crimes. The neuter singular substantive, τὸ κοινόν, occurs frequently and refers to "the state" or "the government." The neuter *plural* substantive, τὰ κοινά, often means "the public treasury" or "public affairs." The neuter singular substantive is also used *without* the article in a number of prepositional phrases: ἐκ κοινοῦ or ἀπὸ κοινοῦ, "at public expense"; εἰς/ἐς κοινόν, "openly," "publicly."

→ The interrogative particle ἆρα is used to introduce a question that expects either a yes or no answer. A **particle** is a word that is not assigned to any other part of speech (e.g., adverb, adjective, etc.). ἆρα is *not required* to mark a question, but when it does appear, ἆρα is always the first word in prose and nearly always the first in poetry. When ἆρα is followed by οὐ, the expected answer is "yes."

> ἆρα τοὺς συμμάχους ἔπειθεν; Was he persuading the allies?
>   (Answer may be "yes" or "no")
> ἆρα οὐ τοὺς συμμάχους ἔπειθεν; Wasn't he persuading the allies?
>   (Expected answer is "yes")

→ γάρ is called a **postpositive** conjunction because it is regularly *placed after* the first word in a sentence. It often introduces a clause or sentence that *explains the reason* for a preceding one (*explanatory* or *causal* γάρ). An explanatory γάρ is translated "for."

> τοὺς σοφοὺς ἐκ τῆς γῆς πέμπει· ἄρχειν γὰρ τοῦ δήμου ἐθέλει.
> He is sending the wise men out from the land; *for* he wishes to rule the people.

When γάρ is used to introduce a clause or sentence that *confirms* a preceding one (*confirming* γάρ), it is translated "indeed" or "in fact."

> τοῖς τούτου λόγοις οὐ πείθομαι· οὐ γὰρ ἐθέλω.
> I am not being persuaded by the words of this man; *indeed,* I am refusing (to be persuaded).

Confirming γάρ often occurs in questions with the omission of several elements, where it is used to seek confirmation, as well as in answers, where another speaker indicates his or her agreement with what was just said. In such cases γάρ is often untranslatable.

> τὴν ἀλήθειαν περὶ τῶν πολῑτῶν ἔλεγον. οὐ γάρ;
> I was speaking the truth about the citizens. (*Indeed*) (was I) not? (seeks confirmation)
>
> Α. τὴν ἀλήθειαν περὶ τῶν πολῑτῶν ἔλεγον.
> Β. περὶ γὰρ τούτων καὶ περὶ τοῦ φόβου.
> A. I was speaking the truth about the citizens.
> B. *Indeed* (you *were* speaking the truth) about these men and about their fear. (indicates agreement with what was just said)

γάρ is often joined with other particles, conjunctions, and adverbs to form **particle combinations** with specialized meanings. Two common ones are extensions of explanatory γάρ: καὶ γάρ, "for in fact," and ἀλλὰ γάρ, "but as a matter of fact."

→ δέ is a postpositive conjunction that introduces a word, clause, or sentence that differs from what precedes. When δέ introduces something *in contrast with* what precedes (*adversative* δέ), it is translated "but"; adversative δέ is weaker than ἀλλά. When δέ introduces something *additional* or *new* (*connective* δέ), it is translated "and." Connective δέ usually indicates that there is continuity in thought from one clause to the next. Context usually makes clear which δέ occurs in a particular sentence.

> τὴν περὶ ψῡχῆς δόξαν ἔλεγεν, τοὺς δὲ πολῑτᾱς οὐκ ἔπειθεν.
> He was speaking his opinion about soul, *but* he was not persuading the citizens. (adversative δέ)
>
> τὴν περὶ ψῡχῆς δόξαν ἔλεγεν, τοὺς δὲ πολῑτᾱς ἔπειθεν.
> He was speaking his opinion about soul, *and* he was persuading the citizens. (connective δέ)

→ In early Greek poetry (Homer, Hesiod, Pindar) the postpositive particle μέν is often used by itself to emphasize a word next to it ("certainly," "indeed"), but in Attic Greek this use is rare and for the most part confined to poetry. Instead, μέν is regularly used in the first of two clauses that are *antithetical* (in opposition) to each other. The second clause very often contains δέ, and it is convenient to translate the words μέν . . . δέ . . . "on the one hand . . . , on the other hand . . . ," or *not* to translate μέν and to translate δέ "but." The first clause is called the μέν **clause** and the second is called the δέ **clause**.

> οἱ μὲν ἀγαθοὶ ὑπὸ τοῦ σοφοῦ διδάσκονται, οἱ δὲ κακοὶ οὐκ ἐθέλουσιν.
> The good men, *on the one hand,* are being taught by the wise man; the bad men, *on the other hand,* are refusing (to be taught by the wise man).
> The good men are being taught by the wise man, but the bad men are refusing.

Sometimes a somewhat sharper contrast is marked by μέν in the first clause and ἀλλά in the second clause.

> οὗτοι μὲν δίκαια λέγουσιν, ἀλλὰ Εὐρῑπίδης τὸν δῆμον ἀδίκοις λόγοις πείθει.
> These men say just things, but Euripides is trying to persuade the people with unjust speeches.

→ The preposition **πρός** expresses a basic relation of each case by which it is followed: genitive, "from"; dative, "at"; accusative, "toward." **πρός** with the genitive case expresses *descent, point of view,* or *agent as the source* ("from," "by"). (For **πρός** with a Genitive of Personal Agent see §37.) In oaths and appeals it is translated "by" or "in the name of."

> *πρὸς Γοργίου πειθόμεθα.*   We are being persuaded *by Gorgias.*
> *πρὸς θεῶν εὖ λέγει Γοργίας.*   *In the name of the gods,* Gorgias is speaking well.

πρός with the dative case expresses *location close to* ("near") when the noun in the dative is a *place*. It may also mean "in the presence of" and "in addition to."

> *πολέμου ἐπαύοντο καὶ ἄρχεσθαι ἤθελον. πρὸς δὲ τούτοις περὶ εἰρήνης ἔλεγον.*
> They were ceasing from war and were willing to be ruled. And *in addition to these things* they were
>   speaking about peace.

πρός with the accusative case expresses *motion toward* a place ("toward"). It may also mean "in the face of," "in relation to," or, in a hostile sense, "against." With verbs of speaking it means "in reply to."

> *τὰ ἔργα τὰ πρὸς τὴν ψῡχὴν ἀγαθὰ διδάξω.*
> I shall teach the good works in relation to the soul.

> *οἱ Λακεδαιμόνιοι τοῦ πολέμου πρὸς τοὺς Ἀθηναίους ἤρχοντο.*
> The Spartans were beginning the war against the Athenians.

→ The interrogative adverb **πῶς** is used to ask "how." It may also ask for an explanation: "How is it that?" Used rhetorically, **πῶς** may express astonishment or doubt, and in replies it may express agreement or raise a strong objection.

> *πῶς οἱ Ἀθηναῖοι τοῦ πολέμου ἄρχονται;*   *How* are the Athenians beginning the war?
>
> *πῶς ὁ Γοργίᾱς ἐν τῇ βουλῇ λέγει;*   *How is it that* Gorgias is speaking in the council?
>
> **Α.** *ταῦτα περὶ τῆς ψῡχῆς ἐλέγομεν.*   A. We were saying these things about the soul.
> **Β.** *πῶς γὰρ οὔ;*   B. Indeed *how* (were we) not (saying these things)?
>   (Agreement)
>
> **Α.** *οὐχ οἱ θεοὶ τῶν ἀνθρώπων ἄρχουσιν.*   A. The gods do not rule men.
> **Β.** *πῶς δὲ ταῦτα λέγεις;*   B. But *how* do (can) you say these things?
>   (Objection)

→ When followed by the genitive case, the preposition **ὑπό** means "(from) under" (the earth, the shadows, one's eyelids), but much more common is the meaning "by" in expressing *agency* with a Genitive of Personal Agent (§37).

> *ὑπὸ τῶν ἀγαθῶν διδάσκομαι.*   I am being taught *by* good men.

With passive verbs and even with intransitive verbs in the active voice, ὑπό in a phrase of cause or agency (with emotions, persons, or things) is translated "impelled by" (e.g., anger) or "at the hands of" (e.g., one's enemies).

When followed by the dative case, ὑπό expresses position or location under and is translated "beneath" or "at the foot of" (the earth, the walls of Troy, mountains). With persons or gods, meanings such as "under the power of" or "under the protection of" are appropriate.

When followed by the accusative case, ὑπό expresses *motion* toward and under, but it may also express position under. In expressions of time ὑπό may be translated "toward," "in the course of," or "during": ὑπὸ τὴν εἰρήνην ("during [the time of] the peace").

Derivatives and Cognates

	Derivatives	*Cognates*
ἄρχω	archaeology, mon**arch**	
γῆ	**ge**ology	
κοινός	**cen**obite, epi**cene**	**ge**mot, **con**nect, **con**trary
λέγω	**lex**icon, pro**leg**omenon	
ξένος	**xen**ophobia, **xen**on	**guest**, **host**age, **hos**pital
οὐρανός	**Uran**us	
παύω	**pau**se	
πείθω		a**bide**, **fi**ancé, **fed**eral, **faith**
πέμπω	**pomp**	
πόνος	geo**pon**ic, litho**pone**	**spin**, su**spend**, **span**, **pound**
ὑπό	**hypo**dermic	**up**, **op**en, **eaves**drop, **sub-**

§22. Accentuation 3: Recessive Accent

There is no given accent to be learned for verbs, as for nouns and adjectives, and the accent on *most* Greek verb forms is **recessive**. A **recessive accent** *recedes* or *moves back* from the ultima as far as it can *while obeying the rules for the possibilities of accent* (§3).[3] For example:

ἐθέλομεν

ἐθέλεις

ἐπαύσω

παῦσον

OBSERVATIONS

1. In the verb form ἐθέλομεν, the ultima is *short,* so the recessive accent moves back as far as the antepenult and must be an acute (§3, rule 4).

2. In the verb form ἐθέλεις, the ultima is *long,* so the recessive accent moves back only as far as the penult and is an acute since the vowel in that syllable is *short* and the ultima is *long* (§3, rule 3).

3. In the verb form ἐπαύσω, the ultima is long, so the recessive accent moves back only as far as the penult and is an acute since the ultima is *long* (§3, rule 3).

4. In the verb form παῦσον, the ultima is *short,* so a recessive accent on the antepenult would be possible. Since this word has only two syllables, however, the recessive accent moves back only as far as the penult. Since the penult is long and the ultima is short, the accent is a circumflex (§3, rule 6).

☛ DRILL 22 MAY NOW BE DONE.

§23. The Finite Greek Verb and Its Properties: Person, Number, Tense, Voice, Mood

A verb is the part of speech that expresses action, existence, or occurrence. It is used to declare or assert something about the subject.[4] Every verb form in Greek *may* have a maximum of five properties—**person, number, tense, voice,** and **mood**—and a **finite verb form** is *defined* or limited by *all five* of these properties.

PERSON—Greek verbs appear in the **first person** when the subject of the verb is the speaker (I, we), in the **second person** when the subject is the person addressed (you, you [pl.]), and in the **third person** when the subject is the person or thing spoken about (he, she, it, they, or any specific noun that could replace these pronouns, such as the boy, Euripides, dangers).

---

3. A one-syllable verb form with a *short* syllable has an acute accent. A one-syllable verb form with a *long* syllable may have either an acute accent or a circumflex. Whenever such a form is introduced in this textbook, its accent is noted.

4. There are, in fact, several kinds of verbs:
  —**transitive** verbs, which carry the action from a subject to a direct object: the dog *chases* the cat.
  —**intransitive** verbs, which do *not* carry the action from a subject to a direct object: the dog *barks.*
  —**linking** verbs, which equate the subject with a noun or adjective in the predicate: my dog *is* beautiful.

NUMBER—Greek verbs appear in the **singular** when the subject is one and in the **plural** when the subject is more than one. Greek verbs *may* appear in the **dual** when the subject is two, but since dual forms are fairly uncommon, they are not introduced in this textbook. The forms of the dual are given in the Morphology Appendix along with the singular and plural forms.

TENSE—The **tense** of a Greek verb *often* indicates *time* and *always* indicates *aspect*:
1. time: present, past, or future
2. aspect: simple, progressive, repeated, or completed

Aspect refers to the way the action of a verb is looked at and in particular indicates *the relation of the action to the passage of time*. A verb that has **simple aspect** represents an action as *simply occurring once*.

Mom, I *hear* a noise! (present time)
That boy *ate* two desserts. (past time)
The candidate *will win* the election tomorrow. (future time)

A verb that has **progressive aspect** represents an action as *being in progress*.

The boys *are making* a noise. (present time)
She *was reading* a book during the lecture. (past time)
I *shall be waiting* right here until you return. (future time)

A verb that has **repeated aspect** represents an action as *repeated* or habitual.

We *walk* at least a mile every day. (present time)
The boy *used to live* in the country. (past time)
I *shall sit* here on and off for days and days. (future time)

A verb that has **completed aspect** represents an action as already *completed*.

She *has read* three books about snakes. (present time)
When I went to bed, I *had cleaned* the whole house. (past time)
He *will have cooked* a three-course dinner by the time Dad gets home. (future time)

Different verb tenses can *share the same time* but *differ in aspect*. The verbs in the following English sentences are all in past time; they differ in *aspect only*.

The boy *sneezed.*	simple aspect
The boy *was sneezing.*	progressive aspect
Every time he smelled pepper, the boy *sneezed.*	repeated aspect
Because the boy *had sneezed,* I offered a hankie.	completed aspect

VOICE—A Greek verb appears in the **active** voice when its subject is *performing* the action of the verb. (The speaker *is persuading* his audience.) A Greek verb appears in the **passive** voice when its subject is *receiving* the action of the verb. (The speaker *is being persuaded* by his mother). A Greek verb may also appear in a third voice, the **middle** voice, when its subject is performing the action of the verb *with reference to itself or upon itself* or *with some special interest in the action*. Vocabularies and dictionaries regularly give active and then middle meanings for Greek verbs.

Mood—A Greek verb occurs in one of four different moods based on the *writer's or speaker's attitude* toward the factuality or likelihood of the action expressed. The **indicative** mood is used to represent an action as factual or to ask a question of fact. (The cat *is scratching* the furniture. Why *is* the cat *scratching* the furniture?) The **imperative** mood is used to give a command. (*Scratch* your scratching post, Whitey.) The **subjunctive** mood is used to represent an action as an exhortation or as a deliberative question. (*Let* us *leave* the cat alone! *Should* we *leave* the cat alone?) The **optative** mood is used to represent an action as *wished for* or as *possible*. (*If only* the cat *would* not *scratch* the furniture. That cat *might scratch* you.)

OBSERVATION

The subjunctive and optative moods are also used to express several other types of actions that are viewed as nonfactual.

§24. The Greek Tenses of the Indicative Mood: Overview

Since Greek tenses have three possible times (*present, past, future*) and four possible aspects (*simple, progressive, repeated, completed*), it would be most efficient if Greek had twelve tenses corresponding to the twelve possible combinations of time and aspect. In fact, Greek has only *seven* tenses in the indicative mood:

1. **Present**: reports an action in *present* time with *simple* or (more often) *progressive* or *repeated* aspect. (She hears. She is hearing. She hears [every day/often/repeatedly].)
2. **Imperfect**: reports an action in *past time* with either *progressive* or *repeated* aspect. (She was hearing. She used to hear. She heard [every day/often/repeatedly].)
3. **Future**: reports an action in *future* time with *simple* or (less often) *progressive* or *repeated* aspect. (She will hear. She will be hearing. She will hear [every day/often/repeatedly].)
4. **Aorist**: reports an action in *past* time with *simple* aspect. (She heard.)
5. **Perfect**: reports an action in *present* time with *completed* aspect. (She has heard.)
6. **Pluperfect**: reports an action in *past* time with *completed* aspect. (She had heard.)
7. **Future Perfect**: reports an action in *future* time with *completed* aspect. (She will have heard.)[5]

OBSERVATIONS

1. All tenses in Greek that may indicate *progressive* aspect (i.e., present, imperfect, and future) may also indicate *repeated* aspect.

2. The present and future indicative may indicate simple, progressive, or repeated aspect. Context usually makes clear the appropriate translation.

The chart below shows the seven tenses of the indicative mood arranged according to time and aspect with a sample verb showing the corresponding verb phrase in English:

5. The Future Perfect is rare in Greek and is not included in this textbook.

The Seven Greek Tenses of the Indicative Mood

A　S　P　E　C　T

		Simple	Progressive/Repeated	Completed
T	Present	Present "he says"	Present "he is saying" "he says (every day)"	Perfect "he has said"
I **M**	Past	Aorist "he said"	Imperfect "he was saying" "he said (every day)" "he used to say"	Pluperfect "he had said"
E	Future	Future "he will say"	Future "he will be saying" "he will say (every day)"	Future perfect "he will have said"

Tenses that are present or future in time are called **primary tenses**. Tenses that are past in time are called **secondary tenses**.

Primary Tenses	Secondary Tenses
Present	Imperfect
Future	Aorist
Perfect	Pluperfect
Future Perfect (rare)	

☞ DRILL 23–24 MAY NOW BE DONE.

§25. The Vocabulary Entry for a Verb: Principal Parts

The full vocabulary entry for a verb contains six **principal parts** and English meanings for the verb. The six principal parts are the *given elements* from which all the forms of a Greek verb are created. For example:

παύω, παύσω, ἔπαυσα, πέπαυκα, πέπαυμαι, ἐπαύθην stop (trans.); *middle,* stop (intrans.), cease

OBSERVATION

When παύω[6] appears in the *active* voice, it is **transitive**; that is, it expresses an action that is directly exerted on a direct object (e.g., "He is stopping the strife of war"). When it appears in the *middle* voice, it is **intransitive**; that is, it expresses an action that is *not* directly exerted on a direct object (e.g., "The strife of war is stopping").

---

6. A Greek verb is referred to by the first principal part (παύω), unlike an English verb, which is referred to by its infinitive (to stop).

Principal Part		
1 παύω	first person sing. present active indicative	"I am stopping" (trans.)
2 παύσω	first person sing. future active indicative	"I shall stop" (trans.)
3 ἔπαυσα	first person sing. aorist active indicative	"I stopped" (trans.)
4 πέπαυκα	first person sing. perfect active indicative	"I have stopped" (trans.)
5 πέπαυμαι[7]	first person sing. perfect middle/passive indicative	"I have stopped" (intrans.)/ "I have been stopped"
6 ἐπαύθην	first person sing. aorist passive indicative	"I was stopped"

OBSERVATION

Each of the six principal parts is a finite form in the first person singular, but from these principal parts stems may be taken for use in creating all the other forms of each Greek verb. THE PRINCIPAL PARTS OF EACH VERB MUST BE MEMORIZED; they cannot be guessed.

§26. Omega Verbs (Thematic Verbs)

To form any finite Greek verb form:

1. take a *stem* from one of the principal parts
2. *sometimes* add a *prefix* that indicates past time
3. add *endings* that indicate three things: person, number, and voice.

Omega verbs are so called from the ending -ω of principal part 1 (the first person singular present active indicative). Omega verbs are also called **thematic verbs** (< θέμα, "primary element") because some of their stems have **thematic vowels** (-o- or -ε-) *at the ends* of the stems before endings indicating person, number, and voice (**personal endings**) are added. The resulting combinations of thematic vowels and personal endings are commonly presented as *endings* for various tenses.[8]

When one generates a complete set of forms of a particular tense and voice of a Greek verb, one is said to **conjugate** the verb in that tense and voice, and the resulting set of forms is called a **conjugation**.

☛   DRILL 25–26 MAY NOW BE DONE.

§27. Present Active Indicative of Omega Verbs

To form the present active indicative of an omega verb:

1. take the **present stem** by removing the -ω from the **first** principal part
2. add the following **primary active endings**:[9]

7. The final -αι of πέπαυμαι counts as *short* for purposes of accent.
8. A second group of verbs have -μι as the ending in principal part 1 and are called -μι **verbs** or **athematic verbs** because they lack thematic vowels. See §55.
9. Tenses that are present or future in time are called primary tenses (§24).

Person	Singular		Plural	
1	-ω	I	-ομεν	we
2	-εις	you	-ετε	you (pl.)
3	-ει	he, she, it	-ουσι(ν)	they

MEMORIZE THESE ENDINGS, DOWN THE SINGULAR AND THEN DOWN THE PLURAL, AND BE PREPARED TO RECITE THEM QUICKLY.

OBSERVATIONS

1. Each of the primary active endings is in origin a combination of a thematic vowel (-o- or -ε-) and one of the *primary active personal endings*. Only in the first and second person plural endings (-ομεν and -ετε) do the thematic vowels (-o- or -ε-) and the personal endings (-μεν, -τε) remain distinct and unchanged.

2. The ending of the third person plural has a nu in parentheses, which is called a nu movable or a movable nu (§8, Observation 5, p. 27). This nu usually appears as part of the third person plural form when the word to which it is attached either is followed by a word beginning with a vowel *or* is the last word in a clause or sentence.

Thus, the present active indicative conjugation of παύω is:

Present Stem: παυ-

Singular
1 παύω   I am stopping (trans.)
2 παύεις   you are stopping (trans.)
3 παύει   he, she, it is stopping (trans.)

Plural
1 παύομεν   we are stopping (trans.)
2 παύετε   you (pl.) are stopping (trans.)
3 παύουσι(ν)   they are stopping (trans.)

OBSERVATIONS

1. The accent on finite verb forms is *recessive*. In the singular forms the accent is on the penult. When the ultima is short (as in the plural forms), the accent moves back to the antepenult.

2. Although there *are* words in Greek for the personal pronouns "I," "you," etc., these are regularly omitted when they are the subjects of verbs. *Because the verb endings supply the subjects, these pronouns are not required.* In the third person singular, if no subject is expressed, the appropriate pronoun ("he," "she," or "it") must be determined from context. If the subject is expressed, *no pronoun should be supplied.*

τὸν λόγον παύει.   He/She is stopping his/her speech.
ὁ ἄνθρωπος τὸν λόγον παύει.   The man is stopping his speech.

3. The English translations for the present tense forms given above have progressive aspect. Because the present tense may also have simple or repeated aspect, alternate translations are possible: "I stop," "I stop (repeatedly)," etc.

§28. Subject-Verb Agreement

A finite verb agrees with its subject in *person and number*. If the subject is singular, the verb must be singular. If the subject is plural, the verb must be plural. However, if the subject is *neuter plural*, the *verb in Greek is regularly singular*. MEMORIZE THIS RULE OF SUBJECT-VERB AGREEMENT. For example:

οἱ θεοὶ τὸν πόλεμον παύουσιν.
The gods the war (d.o.) are stopping.
The gods are stopping the war.
(both subject and verb are plural)

τὰ τῶν θεῶν τέκνα τὸν πόλεμον παύει.
The children of the gods are stopping the war.
(subject is neuter plural; verb is *singular*)

§29. Present Middle and Passive Indicative of Omega Verbs

In the present tense, the middle and passive forms of omega verbs are *identical*. To form the present middle/passive indicative of an omega verb:

1. take the **present stem** by removing the **-ω** from the **first** principal part
2. add the following **primary middle/passive endings**:

Person	Singular		Plural	
1	-ομαι	I	-ομεθα	we
2	-η/-ει	you	-εσθε	you (pl.)
3	-εται	he, she, it	-ονται	they

MEMORIZE THESE ENDINGS, DOWN THE SINGULAR AND THEN DOWN THE PLURAL, AND BE PREPARED TO RECITE THEM QUICKLY.

OBSERVATIONS

1. Each of the primary middle/passive endings is a combination of a thematic vowel (**-o-** or **-ε-**) and one of the *primary middle/passive personal endings,* which are:

Person	Singular		Plural	
1	-μαι	I	-μεθα	we
2	-σαι	you	-σθε	you (pl.)
3	-ται	he, she, it	-νται	they

These primary middle/passive personal endings are used by themselves and in combination with thematic vowels to form many *primary* middle and passive tenses in Greek.

2. With the exception of the second person singular ending, each primary middle/passive ending is a simple combination of a thematic vowel (**-o-** or **-ε-**) and a primary middle/passive *personal* ending.

3. In the second person singular ending, the sigma of the middle/passive *personal* ending -**σαι** became **intervocalic** (between vowels) when it was added after the thematic vowel -**ε**- (*-εσαι).[10] In Attic Greek, a sigma between two vowels—called an **intervocalic sigma**—was regularly dropped, and the remaining vowels contracted according to regular rules to produce the ending -**η** (*-εσαι > *-εαι > -η). The sound of this ending was also written -**ει**, and both endings came to be used. There is *no difference in meaning* between the two endings.

Thus, the present middle/passive indicative conjugation of **παύω** is:

Present Stem: **παυ-**

		Middle Translation	*Passive Translation*
Singular			
1	παύομαι	I am stopping (intrans.)	I am being stopped
2	παύῃ/παύει	you are stopping (intrans.)	you are being stopped
3	παύεται	he, she, it is stopping (intrans.)	he, she, it is being stopped
Plural			
1	παυόμεθα	we are stopping (intrans.)	we are being stopped
2	παύεσθε	you (pl.) are stopping (intrans.)	you (pl.) are being stopped
3	παύονται	they are stopping (intrans.)	they are being stopped

OBSERVATIONS

1. The accent on finite verb forms is *recessive*. The final diphthong -**αι** in the first person singular ending, the third person singular ending, and the third person plural ending counts as *short* for purposes of accent. MEMORIZE THIS ADDITIONAL RULE OF ACCENT.

2. Context usually makes clear whether a form in a particular sentence is middle or passive. For example:

ὁ νεᾱνίᾱς τοῦ λόγου παύεται.
The young man from his speech is stopping. (middle voice)
The young man is stopping from his speech.

ὁ νεᾱνίᾱς τοῖς τοῦ ποιητοῦ λόγοις παύεται.
The young man by the words of the poet is being stopped. (passive voice)
The young man is being stopped by the words of the poet.

3. The alternate second singular present middle/passive indicative form **παύει** is identical with the third person singular present active indicative form:

παύει   he is stopping (trans.) (active voice)
you are stopping (intrans.) (middle voice)
you are being stopped (passive voice)

Context usually makes clear which form occurs in a particular sentence.

4. The English translations for the present tense forms given above have progressive aspect. Because the present tense may also have simple or repeated aspect, alternate translations are possible: "I stop (intrans.)," "I am stopped (repeatedly)," etc.

10. An asterisk next to an ending or a form indicates that the ending or form is original or hypothetical.

§30. Imperfect Active Indicative of Omega Verbs

To form the imperfect active indicative of an omega verb:

1. take the **present stem** by removing the -ω from the **first** principal part
2. add ἐ-, the **past indicative augment**,[11] to the beginning of the stem or lengthen the initial vowel of the stem
3. add the following **secondary active endings**:[12]

Person	Singular		Plural	
1	-ον	I	-ομεν	we
2	-ες	you	-ετε	you (pl.)
3	-ε(ν)	he, she, it	-ον	they

MEMORIZE THESE ENDINGS, DOWN THE SINGULAR AND THEN DOWN THE PLURAL, AND BE PREPARED TO RECITE THEM QUICKLY.

OBSERVATIONS

1. Each of the secondary active endings is a combination of a thematic vowel (-o- or -ε-) and one of the *secondary active personal endings*, which are:

Person	Singular		Plural	
1	-ν	I	-μεν	we
2	-ς	you	-τε	you (pl.)
3	—[13]	he, she, it	-ν	they

These secondary active personal endings are used to form many secondary active tenses in Greek.

2. The ending of the third person singular has a nu movable.

3. The endings of the first person singular and third person plural are identical. Context usually makes clear which form appears in a particular sentence.

Thus, the imperfect active indicative conjugation of παύω is:

Present Stem with Past Indicative Augment: ἐπαυ-	
Singular	
1 ἔπαυον	I was stopping (trans.)
2 ἔπαυες	you were stopping (trans.)
3 ἔπαυε(ν)	he, she, it was stopping (trans.)
Plural	
1 ἐπαύομεν	we were stopping (trans.)
2 ἐπαύετε	you (pl.) were stopping (trans.)
3 ἔπαυον	they were stopping (trans.)

11. The term "past indicative augment" is borrowed from H. Hansen and G. Quinn, *Greek: An Intensive Course* (New York: Fordham University Press, 1992).

12. Tenses that are past in time are called secondary tenses (§24).

13. There is *no* personal ending for the third person singular.

1. The accent on finite verb forms is *recessive*.

2. The English translations for the imperfect tense forms given above have progressive aspect. Because the imperfect tense may also have repeated aspect, alternate translations are possible: "I used to stop," "I stopped (repeatedly)," etc.

The Augmented Present Stem

In any secondary tense of the indicative mood, every form of a verb whose stem begins with a consonant has the past indicative augment, ἐ-, as a prefix. When a stem begins with a *vowel*, however, instead of having ἐ- added as the past indicative augment, the initial vowel is augmented by being lengthened. A present stem to which the past indicative augment has been added *or* whose initial vowel has been lengthened is called an **augmented present stem**. For example:

First Principal Part	Present Stem	Augmented Present Stem
παύω	παυ-	ἐπαυ-
ἐθέλω	ἐθελ-	ἠθελ-
ἄρχω	ἀρχ-	ἠρχ-

OBSERVATIONS

1. The initial vowel of the present stem ἐθελ- is lengthened to the corresponding Greek long vowel in the augmented stem ἠθελ-. Thus, the imperfect active indicative conjugation of ἐθέλω is:

	Singular	Plural
1	ἤθελον	ἠθέλομεν
2	ἤθελες	ἠθέλετε
3	ἤθελε(ν)	ἤθελον

The initial vowels of stems beginning with iota, omicron, and upsilon are also lengthened to the corresponding long vowel when their stems are augmented (ι- > ῑ-, ο- > ω-, υ- > ῡ-).

2. In Attic Greek, a stem beginning with alpha always has eta in its augmented stem. Thus, the present stem ἀρχ- becomes ἠρχ- when augmented.

§31. Imperfect Middle and Passive Indicative of Omega Verbs

In the imperfect tense, the middle and passive forms of omega verbs are *identical*. To form the imperfect middle/passive indicative of an omega verb:

1. take the **present stem** by removing the -ω from the **first** principal part
2. add the past indicative augment or lengthen the initial vowel
3. add the following **secondary middle/passive endings**:

Person	Singular		Plural	
1	-ομην	I	-ομεθα	we
2	-ου	you	-εσθε	you (pl.)
3	-ετο	he, she, it	-οντο	they

MEMORIZE THESE ENDINGS, DOWN THE SINGULAR AND THEN DOWN THE PLURAL, AND BE PREPARED TO RECITE THEM QUICKLY.

OBSERVATIONS

1. Each of the secondary middle/passive endings is a combination of a thematic vowel (-o- or -ε-) and one of the *secondary middle/passive personal endings,* which are:

Person	Singular		Plural	
1	-μην	I	-μεθα	we
2	-σο	you	-σθε	you (pl.)
3	-το	he, she, it	-ντο	they

These secondary middle/passive personal endings are used by themselves and in combination with thematic vowels to form many *secondary* middle and passive tenses in Greek.

2. With the exception of the second person singular ending, each of the secondary middle/passive endings is a simple combination of a thematic vowel and a secondary middle/passive *personal* ending.

3. In the second person singular ending, the -σ- of the ending became an intervocalic sigma (*-εσο) and was lost. In Attic Greek, the remaining vowels contracted according to regular rules to produce the ending -ου (*-εσο > *-εο > -ου). (Cf. the expected second person *present* middle/passive ending *-εσαι and §29, Observation 3, p. 68.)

Thus, the imperfect middle/passive indicative conjugation of παύω is:

Augmented Present Stem: ἐπαυ-		
	Middle Translation	*Passive Translation*
Singular		
1 ἐπαυόμην	I was stopping (intrans.)	I was being stopped
2 ἐπαύου	you were stopping (intrans.)	you were being stopped
3 ἐπαύετο	he, she, it was stopping (intrans.)	he, she, it was being stopped
Plural		
1 ἐπαυόμεθα	we were stopping (intrans.)	we were being stopped
2 ἐπαύεσθε	you (pl.) were stopping (intrans.)	you (pl.) were being stopped
3 ἐπαύοντο	they were stopping (intrans.)	they were being stopped

OBSERVATIONS

1. The accent on finite verb forms is *recessive.*

2. Context usually makes clear whether a form in a particular sentence is middle or passive.

3. The English translations for the imperfect tense forms given above have progressive aspect. Because the imperfect tense may also have repeated aspect, alternate translations are possible: "I stopped (intrans.) (repeatedly)," etc.

§32. The Present Active and Middle/Passive Infinitives of Omega Verbs

The **infinitive** is an *abstract verbal noun* in the *neuter singular*. It is **indeclinable**; that is, although it is a noun, it does not have case endings. The infinitive has the verbal properties of tense (present, future, aorist, or perfect) and voice (active, middle, or passive).[14]

To form the present active infinitive of an omega verb:

1. take the **present stem** by removing the -ω from the **first** principal part
2. add the present active infinitive ending -ειν.

For example:

Present Stem	Present Active Infinitive	
παυ-	παύειν	to be stopping (trans.)/to stop (repeatedly) (trans.)

OBSERVATIONS

1. The original ending of the present active infinitive was -εν. This ending was attached to the present stem and the thematic vowel -ε-, and the resulting form had a recessive accent (*παύεεν). In Attic Greek the two epsilons contracted and created the diphthong -ει-, called a **spurious diphthong**.[15] The accent on the present active infinitive of omega verbs is *recessive*.

2. A present active infinitive *does not always indicate time but always indicates aspect*—either progressive or repeated.

To form the present middle/passive infinitive of an omega verb:

1. take the **present stem** by removing the -ω from the **first** principal part
2. add the present middle/passive infinitive ending -εσθαι.

For example:

Present Stem	Present Middle/ Passive Infinitive	Middle Translation	Passive Translation
παυ-	παύεσθαι	to be stopping (intrans.) to stop (intrans.) (repeatedly)	to be (being) stopped to be stopped (repeatedly)

OBSERVATIONS

1. The original ending of the present middle/passive infinitive was -σθαι. This ending was attached to the present stem and the thematic vowel -ε-, and the accent on the resulting form is *recessive*. The final diphthong -αι counts as *short* for purposes of accent.

2. A present middle/passive infinitive *does not always indicate time but always indicates aspect*—either progressive or repeated.

14. An infinitive (< Latin **infinitīvus**, "not limited") is a verb form that is *not limited* by person and number.
15. The term "spurious diphthong" is used to indicate a diphthong that developed through sound changes such as those described above. There is some linguistic evidence for the view that these spurious dipthongs were at some time pronounced slightly differently from original diphthongs, but this distinction in sound quickly disappeared.

§33. Future Active and Middle Indicative and Infinitives of Omega Verbs

Future Active and Middle Indicative of Omega Verbs

To form the future active indicative of an omega verb:

1. take the **future stem** by removing the -**ω** from the **second** principal part
2. add the **primary active endings**.

To form the future middle indicative of an omega verb:

1. take the **future stem** by removing the -**ω** from the **second** principal part
2. add the **primary middle/passive endings**.

Thus, the future active and middle indicative conjugations of παύω are:

Future Stem: παυσ-

	Active		Middle	
Singular				
1	παύσω	I shall stop (trans.)	παύσομαι	I shall stop (intrans.)
2	παύσεις	you will stop (trans.)	παύσῃ/παύσει	you will stop (intrans.)
3	παύσει	he, she, it will stop (trans.)	παύσεται	he, she, it will stop (intrans.)
Plural				
1	παύσομεν	we shall stop (trans.)	παυσόμεθα	we shall stop (intrans.)
2	παύσετε	you (pl.) will stop (trans.)	παύσεσθε	you (pl.) will stop (intrans.)
3	παύσουσι(ν)	they will stop (trans.)	παύσονται	they will stop (intrans.)

OBSERVATIONS

1. The future stem is used to form the future *active* and *middle* tenses *only*. The future passive indicative tense is formed with a stem from the sixth principal part (§34).

2. The endings of the future active indicative of an omega verb are identical with those of the present active indicative. The forms of these tenses *differ in stem only*.

3. The endings of the future middle indicative of an omega verb are identical with those of the present middle/passive indicative. The forms of these tenses *differ in stem only*.

4. The accent on finite verb forms is *recessive*. The final diphthong -**αι** counts as *short* for purposes of accent.

5. The alternate second person singular future middle indicative παύσει is identical with the third person singular future active indicative:

> παύσει   he will stop (trans.) (active voice)
>   you will stop (intrans.) (middle voice)

Context usually makes clear which form occurs in a particular sentence.

6. The English translations for the future tense forms given above have simple aspect. Because the future tense may also have progressive or repeated aspect, alternate translations are possible: "I shall be stopping," "I shall stop (repeatedly)," etc.

Future Active and Middle Infinitives of Omega Verbs

To form the future active infinitive of an omega verb:

1. take the **future stem** by removing the -ω from the **second** principal part
2. add the ending -ειν.

To form the future middle infinitive of an omega verb:

1. take the **future stem** by removing the -ω from the **second** principal part
2. add the ending -εσθαι.

Thus, the future active and middle infinitives of παύω are:

Future Stem: παυσ-

Future Active Infinitive
παύσειν

to be about to/going to stop (trans.)
to be about to/going to be stopping (trans.)
to be about to/going to stop (repeatedly) (trans.)

Future Middle Infinitive
παύσεσθαι

to be about to/going to stop (intrans.)
to be about to/going to be stopping (intrans.)
to be about to/going to stop (repeatedly) (intrans.)

OBSERVATIONS

1. The future active infinitive ending is identical with the present active infinitive ending. The future middle infinitive ending is identical with the present middle/passive infinitive ending. (For an explanation of the development of the endings -ειν and -εσθαι, see §32.) The accent on each infinitive is *recessive*, and the final diphthong -αι counts as *short* for purposes of accent.
2. A future active or middle infinitive indicates time *subsequent to (after)* the verb on which it depends. It also indicates *aspect—simple, progressive,* or *repeated*.

§34. Future Passive Indicative and Infinitive of Omega Verbs

Future Passive Indicative of Omega Verbs

The future passive indicative and infinitive are formed from the *sixth* principal part, which is the first person singular *aorist* passive indicative (§25). Since the aorist indicative is a secondary tense (§24), it has an augment (either ἐ- or a lengthened initial vowel). When the sixth principal part is used to form the future passive tense, one must obtain an **unaugmented aorist passive stem** by removing the first person singular aorist passive indicative ending -ην and by removing the augment. For example:

Sixth Principal Part	Augmented Aorist Passive Stem	Unaugmented Aorist Passive Stem
ἐπείσθην	ἐπεισθ-	πεισθ-
ἤρχθην	ἠρχθ-	ἀρχθ-

OBSERVATION

Since an initial eta in an augmented form may be either a lengthened alpha or a lengthened epsilon, the appropriate short vowel is determined by looking at the other unaugmented forms of the verb, such as the first principal part.

To form the future passive indicative of an omega verb:

1. take the **unaugmented aorist passive stem** by removing the ending -ην and the augment from the **sixth** principal part
2. add the **infix**[16] -ησ-
3. add the **primary middle/passive endings**.

Thus, the future passive indicative conjugation of παύω is:

Unaugmented Aorist Passive Stem: παυθ-

Singular

1	παυθήσομαι	I shall be stopped
2	παυθήσῃ/παυθήσει	you will be stopped
3	παυθήσεται	he, she, it will be stopped

Plural

1	παυθησόμεθα	we shall be stopped
2	παυθήσεσθε	you (pl.) will be stopped
3	παυθήσονται	they will be stopped

OBSERVATIONS

1. The endings of the future passive indicative of an omega verb are identical with those of the present middle/passive indicative and the future middle indicative.
2. The accent on finite verb forms is *recessive*. The final diphthong -αι counts as *short* for purposes of accent.
3. The English translations for the future tense forms given above have simple aspect. Because the future tense may also have progressive or repeated aspect, alternate translations are possible: "I shall be being stopped," "I shall be stopped (repeatedly)," etc.

Future Passive Infinitive of Omega Verbs

To form the future passive infinitive of an omega verb:

1. take the **unaugmented aorist passive stem** by removing the ending -ην and the augment from the **sixth** principal part
2. add the infix -ησ-
3. add the ending -εσθαι.

---

16. An **infix** is an inflectional element that appears in the middle of a word.

For example:

Unaugmented Aorist Passive Stem παυθ-	Future Passive Infinitive παυθήσεσθαι	to be about to be stopped to be about to be being stopped to be about to be stopped (repeatedly)

OBSERVATIONS

1. The accent on the future passive infinitive is *recessive*. The final diphthong -**αι** counts as *short* for purposes of accent.

2. A future passive infinitive indicates time *subsequent to (after)* the verb on which it depends. It also indicates *aspect—simple, progressive,* or *repeated.*

§35. Synopsis 1: Present, Imperfect, and Future Active, Middle, and Passive Indicative; Present and Future Active, Middle, and Passive Infinitives

A synopsis (σύνοψις, "seeing all together") is a brief summary or condensed view of the forms of a Greek verb, and generating a synopsis is a good systematic way of reviewing verb morphology. To make a synopsis, one chooses a verb and then a person and number for the subject. The principal parts of the verb are written out, followed by its forms in all tenses in the given person and number. Here is a model synopsis for **διδάσκω** in the third person singular.

Principal Parts: διδάσκω, διδάξω, ἐδίδαξα, δεδίδαχα, δεδίδαγμαι, ἐδιδάχθην
Person and Number: **3rd sing.**

	Active	Middle	Passive
Indicative			
Present	διδάσκει he is teaching	διδάσκεται he is causing to be taught	διδάσκεται he is being taught
Imperfect	ἐδίδασκε(ν) he was teaching	ἐδιδάσκετο he was causing to be taught	ἐδιδάσκετο he was being taught
Future	διδάξει he will teach	διδάξεται he will cause to be taught	διδαχθήσεται he will be taught
Infinitives			
Present	διδάσκειν to be teaching	διδάσκεσθαι to be causing to be taught	διδάσκεσθαι to be (being) taught
Future	διδάξειν to be about to teach	διδάξεσθαι to be about to cause to be taught	διδαχθήσεσθαι to be about to be taught

OBSERVATION

Rare forms are *not* included in a synopsis. Basic English translations should be given for indicative and infinitive forms.

☞ DRILL 27–35 MAY NOW BE DONE.

§36. Object Infinitive

The infinitive is a verbal noun and may be used as the direct object of another verb. Such an infinitive is called an **Object Infinitive**. For example:

> οἱ πολῖται ἐθέλουσι τοὺς νεᾱνίᾱς εἰς πόλεμον πέμπειν.
> The citizens wish the young men (d.o.) to war *to send (repeatedly)*.
> The citizens wish *to send (repeatedly)* the young men to war.
>
> ἔπειθε τοὺς πολίτᾱς τοὺς νεᾱνίᾱς εἰς πόλεμον μὴ πέμπειν.
> He was persuading the citizens the young men (d.o.) to war not *to be sending*.
> He was persuading the citizens not *to be sending* the young men to war.

The syntax of each italicized word (πέμπειν) is **Object Infinitive**.

OBSERVATIONS

1. Many verbs of ordering, forbidding, asking, teaching, etc. may be followed by an Object Infinitive.
2. The adverb **μή** is used to negate an Object Infinitive, as in the second sentence.
3. In the second sentence the verb ἔπειθε has *two* direct objects, the noun πολίτᾱς and the Object Infinitive πέμπειν.

§37. Genitive of Personal Agent

The preposition ὑπό followed by a noun in the genitive case is frequently used with verbs in the passive voice to express the *agent* or *person by whom* the action of the verb is done. The preposition ὑπό is translated "by," and a genitive so used is called a **Genitive of Personal Agent**. For example:

> ὑπὸ τοῦ Γοργίου ἐδιδάσκοντο.   *By Gorgias* they were being taught.
>   They were being taught *by Gorgias*.

The preposition πρός may also be used with a Genitive of Personal Agent, particularly in poetry or when there is an emphasis on the agent as the *source* of the action.

> ταῦτα πρὸς τῶν ποιητῶν ἐλέγετο.   These things were being said *by the poets.*

The syntax of each italicized word (Γοργίου, ποιητῶν) is **Genitive of Personal Agent**.

OBSERVATIONS
_____

1. In the second sentence, the use of the preposition πρός instead of ὑπό suggests that the Genitive of Personal Agent, "poets," is to be understood both as the *source* of what is being said and as the *agent* of the verbal action.

2. A Genitive of Personal Agent is most often a person, a god, or a group of people or gods. Occasionally a thing appears in the Genitive of Personal Agent, and that thing is thus personified. For example:

> ὑπὸ φόβου ἐπαυόμην.   I was being stopped by fear. (fear is personified)

§38. Dative of Indirect Object

Both in English and in Greek, with verbs of *giving, showing, telling,* and the like, an *indirect object* often appears with a direct object. A direct object is a person or thing directly receiving the action of a verb; an **indirect object** (i.o.) is a person or thing *indirectly affected by* or *interested in* the action.

In English an indirect object regularly appears *immediately after the verb* and *before the direct object.* An indirect object may also appear without a direct object.

I gave the *boys* money.	(*boys* = i.o.; *money* = d.o.)
The poet will show the *woman* his poems.	(*woman* = i.o.; *poems* = d.o.)
Who told *you*?	(*you* = i.o.)

If the order of indirect object and direct object is reversed in English, the preposition *to* is used, and the indirect object is expressed by a prepositional phrase:

I gave money *to the boys.*
The poet will show his poems *to the woman.*

In Greek, the *dative case* with no preposition is used to express an indirect object. For example:

> ἡ θεὸς ἀνθρώποις τὴν σοφίᾱν πέμπει.
> The goddess *to men* wisdom (d.o.) is sending.
> The goddess is sending *men* wisdom.

> τῷ τέκνῳ τὰ τῶν θεῶν ἔργα ἔλεγον.
> *To* my *child* the of the gods deeds (d.o.) I was telling.
> I was telling my *child* the deeds of the gods.

The syntax of each italicized word (ἀνθρώποις, τέκνῳ) is **Dative of Indirect Object**.

OBSERVATIONS

1. The categories of verbs (giving, showing, telling) that take indirect objects should be broadly understood. *Giving* includes *sending, offering*, etc. *Showing* includes *pointing out, making clear*, etc. *Telling* includes *speaking, answering, promising*, etc.

2. There are no strict rules for the order of direct and indirect objects in Greek sentences.

☛ DRILL 36–38 MAY NOW BE DONE.

§39. Word Order in Greek

Only a few general observations can be made about the order of words in Greek sentences. Many variations in word order can be seen in the different genres of prose writing (philosophy, history, oratory) and in the chosen styles of individual authors. Variations can also be noted across time (from the fifth to the fourth century B.C.E.). Poetic texts, in which each rhythmic line must be viewed as a second unit of meaning in addition to the sentence, offer their own distinctive word orders. One feature of the Greek language, however, underlies and makes possible variations in word order in every Greek sentence and invites comparison with English and English word order.

Greek nouns, adjectives, and verbs have many different inflectional endings that convey information—apart from word order—about grammatical function, tense, voice, etc. English has many fewer such endings. Therefore, fewer orders are available for conveying a particular meaning clearly. In the English sentence "The strangers teach the citizens," *strangers* is understood as the subject of the verb because it appears *before* the verb, and *citizens* is understood as the direct object because it appears *after* the verb. No special endings appear on *strangers* because it is the subject and *citizens* because it is the direct object. The same sentence could theoretically be written in Greek in six different word orders. The three elements—subject, verb, direct object—could appear in any order, and basic syntax and meaning would be clear from the particular inflectional endings on "strangers" (-οι, nominative plural) and "citizens" (-ᾱς, accusative plural).

Other important considerations for understanding Greek word order are *emphasis, hyperbaton,* and *balance and antithesis.*

EMPHASIS—Because basic meaning in Greek sentences may be conveyed by a great variety of orders, considerations of **emphasis** are most important in determining the order of each sentence.[17] Unemphatic or neutral order for a simple Greek sentence is subject, object, verb. Since words placed first receive most emphasis and words in last position occupy a place of secondary emphasis, the **neutral order** of a Greek sentence emphasizes the subject most and gives balancing secondary emphasis to the verb. When the subject is expressed only in the verb ending, that verb or another grammatical element may occupy the emphatic first position.

---

17. Considerations of emphasis also determine the order of words in *clauses* occurring within larger Greek sentences.

οἱ ξένοι τοὺς πολίτᾱς διδάσκουσιν.
The strangers the citizens (d.o.) are teaching.
The strangers are teaching the citizens.

τοὺς πολίτᾱς διδάσκουσιν.
The citizens (d.o.) they are teaching.
They are teaching the citizens.

This neutral order may be changed if different elements are to be differently emphasized.

οἱ ξένοι διδάσκουσι τοὺς πολίτᾱς.
διδάσκουσι τοὺς πολίτᾱς οἱ ξένοι.

OBSERVATIONS

1. In the first sentence, the subject still occupies the neutral, emphatic first position. The direct object (rather than the verb) receives secondary emphasis in last position.

2. In the second sentence, the subject and the verb are the elements receiving emphasis (as in neutral word order), but the verb in first position receives more emphasis than the subject in last position.

Any element in a sentence that the writer wishes to emphasize may be placed first for greater emphasis or last for slightly less emphasis. As a general rule, whatever appears first is most important, and elements following are less important.[18]

περὶ τῶν ἐν Ἅιδου ψῡχῶν λέξω, ὦ Ἀθηναῖοι, πολλάκις.
Concerning the souls in Hades, I shall speak, Athenians, often.

OBSERVATIONS

1. In this sentence a prepositional phrase (περὶ τῶν ἐν Ἅιδου ψῡχῶν) is placed first to emphasize the subject matter of an anticipated speech.

2. The adverb πολλάκις would ordinarily (unemphatically) appear before the verb (πολλάκις λέξω), but delayed and placed last, it receives special emphasis.

HYPERBATON—An important effect of varying neutral word order to emphasize particular elements in a sentence is the creation of liveliness (sometimes even suspense or surprise) in the sentence. One order frequently employed to this end involves dividing several words that belong together by the insertion of another element, often a verb. This separation of words or the displacement of a single word is called **hyberbaton** (ὑπερβατόν, "transposition").

οὗτος δεινῷ ἄρχεται καὶ αἰσχρῷ φόβῳ.
This man is ruled by terrible and shameful fear.

πολλάκις λόγοι πείσουσι τῶν σοφῶν τὸν δῆμον.
Often speeches of wise men will persuade the people.

18. The order of words in a Greek sentence is also influenced by the placement of a particular sentence within a larger context. Often elements that refer to previously mentioned subjects, objects, verbal ideas, and the like appear early in a Greek sentence, and their emphatic placement in a specific sentence is more clearly understood by the position of a sentence within a paragraph.

1. In the first sentence ἄρχεται is inserted after δεινῷ, the first adjective modifying φόβῳ, effectively emphasizing δεινῷ by separating it both from αἰσχρῷ, the second adjective joined to it by καί, and from φόβῳ. The idea of something "terrible" is thus suspended, and what is "terrible" is made clear only at the end of the sentence. Similarly, a syntactical element (dative) is introduced early in the sentence, but its full syntax (Dative of Means) does not become clear until the noun (φόβῳ) appears.

2. In the second sentence πείσουσι is inserted between λόγοι, the subject, and a Subjective Genitive, τῶν σοφῶν, that qualifies it. Although the phrase λόγοι τῶν σοφῶν is interrupted by only a single word, the slight delay in the appearance of τῶν σοφῶν adds color to each element in the phrase: λόγοι, πείσουσι, τῶν σοφῶν.

Certain dramatic effects of word order may be achieved by more radical uses of hyperbaton.

ἔργα τοὺς ἑταίρους σὺν θεοῖς διδάξω καλά.
Beautiful deeds with the aid of the gods I shall teach my companions.

μόνῳ ἐθέλουσιν οἱ ξένοι τούτῳ πείθεσθαι τῷ νόμῳ.
Only this law the strangers are willing to obey.

1. In the first sentence, the placement of the adjective καλά in the last position and far away from the noun it modifies (ἔργα in first position) is an example of radical hyperbaton. This dramatic order gives maximum emphasis to the direct object, "beautiful deeds."

2. In the second sentence, the phrase μόνῳ τούτῳ τῷ νόμῳ is spread across the sentence, occupying first, center, and last positions. By this double hyperbaton the phrase receives great emphasis and serves to bind the entire sentence together in a highly balanced way.

BALANCE AND ANTITHESIS—Many Greek sentences have a two-part structure and express a pointed contrast or antithesis. The order of such sentences often exploits the natural **balance** of the two contrasting clauses.

ὁ μὲν Γοργίας εὖ λέγει, ὁ δὲ νεᾱνίας οὔ.
Gorgias speaks well, *but the young man* (does) not (speak well).

εὖ μὲν λέγει ὁ Γοργίας, κακῶς δὲ ὁ νεᾱνίας.
Well does Gorgias speak, *but badly* does the young man (speak).

1. In the first sentence contrasting subjects (Gorgias and the young man) come first in their clauses and are marked by μέν and δέ. This balanced order allows for the omission or *ellipsis* of εὖ λέγει in the second clause. **Ellipsis** is the omission of one or more words that can be easily supplied from a parallel context.

2. In the second sentence contrasting adverbs are placed in emphatic first position in their clauses and are marked by μέν and δέ. The contrasting subjects receive secondary emphasis in last position.

When reading and translating Greek sentences, students should first *go in order,* noting carefully all effects of word order. A final English translation should make the fewest possible changes to the order of the Greek, while also trying to emphasize the same elements. For example:

μόνῳ	ἐθέλουσιν	οἱ ξένοι	τούτῳ	πείθεσθαι	τῷ νόμῳ.
Only	they are willing	the strangers	this	to obey	law.

Only this law the strangers are willing to obey.

The word order of each Greek sentence joins with the words themselves to convey the writer's intended meaning. Only by paying attention to and attempting to translate in Greek word order can students develop a sense for the levels of meaning imparted to a Greek sentence by the careful placement of words within it.

Short Readings

1. An often quoted Greek proverb, first found in the poetry of Alcaeus of Lesbos

    οἶνος καὶ ἀλήθεια.   (Athenaeus, *Deipnosophistae* II.6.4)

οἶνος, οἴνου, ὁ wine

2. After failing to find Ajax, the Chorus returns and begins speaking.

    πόνος πόνῳ πόνον φέρει.   (Sophocles, *Ajax* 866)

φέρω, οἴσω, ἤνεγκα/ἤνεγκον, ἐνήνοχα,
  ἐνήνεγμαι, ἠνέχθην bear, bring

3. When the Persian general Artabanus advises his king, Xerxes, to be cautious, he bases his advice on the following idea.

    . . . αἱ συμφοραὶ τῶν ἀνθρώπων ἄρχουσι καὶ οὐκὶ ὤνθρωποι τῶν συμφορέων.
                                      (Herodotus, *Inquiries* VII.49.3)

οὐκί (Ionic) = Attic οὐχί, *an emphatic form of* οὐκ   συμφορέων (Ionic) = Attic συμφορῶν
ὤνθρωποι = οἱ ἄνθρωποι

4. Phaedra introduces an account of her desire for Hippolytus.

    λέξω δὲ καί σοι τῆς ἐμῆς γνώμης ὁδόν.   (Euripides, Hippolytus 391)

σοι = *sing. dat. of second person personal pronoun,*
  you

ἐμῆς = *fem. sing. gen. of possessive adj. modifying*
  γνώμης, my

5. A fragment from a tragedy of Euripides

    οἱ γὰρ πόνοι τίκτουσι εὐανδρίᾱν . . .   (Euripides, frag. 1052.7)

τίκτω, τέξομαι, ἔτεκον, τέτοκα, ——, ἐτέχθην
  beget, give birth to

εὐανδρίᾱ, εὐανδρίᾱς, ἡ manliness, manly spirit

6.   The opening words of the second book of the historian's account of the Peloponnesian war

    Ἄρχεται δὲ ὁ πόλεμος ἐνθένδε ἤδη Ἀθηναίων καὶ Πελοποννησίων καὶ τῶν ἑκατέροις
    ξυμμάχων, . . .   (Thucydides, *Pelponnesian War* II.1)

ἐνθένδε (adv.) from here, from this point
ἤδη (adv.) now
Πελοποννήσιοι, Πελοποννησίων, οἱ (the)
  Peloponnesians

ἑκατέροις = *masc. pl. dat. of an adjective used as a*
  noun, to each

7. Socrates cites a poetic expression as an example of how poetry may encourage bad behavior.

      ... δῶρα θεοὺς πείθει ...   (Plato, *Republic* 390e3)

δῶρον, δώρου, τό gift

8. A fragment from a comedy of Philemon

      ψῡχῆς πόνος γὰρ ὑπὸ λόγου κουφίζεται.   (Philemon, frag. 207)

κουφίζω, κουφιῶ, ἐκούφισα, κεκούφικα, ——,
   —— lighten

9. A proverb from a comedy of Menander

      ἄγει τὸ θεῖον τοὺς κακοὺς πρὸς τὴν δίκην.   (Menander, *Sententiae* 16)

ἄγω, ἄξω, ἤγαγον, ἦχα, ἦγμαι, ἤχθην lead   θεῖος, θείᾱ, θεῖον divine

10. A proverb from Aesop

      Κακὸν κακοῦ οὐχ ἅπτεται.   (Aesop, *Proverbs* 30)

ἅπτω, ἅψω, ἦψα, ——, ἧμμαι, ἥφθην fasten, join;
  middle, grasp, perceive (+ gen.)

CHAPTER 4

Vocabulary

→ ἀρετή, ἀρετῆς, ἡ excellence; valor; virtue
→ νίκη, νίκης, ἡ victory
→ τύχη, τύχης, ἡ chance, fortune

→ Ἑρμῆς, Ἑρμοῦ, ὁ Hermes

→ βίος, βίου, ὁ life; livelihood
→ βροτός, βροτοῦ, ὁ mortal
→ θάνατος, θανάτου, ὁ death
   υἱός, υἱοῦ, ὁ son

→ ἔχω, ἕξω/σχήσω, ἔσχον, ἔσχηκα,
   -έσχημαι, —— have, hold; inhabit,
   occupy; *intrans.*, be able (+ inf.); be
   (+ adv.); *middle*, hold on to, cling to
   (+ gen.)

→ ἀδικέω, ἀδικήσω, ἠδίκησα, ἠδίκηκα,
   ἠδίκημαι, ἠδικήθην (do) wrong (to);
   injure
→ ποιέω make; do; *middle*, make; do;
   deem, consider
→ πολεμέω, πολεμήσω, ἐπολέμησα,
   πεπολέμηκα, ——, ἐπολεμήθην make
   war (upon), be at war (with) (+ dat.);
   quarrel; fight; *passive*, be treated as an
   enemy, have war made upon (oneself)
→ φιλέω, φιλήσω, ἐφίλησα, πεφίληκα,
   πεφίλημαι, ἐφιλήθην love, like; be
   accustomed, be fond of (+ inf.)

→ νῑκάω conquer, defeat; prevail (over),
   win
→ τελευτάω, τελευτήσω, ἐτελεύτησα,
   τετελεύτηκα, ——, ἐτελευτήθην
   accomplish, end, finish; die
→ τῑμάω honor; *middle*, value, deem
   worthy

→ ἀξιόω, ἀξιώσω, ἠξίωσα, ἠξίωκα,
   ἠξίωμαι, ἠξιώθην think worthy; think
   (it) right; expect, require
→ δηλόω show, make clear, reveal

ἐκεῖνος, ἐκείνη, ἐκεῖνο (demonstr.
adj./pron.) that; *pl.*, those (§§44, 45)
ὅδε, ἥδε, τόδε (demonstr. adj./pron.)
this; *pl.*, these (§§43, 45)

μέγας, μεγάλη, μέγα great, big (§46)
νέος, νέα, νέον new; young
ὀλίγος, ὀλίγη, ὀλίγον little, small;
pl., few
πολέμιος, πολεμίᾱ, πολέμιον of an
enemy, hostile; *masc. subst.*, enemy
→ πολύς, πολλή, πολύ much, many (§46)
πονηρός, πονηρά, πονηρόν worthless;
wicked
→ χαλεπός, χαλεπή, χαλεπόν severe,
harsh; difficult

→ δή (postpositive particle) certainly,
indeed, of course
→ ἐπί (prep. + gen.) in, on, upon
   (prep. + dat.) in, on; in addition to;
   for (i.e., because of); on condition of
   (prep. + acc.) to; against; for (the
   purpose of)
→ μετά (prep. + gen.) (along) with; with
   the aid of; in accordance with
   (prep. + acc.) after
→ οὕτω(ς) (adv.) in this way, thus, so
   ὧδε (adv.) in this way, so; in the
   following way

Vocabulary Notes

→ ἀρετή, ἀρετῆς, ἡ refers to goodness or "excellence" of any kind, often to excellence in art or workmanship, but also to moral excellence or "virtue." Homer's usage of ἀρετή meaning manly prowess or "valor" reflects the derivation of the word from ἄρρην (old Attic ἄρσην), meaning "male." In the plural ἀρετή may be translated "acts of courage" as well as "virtues."

→ νίκη, νίκης, ἡ, "victory" frequently appears with a Subjective or an Objective Genitive or both.

> διὰ τὴν τῶν Λακεδαιμονίων νίκην
> on account of the victory *of the Spartans* (Subjective Genitive)
> on account of the victory *over the Spartans* (Objective Genitive)

When capitalized, **Νίκη** refers to the goddess Victory.

→ τύχη, τύχης, ἡ not only means "chance" or "fortune" in the sense of a force beyond human control but may also mean the *result* of chance: "fortune" or "success" when positive, "misfortune" if negative. Sometimes τύχη is used to mean "destiny" or "fate," and when capitalized, **Τύχη** refers to the goddess Fortune.

→ Ἑρμῆς, Ἑρμοῦ, ὁ, "Hermes," occurs in the singular only and has a circumflex on the ultima of all its forms. One of the Olympian gods, Hermes is the son of Zeus and Maia. He is associated with wiliness, invention, theft, and deception. In addition, he is a messenger of the gods, and he acts as an escort of souls to and from Hades.

→ βίος, βίου, ὁ means "life" in the sense of the *manner* in which a person lives or the *kind* of life one lives. It may also refer to a person's life as the sum of all he or she has done and experienced. It may also mean "livelihood" or "living," the *means* by which one lives. In most instances, βίος refers to the life or livelihood of a human, although the poets occasionally use it to refer to the manner or means of living of an animal.

→ The highly poetic noun βροτός, βροτοῦ, ὁ is derived from the PIE root *mer-, "die." The Greek word may be translated "mortal" or "human" and lays stress on man as a creature that is subject to death. βροτός is often contrasted with those who are *immortal*.

→ In Homer, Hesiod, and the tragic poets, the capitalized noun **Θάνατος, Θανάτου, ὁ**, "Death," is a god, the brother of Sleep. When not capitalized, it means the "death" of any mortal.

→ ἔχω, ἔξω/σχήσω, ἔσχον, ἔσχηκα, -έσχημαι, —— has *two* second principal parts, ἔξω and σχήσω. ἔξω has *progressive* or *repeated* aspect and requires no special translation. σχήσω has *simple* aspect *only* and means "will acquire" or "will get." When the stem from the first principal part of the verb ἔχω is augmented to form the imperfect tense, the irregularly augmented stem is εἰχ-. The fifth principal part is preceded by a hyphen because it appears only in *compounds* of ἔχω, of which there are many. A **compound verb** is a verb made from a root verb plus one or more than one *prefix* (e.g., συνέχω < συν- + ἔχω).

In the active voice ἔχω may be either transitive or intransitive. Its basic *transitive* meaning is "have, hold" with a variety of direct objects (a house, money, beauty, honor, gratitude). When the direct object is a place (heaven, earth, a city), ἔχω means "inhabit," "occupy."

When ἔχω takes an Object Infinitive, it means "have the means or power" to do something. In this usage ἔχω is regularly translated "be able."

> λέγειν ἔχει.   *He is able* to speak.

When used *intransitively* in the active voice and accompanied by an adverb or a prepositional phrase, ἔχω means "be" (in some state or position).

| ταῦτα οὕτως ἔχει. | These things *are* so. |
| οἱ Γοργίου φίλοι εὖ ἔχουσιν. | The friends of Gorgias *are good* (*are doing well*). |

In the middle voice ἔχω means "hold on to," "cling to," and often takes the genitive case, either objective or partitive in origin.

| τῆς γνώμης ἔχομαι. | *I am holding on to* my opinion. |

ἔχω occurs in the passive voice with meanings such as "be held," "be occupied."

Principal Parts of Contracted Verbs

Many epsilon-, alpha-, and omicron-contracted verbs (§§40–42) are derived from the stems of nouns or adjectives. Such verbs are called **denominative verbs**. The meanings of denominative verbs may often be inferred from the nouns or adjectives from which they are derived. For example:

ἀδικέω do wrong	(< ἄδικος)
φιλέω love	(< φίλος)
νῑκάω conquer, defeat	(< νίκη)

The first principal parts of contracted verbs always appear in dictionaries and vocabulary lists in their *uncontracted* forms in order to make clear whether they are epsilon-contracted, alpha-contracted, or omicron-contracted verbs (ἀδικέω, for example, rather than the actual first person singular present active indicative, ἀδικῶ). Uncontracted forms appear in some dialects but not in Attic Greek.

The principal parts of most epsilon- and alpha-contracted verbs follow closely the pattern of the principal parts of ἀδικέω: ἀδικέω, ἀδικήσω, ἠδίκησα, ἠδίκηκα, ἠδίκημαι, ἠδικήθην. If *only* the first principal part of an epsilon- or alpha-contracted verb is listed in the vocabulary, the remaining principal parts end in -ησω, -ησα, -ηκα, -ημαι, -ηθην, have past indicative augments (or lengthened vowels) in their *third* and *sixth* principal parts, and have regular reduplication in their *fourth* and *fifth* principal parts. No other principal parts are given for these verbs. However, when learning these verbs, ALWAYS WRITE OUT AND/OR SAY ALL SIX PRINCIPAL PARTS. For example, νῑκάω is the *only* principal part given for that verb in the vocabulary list, but on a flash card, the principal parts should be written out in full: νῑκάω, νῑκήσω, ἐνίκησα, νενίκηκα, νενίκημαι, ἐνῑκήθην. If an epsilon- or alpha-contracted verb has principal parts that *differ* from this pattern, they are included in the vocabulary list.

The principal parts of most omicron-contracted verbs follow closely the pattern of the principal parts of ἀξιόω: ἀξιόω, ἀξιώσω, ἠξίωσα, ἠξίωκα, ἠξίωμαι, ἠξιώθην. If *only* the first principal part of an omicron-contracted verb is listed in the vocabulary, the remaining principal parts end in -ωσω, -ωσα, -ωκα, -ωμαι, -ωθην, have past indicative augments (or lengthened vowels) in their *third* and *sixth* principal parts, and have regular reduplication in their *fourth* and *fifth* principal parts. No other principal parts are given for these verbs. However, when learning these verbs, ALWAYS WRITE OUT AND/OR SAY ALL SIX PRINCIPAL PARTS.

→ ἀδικέω, ἀδικήσω, ἠδίκησα, ἠδίκηκα, ἠδίκημαι, ἠδικήθην is an epsilon-contracted verb that means "(do) wrong (to)" or "injure" and usually takes an Accusative, Direct Object. It may also be used absolutely. ἀδικέω occurs regularly in both the active and passive voices but not in the middle.

→ In the active voice the epsilon-contracted verb **ποιέω, ποιήσω, ἐποίησα, πεποίηκα, πεποίημαι, ἐποιήθην** means "make" in the sense of "produce" (works of art, a house, a tomb) or "create" (the race of men, children). After Homer it also means "write" or "compose" (poetry) or "represent in poetry." When **ποιέω** means "do," it may take an Accusative, Direct Object or a Double Accusative.

> **δίκαια ἐποίει.**   He was doing just things.
> **κακὰ τὸν φίλον ποιεῖς.**   You are doing bad things to your friend.

With certain adverbs and people as direct objects **ποιέω** may be translated "treat."

> **εὖ ποιοῦμεν τοὺς ἑταίρους.**   We are treating our companions well.

ποιέω in the active voice may also be used absolutely with the meaning "do" or "act."

> **εὖ ποιεῖ.**   He is doing well.

In the active or middle voice, **ποιέω** meaning "make" may appear with two accusatives, one an Accusative, Direct Object and one a Predicate Accusative.

> **τούτους ποιοῦμεν πολίτᾱς.**   We are making these men citizens.

Often in the middle voice **ποιέω** and certain direct objects are equivalent to certain verbs.

> **ἀρχὴν ποιεῖσθαι**   to make a beginning = to begin
> **βουλὴν ποιεῖσθαι** to make a plan = to plan
> **λόγους ποιεῖσθαι** to make words = to speak

In the middle voice **ποιέω** may also mean "consider." A Genitive of Value (§48) or a prepositional phrase is often part of this usage.

> **ὀλίγου ποιοῦνται τὰ ὅπλα.**   They consider weapons of little value.
> **περὶ πολλοῦ ποιούμεθα τὴν εἰρήνην.**   We consider peace of much value.

ποιέω occurs frequently in the passive voice. In Attic poetry, the iota of the present stem of **ποιέω** is often *dropped* before endings beginning with either epsilon or eta. For example, the present active infinitive may appear as **ποιεῖν** or **ποεῖν**.

→ **πολεμέω, πολεμήσω, ἐπολέμησα, πεπολέμηκα, ——, ἐπολεμήθην** is an epsilon-contracted verb that may be used absolutely and mean "be at war," or it may be accompanied by a Dative of Reference that indicates those *against whom* one is at war or *upon whom* one is making war. Rather than a Dative of Reference, **πρός** with an accusative may appear.

> **ἐπολεμοῦμεν.**
> We were at war.
>
> **τοῖς Λακεδαιμονίοις/πρὸς τοὺς Λακεδαιμονίους ἐπολεμοῦμεν.**
> We were making war upon the Spartans/against the Spartans.

πολεμέω may also be used less concretely to mean "quarrel" with someone (Dative of Reference) or "fight." When πολεμέω appears in the passive voice, it is translated "be treated as an enemy" or "have war made upon (oneself)." It does not appear in the middle voice.

→ φιλέω, φιλήσω, ἐφίλησα, πεφίληκα, πεφίλημαι, ἐφιλήθην is an epsilon-contracted verb that regularly appears in the active and passive voices. It rarely appears in the middle voice, and the meaning in the middle voice is the same as in the active voice. The expected fourth and fifth principal parts of φιλέω are *φεφίληκα and *φεφίλημαι. However, Greek avoids two successive syllables with aspirated consonants, and the aspirate of the first syllable is replaced by its unaspirated, voiceless counterpart (i.e., the aspirated labial φ is replaced by the voiceless labial π). This sound change is called the **dissimilation of aspirates**. In all other respects the principal parts of φιλέω follow the pattern of other epsilon- and alpha-contracted verbs. If *only* the first principal part of an epsilon- or alpha-contracted verb beginning with an aspirated consonant is listed in the vocabulary, then the remaining principal parts end in -ησω, -ησα, -ηκα, -ημαι, -ηθην and *have reduplication with dissimilation of aspirates in their fourth and fifth principal parts.* No other principal parts are given for these verbs. However, when learning these verbs, ALWAYS WRITE OUT AND/OR SAY ALL SIX PRINCIPAL PARTS.

Although in the poets φιλέω may be used to express sexual desire for someone or being in love with someone, it more often means "regard with affection" or "love" in a nonerotic sense and is used of feelings held by gods for mortals, parents for children, and even a politician for the people. In certain contexts it may mean little more than "like," "approve of," but φιλέω is also one of the verbs used to mean "kiss."

After Homer, in both prose and poetry, φιλέω developed the meanings "be accustomed"; "be fond of." With these meanings φιλέω regularly takes an Object Infinitive.

ἡ συμφορὰ σοφίᾱν διδάσκειν φιλεῖ.	Misfortune is accustomed to teach(ing) wisdom.
ἄρχεσθαι φιλεῖ ὁ δῆμος.	The people are fond of being ruled.

→ When the alpha-contracted verb νῑκάω, νῑκήσω, ἐνίκησα, νενίκηκα, νενίκημαι, ἐνῑκήθην means "conquer," "defeat," or "prevail over," it takes an Accusative, Direct Object (usually a person).

τοὺς Ἀθηναίους νῑκᾶν ἐθέλομεν.	We wish to defeat the Athenians.

When νῑκάω is used absolutely, it may mean "conquer," "win," or "prevail." An Accusative or Dative of Respect may accompany the absolute use of νῑκάω.

οἱ σύμμαχοι νῑκῶσιν.	The allies are winning.
ἡ τοῦ σοφοῦ γνώμη νῑκᾷ.	The opinion of the wise man prevails.
μάχην/μάχῃ ἐνῑκῶμεν.	We were conquering in (respect to) battle.

The middle voice of νῑκάω has no special meaning and is rare.

→ τελευτάω, τελευτήσω, ἐτελεύτησα, τετελεύτηκα, ——, ἐτελευτήθην is an alpha-contracted verb that may be transitive or intransitive. It most often occurs in the active voice, rarely in the passive, and never in the middle. The earliest meanings of τελευτάω in the active voice are "bring to pass," "accomplish" (trans.) and "end," "come to an end" (intrans.).

ταῦτα ἐτελεύτᾱ θεός.	A god was accomplishing these things. (trans.)
νῦν τελευτᾷ ὁ πόλεμος.	The war is ending now. (intrans.)

The English verbs "finish" and "end" are useful for translating *both* transitive and intransitive uses. A common specialized meaning of τελευτάω is "end" (one's life) (trans.) or "die" (intrans.).

> οὗτος τελευτᾶν τὸν βίον ἐθέλει.
> This man wishes to end his life.
>
> ὑπὸ ἐχθρῶν τελευτῶσιν.
> They are dying at the hands of enemies. (i.e., they are being killed by enemies.)

→ τῑμάω, τῑμήσω, ἐτίμησα, τετίμηκα, τετίμημαι, ἐτῑμήθην is an alpha-contracted verb that means "honor" and occurs regularly in both the active and passive voices. In the middle voice τῑμάω means "value," "deem worthy," and it appears with a Genitive of Value or a prepositional phrase (§48). In the passive voice τῑμάω may mean "be honored" (passive of the active meaning) or "be deemed worthy" (passive of the middle meaning).

→ ἀξιόω, ἀξιώσω, ἠξίωσα, ἠξίωκα, ἠξίωμαι, ἠξιώθην is an omicron-contracted verb that means "think worthy"; "think (it) right"; "expect," "require." When ἀξιόω means "think worthy," it takes an Accusative, Direct Object and a Genitive of Value (§48). When ἀξιόω means "think (it) right," "expect," "require," it takes an Object Infinitive, sometimes with an accompanying accusative. This accusative is actually the subject of the infinitive (§58), and when the verb is translated "think (it) right," the accusative is preceded by the English word "for."

> τοῦτον λόγου οὐκ ἀξιῶ.   (Acc., D.O. and Genitive of Value)
> I do not think *this man* worthy of *a word* (i.e., worthy of mention).
>
> ἀξιοῦμεν τὸν ποιητὴν ἐν τῇ βουλῇ λέγειν.   (Acc. and Object Infin.)
> We think it right *for the poet to speak* in the council.
> We expect *the poet to speak* in the council.

ἀξιόω appears in the active voice and the passive voice. In Attic poetry it occurs rarely in the middle voice with meanings identical with the active meanings.

→ δηλόω, δηλώσω, ἐδήλωσα, δεδήλωκα, δεδήλωμαι, ἐδηλώθην is an omicron-contracted verb that means "make clear," "show," or "reveal" (a thought, the truth, deeds). It often takes an Accusative, Direct Object and a Dative of Indirect Object. δηλόω appears frequently in the active voice and rarely in the middle or passive voice.

→ When the adjective πολύς, πολλή, πολύ modifies a noun and means "much" (singular) or "many" (plural), it usually appears *without* the article. Substantives of πολύς, πολλή, πολύ frequently take a Partitive Genitive (§46).

> πολλοὺς τῶν Ἀθηναίων   many (Athenians) (d.o.) of the Athenians

When preceded by the article, whether modifying a noun or used substantively, πολύς means "the greater part," "the majority."

> οἱ πολλοί   the many, the majority (subj.) (of the people)
> τὰ πολλὰ τέκνα   the majority of the children (subj. or d.o.)
> τὸ πολὺ τῶν ὅπλων   the greater part (subj. or d.o.) of the weapons

The neuter singular of πολύς is also used with prepositions in two idiomatic phrases, which should be learned:

ἐπὶ (τὸ) πολύ	to a great extent; for the most part
περὶ πολλοῦ	of much value

→ The adjective χαλεπός, χαλεπή, χαλεπόν, "severe," "harsh"; "difficult," may be applied to feelings, experiences, human beings, and gods. The adverb formed from this adjective, χαλεπῶς, may be translated "harshly," but it often means "hardly" or "with difficulty."

→ The postpositive particle δή is often used to intensify an adjective, adverb, pronoun, or conjunction and to indicate *certainty* about a word or idea that precedes it. It may be translated "certainly," "indeed," or "of course."

ὀλίγοι δή	few men (subj.) indeed (= very few)
νῦν δή	now certainly
ἐκεῖνος δή	that man (subj.) of course

Because δή ordinarily indicates certainty about the word it intensifies, it is sometimes used sarcastically.

οὗτος, ὁ σοφὸς δή	this man (subj.), wise *of course*

Often δή is used with conjunctions (ἀλλὰ δή, "but indeed," and καὶ δή or the emphatic καὶ δὴ καί, "and indeed," "and in particular") to indicate that a word, clause, or phrase following is of great importance.

πολλοὶ ἄνθρωποι ἐν ἐκείνῳ ἐτελεύτων τῷ πολέμῳ καὶ δὴ καὶ Ἀθηναῖοι.
Many men were dying in that war *and in particular* Athenians (were dying).

When these particle combinations are separated by a word (ἀλλὰ ... δή, καὶ ... δή), δή emphasizes the word it follows.

ταῦτα κακῶς ποιεῖς καὶ πονηρῶς δὴ νῑκᾷς.
You are doing these things badly, *and wickedly indeed* you are prevailing.

→ When followed by the genitive case, the preposition ἐπί expresses *location in* place or time, but several extended meanings are also possible.

ἐπὶ γῆς	upon the earth
ἐπὶ πολέμου	(engaged) in war
ἐπὶ εἰρήνης	in (time of) peace
γνώμη ἐπὶ τούτου	an opinion (subj.) on this thing

When followed by the dative case, ἐπί expresses a more definite and specific indication of *location in or on* than when followed by the genitive. Ideas of addition ("in addition to"), cause ("for," "because of"), and condition are also often present.

ἐπὶ τῇ γῇ, οὐκ ἐν τῇ θαλάττῃ	on the land, not on the sea
ἐπὶ τούτοις	in addition to these things
ἐπὶ τούτῳ	for (because of) this thing
ἐπὶ ἐκείνοις	on those conditions

When followed by the accusative case, ἐπί expresses *motion to, onto,* or *against.* It may also indicate *purpose.*

ἐπὶ τὴν γῆν	(motion) onto the land
ἐπὶ τοὺς Ἀθηναίους	against the Athenians
ἐπὶ τοῦτο	for (the purpose of) this thing, for this purpose

→ In Attic prose, the preposition μετά, when followed by the genitive case, means "with" in all the same senses as σύν/ξύν followed by the dative case (which it gradually replaced): "along with," "with the aid of," "in accordance with."

μετὰ τῶν συμμάχων	along with the allies
μετὰ τοῦ θεοῦ	with the aid of the god
μετὰ ἀληθείᾱς	in accordance with truth, truly

When μετά is followed by the accusative case, it means "after" in time or in rank.

| μετὰ ταῦτα | after these things |
| μετὰ τοὺς θεούς | after (i.e., next to, following) the gods |

→ οὕτω(ς) (adv.), "in this way," "thus," "so," has a sigma in parentheses, which is called a **sigma movable** or a **movable sigma.** This sigma appears when **οὕτως** is followed by a word beginning with a vowel and is omitted when it is followed by a word beginning with a consonant.

Derivatives and Cognates

	Derivatives	*Cognates*
βίος	**biol**ogy, micro**be**	zoology
βροτός	am**br**osia	**mur**der, **mor**tal, **man**ticore
ἐπί	**epi**logue	**ob**verse
θάνατος	eu**thana**sia	dead, **dw**indle
μέγας	**megal**opolis, o**mega**	much, **mag**nitude, **maj**or
μετά	**meta**physics	**mid**way
νέος	**neo**teric, miso**ne**ism, **neo**logism	new, novice
ὀλίγος	**olig**archy	
ποιέω	onomato**poeia**, poem	cheetah
πολύς	**poly**math	complete, full
τύχη		penta**teuch**, doughty
υἱός		son

§40. Contracted Verbs 1: -έω

Some omega verbs have present stems that end in -ε. For example:

ἀδικέω, ἀδικήσω, ἠδίκησα, ἠδίκηκα, ἠδίκημαι, ἠδικήθην do wrong
ποιέω, ποιήσω, ἐποίησα, πεποίηκα, πεποίημαι, ἐποιήθην make; do

When the omega is removed from principal part 1 of these verbs, the present stems are **ἀδικε-** and **ποιε-**. Verbs such as these are called **contracted verbs** because in Attic Greek the vowel at the end of the stem *contracts* with vowels in the endings according to regular rules. The conjugation of contracted verbs differs from that of other omega verbs in the present and imperfect tenses *only* (i.e., the tenses that are formed from principal part 1). For verbs that have present stems ending in -α see §41; for verbs that have present stems ending in -o see §42. To distinguish among these one regularly refers to *epsilon-contracted verbs, alpha-contracted verbs,* and *omicron-contracted verbs.*[1]

Epsilon-contracted verbs follow regular rules of contraction:

$$\varepsilon + \omega = \omega \qquad \varepsilon + \varepsilon = \varepsilon\iota$$
$$\varepsilon + \varepsilon\iota = \varepsilon\iota \qquad \varepsilon + o = o\upsilon$$
$$\varepsilon + \eta = \eta$$
$$\varepsilon + o\upsilon = o\upsilon$$

MEMORIZE THESE RULES OF ATTIC CONTRACTION.

OBSERVATIONS

1. When an epsilon contracts with a long vowel or diphthong, the epsilon is absorbed by the long vowel or diphthong. Thus, all the contractions in the left-hand column result in *no changes* in the spellings of the endings.

2. When an epsilon contracts with a short vowel, a spurious diphthong (ει or ου) is formed. Thus, both the contractions in the right-hand column result in *changes* to the spellings of the endings.

Thus, the present active and middle/passive indicative conjugations of **ποιέω** are:

Present Stem: ποιε-

	Present Active Indicative		Present Middle/Passive Indicative	
Singular				
1	ποιέω >	ποιῶ	ποιέομαι >	ποιοῦμαι
2	ποιέεις >	ποιεῖς	ποιέῃ/ποιέει >	ποιῇ/ποιεῖ
3	ποιέει >	ποιεῖ	ποιέεται >	ποιεῖται
Plural				
1	ποιέομεν >	ποιοῦμεν	ποιεόμεθα >	ποιούμεθα
2	ποιέετε >	ποιεῖτε	ποιέεσθε >	ποιεῖσθε
3	ποιέουσι(ν) >	ποιοῦσι(ν)	ποιέονται >	ποιοῦνται

1. There are *no* contracted verbs whose stems end in -ι or -υ.

The imperfect active and middle/passive indicative conjugations of ποιέω are:

Augmented Present Stem: ἐποιε-				
	Imperfect Active Indicative		Imperfect Middle/Passive Indicative	
Singular				
1	ἐποίεον >	ἐποίουν	ἐποιεόμην >	ἐποιούμην
2	ἐποίεες >	ἐποίεις	ἐποιέου >	ἐποιοῦ
3	ἐποίεε >	ἐποίει	ἐποιέετο >	ἐποιεῖτο
Plural				
1	ἐποιέομεν >	ἐποιοῦμεν	ἐποιεόμεθα >	ἐποιούμεθα
2	ἐποιέετε >	ἐποιεῖτε	ἐποιέεσθε >	ἐποιεῖσθε
3	ἐποίεον >	ἐποίουν	ἐποιέοντο >	ἐποιοῦντο

The present active and middle/passive infinitives of ποιέω are:

	Present Active Infinitive		Present Middle/Passive Infinitive	
	ποιέεν >	ποιεῖν	ποιέεσθαι >	ποιεῖσθαι

OBSERVATIONS

1. The accent on each contracted verb form is determined by where a *recessive* accent falls on the corresponding *uncontracted* form. *Only* by knowing the accent on an *uncontracted* form of a contracted verb can one place the correct accent on a contracted form.

   If the recessive accent on the uncontracted form falls on either of the syllables to be contracted (e.g., ποιέω, ποιέομεν, ποιεόμεθα), the contracted syllable receives the accent. If this accent falls on the *ultima*, it is a circumflex (e.g., ποιῶ). If this accent falls on the *penult* or *antepenult*, the accent is determined by the rules for the possibilities of accent (e.g., ποιοῦμεν, ποιούμεθα).

   If the recessive accent on the uncontracted form falls *before* the vowels that contract—(e.g., ἐποίεον)—the accent on the contracted form remains recessive according to the rules for the possibilities of accent (e.g., ἐποίουν).

2. A nu movable is *never* used in the third person singular imperfect active indicative form of any contracted verb.

3. In the present active infinitive of epsilon-contracted verbs, the epsilon at the end of the stem contracts first with the thematic vowel epsilon and then with the epsilon of the original present active infinitive ending -εν (§32, Observation 1, p. 72).

4. In Ionic, the Greek dialect most closely related to Attic, and in the epic dialect of Homer, many uncontracted forms of epsilon-contracted verbs are used. BE PREPARED TO RECOGNIZE BOTH UNCONTRACTED AND CONTRACTED FORMS OF EPSILON-CONTRACTED VERBS. Uncontracted forms of epsilon-contracted verbs appear in the Short and Longer Readings.

☛   DRILL 40 MAY NOW BE DONE.

§41. Contracted Verbs 2: -άω

Some omega verbs have present stems that end in -α and are called *alpha-contracted verbs*. For example:

νῑκάω, νῑκήσω, ἐνίκησα, νενίκηκα, νενίκημαι, ἐνῑκήθην   conquer, defeat

τελευτάω, τελευτήσω, ἐτελεύτησα, τετελεύτηκα, ———, ἐτελευτήθην   accomplish, end, finish

When the omega is removed from principal part 1 of these verbs, the present stems are **νῑκα-** and **τελευτα-**.

Alpha-contracted verbs follow regular rules of contraction:

$$\alpha + \omega = \omega \qquad \alpha + \varepsilon = \bar{\alpha}$$
$$\alpha + o = \omega \qquad \alpha + \varepsilon\iota = ᾳ$$
$$\alpha + o\upsilon = \omega \qquad \alpha + \eta = ᾳ$$

MEMORIZE THESE RULES OF ATTIC CONTRACTION.

OBSERVATIONS

1. When an alpha contracts with any vowel or diphthong with an o sound (**ω**, **o**, or **ου**), the resulting contraction is *always* **ω**.

2. When an alpha contracts with any vowel or diphthong with an e sound (**ε**, **ει**, or **η**), the resulting contraction is always **ᾱ**.

3. Any iota (ordinary or subscript) is retained as a subscript (**ᾳ**).

Thus, the present active and middle/passive indicative conjugations of **νῑκάω** are:

Present Stem: **νῑκα-**

	Present Active Indicative		Present Middle/Passive Indicative	
Singular				
1	νῑκάω >	νῑκῶ	νῑκάομαι >	νῑκῶμαι
2	νῑκάεις >	νῑκᾷς	νῑκάῃ/νῑκάει >	νῑκᾷ
3	νῑκάει >	νῑκᾷ	νῑκάεται >	νῑκᾶται
Plural				
1	νῑκάομεν >	νῑκῶμεν	νῑκαόμεθα >	νῑκώμεθα
2	νῑκάετε >	νῑκᾶτε	νῑκάεσθε >	νῑκᾶσθε
3	νῑκάουσι(ν) >	νῑκῶσι(ν)	νῑκάονται >	νῑκῶνται

The imperfect active and middle/passive indicative conjugations of **νῑκάω** are:

Augmented Present Stem: **ἐνῑκα-**

	Imperfect Active Indicative		Imperfect Middle/Passive Indicative	
Singular				
1	ἐνίκαον >	ἐνίκων	ἐνῑκαόμην >	ἐνῑκώμην
2	ἐνίκαες >	ἐνίκᾱς	ἐνῑκάου >	ἐνῑκῶ
3	ἐνίκαε >	ἐνίκᾱ	ἐνῑκάετο >	ἐνῑκᾶτο
Plural				
1	ἐνῑκάομεν >	ἐνῑκῶμεν	ἐνῑκαόμεθα >	ἐνῑκώμεθα
2	ἐνῑκάετε >	ἐνῑκᾶτε	ἐνῑκάεσθε >	ἐνῑκᾶσθε
3	ἐνίκαον >	ἐνίκων	ἐνῑκάοντο >	ἐνῑκῶντο

The present active and middle/passive infinitives of νῑκάω are:

Present Active Infinitive	Present Middle/Passive Infinitive
νῑκάεεν > νῑκᾶν	νῑκάεσθαι > νῑκᾶσθαι

OBSERVATIONS

___

1. The accent on each contracted verb form is determined by where a *recessive* accent falls on the corresponding *uncontracted* form. *Only* by knowing the accent on an *uncontracted* form of a contracted verb can one place the correct accent on a contracted form.

If the recessive accent on the uncontracted form falls on either of the syllables to be contracted (e.g., νῑκάω, νῑκάομεν, νῑκαόμεθα), the contracted syllable receives the accent. If this accent falls on the *ultima*, it is a circumflex (e.g., νῑκῶ). If this accent falls on the *penult* or *antepenult*, the accent is determined by the rules for the possibilities of accent (e.g., νῑκῶμεν, νῑκώμεθα).

If the recessive accent on the uncontracted form falls *before* the vowels that contract—(e.g., ἐνίκαον)—the accent on the contracted form remains recessive according to the rules for the possibilities of accent (e.g., ἐνίκων).

2. A nu movable is *never* used in the third person singular imperfect active indicative form of any contracted verb.

3. In the present active infinitive of alpha-contracted verbs, the alpha at the end of the stem contracts first with the thematic vowel epsilon and then with the epsilon of the original present active infinitive ending -εν (§32, Observation 1, p. 72).

4. In the dialect of Homer, many uncontracted forms of alpha-contracted verbs are used. BE PREPARED TO RECOGNIZE BOTH UNCONTRACTED AND CONTRACTED FORMS OF ALPHA-CONTRACTED VERBS. Uncontracted forms of alpha-contracted verbs appear in the Short and Longer Readings.

☛   DRILL 41 MAY NOW BE DONE.

§42. Contracted Verbs 3: -όω

Some omega verbs have present stems that end in **-o** and are called *omicron-contracted verbs*. For example:

ἀξιόω, ἀξιώσω, ἠξίωσα, ἠξίωκα, ἠξίωμαι, ἠξιώθην   think worthy
δηλόω, δηλώσω, ἐδήλωσα, δεδήλωκα, δεδήλωμαι, ἐδηλώθην   show, make clear

When the omega is removed from principal part 1 of these verbs, the present stems are ἀξιο- and δηλο-.

Omicron-contracted verbs follow regular rules of contraction:

o + ω = ω	o + o = ου
o + ει = οι	o + ε = ου
o + η = οι	o + ου = ου

MEMORIZE THESE RULES OF ATTIC CONTRACTION.

OBSERVATIONS

1. When an omicron contracts with an omega, the omega absorbs the omicron.
2. When an omicron contracts with any diphthong containing an iota (ει or ῃ), the resulting contraction is the spurious diphthong οι.
3. When an omicron contracts with any *short* vowel or the diphthong ου, the resulting contraction is the spurious diphthong ου.

Thus, the present active and middle/passive indicative conjugations of **δηλόω** are:

Present Stem: **δηλο-**

	Present Active Indicative		Present Middle/Passive Indicative	
Singular				
1	δηλόω >	**δηλῶ**	δηλόομαι >	**δηλοῦμαι**
2	δηλόεις >	**δηλοῖς**	δηλόῃ/δηλόει >	**δηλοῖ**
3	δηλόει >	**δηλοῖ**	δηλόεται >	**δηλοῦται**
Plural				
1	δηλόομεν >	**δηλοῦμεν**	δηλοόμεθα >	**δηλούμεθα**
2	δηλόετε >	**δηλοῦτε**	δηλόεσθε >	**δηλοῦσθε**
3	δηλόουσι(ν) >	**δηλοῦσι(ν)**	δηλόονται >	**δηλοῦνται**

The imperfect active and middle/passive indicative conjugations of **δηλόω** are:

Augmented Present Stem: **ἐδηλο-**

	Imperfect Active Indicative		Imperfect Middle/Passive Indicative	
Singular				
1	ἐδήλοον >	**ἐδήλουν**	ἐδηλοόμην >	**ἐδηλούμην**
2	ἐδήλοες >	**ἐδήλους**	ἐδηλόου >	**ἐδηλοῦ**
3	ἐδήλοε >	**ἐδήλου**	ἐδηλόετο >	**ἐδηλοῦτο**
Plural				
1	ἐδηλόομεν >	**ἐδηλοῦμεν**	ἐδηλοόμεθα >	**ἐδηλούμεθα**
2	ἐδηλόετε >	**ἐδηλοῦτε**	ἐδηλόεσθε >	**ἐδηλοῦσθε**
3	ἐδήλοον >	**ἐδήλουν**	ἐδηλόοντο >	**ἐδηλοῦντο**

The present active and middle/passive infinitives of **δηλόω** are:

	Present Active Infinitive		Present Middle/Passive Infinitive	
	δηλόεεν >	**δηλοῦν**	δηλόεσθαι >	**δηλοῦσθαι**

OBSERVATIONS

1. The accent on each contracted verb form is determined by where a *recessive* accent falls on the corresponding *un*contracted form. *Only* by knowing the accent on an *un*contracted form of a contracted verb can one place the correct accent on a contracted form.

If the recessive accent on the uncontracted form falls on either of the syllables to be contracted (e.g., **δηλόω, δηλόομεν, δηλοόμεθα**), the contracted syllable receives the accent. If this accent falls on the *ultima*, it is a circumflex (e.g., δηλῶ). If this accent falls on the *penult* or *antepenult*, the accent is determined by the rules for the possibilities of accent (e.g., δηλοῦμεν, δηλούμεθα).

If the recessive accent on the uncontracted form falls *before* the vowels that contract—(e.g., ἐδήλοον)—the accent on the contracted form remains recessive according to the rules for the possibilities of accent (e.g., ἐδήλουν).

2. A nu movable is *never* used in the third person singular imperfect active indicative form of any contracted verb.

3. In the present active infinitive of omicron-contracted verbs, the omicron at the end of the stem contracts first with the thematic vowel epsilon and then with the epsilon of the original present active infinitive ending -εν (§32, Observation 1, p. 72).

4. Uncontracted forms of omicron-contracted verbs do not appear in any Greek dialect.

☛ DRILL 42 MAY NOW BE DONE.

§43. The Demonstrative Adjective and Pronoun ὅδε, ἥδε, τόδε

The demonstrative adjective and pronoun ὅδε, ἥδε, τόδε, "this (here)" (sing.), "these (here)" (pl.), points to what is near the writer or speaker. ὅδε, ἥδε, τόδε was formed by the addition of the suffix -δε to the article ὁ, ἡ, τό.

	Singular			*Plural*		
	M.	F.	N.	M.	F.	N.
Nom.	ὅδε	ἥδε	τόδε	οἵδε	αἵδε	τάδε
Gen.	τοῦδε	τῆσδε	τοῦδε	τῶνδε	τῶνδε	τῶνδε
Dat.	τῷδε	τῇδε	τῷδε	τοῖσδε	ταῖσδε	τοῖσδε
Acc.	τόνδε	τήνδε	τόδε	τούσδε	τάσδε	τάδε

MEMORIZE THIS DECLENSION ACROSS THE SINGULAR AND ACROSS THE PLURAL.

OBSERVATIONS

1. There are no vocative case forms for ὅδε, ἥδε, τόδε.

2. All the forms of ὅδε, ἥδε, τόδε have the same accents as the corresponding forms of the article *except* the masculine and feminine singular and plural nominative forms, which all have acute accents on their penults. The accents on ἥδε, τήνδε, οἵδε, αἵδε, τούσδε, and τάσδε do not follow the regular rules of accent.[2]

When ὅδε functions as an adjective modifying a noun, it agrees with that noun in gender, number, and case. In prose the noun usually has an article, and the demonstrative is placed before or after the article-noun phrase.[3] The article in such phrases is *omitted* in English translations.

2. For a complete explanation of the accents on these forms, see §54, Observation 2, p. 130.
3. In poetry the article is often *omitted*.

τούσδε τοὺς νεανίας	these young men (d.o.)
διὰ τήνδε τὴν αἰτίᾱν	on account of this cause
τὰ ἀγαθὰ τάδε	these good things (subj. or d.o.)

When ὅδε functions as a pronoun, it is convenient to reflect the gender and number in English translations by supplying the word "man," "woman," or "thing" (sing.) or "men," "women," or "things" (pl.).

οἵδε	these men (subj.)
περὶ τοῦδε	concerning this thing (man)
τήνδε	this woman (d.o.)
τὴν τῶνδε ἀρετήν	the excellence (d.o.) of these men (women/things)

OBSERVATION

When the pronoun ὅδε is used as a Genitive of Possession in prose, it appears in the *attributive* position.

☛ DRILL 43 MAY NOW BE DONE.

§44. The Demonstrative Adjective and Pronoun
ἐκεῖνος, ἐκείνη, ἐκεῖνο

The demonstrative adjective and pronoun ἐκεῖνος, ἐκείνη, ἐκεῖνο, "that" (sing.), "those" (pl.), points to what is far from the writer or speaker.

	M.	F.	N.	M.	F.	N.
	Singular			*Plural*		
Nom.	ἐκεῖνος	ἐκείνη	ἐκεῖνο	ἐκεῖνοι	ἐκεῖναι	ἐκεῖνα
Gen.	ἐκείνου	ἐκείνης	ἐκείνου	ἐκείνων	ἐκείνων	ἐκείνων
Dat.	ἐκείνῳ	ἐκείνῃ	ἐκείνῳ	ἐκείνοις	ἐκείναις	ἐκείνοις
Acc.	ἐκεῖνον	ἐκείνην	ἐκεῖνο	ἐκείνους	ἐκείνᾱς	ἐκεῖνα

OBSERVATION

There are no vocative case forms for ἐκεῖνος, ἐκείνη, ἐκεῖνο. The declension of ἐκεῖνος, ἐκείνη, ἐκεῖνο is identical with that of any first-second-declension adjective *except* in the neuter nominative and accusative singular form, which ends in -o (cf. τό).

When ἐκεῖνος functions as an adjective modifying a noun, it agrees with that noun in gender, number, and case. In prose the noun usually has an article, and the demonstrative is placed before or after the article-noun phrase.[4] The article in such phrases is *omitted* in English translations.

4. In poetry the article is often *omitted*.

ἐκεῖνον τὸν ξένον	that stranger (d.o.)
περὶ τοῦ νόμου ἐκείνου	about that law
ἐκείναις ταῖς καλαῖς	for those beautiful women

When ἐκεῖνος functions as a pronoun, it is convenient to reflect the gender and number in English translations by supplying the word "man," "woman," or "thing" (sing.) or "men," "women," or "things" (pl.).

ἐκείνους	those men (d.o.)
ἐξ ἐκείνων	resulting from those things
τοῖς ἐκείνης τέκνοις	to the children of that woman

OBSERVATION

When the pronoun ἐκεῖνος is used as a Genitive of Possession in prose, it appears in the *attributive* position.

☞ DRILL 44 MAY NOW BE DONE.

§45. Comparison of οὗτος, ὅδε, and ἐκεῖνος

οὗτος, αὕτη, τοῦτο and ὅδε, ἥδε, τόδε are both translated "this" in the singular and "these" in the plural. ὅδε, however, points more *emphatically* to people or things that are close to the speaker or writer (whether in a physical or a mental way) or to something just noticed or mentioned. Thus, ὅδε means "this/these (near me)"; οὗτος is less emphatic.

ἐκεῖνος, ἐκείνη, ἐκεῖνο points to persons or things that are more remote from the speaker or writer in place, time, or thought. Thus, ἐκεῖνος means "that/those (far from me)," "that/those (near him)," or "that/those (of a former time)." Like οὗτος, ἐκεῖνος may point to famous or notorious people or things. When ἐκεῖνος has either of these meanings, it is regularly placed *after* the noun it modifies, and the definite article is regularly omitted. The word "famous" or "notorious" is added to the meaning of the demonstrative adjective.

ὅδε often refers to what *follows,* while οὗτος often refers to what *precedes.*

| διὰ τάδε | on account of the following things |
| διὰ ταῦτα | on account of the preceding things |

When two elements that have already been mentioned are contrasted, οὗτος means "the latter" and ἐκεῖνος "the former."

καὶ ὁ Γοργίᾱς καὶ ὁ Εὐρῑπίδης νεᾱνίᾱς διδάσκουσιν· οὗτος μὲν εὖ διδάσκει, ἐκεῖνος δὲ οὔ.
Both Gorgias and Euripides are teaching young men: *the latter* (Euripides) is teaching (them) well, but *the former* (Gorgias) (is) not (teaching them well).

☞ DRILL 45 MAY NOW BE DONE.

§46. The Irregular Adjectives μέγας, μεγάλη, μέγα and πολύς, πολλή, πολύ

Two common adjectives—μέγας, μεγάλη, μέγα, "great," "big," and πολύς, πολλή, πολύ, "much" (sing.), "many" (pl.)—are first-second-declension adjectives with a few irregular forms in the singular. In the declensions below, the irregular forms are enclosed in boxes. MEMORIZE THESE IRREGULAR FORMS.

| | *Singular* | | | | *Singular* | |
	M.	F.	N.	M.	F.	N.
Nom.	μέγας	μεγάλη	μέγα	πολύς	πολλή	πολύ
Gen.	μεγάλου	μεγάλης	μεγάλου	πολλοῦ	πολλῆς	πολλοῦ
Dat.	μεγάλῳ	μεγάλῃ	μεγάλῳ	πολλῷ	πολλῇ	πολλῷ
Acc.	μέγαν	μεγάλην	μέγα	πολύν	πολλήν	πολύ
Voc.	μεγάλε	μεγάλη	μέγα	—	—	—
	Plural				*Plural*	
Nom.	μεγάλοι	μεγάλαι	μεγάλα	πολλοί	πολλαί	πολλά
Gen.	μεγάλων	μεγάλων	μεγάλων	πολλῶν	πολλῶν	πολλῶν
Dat.	μεγάλοις	μεγάλαις	μεγάλοις	πολλοῖς	πολλαῖς	πολλοῖς
Acc.	μεγάλους	μεγάλᾱς	μεγάλα	πολλούς	πολλάς	πολλά
Voc.	μεγάλοι	μεγάλαι	μεγάλα	—	—	—

OBSERVATIONS

1. Most of the forms of μέγας, μεγάλη, μέγα use the stem μεγαλ-, to which are added the endings of regular first-second-declension adjectives. The persistent accent is given by the feminine singular nominative form.

2. Most of the forms of πολύς, πολλή, πολύ use the stem πολλ-, to which are added the endings of regular first-second-declension adjectives. The persistent accent is an acute on the ultima, which becomes a circumflex in the genitive and dative singular and plural (cf. §13, Observation 2, p. 43). There are *no* vocative forms of πολύς, πολλή, πολύ.

☞ DRILL 46 MAY NOW BE DONE.

§47. Partitive Genitive

When a noun in the genitive case represents the *whole* of which another noun is a *part*, it is called a **Partitive Genitive**.[5] For example:

---

5. The Partitive Genitive is also known as the **Genitive of the Divided Whole**.

> τοῖς ἀγαθοῖς τῶν πολῑτῶν ὅπλα πέμπομεν.
> For the good ones *of* the *citizens* weapons (d.o.) we are sending.
> We are sending weapons for the good ones *of* the *citizens*.
>
> πολλοὶ τῶν Λακεδαιμονίων τοῖς τῶν συμμάχων λόγοις οὐκ ἐπείθοντο.
> Many *of* the *Spartans* were not heeding the words of the allies.

The syntax of each italicized word (πολῑτῶν, Λακεδαιμονίων) is **Partitive Genitive**.

OBSERVATION
___

The Partitive Genitive *does not* regularly stand in the attributive position.

§48. Genitive of Value

With verbs that mean "value," "deem worthy," and the like, the worth or value of someone or something is expressed by a noun or substantive in the genitive case. This use of the genitive is called a **Genitive of Value**. For example:

πολλοῦ ποιοῦμαι ταύτην τὴν γνώμην.	I consider this judgment *of much value.*
θανάτου τούτους ἐτῑμώμεθα.	We were deeming these men worthy *of death.*

The syntax of each italicized word (πολλοῦ, θανάτου) is **Genitive of Value**.

OBSERVATIONS
___

1. A Genitive of Value is often a substantive adjective in the neuter singular. The word "value" may be added in an English translation. In the first sentence πολλοῦ is translated "of much value."

2. Both ποιέω and τῑμάω *in the middle voice* may be accompanied by a Genitive of Value. ἀξιόω in either the active or the passive voice may be accompanied by a Genitive of Value.

3. In the second sentence θανάτου actually expresses the *penalty* that the direct object of ἐτῑμώμεθα *deserves.*

Often a prepositional phrase with an idiomatic translation is used instead of a Genitive of Value.

περὶ πολλοῦ ποιοῦμαι ταύτην τὴν γνώμην.	I consider this judgment *of much value.*

§49. Substantive Use of the Article

An adjective with or without the article may function as a substantive (§15). Although in Attic Greek the *article alone* may not function as a substantive, it often joins with adverbs, prepositional phrases, or other words to create a variety of substantives. For example:

οἱ νῦν	men now (subj.), men of the present day (subj.)
τοὺς μὴ ἐν τῇ ἀγορᾷ	(the class of) men not in the marketplace (d.o.)
ταῖς τῆς χώρᾱς	for the women of the land
ὁ τοῦ Πριάμου	the son (subj.) of Priam

OBSERVATIONS

1. Each of these phrases *in its entirety* functions as a *substantive*. As with adjectives used substantively, the English word "man," "woman," or "thing" (sing.) or "men," "women," or "things" (pl.) is supplied to show gender and number, which are indicated solely by the form of the article that introduces the phrase. In the last phrase the word "son" is supplied, and the name in the genitive indicates the father.

2. When such substantives are negated, it is possible to distinguish clearly between *specific* substantives, negated by **οὐ**, and *generic* substantives, negated by **μή** (§15).

The particles **μέν** and **δέ** may also be combined with forms of the article to form substantives, usually to create a contrast or comparison. For example:

ὁ μὲν εὖ λέγει, ὁ δὲ οὔ.
One man speaks well, *another man* (does) not (speak well).
The one man speaks well, *the other man* (does) not (speak well).

τοὺς μὲν Γοργίᾱς ἐδίδασκεν, τοὺς δὲ διδάσκειν οὐκ ἤθελεν.
Some men (d.o.) Gorgias was teaching, *other men* (d.o.) he was refusing to teach.
Gorgias was teaching *some men,* (but) he was refusing to teach *other men.*

OBSERVATION

When **μέν** and **δέ** create substantives with *singular* forms of the article, the substantives are translated "one ..., another ...." When the two substantives refer to two people or things already mentioned, they are translated "the one ..., the other ...." When **μέν** and **δέ** create substantives with *plural* forms of the article, they are translated "some ..., other ...."

In order to indicate a change of subject from a preceding clause or sentence, **δέ** (*without* **μέν**) may also be combined with a form of the article to form a *new subject*. Often the new subject is part of the preceding sentence but is *not* the subject. For example:

τῷ Ἀλεξάνδρῳ παύεσθαι ὁ Πρίαμος ἔλεγεν, ὁ δὲ οὐκ ἤθελεν.
Priam was telling Alexander to cease, *but he* (Alexander) was refusing (to cease).

OBSERVATION

When **δέ** is combined with an article to indicate a change of subject, the article is translated by a personal pronoun ("he," "she," "it," or "they"). The English personal pronoun reflects the gender and number of the article in Greek. In such cases **δέ** is translated "but" or "and."

§50. Adverbs

An adverb modifies a verb, an adjective, or another adverb. Some examples of English adverbs are *not, justly, well,* and *very*. Many Greek words are identified as adverbs in vocabulary entries (e.g., **οὐ**, **εὖ**), but other adverbs may be formed from adjectives.

To form an adverb from a first-second-declension adjective:

1. take the stem (by dropping the ending of the masculine singular nominative form)
2. add the ending -**ως**.

Adjective	Stem	Adverb	Translation
δίκαιος, δικαίᾱ, δίκαιον	δικαι-	δικαίως	justly
ἄδικος, ἄδικον	ἀδικ-	ἀδίκως	unjustly
καλός, καλή, καλόν	καλ-	καλῶς	beautifully
οὗτος, αὕτη, τοῦτο	οὑτ-	οὕτω(ς)	thus, so, in this way
ὅδε, ἥδε, τόδε	—	ὧδε	in the following way

OBSERVATIONS

1. The accent on an adverb is persistent and is determined by the accent on the masculine singular nominative of the adjective from which it is formed. The rules for the possibilities of accent are observed. If the accent on an adverb falls on the ultima, the accent is *always* a circumflex.

2. The adverb **οὕτω(ς)** has a sigma in parentheses, which is called a **sigma movable**. This sigma appears as part of the word when the adverb is followed by a word beginning with a vowel *or* when the word to which it is attached is the last word in a clause or sentence.

3. The adverb formed from **ὅδε, ἥδε, τόδε** (**ὧδε**) is irregular and must be memorized.

4. The adverb **ἐκείνως** is regularly formed but occurs rarely in Attic Greek. The adverb **μεγάλως** is regularly formed. There is no regularly formed adverb for **πολύς, πολλή, πολύ**.

Close in meaning to many adverbs are certain prepositional phrases. For example, both **δικαίως** and **σὺν δίκῃ** may mean "justly."

☞ DRILL 47–50 MAY NOW BE DONE.

§51. Elision and Crasis

Two types of shortening, *elision* and *crasis*, commonly occur in Greek. Neither elision nor crasis *must* occur, but both appear often in prose and poetry.

Elision is the dropping of a *short vowel* at the end of a word when the next word begins with a vowel or diphthong. An apostrophe marks the omitted letter. For example:

ἀπ' ἀγορᾶς (= ἀπὸ ἀγορᾶς)
ἀλλ' ἄρχομεν (= ἀλλὰ ἄρχομεν)
ταῦτ' ἔλεγεν (= ταῦτα ἔλεγεν)
λέγετ' ἢ οὔ (= λέγετε ἢ οὔ)

κάκ' ἔργα (= κακὰ ἔργα)
ὑφ' ἑταίρων (= ὑπὸ ἑταίρων)
ταῦθ' ὑφ' ἑταίρων (= ταῦτα ὑπὸ ἑταίρων)

OBSERVATIONS

1. Elision is particularly common in disyllabic prepositions and conjunctions, but it may also occur in verbs, nouns, pronouns, adjectives, and adverbs.

2. When a disyllabic *preposition* or *conjunction* has its accent on the elided syllable (e.g., ἀπό, ἀλλά, and ὑπό in the examples above), the accent is dropped. For *other words* accented on the elided syllable, an accent is placed on the penult (e.g., κακά in the example above).

3. Certain consonants become aspirated when a rough breathing appears on the word following an elided syllable. The unaspirated labial pi becomes the aspirated labial phi (e.g., the pi of ὑπό becomes a phi in the phrase ὑφ' ἑταίρων). The unaspirated dental tau becomes the aspirated dental theta (e.g., the second tau of ταῦτα becomes a theta in the phrase ταῦθ' ὑφ' ἑταίρων). The unaspirated palatal kappa becomes the aspirated palatal chi.

Aphaeresis (ἀφαίρεσις, "taking away," "removal"), or **Inverse Elision**, is the loss of an ἐ- at the *beginning* of a word when the *preceding* word ends in a long vowel or diphthong. An apostrophe marks the omitted epsilon. For example:

μὴ 'κ θεοῦ (= μὴ ἐκ θεοῦ)
μὴ 'θελήσειν (= μὴ ἐθελήσειν)

OBSERVATION

Aphaeresis occurs in Attic poetry *only*. In this textbook it appears only in the Short and Longer Readings.

Crasis (κρᾶσις, "mixing") is the *blending of two words into one* by the contraction of a vowel or diphthong at the end of one word with a vowel or diphthong at the beginning of the next word. Crasis occurs most commonly when the first of the two words is καί, ὦ, or a form of ὁ, ἡ, τό. A coronis (') (κορωνίς, "hook") is placed over the contracted syllable if neither of the two words in crasis has a rough breathing. If either word in crasis has a rough breathing, either the first consonant of the resulting form is aspirated, or, if there is no consonant, a rough breathing (') instead of a coronis appears over the contracted syllable. For example:

(crasis with καί)	κἀγαθός (= καὶ ἀγαθός)
	κοὐ (= καὶ οὐ)
	χοἰ (= καὶ οἱ)
	κἀς (= καὶ ἐς)
(crasis with ὦ)	ὦνθρωπε (= ὦ ἄνθρωπε)
(crasis with article)	ἅνθρωπος (= ὁ ἄνθρωπος)
	τἀνθρώπου (= τοῦ ἀνθρώπου)
	οὑκ (= ὁ ἐκ)

1. When elision occurs, two words remain separate. When crasis occurs, two words are pronounced and written as one.

2. When καί is the first word in crasis, the diphthong -αι and its accent are most often dropped, and any short vowel at the beginning of the second word is lengthened: the -αι of καί is dropped, and the first alpha of ἀγαθός becomes long in κἀγαθός.

Most diphthongs and all long vowels at the beginning of the second word in crasis remain unchanged in the resulting form: the -αι of καί is dropped, and οὐ remains unchanged in κοὐ.

When καί appears in crasis with a diphthong or long vowel bearing a rough breathing, the kappa is aspirated, and a coronis is placed over the diphthong or long vowel: the -αι of καί is dropped, kappa becomes chi, and a coronis appears over the diphthong in χοἰ.

In most cases when the word following καί in crasis begins with ε- or εἰ-, the iota of καί is dropped, and the alpha *contracts* with the second word: the iota of καί is dropped, and the alpha contracts with the epsilon of ἐς and becomes long in κἀς.

3. When the interjection ὦ appears in crasis with a noun in the vocative case, the syllable in crasis is always an omega. The resulting word is accented according to the rules for the possibilities of accent.

4. When the article is the first word in crasis, its final vowel or diphthong is dropped *before a word beginning with alpha,* and the alpha is lengthened: the -οῦ of τοῦ is dropped, and the alpha of ἀνθρώπου becomes long in τἀνθρώπου.

5. Other contractions that result from crasis follow the rules for contraction that apply to contracted verbs (§§40–42): ὁ contracts with the epsilon of ἐκ and produces οὑκ.

☞ DRILL 51 MAY NOW BE DONE.

Short Readings

1. A fragment from the works of the philosopher Heraclitus

ἀρηιφάτουc[6] θεοὶ τῑμῶcι καὶ ἄνθρωποι. (Heraclitus, frag. 24)

ἀρείφατοc, ἀρείφατον slain by Ares, slain in war;
 ἀρηιφάτουc (Epic) = Attic ἀρειφάτουc

Fragments from tragedies of Aeschylus

2. μόνοc θεῶν γὰρ Θάνατοc οὐ δώρων ἐρᾷ. (Aeschylus, frag. 161)

δῶρον, δώρου, τό gift   ἐράω love, desire (+ gen.)

3. ἀπάτηc δικαίᾱc οὐκ ἀποcτατεῖ θεόc . . . (Aeschylus, frag. 301)

ἀπάτη, ἀπάτηc, ἡ deception   ἀποcτατέω stand aloof from

Fragments from tragedies of Sophocles

4. οὐ τοῖc ἀθύμοιc ἡ τύχη ξυλλαμβάνει. (Sophocles, frag. 927)

ἄθῡμοc, ἄθῡμον spiritless, faint-hearted
ξυλλαμβάνω (ξυν- + λαμβάνω), ξυλλήψομαι,
 ξυνέλαβον, ξυνείληφα, ξυνείλημμαι,
 ξυνελήφθην take part with, assist (+ dat.)

5. θεοῦ δὲ πληγὴν οὐχ ὑπερπηδᾷ βροτόc. (Sophocles, frag. 961)

πληγή, πληγῆc, ἡ blow, stroke   ὑπερπηδάω (ὑπερ- + πηδάω) leap over; escape from

6. Phaedra's nurse justifies her penchant for giving advice.

πολλὰ διδάcκει μ᾽ ὁ πολὺc βίοτοc· (Euripides, *Hippolytus* 252)

μ᾽ = με = *acc. sing. of first person personal pronoun*, me   βίοτοc, βιότου, ὁ life

---

6. The lunate sigma (**C**, **c**), used in an increasing number of standard Greek texts, appears in the readings of even-numbered chapters in this textbook in order to give students practice in recognizing it.

7. Jocasta responds to the news that her two sons are still alive after a fierce battle at Thebes.

> καλῶϲ τὰ τῶν θεῶν καὶ τὰ τῆϲ τύχηϲ ἔχει. (Euripides, *Phoenician Women* 1202)

8. Hermocrates of Syracuse speaks to a conference of Sicilian leaders about the need for unity against the Athenian menace.

> καὶ οὕτωϲ οὐ πόλεμοϲ πολέμῳ, εἰρήνη δὲ διαφοραὶ ἀπραγμόνωϲ παύονται . . . (Thucydides, *Peloponnesian War* IV.61.7)

διαφορά, διαφορᾶϲ, ἡ difference   ἀπραγμόνωϲ (adv.) without trouble, painlessly

9. A fragment from the works of the philosopher Democritus

> ὁμοφροϲύνη φιλίην ποιέει. (Democritus, frag. 186)

ὁμοφροϲύνη, ὁμοφροϲύνηϲ, ἡ unity of thought, being of the same mind   φιλίᾱ, φιλίᾱϲ, ἡ friendship; φιλίην (Ionic) = Attic φιλίᾱν

10. The orator explains why even false accusations are dangerous.

> οἱ γὰρ πολλοὶ τὴν μὲν ἀλήθειαν ἀγνοοῦϲιν, πρὸϲ δὲ τὴν δόξαν ἀποβλέπουϲιν. (Isocrates, *To Demonicus* 17)

ἀγνοέω (ἀ- + νοέω) not know, be ignorant (of)   ἀποβλέπω (ἀπο- + βλέπω), ——, ἀπέβλεψα, ——, ——, —— look away from (all other objects); gaze; pay attention (to)

11. A fragment from a comedy of Philemon

> τοῦ γὰρ δικαίου κἂν βροτοῖϲι κἂν θεοῖϲ
> ἀθάνατοϲ ἀεὶ δόξα διατελεῖ μόνον. (Philemon, frag. 60)

ἀεί (adv.) always   διατελέω (δια- + τελέω) continue; live

Fragments and proverbial expressions from the comedies of Menander

12.   ... εἰρήνη γεωργὸν κἂν πέτραις τρέφει
         καλῶς, πόλεμος δὲ κἂν πεδίῳ κακῶς.   (Menander frag. 719)

γεωργός, γεωργοῦ, ὁ farmer   τρέφω, τρέψω, ἔτρεψα, τέτροφα, τέθραμμαι,
πέτρᾱ, πέτρᾱς, ἡ rock   ἐτράφην nourish
                                                 πεδίον, πεδίου, τό plain, field

13.   ἐκ τῶν πόνων γὰρ τἀγάθ' αὔξεται βροτοῖς.   (Menander, *Sententiae* 221)

αὐξάνω/αὔξω, αὐξήςω, ηὔξηςα, ηὔξηκα, ηὔξημαι,
   ηὐξήθην *active or middle,* grow, increase (trans.
   and intrans.)

14.   πολλοὶ μὲν εὐτυχοῦςιν, οὐ φρονοῦςιν δέ.   (Menander, *Sententiae* 628)

εὐτυχέω be lucky, be well off, prosper   φρονέω have understanding, be wise; think

15.   χρηςτὸς πονηροῖς οὐ τιτρώςκεται λόγοις.   (Menander, *Sententiae* 822)

χρηςτός, χρηςτή, χρηςτόν useful; good   τιτρώςκω, τρώςω, ἔτρωςα, ——, τέτρωμαι,
                                                 ἐτρώθην wound, hurt

16. A proverb from Aesop

         Τύχη τέχνην ἐπανορθοῖ.   (Aesop, *Proverbs* 97)

τέχνη, τέχνης, ἡ art, skill   ἐπανορθόω (ἐπι- + ἀνα- + ὀρθόω) correct,
                                                 amend

CHAPTER 5

Vocabulary

→ ἀνάγκη, ἀνάγκης, ἡ necessity

→ μαθητής, μαθητοῦ, ὁ student

τέχνη, τέχνης, ἡ skill, art

διδάσκαλος, διδασκάλου, ὁ teacher

→ ἄρχων, ἄρχοντος, ὁ ruler, commander; archon, magistrate

→ δαίμων, δαίμονος, ὁ or ἡ divinity, divine power; spirit

→ Ἕκτωρ, Ἕκτορος, ὁ Hector

→ Ἕλλην, Ἕλληνος, ὁ Hellene, Greek

→ ἐλπίς, ἐλπίδος, ἡ hope; expectation

→ ἔρως, ἔρωτος, ὁ desire, passion, love

→ Ζεύς, Διός, ὁ Zeus

→ παῖς, παιδός, ὁ or ἡ child; slave

→ ῥήτωρ, ῥήτορος, ὁ public speaker, orator; rhetor

→ φρήν, φρενός, ἡ sing. or pl., heart, mind, wits

→ χάρις, χάριτος, ἡ grace, favor, goodwill; delight; gratitude

→ δῶμα, δώματος, τό sing. or pl., house, home

→ σῶμα, σώματος, τό body

→ χρῆμα, χρήματος, τό thing, matter, affair; pl., goods, property, money

ὅς, ἥ, ὅ (relative pron.) who, whose, whom; which, that (§53)

→ ἄγω, ἄξω, ἤγαγον, ἦχα, ἦγμαι, ἤχθην lead, bring; keep; middle, carry away with oneself; marry

→ ἀκούω, ἀκούσομαι, ἤκουσα, ἀκήκοα, ——, ἠκούσθην listen (to), hear (of)

→ ἥκω, ἥξω, ——, ——, ——, —— have come; be present

→ μανθάνω, μαθήσομαι, ἔμαθον, μεμάθηκα, ——, —— learn; understand

→ δεῖ, δεήσει, ἐδέησε(ν), ——, ——, —— (impersonal verb) it is necessary, must; there is need (+ gen.)

→ εἰμί, ἔσομαι, ——, ——, ——, —— be; exist; impersonal, it is possible (§55)

→ ἄλλος, ἄλλη, ἄλλο other, another

βάρβαρος, βάρβαρον non-Greek, foreign; barbarous; masc. pl. subst., foreigners; barbarians

θνητός, θνητή, θνητόν mortal

ῥᾴδιος, ῥᾳδίᾱ, ῥᾴδιον easy

→ ἀεί/αἰεί (adv.) always

→ γε (enclitic particle) limiting, at least, at any rate; emphasizing, indeed

→ κατά (prep. + gen.) down from, beneath; against
(prep. + acc.) according to, in relation to; throughout

μά (particle + acc.) used in oaths, by

νή (particle + acc.) expresses strong affirmation, (yes,) by

→ παρά (prep. + gen.) from (the side of); by
(prep. + dat.) near; at (the house of); among
(prep. + acc.) to (the side of), beside; contrary to

περ (enclitic particle) very, even

→ ποτέ (enclitic adv.) at some time, ever; ποτέ . . . ποτέ . . . at one time . . . , at another time . . . ; sometimes . . . , sometimes . . .

οὔποτε/μήποτε (adv.) never

πως (enclitic adv.) somehow

→ τε (enclitic conj.) and

→ τοι (enclitic particle) surely, you know

→ χάριν (prep. + preceding gen.) for the sake of

Vocabulary Notes

→ ἀνάγκη, ἀνάγκης, ἡ means "necessity" in the sense of force or compulsion (caused by the orders of a commander, a superior force, the demands of the body) or of logical necessity in argument. ἀνάγκη often appears as a Predicate Nominative with a Subject Infinitive, and ἐστί is usually omitted.

ταῦτα ποιεῖν (ἐστιν) ἀνάγκη.	To do these things is a necessity.
	It is a necessity to do these things.

When capitalized in poetry, Ἀνάγκη is personified as the goddess Necessity.

→ μαθητής, μαθητοῦ, ὁ, "student," is related to the verb μανθάνω, "learn"; "understand." A student is one who learns.

→ ἄρχων, ἄρχοντος, ὁ was originally a substantive of a verbal adjective of the verb ἄρχω: "a ruling man." ἄρχων is used of a "ruler" or "commander" in general, and in Athens it is also the title of one of nine annually elected "magistrates" or "archons" who oversaw the political, military, and religious life of the city. Each was assigned a specific actual or symbolic duty, and the name of one of them (the *eponymous* archon) was used to name the year. In addition, ἄρχων may be used more generally of any magistrate.

→ δαίμων, δαίμονος, ὁ or ἡ refers to a "divinity" as the "divine power" of a god, in contrast to θεός, which refers to a god as an individual. δαίμων may mean a "spirit" or "daimon" (both helpful and hurtful) that watches over and controls a person's fate, and it is often used by the poets and occasionally by prose writers to mean "fortune" or "destiny."

→ Ἕκτωρ, Ἕκτορος, ὁ, "Hector," is the most important of the sons of Priam and the greatest defender of Troy. His name is cognate with the verb ἔχω and means "Holder" or "Stayer" (of Troy). He is killed by Achilles.

→ Ἕλλην, Ἕλληνος, ὁ, "Hellene," "Greek," was originally the proper name of the son of Deucalion, Hellen. In Homer the plural form refers to a Thessalian tribe among the Greek forces at Troy, but in Attic Greek it is used of anyone who speaks any dialect of Greek, and the plural is used of the "Greeks" as distinct from the other peoples of the Mediterranean. In poetry Ἕλλην may also be used as an adjective.

→ ἐλπίς, ἐλπίδος, ἡ, "hope," "expectation," is often accompanied by a Subjective or Objective Genitive or both. In the poets it may be personified as the goddess Hope.

→ ἔρως, ἔρωτος, ὁ usually denotes sexual passion or "desire," but it may also refer to a nonerotic desire. The object of one's desire is frequently expressed by an Objective Genitive. An Object Infinitive may appear to express an action one desires to do. ἔρως sometimes refers to the object of one's desire, that is, to one's "love." When capitalized, Ἔρως is the god of love, Eros. In Hesiod he comes into existence without procreation along with Chaos, Earth, and Tartarus, but he is later said to be the child of Aphrodite. The vocative singular of Ἔρως is Ἔρως. MEMORIZE THIS IRREGULAR VOCATIVE.

→ Ζεύς, Διός, ὁ, "Zeus," is king of the Olympian gods, husband and brother of Hera, and father of several other Olympians, including Apollo, Artemis, Athena, Dionysus, and Hermes. In some traditions he is also the father of Aphrodite and Hephaestus. As with other monosyllabic third-declension nouns, the accent on the genitive and dative of Ζεύς shifts to the ultima. The vocative singular of Ζεύς is Ζεῦ. MEMORIZE THIS IRREGULAR VOCATIVE.

→ παῖς, παιδός, ὁ or ἡ means "child" ("son" or "daughter") in relation to descent or age.

> οἱ Πριάμου παῖδες τὰ πολέμου διδάσκονται.
> The sons of Priam are being taught the things of war.
>
> ταῦτα τοῖς παισὶ τοῖς νέοις ἔλεγον.
> I was saying these things to the young children.

In certain contexts **παῖς** refers to one's condition or standing in society and means "slave."

> παύει, ὦ παῖ, τοῦ πόνου;   Are you ceasing from your toil, slave?

Although **παῖς** is monosyllabic in the nominative singular, the accent on the genitive plural in Attic Greek is *persistent* and is *not* on the ultima: **παίδων**. The accent on the vocative singular is a circumflex: **παῖ**. MEMORIZE THESE ACCENTS. The phrases **ἐκ/ἀπὸ παιδός** and **ἐκ/ἀπὸ παίδων** mean "from childhood."

→ **ῥήτωρ, ῥήτορος, ὁ** is often used of a "public speaker" or "orator" (one who speaks about public affairs in assemblies and other public gatherings), and it is also used of a teacher of rhetoric or "rhetor," a man paid to train students in artful speaking. Many rhetors came to Athens in the latter half of the fifth century B.C.E., bringing with them a new level of skill with language that influenced many areas of Athenian life. In Athens rhetors were held in high esteem by many, but others distrusted them and questioned the ethical value of their contribution.

→ **φρήν, φρενός, ἡ** may refer to the midriff or area around the diaphragm of a human being, but more often **φρήν** refers to the "heart" as the seat of the passions or the "mind" as the seat of the mental faculties. It has these meanings in both the singular and the plural, but the plural is more common. Among the prepositional phrases that use **φρήν**, two illustrate its range of meanings: **ἐκ φρενός** means "from the heart," while **ἐκ φρενῶν** means "out of (one's) wits."

→ **χάρις, χάριτος, ἡ** may refer to one's external beauty, "grace," "favor," or "charm." It is also used of a "favor" or "kindness" done or received, or it is used of the "goodwill" that results from such a kindness. By extension of this last meaning, **χάρις** may mean "gratitude" and may be followed by an Objective Genitive.

> χάρις τούτων   gratitude (subj.) for these things

In poetry, **χάρις** may refer to the inward "delight" felt by someone.

> χάρις νίκης   delight (subj.) of (= arising from) victory

When capitalized, **Χάρις** is a Grace, one of two or three goddesses, **αἱ Χάριτες**, the Graces, who attend Aphrodite and symbolize grace, beauty, and charm.

→ **δῶμα, δώματος, τό** means "house" in the singular or the plural. It occasionally means "hall" and is used not only of houses of humans but also of the dwelling places of gods (e.g., **δῶμα Ἄιδου**). Occasionally **δῶμα** is used of the "household" or "family" that lives within. The word appears in Attic poetry only.

→ Although in Homer **σῶμα, σώματος, τό** refers only to a dead "body" or "corpse," in Attic prose and poetry it refers as well to the living body of a human being or an animal. **σῶμα**, "body," is frequently contrasted with **ψῡχή**, "soul."

→ **χρῆμα, χρήματος, τό** is related to a verb that means "use" (**χράομαι**), and its most basic meaning is any "thing" that one *needs* or *uses*. In the plural it often has a *collective* singular meaning of "property" or "goods," and from this meaning grew its common meaning "money." χρῆμα may also refer broadly to any "thing," "matter," or "affair."

➙ ἄγω, ἄξω, ἤγαγον, ἦχα, ἦγμαι, ἤχθην exhibits irregular reduplication *of its entire stem, ἀγ-,* in the third principal part. In the active voice ἄγω means "lead" or "bring." It may also mean "spend" (one's life), "keep" (the peace, silence) or "celebrate," "hold" (holidays, games). In the middle voice ἄγω means "carry away with oneself," and, when used of a man with a woman as a direct object, it means "marry." ἄγω occurs in the passive voice.

➙ ἀκούω, ἀκούσομαι, ἤκουσα, ἀκήκοα, ——, ἠκούσθην is a partial deponent. That is, it lacks active forms in the future tense and has *future middle forms only.* The fourth principal part, ἀκήκοα, shows unusual reduplication, and there is *no* fifth principal part in Attic Greek. ἀκούω means "hear (of)" or "listen (to)" and is regularly followed by an Accusative, Direct Object of the "thing heard" (a speech, words, an explanation) and a genitive of the person *from whom* one hears something. In prose, the genitive may be accompanied by a preposition (ἀπό, ἐκ, παρά, or πρός).

> ταῦτα (ἀπὸ) τοῦ φίλου ἤκουον.   I was hearing these things from my friend.

The active voice of ἀκούω may also be used as the *passive* of λέγω to mean "be spoken of" or "be called." When ἀκούω is so used, it is often accompanied by an adverb or by a Nominative, Predicate Adjective.

> εὖ ἤκουες.   You were hearing (yourself being spoken of) well.
> You were being spoken of well.
>
> κακὸς ἀκούω.   I am hearing (myself called) bad.
> I am called bad.

Other than in the future tense, ἀκούω rarely occurs in the middle voice, but it does occur in the passive voice.

➙ ἥκω, ἥξω, ——, ——, ——, —— appears in the present, imperfect, and future tenses *only,* has forms in the *active voice only,* and has *completed aspect only.* It thus has only two principal parts. Its meaning in the present tense is equivalent to the English present perfect "have come," and it may thus also mean "be present." In the imperfect, it is translated by the English pluperfect "had come" or by the imperfect "was present." In the future, it is translated by the English future perfect "will have come" or by the future "will be present." Since the first letter of ἥκω is a long vowel, no lengthening can take place in the imperfect tense. The majority of its imperfect forms can be recognized by their imperfect endings (e.g., ἧκες), but there is *no* difference between the first and second person plural *present* and *imperfect* forms (ἥκομεν, ἥκετε). These forms are distinguished by *context only.* ἥκω is regularly accompanied by prepositional phrases.

> εἰς τήνδε τὴν χώρᾱν ἥκετε.   You (pl.) have come to (are present in) this land.
> ἧκον πρὸς τὸν Ἀλέξανδρον.   They had come to Alexander.
> ἥξω εἰς ἐκείνην τὴν οἰκίᾱν.   I shall have come to (be present in) that house.

➙ μανθάνω, μαθήσομαι, ἔμαθον, μεμάθηκα, ——, ——, "learn," "understand," is a partial deponent. That is, it lacks active forms in the future tense and has *future middle forms only.* Other than in the future tense, μανθάνω does not occur in the middle voice and is rare in the passive voice. μανθάνω may be accompanied by an Accusative, Direct Object and sometimes also by a noun or pronoun in the genitive case expressing *from whom* one learns something. This genitive is often accompanied by a preposition meaning "from": ἀπό, ἐκ, παρά, πρός. With an Object Infinitive μανθάνω means "learn" or "learn how."

Ἑλένης ἔργα κακὰ μανθάνεις.	You are learning evil deeds from Helen.
ταῦτα ἐξ Εὐρῑπίδου ἐμανθάνομεν.	We were learning these things from Euripides.
εὖ λέγειν μαθήσει, ὦ τέκνον.	You will learn (how) to speak well, child.

→ δεῖ, δεήσει, ἐδέησε(ν), ——, ——, ——, "it is necessary"; "there is need," is an epsilon-contracted impersonal verb. An impersonal verb, usually in the third person singular, is a verb that *has no personal subject* such as "I" or "you." Its principal parts indicate that it is impersonal by appearing in the third, not the first, person. It has regularly formed infinitives. δεῖ originally conveyed the sense of *objective* necessity, but in the latter half of the fifth century B.C.E. and beyond δεῖ could suggest *moral* or *ethical* necessity as well. When δεῖ is accompanied by a Subject Infinitive (§57), with or without a Subject Accusative (§58), it is translated "it is necessary."

δεῖ πολίτᾱς ταῦτα ποιεῖν.	It is necessary for citizens to do these things.
	Citizens must do these things.
ἔδει πολίτᾱς ταῦτα ποιεῖν.	It was necessary for citizens to do these things.
	Citizens had to do these things.
δεήσει πολίτᾱς ταῦτα ποιεῖν.	It will be necessary for citizens to do these things.
	Citizens will have to do these things.

In each of the second translations, the Subject Accusative may become the subject of the English auxiliary verbs "must" (for δεῖ), "had" (ἔδει), or "will have" (δεήσει).

If δεῖ is negated, two meanings are possible: "it is not necessary" or "must not."

οὐ δεῖ πολίτᾱς ταῦτα ποιεῖν.	*It is not necessary* for the citizens to do these things.
	The citizens *must not* do these things.

If the Subject Infinitive is negated, δεῖ is translated "must not."

δεῖ πολίτᾱς ταῦτα μὴ ποιεῖν.	The citizens *must not* do these things.

When δεῖ is accompanied by a Genitive of Separation (with *no* preposition) representing the *thing needed*, it is translated "there is need."

νῦν τῆς ἀρετῆς δεῖ.	Now there is need *of excellence*.

→ εἰμί, ἔσομαι, ——, ——, ——, ——, "be"; "exist," is a partial deponent. That is, it lacks active forms in the future tense and has *future middle forms only*. The irregular conjugations of εἰμί are presented in §55. Other than in the future tense, εἰμί occurs in the active voice only. For the uses and meanings of εἰμί see §56.

The third person singular forms of εἰμί—ἔστι(ν) (with an acute accent on the penult), ἦν, ἔσται—may be used impersonally to express possibility with a Subject Infinitive.

ἔστι (ἦν, ἔσται) λέγειν.   It is possible (was possible, will be possible) to speak.

→ The declension of the adjective ἄλλος, ἄλλη, ἄλλο, "other," "another," is identical with that of any first-second-declension adjective *except* in the neuter nominative and accusative singular forms, which end in omicron (cf. ἐκεῖνο). Sometimes ἄλλος is used in *parallel* constructions, and special translations are required.

ἄλλος τοὺς ποιητὰς τῑμᾷ, ἄλλος δὲ τοὺς ῥήτορας.
One man honors poets, but *another man* (honors) rhetors.

τοῖς λόγοις ἄλλους μὲν ἔπειθες, ἄλλους δὲ οὔ.
Some men you were persuading with your words, but *others* (you were) not (persuading with your words).

When ἄλλος is used in such parallel constructions, its forms have the same gender, number, and case. Singular forms of ἄλλος so arranged are translated "one . . . , another . . . ." Plural forms of ἄλλος are translated "some . . . , others . . . ." Often these parallel constructions are reinforced by the particles μέν and δέ.
    If two different forms of ἄλλος (*including* the adverbial form) appear in the *same* clause or sentence, a comparison is implied, and the first part of the comparison *must be supplied* in an English translation.

ἄλλος ἄλλο λέγει.
One man says one thing, another man says another thing.

τῶν συμμάχων ἄλλοι ἄλλως ἐνίκων.
Of the allies *some were winning in one way,* others were winning in another way.

When a form of ἄλλος occurs in the attributive position, it should be translated "the rest (of)."

τοὺς ἄλλους Ἀθηναίους   *the rest of the* Athenians (d.o.)

When ἄλλος is paired and contrasted with another, more specific or important element, it often *precedes* that element. This order is in contrast to the usual English order.

ἄλλους τε καὶ τὸν σοφὸν ποιητὴν ἔπειθεν.
He was persuading other men and the wise poet (= the wise poet and others).

→ The older form of the adverb meaning "always" is αἰεί. As the fifth century B.C.E. progressed, the form ἀεί, whose long alpha is a result of compensatory lengthening after the loss of iota, gradually became the dominant form and was the *only* form employed by the Attic orators. In poetry the alpha may be long *or* short: ἀεί or ἀεί. The adverbial expression εἰς/ἐς ἀεί/αἰεί means "with a view to always" or "forever."

→ γε is an enclitic particle that serves either to *limit* or to *emphasize* a word, phrase, or clause. The force of γε is sometimes best translated in writing with italics and in speech with a raised intonation or stress on the word or phrase that is limited or emphasized. It is useful, however, to translate *limiting* γε with the phrases "at least" or "at any rate" and to translate *emphasizing* γε with the word "indeed." Context usually makes clear whether γε is being used to limit or to emphasize.

γε is placed immediately *after* the word it limits or emphasizes. Often it is placed between a noun and its article. When γε limits or emphasizes a prepositional phrase, it is often placed immediately after the preposition and before the rest of the phrase.

ὅ γε πόλεμος	the war (subj.) at any rate (limiting)
τῶν γε νῦν	of men now at least (limiting)
ποιηταί γε	*poets* (subj.) (emphasizing)
παρά γε τοὺς νόμους	contrary indeed to the laws (emphasizing)

→ Although the preposition κατά has a wide variety of uses in Attic Greek and may be translated in many ways, the idea of *down* and the idea of *being fitted* or *suited* to are at its core. When κατά is followed by the genitive case, it may refer to motion "down from" (the sky, a mountain, a rock, the mouth), "down over" (the earth, eyes, the head), or "down into" (the earth, nostrils).

κατ᾽ οὐρανοῦ	down from the sky
κατὰ γῆς	down over/down into the earth

At times this use of κατά may be translated "beneath" (i.e., the *result* of having moved under).

οἱ κατὰ γῆς	the men (subj.) beneath the earth

κατά followed by a genitive of a *person* often means "against.

λόγος καθ᾽ Ἑλένης	a speech (subj.) against Helen

The most common meaning of κατά followed by the *accusative* case is "according to."

κατὰ νόμον ἄρχομεν.	We are ruling according to custom.
κατ᾽ Εὐρῑπίδην	according to Euripides

Closely related to this meaning of κατά is one best rendered "in relation to."

τὰ κατὰ θεούς	the things (subj. or d.o.) in relation to gods

With the accusative case κατά may also mean motion "down along" (rivers, mountains) or "throughout" (a city, a country, the sea).

κατὰ ταύτην τὴν χώρᾱν	throughout this land

→ παρά is a preposition that is followed by nouns in the genitive, dative, and accusative cases. Its many uses and corresponding translations all develop from the basic ideas of motion "from the side of" a person (genitive), location "at" or "near" a person (dative), and motion "to (the side of)" or "beside" (accusative) a person or thing.

When followed by the genitive case, παρά most often means "from (the side of)," and the noun in the genitive case is nearly always a person or a personified thing (chance, justice). In certain Attic prose writers (Xenophon, Plato, Demosthenes), παρά is used with a Genitive of Personal Agent. In such cases the idea of personal agency arises from and often blends with the idea of "source" that is inherent in the genitive case.

τὰ παρὰ τῶν ἀρχόντων	the things (subj. or d.o.) from the rulers
ἐκεῖνα παρὰ τῶν ἀρχόντων ἐλέγετο.	Those things were being said by (i.e., *coming from*) the rulers.

When followed by the dative case, παρά means "at" or "near" a person or "among" a group of people. It may also mean "at (the house of)" or "in the opinion of."

παρὰ τοῖς θεοῖς	among the gods
παρὰ τῷ Ἕκτορι	at (the house of) Hector
παρὰ τῷ δήμῳ	in the power of/in the opinion of the people

When followed by the accusative case, παρά means "to (the side of)" people, places, or things. With verbs of motion παρά may also mean "beside" or "along."

παρὰ τοὺς πολίτᾱς	to (the side of) the citizens
παρὰ τὴν θάλατταν	beside the sea

From the idea of something being placed beside or along come a variety of meanings that may be translated "compared with" or "contrary to."

παρὰ ζῷα	compared with animals
παρὰ νόμον	contrary to custom

→ The disyllabic enclitic adverb ποτέ means "at some time," "ever." οὔ ποτε/μή ποτε, "not ever," "never," is often written as a single word: οὔποτε/μήποτε. Especially following interrogative words ποτέ adds broad indefiniteness to the question and may be translated "in the world."

πῶς ποτε ταῦτα λέγειν ἔχεις;	How ever/in the world are you able to say these things?

When ποτέ appears twice in parallel clauses, it is translated "at one time . . . , at another time . . ." or "sometimes . . . , sometimes . . . ."

νῑκῶμέν ποτε, ποτὲ νῑκώμεθα.	Sometimes we win, sometimes we are conquered.

The adverbs πότε ("when") and πῶς ("how") are interrogative and *have accents*. The adverbs ποτέ ("at some time") and πως ("somehow") are indefinite and are *enclitics*.

	Interrogative Adverb		*Indefinite Adverb*	
	πότε	when	ποτέ	at some time
	πῶς	how	πως	somehow

→ The enclitic conjunction τε, "and," is used in four ways. In prose τε usually appears with καί to connect parallel words or clauses. The *two words* τε καί are *together* translated "and." When τε appears *before* and is separated from καί, it is *not* translated, but it serves to indicate that another element parallel to the one marked by τε is soon to appear.

> οἱ ξένοι τε καὶ οἱ Ἀθηναῖοι ἀρετὴν διδάσκονται.
> οἵ τε ξένοι καὶ οἱ Ἀθηναῖοι ἀρετὴν διδάσκονται.
> The foreigners and the Athenians are being taught virtue.

Often in poetry and sometimes in prose single or double τε may connect two closely related words or clauses.

> Μοῖρα ἀνθρώπων θεῶν τε ἄρχει.   Fate rules men and gods.
> Μοῖρα ἀνθρώπων τε θεῶν τε ἄρχει.   Fate rules men and gods.

When single τε is used, it is *placed* after the *second* of the two elements being connected, but it is *translated* after the *first* element. Although it marks each balanced element, double τε is weaker than καί . . . καί . . . , "both . . . and . . . ." The uses of τε may be represented as follows:

> A τε καὶ B   A B τε
> A τε . . . καὶ B   A τε B τε

→ In origin the enclitic particle τοι was a dative singular form of the second person personal pronoun ("to/for you"), a Dative of Reference used to establish a close connection between speaker and listener. τοι occurs early in phrases and sentences, often coming between an article and its noun. It imparts a friendly, cajoling tone to a statement that the speaker or writer wishes the listener or reader to accept without argument or by appeal to proverbial truth, and it may be translated "surely" or "you know."

> ἀγαθόν τοί ἐστιν τοὺς θεοὺς τῑμᾶν.   To honor the gods is *surely* good.

οὔτοι (rarely μήτοι) is often written as a single word, although its accent is determined by the rules for enclitics: οὔτοι, not *οὖτοι.

→ The accusative singular of χάρις, χάριν, is sometimes used as a preposition with a *preceding* genitive and means "for the sake of."

> τοῦ λόγου χάριν   for the sake of the argument

Derivatives and Cognates

	Derivatives	*Cognates*
ἄγω	agony, stratagem, demagogue	agent, transact, agile
ἀεί, αἰεί		coeval, longevity, age, eon
ἀκούω	acoustic	hear
ἄλλος	allegory, parallel	alarm, else, ulterior
δαίμων	demon	
δεῖ	deontology	Deuterium, tire
δῶμα	dome	domestic, timber
εἰμί	ontology	is, yes, sin, essence
ἐλπίς		will, volition, voluptuous
Ζεύς	Dioscuri	Jupiter, jovial, Tuesday, deism
μανθάνω	mathematics, polymath	
παῖς	pediatrist	
ῥήτωρ	rhetoric	word, verb, irony
σῶμα	psychosomatic, chromosome	thigh, tumescent, tumor, tomb
τέχνη	technical	text, toil, architect, dachshund
φρήν	phrenology, frantic, frenzy	phrase
χάρις	charisma, eucharist	yearn, greedy, exhort

§52. Noun Morphology: Third Declension, Consonant Stems

The third declension contains masculine nouns and feminine nouns, which have a common set of endings, and neuter nouns, which have endings slightly different from those of the masculine/feminine nouns.

| | Case Endings of the Third Declension | | | |
| | Masculine/Feminine | | Neuter | |
	Singular	*Plural*	*Singular*	*Plural*
Nominative	—	-ες	—	-α
Genitive	-ος	-ων	-ος	-ων
Dative	-ι	-σι(ν)	-ι	-σι(ν)
Accusative	-α/-ν	-ας	—	-α
Vocative	—	-ες	—	-α

MEMORIZE EACH SET OF ENDINGS, PROCEEDING DOWN THE SINGULAR COLUMN AND THEN DOWN THE PLURAL COLUMN. BE PREPARED TO RECITE THE ENDINGS QUICKLY.

OBSERVATIONS

1. A blank is given for the nominative singular above because third-declension nouns show considerable variation in the nominative singular form. MEMORIZE A BLANK IN PLACE OF A NOMINATIVE SINGULAR ENDING. The nominative singular of each third-declension noun is the first element in the vocabulary entry for that noun and must be memorized.

2. Although -α is the more common accusative singular ending of masculine/feminine third-declension nouns, some third-declension nouns use -ν instead. Although there is no difference in meaning between these two endings, they are *not* interchangeable.[1]

3. A blank is given for the vocative singular of masculine/feminine nouns because third-declension nouns show considerable variation in the vocative singular form. MEMORIZE A BLANK IN PLACE OF A VOCATIVE SINGULAR ENDING.

4. A blank is given for the accusative singular of third-declension neuter nouns because the accusative singular is identical with the nominative singular. FOR NEUTER NOUNS MEMORIZE A BLANK IN PLACE OF AN ACCUSATIVE SINGULAR ENDING. A blank is also given for the vocative singular of third-declension neuter nouns because the vocative singular is identical with the nominative singular. FOR NEUTER NOUNS MEMORIZE A BLANK IN PLACE OF A VOCATIVE SINGULAR ENDING.

5. The dative plural ending of third-declension nouns has a movable nu.

There are slight variations in the declensions of some groups of third-declension nouns, and these variations are determined by the *final letters of their stems*. Nouns of the third declension whose stems end in consonants are called **consonant stems**, while those ending in vowels are called **vowel stems**. This section presents consonant stems ending in the liquid rho or the nasal nu and the dentals, tau, delta, and theta.

1. The third-declension accusative singular endings -α and -ν are derived from a single IE semi-consonant, *ṇ. A **semiconsonant** is a sound that has both a vocalic and a consonantal element, and the ₒ below the letter *n* indicates that the letter has a vocalic element. In Greek, the semi-consonant *ṇ sometimes appears as a vowel (-α) and sometimes as a consonant (-ν), depending on the sound that appears next to it in a word.

To decline a noun of the third declension with a stem ending in rho or nu, or in tau, delta, or theta, add the appropriate masculine/feminine or neuter endings to the stem. The stem for these nouns is found by removing the ending from the genitive singular form. For example:

	ῥήτωρ, ῥήτορος, ὁ public speaker Stem = ῥητορ-	δαίμων, δαίμονος, ὁ or ἡ divinity Stem = δαιμον-	ἐλπίς, ἐλπίδος, ἡ hope Stem = ἐλπιδ-	σῶμα, σώματος, τό body Stem = σωματ-
Singular				
Nom.	ῥήτωρ	δαίμων	ἐλπίς	σῶμα
Gen.	ῥήτορος	δαίμονος	ἐλπίδος	σώματος
Dat.	ῥήτορι	δαίμονι	ἐλπίδι	σώματι
Acc.	ῥήτορα	δαίμονα	ἐλπίδα	σῶμα
Voc.	ῥῆτορ	δαῖμον	ἐλπί	σῶμα
Plural				
Nom./Voc.	ῥήτορες	δαίμονες	ἐλπίδες	σώματα
Gen.	ῥητόρων	δαιμόνων	ἐλπίδων	σωμάτων
Dat.	ῥήτορσι(ν)	δαίμοσι(ν)	ἐλπίσι(ν)	σώμασι(ν)
Acc.	ῥήτορας	δαίμονας	ἐλπίδας	σώματα

OBSERVATIONS

1. The accent on *all* third-declension nouns is *persistent*.

2. The vocative singular of a third-declension noun whose stem ends in a liquid or the nasal nu is identical with that stem *when the accent does **not** fall on the last syllable of the stem*. Thus, ῥῆτορ and δαῖμον are both stems and vocative singular forms.

3. The vocative singular of every masculine/feminine third-declension noun ending in a dental is the stem *without the final dental*. Thus, ἐλπί is ἐλπιδ- with the delta dropped.

4. When the dative plural ending -σι(ν) was added to a stem ending in nu, the nu was dropped: *δαίμονσι(ν) > δαίμοσι(ν).

5. When the dative plural ending -σι(ν) was added to a stem ending in a dental, the dental first **assimilated**—altered to become similar—to the sigma of the ending and was then dropped: *ἐλπίδσι(ν) > *ἐλπίσσι(ν) > ἐλπίσι(ν); *σώματσι(ν) > *σώμασσι(ν) > σώμασι(ν). **Assimilation**, the process by which one sound is altered to become similar to another next to it, is a common feature of Greek morphology.

To the declensions of ῥήτωρ, δαίμων, ἐλπίς, and σῶμα one may compare the following declensions:

	χάρις, χάριτος, ἡ grace Stem = χαριτ-	φρήν, φρενός, ἡ sing. or pl., heart Stem = φρεν-	ἄρχων, ἄρχοντος, ὁ ruler Stem = ἀρχοντ-
Singular			
Nom.	χάρις	φρήν	ἄρχων
Gen.	χάριτος	φρενός	ἄρχοντος
Dat.	χάριτι	φρενί	ἄρχοντι
Acc.	χάριν	φρένα	ἄρχοντα
Voc.	χάρι	φρήν	ἄρχον
Plural			
Nom./Voc.	χάριτες	φρένες	ἄρχοντες
Gen.	χαρίτων	φρενῶν	ἀρχόντων
Dat.	χάρισι(ν)	φρεσί(ν)	αρχόυσι(ν)
Acc.	χάριτας	φρένας	ἄρχοντας

OBSERVATIONS

1. When the stem of a third-declension noun ends in a dental preceded by iota or upsilon *and* the persistent accent is *not* on the last syllable of the stem, the accusative singular ending is nu. One may compare the stems ἐλπίδ- and χαριτ- and the accusative singular forms ἐλπίδα and χάριν.

2. In third-declension nouns such as φρήν, which are *monosyllabic*—having one syllable only—in the nominative singular, the accent shifts to the ultima in the genitive and dative singular *and* plural. The accent on the genitive plural is usually a circumflex over the ending -ων. MEMORIZE THIS ADDITIONAL RULE OF ACCENT.

3. The vocative singular of a third-declension noun ending in a liquid or the nasal nu *is identical with the nominative singular when the accent in the nominative singular is on the ultima.* Thus, the vocative singular of φρήν is φρήν.

4. When the dative plural ending -σι(ν) was added to a stem ending in -ντ, the following sound changes produced the Attic Greek dative plural ending -ουσι(ν):

   *ἄρχοντσι(ν) > *ἄρχονσσι(ν) > *ἄρχονσι(ν) > ἄρχουσι(ν).

The tau assimilated to the following sigma and was then dropped. The nu before the sigma was also dropped, and the vowel before it was lengthened into a spurious diphthong (-ου-). This lengthening is called **compensatory lengthening** (it *compensates* for the loss of the nu).

Summary of Special Morphology Rules for Third-Declension Nouns	
Acc. Sing.	**-ν** when stem ends in dental preceded by **-ι-** or **-υ-** *and* last syllable of stem is *not* accented (stem = χάριτ-; acc sing. = χάριν)
Voc. Sing.	**stem** when stem ends in **-ρ, -λ,** or **-ν** and accent does *not* fall on last syllable of the stem **stem with final dental dropped** when stem ends in dental **nom. sing.** when stem ends in **-ρ, -λ,** or **-ν** and accent is on the ultima
Dat. Pl.	*-νσι(ν) > **-σι(ν)** (drop **-ν**) *-τσι(ν), -δσι(ν), -θσι(ν) > **-σι(ν)** (drop dental) *-οντσι(ν) > **-ουσι(ν)** (assimilation, compensatory lengthening, spurious diphthong)

☞   DRILL 52 MAY NOW BE DONE.

§53. The Relative Pronoun and the Relative Clause

There are in Greek, as in English, three types of sentences: simple, compound, and complex. A **simple sentence** has only one subject and one predicate (e.g., "Gorgias speaks well."). A **compound sentence** has more than one subject and predicate, each joined together by a coordinating conjunction such as *and, but, for, or, nor* (e.g., "Gorgias speaks well, and the citizens are being persuaded by his words").[2]

A **complex sentence** has one or more than one *independent* or *main* clause and one or more than one *dependent* or *subordinate* clause.[3]

Gorgias, who speaks well, persuades the citizens.

The subordinate clause in this example ("who speaks well") functions as an adjective describing "Gorgias" and is called a *relative clause*.[4] A **relative clause** is introduced by a **relative pronoun** (*who* in this example), and the clause describes or qualifies an antecedent. An **antecedent** (*Gorgias* in this example) is a word that usually goes before the relative pronoun, and it is the word to which the relative pronoun refers.

> **Relative Clause**: an adjectival subordinate clause that describes an antecedent and is introduced by a relative pronoun[5]
> **Relative Pronoun**: a word that introduces a relative clause and refers to an antecedent (in English: *who, whose, whom, which, that,* and sometimes *what*)
> **Antecedent**: a word described by the relative clause and referred to by the relative pronoun

---

2. Simple and compound sentences contain independent clauses *only*. An **independent clause** contains a subject and a verb and expresses a complete thought, and it may stand alone as a simple sentence. If it is part of a complex sentence, an independent clause is often called a **main clause**.
3. A **subordinate clause** contains a subject and a finite verb, but it *cannot* stand alone as a complete sentence.
4. For subordinate clauses that function as adverbs see Part 2, §147; as nouns see §69.
5. There are also relative adjectives, adverbs, and conjunctions, all of which may introduce relative clauses.

In the following sentences containing relative clauses, the antecedent is italicized, the relative pronoun is boldfaced, and the relative clause is underlined.

> The *weapons* **that** <u>the allies asked for</u> have been sent.
> I pity the *woman* **whose** <u>husband has gone to war.</u>
> A *poet* <u>**to whom** the Muses are friendly</u> makes good poems.

The relative pronoun in Greek has singular and plural forms in all three genders. MEMORIZE THE DECLENSION OF THE RELATIVE PRONOUN ACROSS THE SINGULAR AND THEN ACROSS THE PLURAL.

	Singular			*Plural*		
	M.	F.	N.	M.	F.	N.
Nom.	ὅς	ἥ	ὅ	οἵ	αἵ	ἅ
Gen.	οὗ	ἧς	οὗ	ὧν	ὧν	ὧν
Dat.	ᾧ	ᾗ	ᾧ	οἷς	αἷς	οἷς
Acc.	ὅν	ἥν	ὅ	οὕς	ἅς	ἅ

OBSERVATIONS

1. The relative pronoun has *no* vocative case forms.
2. Almost all the forms of the relative pronoun are identical with corresponding forms of the article, except that while the article has initial tau, the relative pronoun has a rough breathing for every form. The masculine nominative singular of the relative pronoun, ὅς, is *not* identical with the corresponding form of the article, ὁ.
3. All the forms of the relative pronoun have accents, acute in the nominative and accusative, circumflex in the genitive and dative.

MEMORIZE THE FOLLOWING RULE: THE RELATIVE PRONOUN AGREES WITH ITS ANTECEDENT IN GENDER AND NUMBER. ITS CASE, HOWEVER, IS DETERMINED BY ITS SYNTAX WITHIN THE RELATIVE CLAUSE. For example:

> τοῖς λόγοις οὓς ὁ Γοργίᾱς ἔλεγεν οὐκ ἐπειθόμην.
> *By the words that* Gorgias was saying I was not being persuaded.
> I was not being persuaded *by the words that* Gorgias was saying.

The relative pronoun (οὕς) introduces a relative clause (οὓς ὁ Γοργίᾱς ἔλεγεν) that describes the antecedent (τοῖς λόγοις). οὕς is *masculine* and *plural* to agree with λόγοις, its antecedent. It is *accusative,* however, because it is the direct object of ἔλεγεν, the verb in the relative clause.

> τῇ ἀγαθῇ ἣ ἐκ τῆς γῆς πέμπεται λέγειν ἐθέλουσιν.
> *To the good woman who* out from the land is being sent to speak they are willing.
> They are willing to speak *to the good woman who* is being sent out from the land.

ἥ is *feminine* and *singular* to agree with ἀγαθῇ, its antecedent. It is *nominative,* however, because it is the subject of πέμπεται, the verb in the relative clause.

> ταῦτα ἃ ἔλεγον καὶ ὁ Πρίαμος ἔλεγεν.
> *These things (d.o.) that* I was saying also Priam was saying.
> Priam also was saying *these things that* I was saying.

ἅ is *neuter* and *plural* to agree with ταῦτα, its antecedent. It is *accusative,* however, because it is the direct object of ἔλεγον, the verb in the relative clause.

τῷ πολίτῃ πειθόμεθα οὗ διὰ βουλὴν παύεται ὁ πόλεμος.
The citizen we heed *of whom* on account of the advice is being stopped the war.
We heed *the citizen* on account of *whose* advice the war is being stopped.

οὗ is *masculine* and *singular* to agree with πολίτῃ, its antecedent. It is *genitive,* however, because its syntax in the relative clause is Subjective Genitive.

OBSERVATIONS
___

1. The relative pronoun usually comes first in its clause. It may come second if it is the object of a preposition.
2. The relative pronoun is often placed immediately after its antecedent.
3. Translations of relative pronoun forms in Greek require mastery of the uses of the relative pronoun forms in English:

	Beings (sing. or pl.)	*Things (sing. or pl.)*
Subject	who	that/which
Possessive	whose	whose
Object of verbs and prepositions	whom	that/which

Restrictive and Nonrestrictive Relative Clauses

In both Greek and English there are two different kinds of relative clauses. A **restrictive** relative clause contains information about the antecedent that is *essential* to the meaning of the sentence. In English such a clause is *not set off by commas,* and an antecedent that is not a person is referred to in English by the relative pronoun *that.*

Men *who are without weapons* will not fight.
I lost the book *that you lent me.*

In each of these sentences the relative clause *restricts* the meaning of the antecedent in a way that is essential for the sense of the sentence. The men who "will not fight" are not men in general, but "men who are without weapons." The book that "I lost" is not any book, but "the book that you lent me." Such restrictive relative clauses are not set off by commas. *That* is used when the antecedent is not a person.

A **nonrestrictive** relative clause contains information about the antecedent that is *not essential* to the meaning of the sentence. In English such a clause *is always set off by commas,* and an antecedent that is not a person is referred to in English by the relative pronoun *which.*

Hades, *who rules the Underworld,* is a brother of Zeus.
You would enjoy this book, *which was written by my sister.*

Chapter 5

In each of these sentences the relative clause contains additional but *nonessential* information about the antecedent. Such *nonrestrictive* clauses are always set off by commas. *Which* is used when the antecedent is not a person.

In Greek the *same pronouns* are used for *both* restrictive *and* nonrestrictive clauses. The two types can be distinguished *by punctuation only.*[6]

☞ DRILL 53 A–C MAY NOW BE DONE.

Connective Relative

Sometimes a Greek sentence begins with a relative pronoun, and its antecedent is a word in the preceding sentence or the entire content of that sentence. For example:

οἱ Λακεδαιμόνιοι τὴν μάχην ἐνίκων. ὃ τῷ δήμῳ ἔδει λέγειν.
The Spartans were prevailing in the battle. *Which thing* to the people it was necessary to tell.
The Spartans were prevailing in the battle. *And* it was necessary to tell the people *this thing.*

OBSERVATIONS

1. The relative pronoun ὅ is neuter and singular to agree with the entire content of the preceding sentence, which serves as its antecedent. It is accusative, however, because its syntax in the relative clause is Accusative, Direct Object.
2. A connective relative is often best translated with a conjunction such as "and" and a demonstrative pronoun (i.e., "this thing").

The Generic Antecedent

Sometimes a relative clause appears with no *expressed* antecedent. When this occurs, a *generic* antecedent must be supplied in an English translation. For example:

οἳ τῆς θαλάττης ἦρχον καὶ τῆς γῆς τὴν τῶν νήσων ἀρχὴν εἶχον.
(Those men/The men) who the sea were ruling and the land the rule (d.o.) of the islands they were holding.
Those men who were ruling the sea and the land were holding the rule of the islands.

μανθάνειν ἐθέλω ἅπερ οὗτος διδάσκει. (περ [enclitic particle] very, even)
To learn I wish *(the very things) that* this man is teaching.
I wish to learn *the very things that* this man is teaching.

ὃς ὑπὸ τῶν θεῶν μὴ φιλεῖται πολλοὺς ἔχει πόνους.
(He/The one) who by the gods is not loved many toils (d.o.) has.
He who is not loved by the gods has many toils.

6. In Greek texts different conventions of punctuation make even punctuation an unreliable method of distinguishing between restrictive and nonrestrictive clauses.

1. In the first sentence the relative pronoun οἵ has no expressed antecedent. Since οἵ is masculine plural, a generic masculine plural antecedent, "those men/the men," is supplied as the subject of the verb "were holding" in the main clause.

2. In the second sentence the enclitic particle περ has been added to the relative pronoun. (For enclitics see §54.) This particle, which may also stand apart from the word it emphasizes (e.g., ἅ περ) means "very," "even." It often appears with a form of the relative pronoun and may emphasize other words as well.

The relative pronoun ἅπερ has no expressed antecedent. Since ἅπερ is neuter plural, a generic neuter plural antecedent, "the very things," is supplied as the direct object of the verb "learn" in the main clause.

3. In the third sentence the relative pronoun ὅς has no expressed antecedent. Since ὅς is masculine singular, a generic masculine singular antecedent, "He/The one," is supplied as the subject of the verb "has" in the main clause.

The negation μή is used whenever a relative pronoun in a relative clause refers to a generic antecedent.

A demonstrative pronoun in the main clause (placed *after* the relative clause) may be included to refer with *emphasis* to a relative pronoun with no expressed antecedent that precedes it.

ἃ οὗτος διδάσκει, ταῦτα μανθάνειν ἐθέλω.
The things that this man is teaching, *these things* I wish to learn.

In this sentence ταῦτα refers with emphasis and points back to the relative pronoun ἅ.

Attraction

Sometimes the *case* of a relative pronoun *is attracted* (changed) *into the case of its antecedent.* This may occur when (1) the information contained in the relative clause provides an *essential* description of the antecedent and (2) the relative pronoun would have been in the accusative case (had attraction not occurred) and the antecedent is in either the genitive or dative case. For example:

πολλὰ ἐμανθάνομεν ἐκ τῶν λόγων ὧν ἔλεγον οἱ σοφοί.
We were learning many things from the words *that* the wise men were saying.

πρὸς τὸ ἀγαθὸν ἄγονται οἱ νεᾱνίαι τοῖς ἀγαθοῖς ἔργοις οἷς ποιεῖς.
The young men are led toward the good by the good deeds *that* you are doing.

1. In the first sentence the relative pronoun ὧν has been attracted into the case of its antecedent, λόγων. If attraction had not occurred, the relative pronoun would have been οὕς, direct object of ἔλεγον: ἐκ τῶν λόγων οὕς ἔλεγον. Even when attraction occurs, the relative is translated with its proper syntax within the relative clause.

2. In the second sentence the relative pronoun οἷς has been attracted into the case of its ante-

cedent, ἔργοις. If attraction had not occurred, the relative pronoun would have been ἅ, direct object of ποιεῖς: τοῖς ἀγαθοῖς ἔργοις ἃ ποιεῖς.

3. A relative pronoun in the accusative case is *often but not always* attracted into the case of an antecedent in the genitive or dative case.

When a relative pronoun is attracted into the case of an antecedent that is a *demonstrative pronoun*, the antecedent is often omitted, but it must be supplied in translation. For example:

πολλοὶ ὧν τῑμῶμεν ἐν τῷδε τῷ πολέμῳ τελευτήσουσιν.
Many *of those men whom* we honor will die in this war.

τοῦτον τὸν ποιητὴν φιλῶ ἐφ' οἷς λέγει.
I love this poet *for those things that* he says.

OBSERVATIONS

___

1. In the first sentence the relative pronoun ὧν appears in the place of the fuller expression ἐκείνων οὕς. ἐκείνων would have been a Partitive Genitive and the antecedent of οὕς, the expected direct object of τῑμῶμεν. When the relative pronoun is attracted into the case of the antecedent, the antecedent is dropped.

2. In the second sentence the phrase ἐφ' οἷς appears in place of the fuller expression ἐπὶ ἐκείνοις ἅ. ἐκείνοις would have been the object of the preposition ἐπί and the antecedent for the relative pronoun ἅ, the expected direct object of λέγει. When the relative pronoun is attracted into the case of the antecedent, the antecedent is dropped, and the preposition is *retained*.

3. When a relative pronoun is attracted into the case of an antecedent that is dropped, the antecedent is supplied in an English translation, and the correct case of the relative pronoun is restored. Thus, ὧν is translated "of those men whom" and ἐφ' οἷς is translated "for those things that."

☛   DRILL 53 D–E MAY NOW BE DONE.

§54. Enclitics

In addition to proclitics (§10, Observation 1, p. 32), there are other words in Greek that have no accents of their own. These words are called **enclitics** (< ἐγκλίνω, "lean on"), and they differ from proclitics in that they are pronounced closely with *preceding* words. Five enclitics are:

γε	at least, at any rate (limits); indeed (emphasizes)
περ	even, very
πως	somehow
τοι	surely, you know
ποτέ	at some time, ever

OBSERVATION

___

Enclitics are either *monosyllabic* (having one syllable) or *disyllabic* (having two syllables). When a disyllabic enclitic is listed in a vocabulary entry, an acute accent is placed on its ultima.

Enclitics and the words they lean back on follow certain rules of accent:

1.	a	p	ú	+ e *or* e-e	(no change)
2.	a	p	û	+ e *or* e-e	(no change)
3.	a	p̂	ú	+ e *or* e-e	(acute added to ultima)
4.	á	p	ú	+ e *or* e-e	(acute added to ultima)
5.	a	ṕ	u	+ e	(no change)
6.	a	ṕ	u	+ e-é	(acute added to ultima of *enclitic*)

OBSERVATIONS

1. In the rules pictured above, "e" stands for a monosyllabic enclitic and "e-e" for a disyllabic enclitic.

2. When an enclitic (of one *or* two syllables) directly follows a word with an acute accent or a circumflex on the ultima, the acute accent *does not change to a grave* (rule 1), and the circumflex *remains unchanged* (rule 2).

ἀγαθός γε ποιητής   a *good* poet (subj.)
ἀδικεῖν τοι   to do wrong, you know
(Italics indicate the emphasis placed on a word by the enclitic γε.)

3. When an enclitic (of one *or* two syllables) directly follows a word with a circumflex on the penult, the ultima of that word receives an acute accent in addition (rule 3).

ταῦτά τοι   these things (subj. or d.o.), you know

4. When an enclitic (of one *or* two syllables) directly follows a word with an acute accent on the antepenult, the ultima of that word receives an acute accent in addition (rule 4).

οὐ πείθεταί ποτε.   He does not obey ever.

5. When a *monosyllabic* enclitic directly follows a word with an acute accent on the penult, *no change* of accent occurs (rule 5). However, when a *disyllabic* enclitic directly follows a word with an acute accent on the penult, the *enclitic* receives an acute accent on the ultima (rule 6). If an enclitic is followed by another word, the acute on its ultima follows the regular rules for the possibilities of accent and is changed to a grave.

ἑταίρους γε   *companions* (d.o.)
τοῦτο οὐ λέγω ποτέ.   I do not say this thing ever.
οὐ λέγω ποτὲ τοῦτο.   I do not say this thing ever.

When an enclitic (of one or two syllables) directly follows a *proclitic,* the proclitic receives an acute accent. Even when the vowel of the enclitic is lost through elision, the proclitic receives an acute accent.

οἵ γε πολῖται   the citizens, at least (subj.)
αἵ γ' ἀρεταί   the virtues, at least (subj.)
οὔτοι ἐθέλουσιν.   They are not, you know, willing.

1. οὔ τοι and οὔ ποτε are often written as single words, although their accents are determined by the rules for enclitics: οὔτοι (not *οὖτοι) and οὔποτε.

2. The accents on many forms of the demonstrative adjective and pronoun ὅδε, ἥδε, τόδε reflect the word's origin as a combination of the article with the *originally enclitic* particle -δε: ὁ δε > ὅδε (enclitic follows proclitic); τάς δε > τάσδε (acute accent on ultima remains acute).

When an enclitic (of one or two syllables) directly follows one or more than one *other enclitic,* each preceding enclitic (except the last in the series) receives an acute accent.

τοῦτό γέ τοι   *this thing,* you know

A disyllabic enclitic sometimes begins a sentence or clause and in this position has an accent on the ultima.

ποτὲ διδάσκει, ποτὲ διδάσκεται.   (ποτέ ..., ποτέ ... sometimes ..., sometimes ...)
Sometimes he is teaching, sometimes he is being taught.

☛ DRILL 54 MAY NOW BE DONE.

§55. The Verb εἰμί

Unlike the verbs presented thus far, the Greek verb εἰμί, ἔσομαι, ——, ——, ——, ——, "be"; "exist," does *not* have a first principal part ending in -ω and is *not* an omega verb. Rather, it is called a -μι **verb** because its first principal part ends in -μι.[7]

The Present and Imperfect Active Indicative of εἰμί

In the present and imperfect indicative, εἰμί has *irregular* active voice forms only.

	Present Active Indicative		Imperfect Active Indicative	
Singular				
1	εἰμί	I am	ἦ or ἦν	I was
2	εἶ	you are	ἦσθα	you were
3	ἐστί(ν)	he, she, it is	ἦν	he, she, it was
Plural				
1	ἐσμέν	we are	ἦμεν	we were
2	ἐστέ	you (pl.) are	ἦτε	you (pl.) were
3	εἰσί(ν)	they are	ἦσαν	they were

MEMORIZE THESE FORMS, PAYING SPECIAL ATTENTION TO ACCENT, AND BE PREPARED TO RECITE THEM QUICKLY.

---

7. -μι verbs are also called **athematic verbs** because, unlike omega verbs, their endings are attached directly to their stems with no intervening thematic vowels (-ο- or -ε-); see §26.

1. Except for the monosyllabic second person singular, which has a circumflex, forms of εἰμί in the present tense are *disyllabic enclitics*. In vocabulary lists and model conjugations they are written with acute accents on the ultima, but in sentences the rules for accent with enclitics are observed (§54).

2. Both the third person singular and the third person plural present active indicative have a nu movable.

3. Forms of εἰμί in the imperfect tense are *not* enclitics and have recessive accents. The imperfect conjugation uses the augmented tense stem ἠ-.

4. The alternate first person singular imperfect active indicative ἦν is identical with the third person singular imperfect active indicative ἦν. Context usually makes clear whether a form is first or third person.

5. εἰμί is intransitive, and it has no middle or passive forms in the present and imperfect tenses.

6. The English translations given above for the imperfect forms of εἰμί ("I was," etc.) are idiomatic and are used instead of the less natural but more accurate translations ("I was being," etc.). The imperfect tense in Greek may have *progressive* or *repeated* aspect *only* (*not* simple), and alternate translations that convey these aspects are also possible: "I used to be," "I was (repeatedly)," etc.

The third person singular present active indicative of εἰμί is accented on the penult—ἔστι(ν)—when it is the first word in a sentence. In this position with this accent, ἔστι(ν) usually indicates existence ("there is") or possibility ("it is possible"). ἔστι(ν) is also accented on the penult when it follows οὐκ, μή, καί, ἀλλ' or ἀλλά, and τοῦτ' or τοῦτο. When any of the other enclitic forms of εἰμί (first person singular or first, second, or third person plural) follows these words or is the first word in a sentence, it is accented on the ultima. When any disyllabic enclitic form of εἰμί follows a word in elision, it retains its accent on the ultima.

> πολλοὶ δ' εἰσὶν ἐν ἀγορᾷ.   And many men are in the agora.

The Future Indicative of εἰμί; Partial Deponents

In the future indicative, the verb εἰμί has *middle* voice forms *only,* and it is conjugated almost identically with *omega* verbs. Many Greek verbs *lack active voice forms in the future tense* and in this tense are conjugated *in the middle voice only*. Such verbs are called **Partial Deponents**.[8] A partial deponent verb may be identified by a second principal part that ends in -ομαι. *There is no special middle voice significance and no special translation for the middle voice forms of a partial deponent.*

---

8. *Deponent* means "putting aside." Partial deponents are "putting aside" (lack) active voice forms in the future tense.

	Future Middle Indicative	
Future Stem: ἐσ-		
Singular		
1	ἔσομαι	I shall be
2	ἔσῃ/ἔσει	you will be
3	ἔσται	he, she, it will be
Plural		
1	ἐσόμεθα	we shall be
2	ἔσεσθε	you (pl.) will be
3	ἔσονται	they will be

OBSERVATIONS

1. The future stem of a partial deponent is found by dropping the first person singular ending -ομαι from the second principal part. To this stem are added the regular future middle endings.

2. The third person singular future middle indicative of εἰμί is *irregular*: ἔσται (*not* *ἔσεται). MEMORIZE THIS IRREGULAR FORM.

The Present Active and Future Middle Infinitives of εἰμί

εἰμί has two infinitives. The present active infinitive is irregular. The future middle infinitive is formed regularly from the stem ἐσ-:

Present Active Infinitive	εἶναι	to be
Future Middle Infinitive	ἔσεσθαι	to be about to be

OBSERVATION

The accent on the present active infinitive is *persistent on the penult*. Final -αι counts as *short* for purposes of accent. The accent on the future middle infinitive is *recessive*. Final -αι counts as *short* for purposes of accent.

MEMORIZE THESE INFINITIVE FORMS.

☞ DRILL 55 MAY NOW BE DONE.

§56. The Uses of εἰμί and the Nominal Sentence; Predicate Adjective

εἰμί as a Copulative Verb

In many sentences the verb "be" is used to express an *equivalency* between the subject and an element in the predicate (§6, p. 23). This element may be either a noun or an adjective. For example:

οὗτός ἐστι *ποιητής*.	This man is a *poet*.
τέκνον εἰμὶ Πριάμου.	I am a *child* of Priam.
οἱ Γοργίου λόγοι εἰσὶν *ἄδικοι*.	The speeches of Gorgias are *unjust*.
μεγάλα ἦν τὰ ἐκείνων ἔργα.	The deeds of those men were *great*.

The syntax of each of the italicized words in the first two sentences (ποιητής, τέκνον) is **Predicate Nominative**. The syntax of each of the italicized words in the third and fourth sentences (ἄδικοι, μεγάλα) is **Nominative, Predicate Adjective**.

OBSERVATIONS

1. A predicate adjective agrees with the noun it modifies (the subject) in gender, number, and case.

2. Although the copulative verb is frequently placed *between* the subject and the predicate nominative or predicate adjective, the order of these three elements (subject, copulative verb, predicate nominative or predicate adjective) is determined by the particular emphasis sought by the writer or speaker. Each element may appear in any of the three possible positions.

The Nominal Sentence and the Predicate Position

Especially in a timeless proverbial statement, a form of the copulative verb εἰμί is frequently omitted in Greek but must be supplied in English. Such a statement *with no expressed verb* is called a nominal sentence. For example:

ἡ ψῡχὴ ἀθάνατος.	The soul (is) immortal.
μοῖρα πολλῶν ἡ συμφορά.	Misfortune (is) the fate of many men.

OBSERVATIONS

1. When an adjective is placed *outside the attributive position*—that is, when it is *not* directly preceded by a form of the article—it is said to be in the **predicate position**. Adjectives in nominal sentences are always in the predicate position. The syntax of ἀθάνατος in the first sentence is Nominative, Predicate Adjective.

2. The first sentence could also be written ἀθάνατος ἡ ψῡχή. With such *sentences* one may contrast the *phrase* ἡ ἀθάνατος ψῡχή, "the immortal soul."

3. The verb to be supplied in nominal sentences is almost always the third person singular present active indicative of "be," "is."

4. When two nouns are equated in a nominal sentence, the subject is often distinguished from the predicate nominative by the article, as in the second sentence.

εἰμί Meaning "Exist"

In addition to functioning as a copulative verb joining subjects to predicate nominatives and predicate adjectives, εἰμί may be used to *assert the existence* of people or things. For example:

εἰσὶ τῇ ἀληθείᾳ θεοί.	There are truly gods.
	Gods truly exist.
ἦν φόβος ἐν τῇ γῇ.	There was fear in the land.
ἆρ' ἔστι νόμος δίκαιος;	Is there a just law?
	Does a just law exist?

OBSERVATIONS

    1. When εἰμί means "exist," it is often the first word in its sentence or clause.

    2. When the third person singular present active indicative of εἰμί is used to assert existence, it is usually accented on the penult: ἔστι(ν). When the third person plural present active indicative of εἰμί is used to assert existence and is the first word in a sentence, it is accented on the ultima: εἰσί(ν).

    3. In these sentences each form of εἰμί (εἰσί, ἦν, ἔστι) is the *entire predicate*. Such predicates may be modified by adverbs or adverbial expressions (τῇ ἀληθείᾳ, ἐν τῇ γῇ), but they do *not* contain predicate nominatives or predicate adjectives. The things that are said to exist (θεοί, φόβος, νόμος) are the *subjects* of the forms of εἰμί.

    4. It is convenient to use the English expletive "there" when translating statements of existence.[9]

§57. Subject Infinitive

The infinitive, which is a verbal noun, may function as the object of another verb (§36). It may also be the *subject* of a verb, and when it is so used, it is called a **Subject Infinitive**. For example:

ἀγαθόν ἐστιν εὖ λέγειν.	*To speak* well is good.
	Speaking well is good.
	It is good (a good thing) *to speak* well.
κακὸν τοῖς νόμοις μὴ πείθεσθαι.	*Not to obey* the laws is bad.
	It is bad (a bad thing) *not to obey* the laws.
ὀλίγων δικαίως ἄρχειν.	*To rule* justly is of few men.
	To rule justly belongs to few men.
	It belongs to few men *to rule* justly.
ἆρ' ἔστι φιλεῖσθαι;	Is it possible *to be loved?*
δεῖ πολέμου ἄρχεσθαι.	It is necessary *to begin* a war.
(δεῖ, δεήσει, ἐδέησε(ν), ——, ——, —— *impersonal verb, it is necessary*)	

---

9. An **expletive** is a word that stands in place of or anticipates a following word or phrase.

The syntax of each italicized word (λέγειν, πείθεσθαι, ἄρχειν, φιλεῖσθαι, ἄρχεσθαι) is **Subject Infinitive**.

OBSERVATIONS

1. The Subject Infinitive is a *neuter* singular noun. In the first two sentences, the predicate adjectives ἀγαθόν and κακόν are neuter nominative singular. (It is also possible to view ἀγαθόν and κακόν as substantives ["a good thing," "a bad thing"] functioning as Predicate Nominatives.)

2. The adverb μή is used to negate a Subject Infinitive, as in the second sentence.

3. A Subject Infinitive is often the subject of a nominal sentence, as in the second and third sentences.

4. The Genitive of Possession may appear in the predicate position with a Subject Infinitive, as in the third sentence. A Genitive of Possession in the predicate position may be translated with the words "belongs to."

5. When ἔστι(ν) means "it is possible," it functions as an *impersonal verb*. An **impersonal verb**, usually in the third person singular, is a verb that *has no personal subject* such as "I" or "you." δεῖ is also an impersonal verb. In the fourth sentence, the Subject Infinitive φιλεῖσθαι is the subject of ἔστι: "Is to be loved possible?" In the fifth sentence, the Subject Infinitive ἄρχεσθαι is the subject of δεῖ: "To begin a war is necessary."

6. It is convenient in English to add the pronoun "it" when translating sentences with impersonal verbs, but "it" is an expletive that merely anticipates the Subject Infinitive. Since it is a verbal noun, the Subject Infinitive may be translated with the English gerund,[10] as in the second translation of the first sentence.

§58. Subject Accusative

The subject of a conjugated or finite verb is in the nominative case, but the subject of an *infinitive* is in the *accusative* case. A noun or pronoun so used is called a **Subject Accusative**. For example:

καλόν ἐστι τοῦτον τὸν *νεᾱνίᾱν* εὖ διδάσκεσθαι.
It is a fine thing for this *young man* to be taught well.

ἔδει τοὺς *Ἀθηναίους* πολεμεῖν.
It was necessary for the *Athenians* to be at war.

δεῖ τοὺς *πολί̄τᾱς* τοὺς θεοὺς τῑμᾶν.
It is necessary for the *citizens* to honor the gods.
(δεῖ, δεήσει, ἐδέησε(ν), ——, ——, —— *impersonal verb*, it is necessary)

The syntax of each italicized word (νεᾱνίᾱν, πολί̄τᾱς, Ἀθηναίους) is **Subject Accusative**.

10. A **gerund** is a verbal noun ending in "-ing."

OBSERVATIONS
_____

1. In each of these sentences, a Subject Infinitive has with it a Subject Accusative: νεᾱνίᾱν is the subject of διδάσκεσθαι; Ἀθηναίους is the subject of πολεμεῖν; and πολίτᾱς is the subject of τῑμᾶν.

2. It is possible for a Subject Infinitive to appear with *both* a Subject Accusative *and* an Accusative, Direct Object. In the third sentence, θεούς is the direct object of τῑμᾶν.

3. In an English translation of a sentence containing a Subject Accusative and a Subject Infinitive, the word "for" is added before the Subject Accusative.

☞   DRILL 56–58 MAY NOW BE DONE.

Short Readings

1. A fragment from the Lesbian poet Alcaeus

οἶνος γὰρ ἀνθρώπῳ δίοπτρον . . .   (Alcaeus, frag. 333)

οἶνος, οἴνου, ὁ wine
ἀνθρώπῳ (Lesbian) = Attic ἀνθρώπου

δίοπτρον, διόπτρου, τό means for seeing through
(+ gen.)

Fragments from the works of the philosopher Heraclitus

2.   τῷ οὖν τόξῳ ὄνομα βίος,† ἔργον δὲ θάνατος.   (Heraclitus, frag. 48)

οὖν (postpositive particle) therefore
τόξον, τόξου, τό bow

ὄνομα, ὀνόματος, τό name
†βίος, cf. βιός, βιοῦ, ὁ bow

3.   ὁ ἄναξ οὗ τὸ μαντεῖόν ἐστι τὸ ἐν Δελφοῖς οὔτε λέγει οὔτε κρύπτει ἀλλὰ σημαίνει.
                                                                           (Heraclitus, frag. 93)

ἄναξ, ἄνακτος, ὁ lord
μαντεῖον, μαντείου, τό oracle
Δελφοί, Δελφῶν, οἱ Delphi (the place of Apollo's
    most famous temple)
οὔτε . . . οὔτε . . . neither . . . nor . . .

κρύπτω, κρύψω, ἔκρυψα, ——, κέκρυμμαι,
    ἐκρύφθην hide, conceal
σημαίνω, σημανῶ, ἐσήμηνα, ——, σεσήμασμαι,
    ἐσημάνθην indicate, give a sign

4.   An observation of the Chorus

. . . σοφῷ γὰρ αἰσχρὸν ἐξαμαρτάνειν.   (Aeschylus, *Prometheus Bound* 1039)

ἐξαμαρτάνω (ἐξ- + ἁμαρτάνω), ἐξαμαρτήσομαι,
    ἐξήμαρτον, ἐξημάρτηκα, ἐξημάρτημαι,
    ἐξημαρτήθην miss the mark, err greatly

5. A messenger gives two characterizations of the seer Amphiaraus, set to defend one of the seven gates of Thebes.

οὐ γὰρ δοκεῖν ἄριστος, ἀλλ᾿ εἶναι θέλει.   (Aeschylus, *Seven Against Thebes* 592)

δοκέω, δόξω, ἔδοξα, ——, δέδογμαι, —— seem

ἄριστος, ἀρίστη, ἄριστον best

δεινὸς ὃς θεοὺς σέβει.   (Aeschylus, *Seven Against Thebes* 596)

σέβω, ——, ——, ——, ——, —— worship,
    honor

6. The Chorus states a truism.

> Διὸς οὐ παρβατός ἐστιν
> μεγάλā φρὴν ἀπέρāτος.

(Aeschylus, *Suppliant Women* 1048–49)

παρβατός, παρβατόν to be overcome
μεγάλā (Doric) = Attic μεγάλη

ἀπέρāτος, ἀπέρāτον boundless, infinite

7. An utterance of Achilles in Aeschylus's *Myrmidons*

> ὅπλων, ὅπλων δεῖ.

(Aeschylus, frag. 232)

Fragments from tragedies of Aeschylus

8. ὡς οὐ δικαίως θάνατον ἔχθουσιν βροτοί,
    ὅσπερ μέγιστον ῥῦμα τῶν πολλῶν κακῶν.

(Aeschylus, frag. 353)

ὡς (exclam. adv.) how
ἔχθω, ——, ——, ——, ——, —— hate
μέγιστος, μεγίστη, μέγιστον greatest

ῥῦμα, ῥύματος, τό protection, defense,
  deliverance

9. οἵ τοι στεναγμοὶ τῶν πόνων ἐρείσματα.

(Aeschylus, frag. 385)

στεναγμός, στεναγμοῦ, ὁ groan, moan

ἔρεισμα, ἐρείσματος, τό prop, support

10. καλὸν δὲ καὶ γέροντι μανθάνειν σοφά.

(Aeschylus, frag. 396)

γέρων, γέροντος, ὁ old man

11. Creon reacts to news of his wife's death.

> ὤμοι μοι, τάδ᾽ οὐκ ἐπ᾽ ἄλλον βροτῶν
> ἐμᾶς ἁρμόσει ποτ᾽ ἐξ αἰτίας.

(Sophocles, *Antigone* 1317–18)

ὤμοι μοι (interj.) alas! ah me!
ἐμός, ἐμή, ἐμόν my; ἐμᾶς (Doric) = Attic ἐμῆς

ἁρμόζω, ἁρμόσω, ἥρμοσα, ἥρμοκα, ἥρμοσμαι,
  ἡρμόσθην be adapted; fit; apply

Fragments from tragedies of Sophocles

12. **ἄνθρωπός ἐστι πνεῦμα καὶ σκιὰ μόνον.** (Sophocles, frag. 13)

πνεῦμα, πνεύματος, τό wind, air; breath   σκιά, σκιᾶς, ἡ shadow

13. **σοφοὶ τύραννοι τῶν σοφῶν ξυνουσίᾳ.** (Sophocles, frag. 14)

τύραννος, τυράννου, ὁ absolute ruler, monarch;   ξυνουσίᾱ, ξυνουσίᾱς, ἡ being together,
    tyrant   association

14. **τοῖς γὰρ δικαίοις ἀντέχειν οὐ ῥᾴδιον.** (Sophocles, frag. 78)

ἀντέχω (ἀντι- + ἔχω) withstand, hold out
    against (+ dat.)

15. **καλὸν φρονεῖν τὸν θνητὸν ἀνθρώποις ἴσα.** (Sophocles, frag. 346)

φρονέω think   ἴσος, ἴση, ἴσον equal

16. **ἀλλ' εἰσὶ μητρὶ παῖδες ἄγκυραι βίου.** (Sophocles, frag. 685)

μήτηρ, μητρός, ἡ mother   ἄγκῡρα, ἀγκύρᾱς, ἡ anchor

17. **ἀλλ' ἔσθ' ὁ θάνατος λοῖσθος ἰᾱτρὸς νόσων.** (Sophocles, frag. 698)

λοῖσθος, λοῖσθον last (of all)   νόσος, νόσου, ἡ sickness, disease
ἰᾱτρός, ἰᾱτροῦ, ὁ doctor, healer

18. **ἀεὶ γὰρ εὖ πίπτουσιν οἱ Διὸς κύβοι.** (Sophocles, frag. 895)

πίπτω, πεσοῦμαι, ἔπεσον, πέπτωκα, ——, —— fall   κύβος, κύβου, ὁ cube; *pl.*, dice

19. A Spartan envoy, Melesippus, makes this prediction to his escort as he departs from Athenian territory.

> ἥδε ἡ ἡμέρᾱ τοῖς Ἕλλησι μεγάλων κακῶν ἄρξει.   (Thucydides, *Peloponnesian War* II.12.4)

ἡμέρᾱ, ἡμέρᾱς, ἡ day

20. Conversing with Creon, who has banished her, Medea makes a despairing remark.

> φεῦ φεῦ, βροτοῖς ἔρωτες ὡς κακὸν μέγα.   (Euripides, *Medea* 330)

φεῦ (interj.) alas! oh!   ὡς (exclam. adv.) how

Fragments from the tragedies of Euripides

21.   λόγος γὰρ τοὖργον οὐ νῑκᾷ ποτε.   (Euripides, frag. 97N)

22.   πτηνὰς διώκεις, ὦ τέκνον, τὰς ἐλπίδας.   (Euripides, frag. 271N)

πτηνός, πτηνή, πτηνόν winged; swift-moving;   διώκω, διώξω, ἐδίωξα, ——, δεδίωγμαι,
    fleeting   ἐδιώχθην pursue, chase

23.   οὐ δῆκταί πως κύνες οἱ θεοί,
        ἀλλ' ἡ Δίκη γὰρ καὶ διὰ σκότου βλέπει.   (Euripides, frag. 555N)

δήκτης, δήκτου, ὁ biter   σκότος, σκότου, ὁ darkness
κύων, κυνός, ὁ or ἡ dog   βλέπω, ——, ἔβλεψα, ——, ——, —— see, look (at)

24.   ἀρετὴ μέγιστον τῶν ἐν ἀνθρώποις καλόν.   (Euripides, frag. 1030N)

μέγιστος, μεγίστη, μέγιστον greatest

25. The hoopoe gives the other birds at least one reason to speak with humans.

> ἀλλ' ἀπ' ἐχθρῶν δῆτα πολλὰ μανθάνουσιν οἱ σοφοί.   (Aristophanes, *Birds* 375)

δῆτα (adv.) certainly, of course

26. The Chorus of Knights begins a song.

> ὦ Δῆμε, καλήν γ᾽ ἔχεις
> ἀρχήν ...   (Aristophanes, *Knights* 1111)

27. Caught and bound by a Scythian archer, a comic character utters a truism.

> θεοί, Ζεῦ σῶτερ, εἰσὶν ἐλπίδες.   (Aristophanes, *Thesmophoriazousae* 1009)

σωτήρ, σωτῆρος, ὁ savior; σῶτερ = *voc. sing.*

28. A fragment from a comedy

> ἄγροικός εἰμι· τὴν σκάφην σκάφην λέγω.   ([Aristophanes] frag. 901b)

ἄγροικος, ἄγροικον living or grown in the coun-   σκάφη, σκάφης, ἡ tub, trough
   try, rustic, countrified

29. Xenophon explains to his men why they must take seriously Spartan Cleander's threat to ban them from all the Greek cities in Asia Minor.

> ... χαλεπὸν ἔσται καὶ μένειν καὶ ἀποπλεῖν· καὶ γὰρ ἐν τῇ γῇ ἄρχουσι Λακεδαιμόνιοι
> καὶ ἐν τῇ θαλάττῃ ...   (Xenophon, *Anabasis* VI.6.13)

μένω, μενῶ, ἔμεινα, μεμένηκα, ——, —— remain   ἀποπλέω (ἀπο- + πλέω) sail away

30. Xenophon assures his wife of the value of her many domestic tasks.

> τὰ γὰρ καλά τε κἀγαθά ... οὐ διὰ τὰς ὡραιότητας, ἀλλὰ διὰ τὰς ἐν τῷ βίῳ ἀρετὰς τοῖς
> ἀνθρώποις ἐπαύξεται.   (Xenophon, *Oeconomicus* 7.43)

ὡραιότης, ὡραιότητος, ἡ bloom of youth; *pl.*,   ἐπαύξω (ἐπι- + αὔξω), ἐπαυξήσω, ——, ——,
   signs of youthful beauty   ——, —— increase, augment

31. Socrates sums up his comparison of poets to bees.

> κοῦφον γὰρ χρῆμα ποιητής ἐστιν καὶ πτηνὸν καὶ ἱερόν, ...　　(Plato, *Ion* 534b4)

κοῦφος, κούφη, κοῦφον light, nimble　　　　ἱερός, ἱερά, ἱερόν sacred, holy
πτηνός, πτηνή, πτηνόν winged

32. While discussing what a lawgiver ought to teach, the Spartan Cleinias utters a truism.

> καλὸν μὲν ἡ ἀλήθεια, ὦ ξένε, καὶ μόνιμον·　　(Plato, *Laws* 663e3)

μόνιμος, μονίμη, μόνιμον stable, lasting, steadfast

33. Socrates offers a definition.

> ἔστι γὰρ λήθη μνήμης ἔξοδος.　　(Plato, *Philebus* 33e3)

λήθη, λήθης, ἡ forgetfulness　　　　ἔξοδος, ἐξόδου, ἡ going out; way out
μνήμη, μνήμης, ἡ memory

34. Glaucon quotes a proverb.

> ... χαλεπὰ τὰ καλά.　　(Plato, *Republic* 435c8)

35. The philosopher explains why the soul is a particularly interesting subject.

> ἔστι† γὰρ οἷον ἀρχὴ ζῴων.　　(Aristotle, *About the Soul* 402a6)

†ἔστι, *subject is the soul*　　　　οἷον (adv.) as it were

36. The philosopher defines two types of law.

> νόμος δ' ἐστὶν ὁ μὲν ἴδιος, ὁ δὲ κοινός.　　(Aristotle, *Rhetoric* 1368b7)

ἴδιος, ἰδίᾱ, ἴδιον private

Fragments and proverbial expressions from the comedies of Menander

37.   κοινὰ τὰ τῶν φίλων.   (Menander, frag. 9)

38.   λύπης ἰᾱτρός ἐστιν ἀνθρώποις λόγος·
      ψῡχῆς γὰρ οὗτος μόνος ἔχει θελκτήρια.   (Menander, frag. 559)

λύπη, λύπης, ἡ pain; grief   θελκτήριον, θελκτηρίου, τό charm, spell; means
ἰᾱτρός, ἰᾱτροῦ, ὁ doctor, healer   of lightening, soothing

39.   ἀρχὴ μεγίστη τῶν ἐν ἀνθρώποις κακῶν
      ἀγαθά, τὰ λίᾱν ἀγαθά.   (Menander, frag. 724)

μέγιστος, μεγίστη, μέγιστον greatest   λίᾱν (adv.) excessively

40.   ἄγει δὲ πρὸς φῶς τὴν ἀλήθειαν χρόνος.   (Menander, *Sententiae* 13)

φῶς, φωτός, τό (day)light   χρόνος, χρόνου, ὁ time

41.   αἱ δ' ἐλπίδες βόσκουσι τοὺς κενοὺς βροτῶν.   (Menander, *Sententiae* 51)

βόσκω, βοσκήσω, ——, ——, ——,   κενός, κενή, κενόν empty
   ἐβοσκήθην feed, nourish

42.   ὃν γὰρ θεοὶ φιλοῦσιν ἀποθνῄσκει νέος.   (Menander, *Sententiae* 425)

ἀποθνῄσκω (ἀπο- + θνῄσκω), ἀποθανοῦμαι,
   ἀπέθανον, τέθνηκα, ——, —— die

43.   νῑκᾷ παλαιὰς χάριτας ἡ νέᾱ χάρις.   (Menander, *Sententiae* 533)

παλαιός, παλαιά, παλαιόν old

44.   ὅπλον μέγιστον ἐν βροτοῖς τὰ χρήματα.   (Menander, *Sententiae* 612)

μέγιστος, μεγίστη, μέγιστον greatest

45.   ὁ λόγος ἰᾱτρὸς τῶν κατὰ ψῡχὴν σοφοῦ.   (Menander, *Sententiae* 622)

ἰᾱτρός, ἰᾱτροῦ, ὁ doctor, healer

46.   τυφλὸν δὲ καὶ δύστηνον ἀνθρώποις τύχη.   (Menander, *Sententiae* 741)

τυφλός, τυφλή, τυφλόν blind   δύστηνος, δύστηνον wretched

47.   τῶν γὰρ πενήτων εἰσὶν οἱ λόγοι κενοί.   (Menander, *Sententiae* 752)

πένης, πένητος, ὁ poor man   κενός, κενή, κενόν empty; to no purpose

48.   ψῡχῆς ὄλεθρός ἐστι σωμάτων ἔρως.   (Menander, *Sententiae* 851)

ὄλεθρος, ὀλέθρου, ὁ destruction, ruin

49. A proverb from the school of Pythagoras

      ψῡχὴ ταμεῖόν ἐστι, ἀγαθοῦ μὲν ἀγαθῶν, κακοῦ δὲ κακῶν.   (*Opinions of the Pythagoreans* 117)

ταμεῖον, ταμείου, τό treasury, storehouse

50. The title of one of Plutarch's works

      πῶς δεῖ τὸν νέον ποιημάτων ἀκούειν†;   (Plutarch)

ποίημα, ποιήματος, τό poem   †ἀκούω, *here*, hear and understand (+ gen.)

51. The biographer reports a saying of Democritus, a philosopher from Thrace.

      λόγος ἔργου σκιή.   (Diogenes Laertius, *Lives of the Philosophers* IX.37)

σκιᾱ́, σκιᾶς, ἡ shadow; σκιή (Ionic) = Attic σκιᾱ́

Proverbs from Aesop

52. **ἀεὶ τὰ πέρυσι καλά.** (Aesop, *Proverbs* 1)

πέρυσι(ν) (adv.) a year ago, last year

53. **ποτὲ βοῦς, ποτὲ βοτάνη.** (Aesop, *Proverbs* 143)

βοῦς, βοός, ὁ or ἡ bull; cow   βοτάνη, βοτάνης, ἡ pasture; fodder

54. **φίλος καὶ ἵππος ἐν ἀνάγκῃ δοκιμάζονται.** (Aesop, *Proverbs* 171)

ἵππος, ἵππου, ὁ or ἡ horse; mare   δοκιμάζω, δοκιμάσω, ἐδοκίμασα, ——,
δεδοκίμασμαι, ἐδοκιμάσθην test; prove

§59. Names of the Greek Gods

The names of Greek gods belong to all three declensions. Here are the names of the most prominent Greek gods.

Ζεύς, Διός, ὁ (voc. = Ζεῦ) Zeus	king of the gods, god of sky and weather
Ἥρᾱ, Ἥρᾱς, ἡ Hera	queen of the gods, goddess of marriage
Ποσειδῶν, Ποσειδῶνος, ὁ	
(voc. = Πόσειδον) Poseidon	god of the sea
Ἅιδης, Ἅιδου, ὁ Hades	god of the underworld
Δημήτηρ, Δημητρός, ἡ	
(voc. = Δήμητερ) Demeter	goddess of agriculture
Ἑστίᾱ, Ἑστίᾱς, ἡ Hestia	goddess of the hearth
Ἀθηνᾶ, Ἀθηνᾶς, ἡ Athena	goddess of wisdom, war, Athens
Ἀπόλλων, Ἀπόλλωνος, ὁ	
(voc. = Ἄπολλον) Apollo	god of medicine, music, poetry, prophecy
Φοῖβος, Φοίβου, ὁ Phoebus (= Apollo)	
Ἄρτεμις, Ἀρτέμιδος, ἡ Artemis	goddess of the hunt
Ἄρης, Ἄρεος/Ἄρεως, ὁ (voc. = Ἄρες) Ares	god of war
Ἑρμῆς, Ἑρμοῦ, ὁ Hermes	messenger god, conductor of souls
Ἥφαιστος, Ἡφαίστου, ὁ Hephaestus	god of fire, craft
Διόνῦσος, Διονύσου, ὁ Dionysus	god of wine, ecstasy
Ἀφροδίτη, Ἀφροδίτης, ἡ Aphrodite	goddess of pleasure, desire, love
Ἔρως, Ἔρωτος, ὁ (voc. = Ἔρως) Eros	god of desire, love

OBSERVATIONS

1. If no vocative form is given, the vocative is formed regularly.

2. In Attic poetry there are additional third-declension forms of Zeus's name, which are derived from the stem Ζην-: Ζηνός (*gen. sing.*), Ζηνί (*dat. sing.*), Ζῆνα (*acc. sing.*). Be prepared to recognize these forms when they occur in readings.

3. Ἀθηνᾶ is a *contracted* first-declension noun. Its stem is Ἀθηνα-, to which are added the endings of *long-alpha* first-declension nouns. When an alpha contracts with a long alpha, a long alpha is produced ($α + ᾱ > ᾱ$). MEMORIZE THIS ADDITIONAL RULE OF ATTIC CONTRACTION.

4. Although Ἀπόλλων does have a regularly formed accusative singular (Ἀπόλλωνα), the more common accusative is the irregular Ἀπόλλω, particularly in oaths (e.g., νὴ τὸν Ἀπόλλω). Φοῖβος, an alternate name for Apollo, was in origin an adjective meaning "bright." The two names often appear together.

5. Ἄρης is an *irregular* third-declension noun.

Nom.	Ἄρης
Gen.	Ἄρεος/Ἄρεως
Dat.	Ἄρει
Acc.	Ἄρη
Voc.	Ἄρες

The accent on the form Ἄρεως is retained from an earlier Homeric form, Ἄρηος. The length of the final two vowels was *exchanged:* -ηο- > -εω-. This exchange of length is called **quantitative metathesis**. *Contrary to* the rules for the possiblities of accent, the accent on the resulting form (Ἄρεως) *remains* the accent on the form *prior* to quantitative metathesis (Ἄρηος).

6. The first six gods on the list are all siblings. They are the children of the Titans Cronus and Rhea. The next seven gods are the children of Zeus by various mothers. Aphrodite and Eros have varying genealogical traditions.

7. With the exception of Eros and (usually) Hades, the gods on this list are often referred to as the Olympian gods, the gods who displaced the preceding generation of gods (the Titans) and dwell on Mount Olympus.

In addition to begetting many of the Olympian gods, Zeus also fathered the divine Muses, whose mother was Memory (**Μνημοσύνη, Μνημοσύνης, ἡ**). Collectively the Muses are the goddesses of the arts, and each Muse was eventually associated with a particular art. (LEARN THIS NOUN: **Μοῦσα, Μούσης, ἡ** Muse.) Here are the names of the nine Muses.

Ἐρατώ, Ἐρατοῦς, ἡ Erato	"Lovely," muse of erotic or lyric poetry
Εὐτέρπη, Εὐτέρπης, ἡ Euterpe	"Delightful," muse of music
Θάλεια, Θαλείας, ἡ Thalia	"Blooming," muse of comedy
Καλλιόπη, Καλλιόπης, ἡ Calliope	"Beautiful Voice," muse of epic poetry
Κλειώ, Κλειοῦς, ἡ Clio	"Celebrator," muse of history
Μελπομένη, Μελπομένης, ἡ Melpomene	"Songstress," muse of tragedy
Οὐρανίᾱ, Οὐρανίᾱς, ἡ Urania	"Heavenly," muse of astronomy
Πολύμνια, Πολυμνίᾱς, ἡ Polymnia	"Of Many Hymns," muse of choral poetry, song
Τερψιχόρᾱ, Τερψιχόρᾱς, ἡ Terpsichore	"Delighting in Dance," muse of dance

OBSERVATION

Ἐρατώ and Κλειώ are irregular, *contracted* third-declension nouns. They are declined identically:

Nom./Voc.	Ἐρατώ	Κλειώ
Gen.	Ἐρατοῦς	Κλειοῦς
Dat.	Ἐρατοῖ	Κλειοῖ
Acc.	Ἐρατώ	Κλειώ

FAMILIARIZE YOURSELF WITH THE NAMES AND DECLENSIONS OF THE GODS GIVEN HERE AND BE PREPARED TO RECOGNIZE THEM WHEN THEY OCCUR IN READINGS.

CHAPTER 6

Vocabulary

Ἀθῆναι, Ἀθηνῶν, αἱ Athens
→ δεσπότης, δεσπότου, ὁ master, lord;
absolute ruler
→ ἐλευθερίᾱ, ἐλευθερίᾱς, ἡ freedom

δοῦλος, δούλου, ὁ slave

→ ἀγών, ἀγῶνος, ὁ contest; struggle
→ ἀνήρ, ἀνδρός, ὁ man; husband

ἐγώ, ἐμοῦ/μου I; me (§67)
ἡμεῖς, ἡμῶν we; us (§67)
σύ, σοῦ/σου you (§67)
ὑμεῖς, ὑμῶν you (pl.) (§67)
αὐτοῦ, αὐτῆς, αὐτοῦ him, her, it;
them (§67)

→ βούλομαι, βουλήσομαι, ——, ——,
βεβούλημαι, ἐβουλήθην want, wish
→ γίγνομαι, γενήσομαι, ἐγενόμην,
γέγονα, γεγένημαι, —— become;
happen; arise, be born
→ δέχομαι, δέξομαι, ἐδεξάμην, ——,
δέδεγμαι, —— accept, receive;
welcome
→ ἔρχομαι, ἐλεύσομαι, ἦλθον, ἐλήλυθα,
——, —— go, come
→ ὁράω, ὄψομαι, εἶδον, ἑώρᾱκα/ἑόρᾱκα,
ἑώρᾱμαι/ὦμμαι, ὤφθην see

αὐτός, αὐτή, αὐτό -self, very; same
(§66)
δῆλος, δήλη, δῆλον clear
ἄδηλος, ἄδηλον unclear
→ ἐλεύθερος, ἐλευθέρᾱ, ἐλεύθερον free
ἐμός, ἐμή, ἐμόν my (§67)
ἡμέτερος, ἡμετέρᾱ, ἡμέτερον our (§67)
→ ὀρθός, ὀρθή, ὀρθόν straight; correct
σός, σή, σόν your (§67)
ὑμέτερος, ὑμετέρᾱ, ὑμέτερον your (pl.)
(§67)
χρηστός, χρηστή, χρηστόν useful;
good

πᾶς, πᾶσα, πᾶν all, every; whole (§68)
ἅπᾱς, ἅπᾱσα, ἅπαν (quite) all,
every; whole (§68)

ἄνευ (prep. + gen.) without
→ ὅτι (conj.) that; because
→ οὖν (postpositive conj.) then, therefore
→ οὔτε/μήτε . . . οὔτε/μήτε . . . (conj.)
neither . . . nor . . .
πόθεν (interrog. adv.) from where
ποῖ (interrog. adv.) to where
ποῦ (interrog. adv.) where
→ ὑπέρ (prep. + gen.) over; on behalf of
(prep. + acc.) beyond
→ ὡς (proclitic conj.) that; as
→ ὥσπερ (conj.) just as

Vocabulary Notes

→ The vocative singular of δεσπότης, δεσπότου, ὁ, "master," "lord," is δέσποτα, with an acute accent on the antepenult. MEMORIZE THIS IRREGULAR ACCENT. δεσπότης refers either to the master of a household or to the master of a slave or slaves. In some contexts δεσπότης means "despot" or "absolute ruler." δεσπότης may also be used of the gods, the masters of men and animals.

→ ἐλευθερίᾱ, ἐλευθερίᾱς, ἡ, "freedom," is an abstract noun used primarily of political freedom (as opposed to slavery). It is formed by the addition of the first-declension abstract noun suffix -ίᾱ to ἐλεύθερ-, the stem of the adjective ἐλεύθερος.

→ ἀγών, ἀγῶνος, ὁ is a noun derived from the root of the verb ἄγω, ἀγ-, and its original meaning was an "assembly," the result of a group's being led together. Because ἀγών was the word used for an assembly for an athletic competition such as the Olympic games (ὁ Ὀλυμπιακὸς ἀγών), it came to mean "contest," its more common meaning in Attic Greek. By extension of this idea ἀγών was used of any "struggle" or "battle."

→ ἀνήρ, ἀνδρός, ὁ, an *irregular* third-declension noun, means "man" as opposed to woman, god, or youth. ἀνήρ may also mean "husband," and it is often used of a man in the prime of his life or of one who possesses courage.
MEMORIZE THE FOLLOWING DECLENSION, PAYING PARTICULAR ATTENTION TO ACCENTS:

Stems				*Singular*	*Plural*
long-vowel grade:	ἀνηρ-		Nom.	ἀνήρ	ἄνδρες
short-vowel grade:	ἀνερ-		Gen.	ἀνδρός	ἀνδρῶν
zero grade:	ἀνδρ-		Dat.	ἀνδρί	ἀνδράσι(ν)
			Acc.	ἄνδρα	ἄνδρας
			Voc.	ἄνερ	ἄνδρες

ἀνήρ has a stem with *three different forms:* a **long-vowel grade** with a long vowel between the nu and the rho (ἀνηρ-); a **short-vowel grade** with a short vowel between the nu and the rho (ἀνερ-); and a **zero grade** with *no vowel* between the nu and the rho (ἀνδρ-). The expected zero grade of ἀνήρ, *ἀνρ-, is replaced by ἀνδρ- in accordance with a regular sound change that occurred in Greek (*-νρ- > -νδρ-). In the dative plural form an alpha is added before the ending. With the exception of the vocative singular and the dative plural, the accentual pattern of ἀνήρ is identical with the one for third-declension nouns with monosyllabic nominative singulars (cf. the declension of φρήν and §52, Observation 2, p. 122).

→ βούλομαι, βουλήσομαι, ——, ——, βεβούλημαι, ἐβουλήθην is a passive-in-the-aorist deponent verb (§65). That is, all its forms are middle *except* for its aorist forms, which are *passive*. βούλομαι means "want" or "wish," and it often takes an Object Infinitive. It may also be used absolutely. It sometimes takes an Accusative, Direct Object, particularly when the direct object is a neuter pronoun. Although βούλομαι and ἐθέλω may both express an idea of wishing or wanting, in Attic prose βούλομαι is used when a subject *desires* or *chooses* an action, but ἐθέλω is used when a subject *is open to* or *accepts* an action.

→ γίγνομαι, γενήσομαι, ἐγενόμην, γέγονα, γεγένημαι, —— is an irregular middle deponent verb (§65). The ending -ομην in the third principal part indicates that this verb has a second aorist. The additional fourth principal part—the first person singular perfect active indicative—is used to form perfect *active* forms, which do not differ in meaning from the perfect middle forms made from the fifth principal part (§83). γίγνομαι means "become," "happen," "arise," "be born," and may be used of both people and things. When γίγνομαι is used as a copulative verb with a Predicate Nominative or a Nominative, Predicate Adjective, it may be translated "become." Its aorist may also be used as the simple past of εἰμί and translated accordingly.

γίγνονται παῖδες ἐκ τούτου.	Children are born from this man.
πολλὰ ἐγίγνετο ἐκ τούτων.	Many things were arising from these things.
ἄρχων ἐγένετο οὗτος.	This man became (i.e., was) archon.

→ δέχομαι, δέξομαι, ἐδεξάμην, ——, δέδεγμαι, —— is a middle deponent verb (§65). That is, all its principal parts and all its forms are middle. The ending **-αμην** in the third principal part indicates that this verb has a first aorist. δέχομαι means "accept" or "receive" with a great variety of direct objects (pay, a gift, a story, an oracle, death). The person *from whom* someone accepts or receives something is regularly expressed by παρά and the genitive case. When the direct object of δέχομαι is a *person* rather than a thing, the appropriate meaning for the verb is "welcome" or "receive favorably."

→ ἔρχομαι, ἐλεύσομαι, ἦλθον, ἐλήλυθα, ——, —— is an intransitive verb that means either "go" or "come." It is a middle deponent in the first two principal parts. Its present and future tenses have *middle forms only*. Its imperfect tense is supplied by another verb. Future tense forms using a stem from ἐλεύσομαι are rare and appear chiefly in Homer and tragedy. In Greek prose the future tense of ἔρχομαι is supplied by another verb, εἶμι (Part 2, §145). ἔρχομαι has a second aorist with *active forms only*. Perfect and pluperfect forms made from the fourth principal part are also *active only* (§83).

→ ὁράω, ὄψομαι, εἶδον, ἑώρᾱκα/ἑόρᾱκα, ἑώρᾱμαι/ὦμμαι, ὤφθην, "see," is an alpha-contracted verb in the present and imperfect tenses (§41). The imperfect indicative, however, has a *double augment* with the initial omicron lengthened *and* an epsilon with a rough breathing added:

ἑώρων, ἑώρᾱς, ἑώρᾱ, etc. (imperfect active indic.)
ἑωρώμην, ἑωρῶ, ἑωρᾶτο, etc. (imperfect passive indic.)

The middle ending, **-ομαι**, in the second principal part indicates that ὁράω is a partial deponent. As the **-ον** ending of the third principal part indicates, ὁράω has a second aorist. The unaugmented aorist stem of εἶδον is **ἰδ-**. Thus, for example, the aorist active infinitive is **ἰδεῖν**. There are no differences in meaning, only differences in form, between the two forms of the fourth principal part and the two forms of the fifth principal part. The unaugmented aorist passive stem from the sixth principal part is **ὀφθ-**. Thus, for example, the future passive indicative is **ὀφθήσομαι, ὀφθήσει/ὀφθήσῃ**, etc. Other than in the future, ὁράω appears rarely in the middle voice and only in poetry. It does appear in the passive voice.

→ ἐλεύθερος, ἐλευθέρᾱ, ἐλεύθερον, "free," may be used to indicate a person's legal status (free as opposed to enslaved), or it may be accompanied by a Genitive of Separation (free from pain, fear). When used of things, ἐλεύθερος may mean "open to all" (a marketplace) or "fit for a free person" (a speech, thoughts).

→ ὀρθός, ὀρθή, ὀρθόν means "straight" as opposed to crooked (e.g., a straight road) and is also applied to "erect" or "upright" posture. It may also denote a person or thing that is "right" or "correct" (a messenger, a speech, a mind, an opinion).

→ After certain verbs and expressions of perceiving, knowing, thinking, and saying, the subordinating conjunction ὅτι means "that" and introduces a *noun* clause called an indirect statement (§69).

    The subordinating conjunction ὅτι may also mean "because." When it has this meaning, it introduces an *adverbial* clause that gives the reason for the main verb.

> τὸν ἑταῖρον φιλῶ ὅτι με φιλεῖ.   I love my companion because he loves me.

→ The postpositive conjunction οὖν joins a sentence with a preceding one and indicates a consequence of or an inference from a preceding idea. It is translated "then," "therefore."

> A. χαλεπὸν εὖ ἄρχειν.
> B. δεῖ οὖν τὴν τῶν ποιητῶν σοφίᾱν εὖ μανθάνειν.
> A. It is difficult to rule well.
> B. It is necessary, *then,* to learn well the wisdom of the poets.

The particle combination μὲν οὖν has these meanings: (1) *in affirmations,* "certainly," "by all means"; (2) *in corrections,* "no," "on the contrary"; (3) *in transitions to a new subject,* "so then," "therefore."

→ οὔτε has an acute accent on the penult because this word is the adverb οὐ, a proclitic, combined with the enclitic connective particle τε. μήτε has an acute accent on the penult because this word is the adverb μή combined with the enclitic connective particle τε. Both the conjunctions οὔτε ... οὔτε ... and μήτε ... μήτε ... mean "neither ... nor ...." The particular elements being negated determine which conjunctions are used.

> οὔτε φίλους ἔχομεν οὔτε συμμάχους.
> Neither do we have friends nor (do we have) allies. (Finite indicative verbs receive negation.)
>
> τὸν ἄδικον μήτε φιλεῖν μήτε τῑμᾶν σοι λέγω.
> I tell you neither to love nor to honor the unjust man. (Object infinitives receive negation.)

Both οὔτε ... οὔτε ... and μήτε ... μήτε ... are often preceded by a simple negative adverb called a *redundant negative.* A **redundant negative** *strengthens* a negative idea, and it should *not* be translated into English.

> οὐκ ἐφίλουν οὔτε δεσπότην οὔτε δούλους.
> I was (not) loving neither master nor slaves.
> I was loving neither master nor slaves.

→ When followed by a noun or pronoun in the genitive case, the preposition ὑπέρ means "over" or "above" and expresses a relation opposite to that of ὑπό, "under," "beneath." From a location in space, "over" is extended to mean "on behalf of."

> καλὴ ἡ ὑπὲρ τῆς ἐλευθερίᾱς μάχη.   Noble is the battle *over/on behalf of* freedom.

When followed by a noun or pronoun in the accusative case, ὑπέρ means "over" or "beyond."

> ὑπὲρ ἐλπίδας ἐνῑκῶμεν.   *Beyond* (our) hopes we were winning.

→ After certain verbs and expressions of perceiving, knowing, thinking, and saying, the subordinating conjunction ὡς means "that" and introduces a *noun* clause called an indirect statement (§69). When ὡς introduces an indirect statement, it differs slightly in usage from ὅτι in that ὅτι often introduces a statement of fact, but ὡς may suggest that an indirect statement is merely an opinion, true or untrue. The subordinating conjunction ὡς may also mean "as." With this meaning, it introduces an *adverbial* clause that modifies the main clause.

ἐκεῖνος ὁ ἀνὴρ τὸν ἀγῶνα νῑκᾷ, ὡς ἀκούσει.
That man is winning in (respect to) the contest, *as* you will hear.

When ὡς meaning "as" is balanced by the adverb οὕτω(ς), "so," in the main clause, a comparison is indicated.

ὡς δοῦλοι δεσπόταις, οὕτως ἐλεύθεροι ἄρχουσι πείθονται.
As slaves (obey) masters, *so* free men obey rulers.

When preceded by ὡς, the third person singular present active indicative of εἰμί, ἐστί(ν), is accented on the *penult*: ἔστι(ν).

→ ὥσπερ has an acute accent on the penult because this word is the conjunction ὡς, a proclitic, combined with the enclitic particle -περ.

Derivatives and Cognates

	Derivatives	*Cognates*
ἀνήρ	**andro**gyny, phil**ander**	
γίγνομαι		kin, **nat**ion, in**nat**e, **gene**alogy
δεσπότης	despot	
δέχομαι	pand**ect**, synec**doche**	dogma, **dec**ent
ἐγώ		ego, I
ἐμοῦ		me
ἐλεύθερος		liberate, deliver
ἔρχομαι		**or**ient, **or**igin, are
ἡμεῖς		us
ὁράω	panorama	a**ware**, **ware**, **ward**, guard
ὄψομαι	myopia	syn**ops**is, **opt**ic, oculus, eye
εἶδον		video, guide, **wis**dom, **id**ol
ὀρθός	**ortho**graphy, **ortho**dox	
πᾶς	**panto**mime, **pan**demic, **pan**creas	
σύ		thou, thee
ὑμεῖς		you
ὑπέρ	**hyper**active	over, **super**b, **sir**loin

§60. First Aorist Active and Middle Indicative and Infinitives of Omega Verbs

The aorist[1] indicative has *past* time with *simple* aspect (§24) and so differs from the imperfect indicative, which also has past time but with progressive or repeated aspect.

I said	aorist (past simple)
I was saying	imperfect (past progressive)
I used to say	imperfect (past repeated)

The aorist *active* and *middle* tenses of an omega verb are formed from the third principal part (first person singular aorist active indicative), and there are *two different* conjugations for these tenses. The conjugation employed by a particular verb is determined by the *ending* of the third principal part.

παύω, παύσω, ἔπαυσα, πέπαυκα, πέπαυμαι, ἐπαύθην
ἄγω, ἄξω, ἤγαγον, ἦχα, ἦγμαι, ἤχθην

When the third principal part ends in -**α**, the verb is said to have a **first aorist**, and most of its aorist active and middle endings have an -**α**-. When the third principal part of a verb ends in -**ov**, the verb is said to have a **second aorist**, and all its aorist active and middle endings have thematic vowels (-**o**- or -**ε**-). Thus, παύω has a first aorist, and ἄγω has a second aorist. Most omega verbs have first aorists, some have second aorists, and a very few—with *two* third principal parts—have *both* a first *and* a second aorist.

First Aorist Active and Middle Indicative of Omega Verbs

To form the first aorist active indicative of an omega verb:

1. take the **augmented**[2] **aorist active and middle stem** by removing the -**α** from the **third** principal part
2. add the following aorist active indicative endings:

Person	Singular	Plural
1	-α	-αμεν
2	-ας	-ατε
3	-ε(ν)	-αν

MEMORIZE THESE ENDINGS, DOWN THE SINGULAR AND THEN DOWN THE PLURAL, AND BE PREPARED TO RECITE THEM QUICKLY.

---

1. "Aorist" (< ἀόριστος, "unlimited") refers to the fact that this tense reports a *simple occurrence* that is *not limited* as to continuance, repetition, or completion.
2. Since principal part 3 is the first person singular aorist active indicative, it already has an augment.

To form the first aorist middle indicative of an omega verb:

1. take the **augmented aorist active and middle stem** by removing the -α from the **third** principal part

2. add the following aorist middle indicative endings:

Person	Singular	Plural
1	-αμην	-αμεθα
2	-ω	-ασθε
3	-ατο	-αντο

MEMORIZE THESE ENDINGS, DOWN THE SINGULAR AND THEN DOWN THE PLURAL, AND BE PREPARED TO RECITE THEM QUICKLY.

Thus, the first aorist active and middle indicative conjugations of παύω are:

Augmented First Aorist Active/Middle Stem: ἐπαυσ-

		Active		Middle
Singular				
1	ἔπαυσα	I stopped (trans.)	ἐπαυσάμην	I stopped (intrans.)
2	ἔπαυσας	you stopped (trans.)	ἐπαύσω	you stopped (intrans.)
3	ἔπαυσε(ν)	he, she, it stopped (trans.)	ἐπαύσατο	he, she, it stopped (intrans.)
Plural				
1	ἐπαύσαμεν	we stopped (trans.)	ἐπαυσάμεθα	we stopped (intrans.)
2	ἐπαύσατε	you (pl.) stopped (trans.)	ἐπαύσασθε	you (pl.) stopped (intrans.)
3	ἔπαυσαν	they stopped (trans.)	ἐπαύσαντο	they stopped (intrans.)

OBSERVATIONS

1. The stem from the third principal part is used to form the aorist active and middle tenses *only*. (The stem for the aorist passive is taken from the sixth principal part [§62].)

2. The accent on finite verb forms is *recessive*.

3. The ending of the third person singular first aorist active indicative has a movable nu.

4. Each of the endings of the aorist middle indicative is a combination of -α- and one of the secondary middle/passive *personal* endings (-μην, -σο, -το, -μεθα, -σθε, -ντο). In the second person singular ending, the -σ- of the ending -σο became intervocalic (*-ασο) and was lost. The remaining vowels contracted according to regular rules of Attic contraction to produce the ending -ω (*-ασο > *-αο > -ω).

First Aorist Active and Middle Infinitives of Omega Verbs

To form the first aorist active infinitive of an omega verb:

1. take the **unaugmented aorist active and middle stem** by removing the -α and augment from the **third** principal part[3]

---

3. Thus, ἔπαυσα > παυσ-; ἠθέλησα > ἐθελησ-.

2. add the first aorist active infinitive ending **-αι**.

To form the first aorist middle infinitive of an omega verb:

1. take the **unaugmented aorist active and middle stem** by removing the **-α** and the augment from the **third** principal part
2. add the first aorist middle infinitive ending **-ασθαι**.
   For example:

Unaugmented Aorist Active/Middle Stem: **παυσ-**

First Aorist Active Infinitive	παῦσαι	to stop (trans.) (once)
First Aorist Middle Infinitive	παύσασθαι	to stop (intrans.) (once)

OBSERVATIONS

1. The accent on the first aorist *active* infinitive is *persistent on the penult,* and the final diphthong, **-αι**, counts as *short* for purposes of accent. The persistent accent is seen clearly in an infinitive of more than two syllables. For example: ἐθελῆσαι. The accent on the first aorist *middle* infinitive is *recessive,* and the final diphthong, **-αι**, counts as *short* for purposes of accent.
2. The aorist active and middle infinitives do *not always indicate past time,* but *always indicate simple aspect.*

☛ DRILL 60 MAY NOW BE DONE.

§61. Second Aorist Active and Middle Indicative and Infinitives of Omega Verbs

Second Aorist Active and Middle Indicative of Omega Verbs

Some verbs have a third principal part (first person singular aorist active indicative) that ends in **-ον**. For example:

ἄγω, ἄξω, ⌈ἤγαγον⌉, ἦχα, ἦγμαι, ἤχθην

Such a verb is said to have a **second aorist,** which uses secondary endings familiar from the imperfect indicative. There is *no* difference in *meaning* between a first aorist and a second aorist, only a difference in *form.*

To form the second aorist active indicative of an omega verb:

1. take the **augmented aorist active and middle stem** by removing the **-ον** from the **third** principal part
2. add the secondary active endings.

To form the second aorist middle indicative of an omega verb:

1. take the **augmented aorist active and middle stem** by removing the **-ον** from the **third** principal part
2. add the secondary middle/passive endings.

Thus, the second aorist active and middle indicative conjugations of ἄγω are:

Augmented Aorist Active/Middle Stem: ἠγαγ-			
	Active		Middle
Singular			
1	ἤγαγον	I led	ἠγαγόμην	I married
2	ἤγαγες	you led	ἠγάγου	you married
3	ἤγαγε(ν)	he, she, it led	ἠγάγετο	he married
Plural			
1	ἠγάγομεν	we led	ἠγαγόμεθα	we married
2	ἠγάγετε	you (pl.) led	ἠγάγεσθε	you (pl.) married
3	ἤγαγον	they led	ἠγάγοντο	they married

OBSERVATIONS

1. The stem from the third principal part is used to form the aorist active and middle *only*. (The stem for the aorist passive is taken from the sixth principal part [§62].)
2. The accent on finite verb forms is *recessive*.
3. The forms of the *imperfect* and the *second aorist* active and middle indicative differ in *stem only*. For example:

ἦγ ον	I was leading (imperfect)
ἤγαγ ον	I led (aorist)
ἦγ ετο	he was marrying (imperfect)
	he was being led
ἠγάγ ετο	he married (aorist)

Second Aorist Active and Middle Infinitives of Omega Verbs

To form the second aorist active infinitive of an omega verb:

1. take the **unaugmented aorist active and middle stem** by removing the **-ον** and the augment from the **third** principal part[4]
2. add the second aorist active infinitive ending **-εῖν**.

To form the second aorist middle infinitive of an omega verb:

1. take the **unaugmented aorist active and middle stem** by removing the **-ον** and the augment from the **third** principal part
2. add the second aorist middle infinitive ending **-έσθαι**.

4. Thus, ἤγαγον > ἀγαγ-; ἔσχον > σχ-.

For example:

> Unaugmented Aorist Active/Middle Stem: ἀγαγ-
>
> Second Aorist Active Infinitive   ἀγαγεῖν   to lead (once)
> Second Aorist Middle Infinitive   ἀγαγέσθαι   to marry (once)

OBSERVATIONS

1. The accent on the second aorist *active* infinitive is *persistent on the ultima*. MEMORIZE THE ACCENT AS PART OF THE ENDING. The accent on the second aorist *middle* infinitive is *persistent on the penult,* and the final diphthong -αι counts as *short* for purposes of accent. MEMORIZE THE ACCENT AS PART OF THE ENDING.

2. The aorist active and middle infinitives do *not always indicate past time,* but *always indicate simple aspect.*

The verb λέγω has both a first and a second aorist with *no* difference in meaning. The first aorist is formed regularly from the third principal part ἔλεξα, and the second aorist is formed regularly from the third principal part εἶπον. There is an *alternate* second person aorist active indicative form, εἶπας, which is more common in Attic Greek than the regularly formed εἶπες. MEMORIZE THIS IRREGULAR FORM. The augmented second aorist active stem, εἰπ-, is also used for the second aorist active infinitive, εἰπεῖν: there is *no unaugmented aorist active/middle stem.*

☛ DRILL 61 MAY NOW BE DONE.

§62. Aorist Passive Indicative and Infinitive of Omega Verbs

All omega verbs form the aorist passive indicative and infinitive in the same way.

Aorist Passive Indicative of Omega Verbs

To form the aorist passive indicative of an omega verb:

1. take the **augmented**[5] **aorist passive stem** by removing the -ην from the **sixth** principal part
2. add the following endings

Person	Singular	Plural
1	-ην	-ημεν
2	-ης	-ητε
3	-η	-ησαν

MEMORIZE THESE ENDINGS, DOWN THE SINGULAR AND THEN DOWN THE PLURAL, AND BE PREPARED TO RECITE THEM QUICKLY.

5. Since principal part 6 is the first person singular aorist passive indicative, it already has an augment.

Thus, the aorist passive indicative conjugation of παύω is:

Augmented Aorist Passive Stem: ἐπαυθ-

Singular
1	ἐπαύθην	I was stopped
2	ἐπαύθης	you were stopped
3	ἐπαύθη	he, she, it was stopped

Plural
1	ἐπαύθημεν	we were stopped
2	ἐπαύθητε	you (pl.) were stopped
3	ἐπαύθησαν	they were stopped

OBSERVATIONS

1. The accent on finite verb forms is *recessive*.
2. Verbs having first aorists and verbs having second aorists form the aorist passive in the same way.

Aorist Passive Infinitive of Omega Verbs

To form the aorist passive infinitive of an omega verb:

1. take the **unaugmented aorist passive stem** by removing the -ην and the augment from the **sixth** principal part
2. add the aorist passive infinitive ending -ῆναι

For example:

Unaugmented Aorist Passive Stem: παυθ-

| Aorist Passive Infinitive | παυθῆναι | to be stopped (once) |

OBSERVATIONS

1. The accent on the aorist passive infinitive is *persistent on the penult*. MEMORIZE THE ACCENT AS PART OF THE ENDING. The final diphthong -αι counts as *short* for purposes of accent.
2. An aorist passive infinitive does *not always indicate past time,* but *always indicates simple aspect.*

§63. Synopsis 2: Present, Imperfect, Future, and Aorist Indicative; Present, Future, and Aorist Infinitives

Here is a model synopsis for ἄρχω in the second person plural. It includes the aorist indicative and infinitives.

Principal Parts: ἄρχω, ἄρξω, ἦρξα, ἦρχα, ἦργμαι, ἤρχθην
Person and Number: **2nd pl.**

	Active	*Middle*	*Passive*
Indicative			
Present	ἄρχετε you (pl.) are ruling	ἄρχεσθε you (pl.) are beginning	ἄρχεσθε you (pl.) are being ruled
Imperfect	ἤρχετε you (pl.) were ruling	ἤρχεσθε you (pl.) were beginning	ἤρχεσθε you (pl.) were being ruled
Future	ἄρξετε you (pl.) will rule	ἄρξεσθε you (pl.) will begin	ἀρχθήσεσθε you (pl.) will be ruled
Aorist	ἤρξατε you (pl.) ruled	ἤρξασθε you (pl.) began	ἤρχθητε you (pl.) were ruled
Infinitives			
Present	ἄρχειν to rule (repeatedly)	ἄρχεσθαι to begin (repeatedly)	ἄρχεσθαι to be ruled (repeatedly)
Future	ἄρξειν to be about to rule	ἄρξεσθαι to be about to begin	ἀρχθήσεσθαι to be about to be ruled
Aorist	ἄρξαι to rule (once)	ἄρξασθαι to begin (once)	ἀρχθῆναι to be ruled (once)

OBSERVATION

In a synopsis basic English translations should be given for indicative and infinitive forms.

☛ DRILL 62–63 MAY NOW BE DONE.

§64. Additional Uses of the Aorist Indicative

Ingressive Aorist

For certain verbs the simple aspect in past time of the aorist tense sometimes expresses the *moment* when something became the case or occurred. This use of the aorist is called the **Ingressive Aorist**,[6] and a special translation, different from that used for other tenses, may be given. For example:

ἦρχον	I was ruling	ἦρξα	I became ruler
ἐπολέμουν	they were making war	ἐπολέμησαν	they began a war
εἶχεν	he was possessing	ἔσχεν	he got

---

6. The Ingressive Aorist is sometimes called the **Inceptive Aorist**.

Gnomic Aorist

In addition to the present tense, the aorist tense may express a timeless general truth. This use of the aorist is called the **Gnomic Aorist** (< γνώμη, "proverb").

ὁ πόλεμος πολλὰς ἀνθρώποις συμφορὰς ποιεῖ/ἐποίησεν.
War makes many misfortunes for men.

OBSERVATIONS

1. In this sentence, the present tense (with repeated aspect) indicates that war *repeatedly* or *always* makes many misfortunes for men. The gnomic aorist (with simple aspect) uses one past occurrence to vividly express all possible occurrences: war *once* made many misfortunes for men, and this has proved to be true *always*.
2. The gnomic aorist is best translated with the English present tense.

☞ DRILL 60–64 MAY NOW BE DONE.

§65. Deponents

Verbs whose second principal parts end in -ομαι (e.g., εἰμί, ἔσομαι, ——, ——, ——, ——; μανθάνω, μαθήσομαι, ἔμαθον, μεμάθηκα, ——, ——) are called Partial Deponents because they lack future active forms and have future middle forms in principal part 2 (§55). Other deponents lack *all* active forms and have middle voice forms *only*. Such verbs are called **Middle Deponent Verbs**. A third group of deponents has middle voice forms in most tenses but *passive* forms in the aorist tense. Such verbs are called **Passive-in-the-Aorist Deponent Verbs**. Each type of deponent is distinguished in dictionaries and in vocabulary lists by its principal parts. That is, the principal parts make clear whether a verb is a middle or a passive-in-the-aorist deponent. For example:

δέχομαι, δέξομαι, ἐδεξάμην, ——, δέδεγμαι, —— accept, receive; welcome
βούλομαι, βουλήσομαι, ——, ——, βεβούλημαι, ἐβουλήθην want, wish

OBSERVATIONS

1. The first principal part of each of these verbs identifies the verb as a deponent because it ends in -ομαι, a middle/passive personal ending, and not -ω, an active personal ending. The present stem for these verbs is obtained by dropping the ending -ομαι.
2. δέχομαι has neither a fourth principal part (first person singular perfect *active* indicative) nor a sixth principal part (first person singular aorist *passive* indicative). All its principal parts are in the middle voice, and it has forms in the *middle voice only*: δέχομαι is a *middle* deponent.
3. βούλομαι has neither a third principal part (first person singular aorist *active* indicative) nor a fourth principal part (first person singular perfect *active* indicative). Instead of aorist *middle* forms, βούλομαι has aorist *passive* forms with *middle* meanings: βούλομαι is a *passive-in-the-aorist* deponent.
4. The ending of the third principal part of δέχομαι, -αμην, indicates that this middle deponent

has a *first* aorist. When a deponent has a third principal part that ends in **-ομην**, it has a *second* aorist.

5. With few exceptions, middle deponents do not have passive forms and cannot have passive meanings (e.g., **δέχεται** means "he receives," *not* "he is being received").

6. The verb **πείθω** was originally a passive-in-the-aorist deponent and had the principal parts **πείθομαι, πείσομαι, ——, ——, πέπεισμαι, ἐπείσθην**. In the Attic Greek version of this verb, aorist middle tense forms do not appear, and some aorist passive forms have *middle* meanings.

Here are synopses of **δέχομαι** and **βούλομαι** in the first person plural.

	Principal Parts: **δέχομαι, δέξομαι, ἐδεξάμην, ——, δέδεγμαι, ——** Person and Number: **1st pl.**			Principal Parts: **βούλομαι, βουλήσομαι, ——, ——, βεβούλημαι, ἐβουλήθην** Person and Number: **1st pl.**		
	Active	*Middle*	*Passive*	*Active*	*Middle*	*Passive*
Indicative Present	——	**δεχόμεθα** we are receiving	——	——	**βουλόμεθα** we are wanting	——
Imperfect	——	**ἐδεχόμεθα** we were receiving	——	——	**ἐβουλόμεθα** we were wanting	——
Future	——	**δεξόμεθα** we shall receive	——	——	**βουλησόμεθα** we shall want	——
Aorist	——	**ἐδεξάμεθα** we received	——	——	——	**ἐβουλήθημεν** we wanted
Infinitives Present	——	**δέχεσθαι** to be receiving	——	——	**βούλεσθαι** to be wanting	——
Future	——	**δέξεσθαι** to be about to receive	——	——	**βουλήσεσθαι** to be about to want	——
Aorist	——	**δέξασθαι** to receive (once)	——	——	——	**βουληθῆναι** to want (once)

☞ DRILL 65 MAY NOW BE DONE.

§66. The Intensive Adjective **αὐτός, αὐτή, αὐτό**

The declension of **αὐτός, αὐτή, αὐτό**, "-self," "very"; "same," is identical with the declension of **ἐκεῖνος, ἐκείνη, ἐκεῖνο**:

	Singular			*Plural*		
	M.	F.	N.	M.	F.	N.
Nom.	αὐτός	αὐτή	αὐτό	αὐτοί	αὐταί	αὐτά
Gen.	αὐτοῦ	αὐτῆς	αὐτοῦ	αὐτῶν	αὐτῶν	αὐτῶν
Dat.	αὐτῷ	αὐτῇ	αὐτῷ	αὐτοῖς	αὐταῖς	αὐτοῖς
Acc.	αὐτόν	αὐτήν	αὐτό	αὐτούς	αὐτάς	αὐτά

MEMORIZE THIS DECLENSION ACROSS THE SINGULAR AND ACROSS THE PLURAL.

OBSERVATION

There are no vocative case forms for αὐτός, αὐτή, αὐτό.

The adjective αὐτός, αὐτή, αὐτό has two distinct uses. When it appears in the *predicate* position, it intensifies nouns or pronouns and is translated "-self" or "very."

ταῦτα Γοργίᾳ αὐτῷ λέξω.	I shall say these things to Gorgias *himself*.
αὐτοὶ οἱ θεοὶ ἀδικοῦσιν.	The *very* gods do wrong.
αὐτή εἰμι ποιητής.	I *myself* (f.) am a poet.

OBSERVATION

In the third sentence the nominative singular form αὐτή intensifies the subject "I" expressed in the ending of the verb εἰμι.

When αὐτός, αὐτή, αὐτό appears in the *attributive* position *or* as a substantive with the article, it means "same."

οἱ αὐτοὶ πολῖται καὶ εἰρήνην ἦγον καὶ πολεμεῖν ἤθελον.
The *same* citizens were both keeping the peace and wishing to make war.

τὰ αὐτὰ τούτῳ τῷ ποιητῇ λέγετε.
You (pl.) are saying the *same* things as this poet.

OBSERVATION

When a comparison is expressed with αὐτός, "same," a Dative of Reference is translated with the word "as," as in the second sentence.

When certain forms of the article join with forms of αὐτός, αὐτή, αὐτό in crasis, the resulting contractions must be carefully analyzed. One may compare, for example, these similar forms:

ταὐτά (= τὰ αὐτά)	the same things (subj. or d.o.)
ταῦτα	these things (subj. or d.o.)
αὑτή (= ἡ αὐτή)	the same woman (subj.)
αὕτη	this woman (subj.)

When the neuter singular nominative and accusative form of **αὐτός** appears in crasis with the article, it usually ends in **-ον** rather than **-ο**. Thus, both **τὸ αὐτό** and **ταὐτόν** mean "the same thing" (subj. or d.o.).

☞ DRILL 66 MAY NOW BE DONE.

§67. Personal Pronouns and Possessive Adjectives

A pronoun is a word used instead of a noun, and a **personal pronoun** represents the speaker(s) or writer(s) (I, we), the one(s) spoken to (you, you [pl.]), or the one(s) spoken about (he, she, it, they). Like nouns, personal pronouns in Greek are declined. These declensions are somewhat irregular and must be memorized.

	First Person *Singular*		Second Person *Singular*	
Nom.	ἐγώ	I	σύ	you
Gen.	ἐμοῦ, μου	of me	σοῦ, σου	of you
Dat.	ἐμοί, μοι	to/for me	σοί, σοι	to/for you
Acc.	ἐμέ, με	me (d.o.)	σέ, σε	you (d.o.)
	Plural		*Plural*	
Nom.	ἡμεῖς	we	ὑμεῖς	you (pl.)
Gen.	ἡμῶν	of us	ὑμῶν	of you (pl.)
Dat.	ἡμῖν	to/for us	ὑμῖν	to/for you (pl.)
Acc.	ἡμᾶς	us (d.o.)	ὑμᾶς	you (pl.) (d.o.)

MEMORIZE THESE DECLENSIONS DOWN THE SINGULAR AND DOWN THE PLURAL.

OBSERVATIONS
_____

1. There are no vocative case forms for personal pronouns.

2. The unaccented alternate forms given in the genitive, dative, and accusative of **ἐγώ** and **σύ** are monosyllabic enclitics. The accented forms are more emphatic than the enclitic forms.

3. The enclitic particle **γε** is frequently attached directly to the nominative and dative singular forms of the first person personal pronoun. The resulting words have *recessive* accents:

ἔγωγε	I, at least; *I*
ἔμοιγε	to me, at least; to *me*

4. Since finite verb forms in Greek indicate the person and number of the subject by their endings, the nominative case forms of the personal pronouns are used only to give added emphasis to the subject.

ἐγὼ λέγω, οὐ σύ.	*I* am speaking, not *you*.

5. Especially after personal or demonstrative pronouns, the particle **μέν** appears but is not followed by a balancing **δέ**. This usage is called **μέν solitarium** (**μέν** alone), and a simple **δέ** clause is implied but not expressed.

ἐγὼ μὲν Ἀλέξανδρον πολλοῦ ἀξιῶ.
I, on the one hand, think Alexander worthy of much.
(You/others, on the other hand, may not.)

6. When the genitive case forms of personal pronouns are used as Genitives of Possession, they appear in the *predicate* position. The enclitic forms in the first and second person singular are common.

ὁ φίλος μου	the friend (subj.) of me, my friend (subj.)
οἱ παῖδες ἡμῶν	the children (subj.) of us, our children (subj.)
τὴν ἀρετήν σου	the virtue (d.o.) of you, your virtue (d.o.)
τοὺς συμμάχους ὑμῶν	the allies (d.o.) of you (pl.), your (pl.) allies (d.o.)

Although the personal pronouns in the predicate position may be used as Genitives of Possession, there are also **possessive adjectives** that may be used in the *attributive* position to express possession. These adjectives are all regularly declined first-second-declension adjectives.

ἐμός, ἐμή, ἐμόν	my
ἡμέτερος, ἡμετέρᾱ, ἡμέτερον	our
σός, σή, σόν	your
ὑμέτερος, ὑμετέρᾱ, ὑμέτερον	your (pl.)

ὁ ἐμὸς φίλος	my friend (subj.)
οἱ ἡμέτεροι παῖδες	our children (subj.)
τὴν σὴν ἀρετήν	your virtue (d.o.)
τοὺς ὑμετέρους συμμάχους	your (pl.) allies (d.o.)

The third person personal pronoun in Greek is supplied by forms of the intensive adjective αὐτός, αὐτή, αὐτό, but the *nominative case forms are not used*.

	Singular			Plural		
	M.	F.	N.	M.	F.	N.
Nom.	—	—	—			
Gen.	αὐτοῦ	αὐτῆς	αὐτοῦ	αὐτῶν	αὐτῶν	αὐτῶν
	of him	of her	of it	of them (m.)	of them (f.)	of them (n.)
Dat.	αὐτῷ	αὐτῇ	αὐτῷ	αὐτοῖς	αὐταῖς	αὐτοῖς
	to him	to her	to it	to them (m.)	to them (f.)	to them (n.)
Acc.	αὐτόν	αὐτήν	αὐτό	αὐτούς	αὐτάς	αὐτά
	him	her	it	them (m.)	them (f.)	them (n.)

MEMORIZE THIS DECLENSION ACROSS THE SINGULAR AND ACROSS THE PLURAL.

OBSERVATIONS

1. Nominative case forms of the third person personal pronoun are supplied by the nominative forms of the demonstrative pronouns, οὗτος, ὅδε, and ἐκεῖνος, but these pronouns *retain their demonstrative force*. Thus, ἐκεῖνος means "that man" rather than "he."

2. The genitive case forms αὐτοῦ, αὐτῆς, αὐτοῦ, and αὐτῶν may be used to express possession in the *predicate* position.

τοῖς φίλοις αὐτοῦ	for the friends of him, for his friends
τὴν ψῡχὴν αὐτῆς	the soul (d.o.) of her, her soul (d.o.)
αἱ δόξαι αὐτῶν	the opinions (subj.) of them, their opinions (subj.)

There is no third person possessive adjective in Attic Greek, but the genitives of the demonstrative pronouns may be used in the attributive position instead of the personal pronouns in the predicate position.

τοῖς τούτου φίλοις	for the friends *of this man*
τὴν τῆσδε ψῡχήν	the soul (d.o.) *of this woman*
αἱ ἐκείνων δόξαι	the opinions (subj.) *of those men*

Summary of Possession

	Attributive Position possessive adjectives; demonstrative pronouns	Predicate Position genitives of personal pronouns
1st person	ἐμός, ἐμή, ἐμόν ἡμέτερος, ἡμετέρᾱ, ἡμέτερον	ἐμοῦ/μου, ἡμῶν
2nd person	σός, σή, σόν ῡ̔μέτερος, ῡ̔μετέρᾱ, ῡ̔μέτερον	σοῦ/σου, ῡ̔μῶν
3rd person	τούτου, ταύτης, τούτου, τούτων ἐκείνου, ἐκείνης, ἐκείνου, ἐκείνων τοῦδε, τῆσδε, τοῦδε, τῶνδε	αὐτοῦ, αὐτῆς, αὐτοῦ, αὐτῶν

☛ DRILL 67 MAY NOW BE DONE.

§68. The Adjectives πᾶς, πᾶσα, πᾶν and ἅπᾶς, ἅπᾶσα, ἅπαν

The adjectives πᾶς, πᾶσα, πᾶν, "all," "every"; "whole," and ἅπᾶς, ἅπᾶσα, ἅπαν, "(quite) all," "every"; "whole," have third-declension endings in the masculine and neuter and first-declension short-alpha endings in the feminine.

	Singular			*Singular*		
Nom./Voc.	πᾶς	πᾶσα	πᾶν	ἅπᾶς	ἅπᾶσα	ἅπαν
Gen.	παντός	πάσης	παντός	ἅπαντος	ἁπάσης	ἅπαντος
Dat.	παντί	πάσῃ	παντί	ἅπαντι	ἁπάσῃ	ἅπαντι
Acc.	πάντα	πᾶσαν	πᾶν	ἅπαντα	ἅπᾶσαν	ἅπαν
	Plural			*Plural*		
Nom./Voc.	πάντες	πᾶσαι	πάντα	ἅπαντες	ἅπᾶσαι	ἅπαντα
Gen.	πάντων	πᾶσῶν	πάντων	ἁπάντων	ἁπᾶσῶν	ἁπάντων
Dat.	πᾶσι(ν)	πάσαις	πᾶσι(ν)	ἅπᾶσι(ν)	ἁπάσαις	ἅπᾶσι(ν)
Acc.	πάντας	πάσᾱς	πάντα	ἅπαντας	ἁπάσᾱς	ἅπαντα

MEMORIZE THESE DECLENSIONS, PAYING PARTICULAR ATTENTION TO ACCENTS.

1. The stem of πᾶς in the masculine and neuter is παντ- and is found in the genitive singular. The stem of πᾶς in the feminine is πᾱσ-. The ending of the masculine and neuter plural dative has a long alpha because of the loss of -ντ- and compensatory lengthening: *πάντσι(ν) > *πάνσσι(ν) > *πάνσι(ν) > πᾶσι(ν).

2. The accent on πᾶς, πᾶσα, πᾶν is *persistent on the penult except* in the masculine and neuter singular genitive and dative, where it is an acute on the ultima, and in the feminine plural genitive plural, where it is a circumflex on the ultima.

3. The stem of ἅπᾱς in the masculine and neuter is ἁπαντ-. The stem of ἅπᾱς in the feminine is ἁπᾱσ-. The ending of the masculine and neuter plural dative has a long alpha because of the loss of -ντ- and compensatory lengthening: *ἅπαντσι(ν) > *ἅπανσσι(ν) > *ἅπανσι(ν) > ἅπᾱσι(ν).

4. The accent on ἅπᾱς, ἅπᾱσα, ἅπαν is *persistent on the first alpha except* in the feminine plural genitive, where it is a circumflex on the ultima.

5. Although ἅπᾱς is an emphatic form of πᾶς, this emphasis need not always be conveyed in translation.

πᾶς or ἅπᾱς most often appears in the *predicate* position and means "every" (with singulars) and "all" (with plurals and collective singulars).

τὴν ὁδὸν ἅπᾱσαν	every road (d.o.)
πάντας τοὺς πολίτᾱς	all the citizens (d.o.)
παντὶ τῷ δήμῳ	for all the people
ἅπᾱσαι αἱ τέχναι	quite all the arts (subj.)

πᾶς or ἅπᾱς may also appear with a noun *without* the article.

πᾶσιν ἄρχουσι	for all rulers
ἐξ ἅπαντος λόγου	(resulting) from every reason

When πᾶς or ἅπᾱς appears in the *attributive position,* it means "whole" or "as a whole."

τὸν πάντα λόγον	the whole speech (d.o.)
οἱ πάντες Ἕλληνες	the Greeks as a whole (subj.)

πᾶς and ἅπᾱς are frequently used substantively, and this substantive use appears in certain common prepositional phrases.

πάντα	all things (subj. or d.o.)
τὸ πᾶν	the whole (subj. or d.o.)
εἰς (τὸ) πᾶν	with a view to the whole thing; altogether; in general

☛ DRILL 68 MAY NOW BE DONE.

§69. Indirect Statement 1

In both English and Greek it is possible to report the words of another *directly*. In English this is called **direct quotation**, and in Greek **direct statement**.

Gorgias says, "The young men wish to be taught."
ὁ Γοργίᾱς λέγει· Οἱ νεᾱνίαι διδάσκεσθαι ἐθέλουσιν.

The allies say the following things: "We are obeying the laws of the Athenians."
οἱ σύμμαχοι λέγουσι τάδε· Τοῖς τῶν Ἀθηναίων νόμοις πειθόμεθα.

OBSERVATION

When a speaker's exact words are quoted in English, the quotation is preceded by a comma or a colon and is set off by quotation marks. In Greek a direct quotation is also usually preceded by a comma or a colon. The first word of a direct quotation is often capitalized, but quotation marks are only sometimes used.

It is also possible to report the words of another *indirectly*. This is called **indirect quotation** in English and **indirect statement** in Greek.

Gorgias says *that* the young men wish to be taught.
ὁ Γοργίᾱς λέγει ὅτι οἱ νεᾱνίαι διδάσκεσθαι ἐθέλουσιν.

The allies say *that* they are obeying the laws of the Athenians.
οἱ σύμμαχοι λέγουσιν ὡς τοῖς τῶν Ἀθηναίων νόμοις πείθονται.

OBSERVATIONS

1. In indirect quotation in English, no comma or colon is used. The subordinating conjunction "that" introduces the indirect quotation, and a change of person sometimes occurs: "We" becomes "they" in the second sentence.

2. In the type of indirect statement in Greek that most closely resembles indirect quotation in English, a subordinating conjunction—either ὅτι or ὡς—corresponding to the English "that" is used. As in English, no preceding punctuation or quotation marks are used, and a change of person sometimes occurs: πειθόμεθα becomes πείθονται.

3. Indirect statement with ὅτι or ὡς is most often introduced in Greek by verbs of saying, reporting, answering, etc. The most common such verb is λέγω.

In Greek the *tense* and *mood* of the verb in an indirect statement with ὅτι/ὡς *always remain unchanged* from the direct statement when the introductory verb of saying is in a *primary* tense (present, future, or perfect). When the introductory verb of saying is in a *secondary* tense (imperfect, aorist, pluperfect), the tense and mood of the indirect statement *often* remain unchanged, but the mood may also be changed to the optative (Part 2, §142). For example:

direct statement:	οἱ Ἀθηναῖοι τῶν νήσων ἄρχουσιν. The Athenians are ruling the islands.
indirect statements:	λέγει ὅτι/ὡς οἱ Ἀθηναῖοι τῶν νήσων ἄρχουσιν. He says that the Athenians *are ruling* the islands. ἔλεγεν ὅτι/ὡς οἱ Ἀθηναῖοι τῶν νήσων ἄρχουσιν. He was saying that the Athenians *were ruling* the islands. λέξει ὅτι/ὡς οἱ Ἀθηναῖοι τῶν νήσων ἄρχουσιν. He will say that the Athenians *are ruling* the islands.

OBSERVATIONS

1. In the first indirect statement, both the introductory verb of saying and the verb in the indirect statement are present indicative, *both in Greek and in English*. The saying and the ruling are occurring *simultaneously* (at the same time). Both actions are happening in the present.

2. In the second indirect statement, the introductory verb of saying is in the imperfect tense, but the verb in the indirect statement remains present indicative, just as in the original direct statement. This vivid representation of the tense and mood of the verb in the direct statement is usually *not* reproduced in English. In the English translation ἄρχουσιν is translated "were ruling" to indicate clearly that the ruling *was simultaneous with* the saying. Both actions were happening in the past.

3. In the third indirect statement, the introductory verb of saying is in the future tense, but the verb in the indirect statement remains present indicative, just as in the original direct statement. In the English translation ἄρχουσιν is translated "are ruling" to indicate that the ruling *is simultaneous with* the saying. Both actions will happen in the future.

direct statement:	οἱ Ἀθηναῖοι τῶν νήσων ἄρξουσιν. The Athenians will rule the islands.
indirect statements:	λέγει ὅτι/ὡς οἱ Ἀθηναῖοι τῶν νήσων ἄρξουσιν. He says that the Athenians *will rule* the islands. ἔλεγεν ὅτι/ὡς οἱ Ἀθηναῖοι τῶν νήσων ἄρξουσιν. He was saying that the Athenians *would rule* the islands. λέξει ὅτι/ὡς οἱ Ἀθηναῖοι τῶν νήσων ἄρξουσιν. He will say that the Athenians *will rule* the islands.

OBSERVATION

The future tense verb in each indirect statement indicates an action *subsequent to* (after) the time of the introductory verb of saying. This subsequent time is indicated in the English translations by "will rule" when the verb of saying is present or future and "would rule" when the verb of saying is in the past.

direct statement:	οἱ Ἀθηναῖοι τῶν νήσων ἦρξαν.
	The Athenians ruled the islands.
indirect statements:	λέγει ὅτι/ὡς οἱ Ἀθηναῖοι τῶν νήσων ἦρξαν.
	He says that the Athenians *ruled* the islands.
	ἔλεγεν ὅτι/ὡς οἱ Ἀθηναῖοι τῶν νήσων ἦρξαν.
	He was saying that the Athenians *had ruled* the islands.
	λέξει ὅτι/ὡς οἱ Ἀθηναῖοι τῶν νήσων ἦρξαν.
	He will say that the Athenians *ruled* the islands.

OBSERVATION

The aorist tense verb in each indirect statement indicates an action *prior to* (before) the time of the introductory verb of saying. This prior time is indicated in the English translations by the simple past tense "ruled" when the verb of saying is present or future and by the pluperfect tense "had ruled" when the verb of saying is in the past.

If the verb in a direct statement is negated, the negative remains unchanged in indirect statement.

direct statement:	οἱ Ἀθηναῖοι τοῖς συμμάχοις οὐκ ἐπολέμησαν.
	The Athenians did not make war on their allies.
indirect statement:	λέγει ὅτι/ὡς οἱ Ἀθηναῖοι τοῖς συμμάχοις οὐκ ἐπολέμησαν.
	He says that the Athenians did not make war on their allies.

In addition to reporting speech after the verb λέγω, indirect statement with ὅτι/ὡς may follow other verbs and expressions of perception or intellection.

μανθάνω ὅτι/ὡς ...	I understand that ...
πείθομαι ὅτι/ὡς ...	I believe that/I am persuaded that ...
δῆλόν ἐστιν ὅτι/ὡς ...	It is clear that ...
δηλόω ὅτι/ὡς ...	I make clear that ...
ὁράω ὅτι/ὡς ...	I see that ...
(ὁράω, ὄψομαι, εἶδον, ἑώρᾱκα/ἑόρᾱκα, ἑώρᾱμαι/ὦμμαι, ὤφθην see)	

An indirect statement introduced by ὅτι or ὡς and containing a finite verb is a *subordinate clause*, and thus a Greek sentence containing an indirect statement is a complex sentence (§53). Furthermore, an indirect statement is a *noun clause*: A **noun clause** functions as an *object* (or sometimes as a *subject*) of an introductory verb of saying or perceiving.

| λέγω ὅτι χαλεπόν ἐστιν ὁ βίος. | I say that life is a difficult thing. |
| δῆλόν ἐστιν ὅτι ἠδίκησας. | It is clear that you did wrong. |

> In the first sentence the indirect statement (ὅτι . . . βίος) is the *direct object* of λέγω. In the second sentence the indirect statement (ὅτι ἠδίκησας) is the *subject* of ἐστιν, and δῆλον is a predicate adjective in the neuter singular nominative: "That you did wrong is clear."

Sometimes an indirect statement is introduced by a verb in the *passive* voice.

> **ἐπείσθην ὅτι δεῖ πολεμεῖν.**
> I was persuaded that it was necessary to make war.

> **διδασκόμεθα ὡς καὶ οἱ θεοὶ ἀδικοῦσιν.**
> We are being taught that even the gods do wrong.

Such indirect statements are best understood as noun clauses analogous to Retained Accusatives. (For the Retained Accusative see the vocabulary note on διδάσκω, p. 54.)

☞ DRILL 69 MAY NOW BE DONE.

§70. The Binary Construction (Prolepsis)

Sometimes a verb that has an indirect statement as a direct object has a *second direct object* that is placed *before* the indirect statement and is someone or something that appears in or is referred to by the indirect statement. For example:

> **ἆρ᾽ ἐκεῖνον ὁρᾷς, ὅτι ἀδικεῖ;**
> Do you see that man, that he is doing wrong?
> Do you see that that man is doing wrong?

> 1. In this sentence the verb ὁρᾷς has two direct objects, the demonstrative pronoun ἐκεῖνον and the indirect statement ὅτι ἀδικεῖ, which is a noun clause. The subject of the indirect statement is emphasized by being expressed *before* the indirect statement as the direct object of the main verb.
> 2. In the second translation the direct object ἐκεῖνον is translated as the subject of the indirect statement.
> 3. The binary construction may also be described as **anticipation**, or **prolepsis** (πρόληψις, "taking before"), since the direct object of the verb *anticipates* the subject of the indirect statement.

§71. Dative of the Possessor

The dative case may be used to indicate the *person who possesses* something. This use is an extension of the case's referential function, and a dative so used is called a **Dative of the Possessor**. For example:

> τῷ *δικαίῳ* ἐστὶν ὁ βίος τῶν θεῶν.
> *To* the *just man* there is the life of the gods.
> The *just man* has the life of the gods.
>
> τούτῳ τῷ *ἀνθρώπῳ* ἦν πολλὰ ἀγαθά.
> *To* this *man* there were many good things.
> This *man* had many good things.

The syntax of each italicized word (*δικαίῳ*, *ἀνθρώπῳ*) is **Dative of the Possessor**.

OBSERVATIONS

---

1. In a sentence containing a Dative of the Possessor, the thing *possessed* appears in the nominative case as the subject of the verb.

2. In each of the second, less literal translations, the Dative of the Possessor is translated into English as the *subject* of the verb "have," and the thing possessed is translated as the *direct object*.

Short Readings

1. Rescued by Aphrodite from single combat with Menelaus, Paris speaks to Helen.

> νῦν μὲν γὰρ Μενέλᾱος ἐνίκηϲεν ϲὺν Ἀθήνῃ,
> κεῖνον δ' αὖτιϲ ἐγώ· παρὰ[†] γὰρ θεοί εἰϲι καὶ ἡμῖν.

(Homer, *Iliad* III.439–40)

Μενέλᾱοϲ, Μενελᾱου, ὁ Menelaus	αὖτιϲ (adv.) again, in turn
Ἀθήνη (Epic) = Attic Ἀθηνᾷ	[†]παρά, *here,* beside
κεῖνον = ἐκεῖνον	

2. When Odysseus falls asleep, his companions argue over whether to open the mysterious bag given to him by the king of the winds.

> … βουλὴ δὲ κακὴ νίκηϲεν ἑταίρων·
> ἀϲκὸν μὲν λῦϲαν, ἄνεμοι δ' ἐκ[†] πάντεϲ ὄρουϲαν.

(Homer, *Odyssey* x.46–47)

νίκηϲεν (Epic) = Attic ἐνίκηϲεν	ἄνεμοϲ, ἀνέμου, ὁ breeze, wind
ἀϲκόϲ, ἀϲκοῦ, ὁ skin, hide	[†]ἐκ, *here* (adv.) out
λύω, λύϲω, ἔλῡϲα, λέλυκα, λέλυμαι, ἐλύθην	ὀρούω, ——, ὤρουϲα, ——, ——, —— rush
loosen; λῦϲαν (Epic) = Attic ἔλῡϲαν	(forth); ὄρουϲαν (Epic) = Attic ὤρουϲαν

3. The poet recalls the names of the Muses.

> Κλειώ τ' Εὐτέρπη τε Θάλειά τε Μελπομένη τε
> Τερψιχόρη[†] τ' Ἐρατώ τε Πολύμνιά τ' Οὐρανίη[†] τε
> Καλλιόπη θ'· ἡ δὲ προφερεϲτάτη ἐϲτὶν ἁπᾱϲέων.

(Hesiod, *Theogony* 77–79)

[†]Τερψιχόρη, Οὐρανίη (Ionic) = Attic	προφερέϲτατοϲ, προφερεϲτάτη, προφερέϲτατον
Τερψιχόρᾱ, Οὐρανίᾱ	eldest
	ἁπᾱϲέων (Epic) = Attic ἁπᾱϲῶν

4. A fragment from the works of the philosopher Pythagoras

> ἀρχὴ δέ τοι ἥμιϲυ παντόϲ.

(Pythagoras, frag. 159)

ἥμιϲυ, ἡμίϲεοϲ, τό half

5. An elegiac couplet

οὔποθ' ὕδωρ καὶ πῦρ συμμείξεται· οὐδέ ποθ' ἡμεῖς
πιcτοὶ ἐπ' ἀλλήλοιc καὶ φίλοι ἐccόμεθα. (Theognis *Elegies* II.1245–46)

ὕδωρ, ὕδατοc, τό water
πῦρ, πυρόc, τό fire
cυμμείγνῡμι (cυν- + μείγνῡμι), cυμμείξω,
cυνέμειξα, cυμμέμιχα, cυμμέμιγμαι,
cυνεμίχθην *active or middle,* mix (together);
intrans., commingle

οὐδέ (conj.) and not
πιcτόc, πιcτή, πιcτόν trustworthy, faithful;
believing
——, ἀλλήλων (reciprocal pron.) one another,
each other
ἐccόμεθα = ἐcόμεθα

6. A tombstone inscription

Καρτερὸc ἐν πολέμοιc Τῑμόκριτοc, οὗ τόδε cᾶμα·
Ἄρηc δ' οὐκ ἀγαθῶν φείδεται, ἀλλὰ κακῶν. (Anacreon 7.160)

καρτερόc, καρτερά, καρτερόν strong, mighty
Τῑμόκριτοc, Τῑμοκρίτου, ὁ Timocritus
cῆμα, cήματοc, τό tomb; cᾶμα (Doric) = Attic cῆμα

φείδομαι, φείcομαι, ἐφειcάμην, ——, ——, ——
spare (+ gen.)

Fragments from the works of the philosopher Heraclitus

7. ψῡχῆιcιν θάνατοc ὕδωρ† γενέcθαι, ὕδατι δὲ θάνατοc γῆν† γενέcθαι· ἐκ γῆc δὲ ὕδωρ
γίνεται, ἐξ ὕδατοc δὲ ψῡχή. (Heraclitus, frag. 36)

ψῡχῆιcιν (Ionic) = Attic ψῡχαῖc
ὕδωρ, ὕδατοc, τό water

†ὕδωρ, γῆν, *Predicate Accusatives agreeing with
implied Subject Accusatives*
γίνεται (Ionic) = Attic γίγνεται

8. πόλεμοc πάντων μὲν πατήρ ἐcτι, πάντων δὲ βαcιλεύc, καὶ τοὺc μὲν θεοὺc ἔδειξε, τοὺc δὲ
ἀνθρώπουc, τοὺc μὲν δούλουc ἐποίηcε, τοὺc δὲ ἐλευθέρουc. (Heraclitus, frag. 53)

πατήρ, πατρόc, ὁ father
βαcιλεύc, βαcιλέωc, ὁ king

δείκνῡμι, δείξω, ἔδειξα, δέδειχα, δέδειγμαι,
ἐδείχθην show

9. ἀνὴρ νήπιοc ἤκουcε πρὸc δαίμονοc ὅκωcπερ παῖc πρὸc ἀνδρόc. (Heraclitus, frag. 79)

νήπιοc, νηπίᾱ, νήπιον foolish

ὅκωcπερ (Ionic) = Attic ὥcπερ (conj.) just as

10. Prometheus and the Chorus discuss one of his great gifts to men.

> **Πρ.** τυφλὰς ἐν αὐτοῖς ἐλπίδας κατῴκιςα.
> **Χο.** μέγ' ὠφέλημα τοῦτ' ἐδωρήςω βροτοῖς.   (Aeschylus, *Prometheus Bound* 250–51)

Πρ. = Prometheus
τυφλός, τυφλή, τυφλόν blind
κατοικίζω (κατα- + οἰκίζω), κατοικιῶ, κατῴκιςα,
——, κατῴκιςμαι, κατῳκίςθην establish; plant

Χο. = Chorus
ὠφέλημα, ὠφελήματος, τό advantage, benefit
δωρέω *active or middle*, give, present

11. The Chorus of Furies explains why it is sure that Orestes will be punished for the murder of his mother.

> μέγας γὰρ Ἅιδης ἐςτὶν εὔθυνος βροτῶν
> ἔνερθε χθονός,
> δελτογράφῳ δὲ πάντ' ἐπωπᾷ φρενί.   (Aeschylus, *Eumenides* 273–75)

εὔθῡνος, εὐθύνου, ὁ investigator; corrector,
chastiser
ἔνερθε (prep. + gen.) beneath, below
χθών, χθονός, ἡ earth, land

δελτογράφος, δελτογράφον writing on a tablet,
recording
ἐπωπάω watch over, observe

Fragments from tragedies of Aeschylus

12.   **ςοὶ μὲν γαμεῖςθαι μόρςιμον, γαμεῖν δ' ἐμοί.**   (Aeschylus, frag. 13)

γαμέω marry (of a man); *middle,* marry (of a
woman)

μόρςιμος, μόρςιμον fated, destined

13.   **. . . ἀλλ' Ἄρης φιλεῖ**
                ἀεὶ τὰ λῷςτα πάντ' ἀπανθίζειν ςτρατοῦ.   (Aeschylus, frag. 146)

λῷςτος, λῴςτη, λῷςτον most desirable; best
ἀπανθίζω (ἀπο- + ἀνθίζω), ἀπανθίςω, ἀπήνθιςα,
——, ——, —— pluck off (flowers)

ςτρατός, ςτρατοῦ, ὁ army

Fragments from tragedies of Sophocles

14.   **ἀνδρῶν γὰρ ἐςθλῶν ςτέρνον οὐ μαλάςςεται.**   (Sophocles, frag. 201e)

ἐςθλός, ἐςθλή, ἐςθλόν good
ςτέρνον, ςτέρνου, τό chest; heart

μαλάςςω, μαλάξω, ἐμάλαξα, ——, ——,
ἐμαλάχθην soften

15.   φιλεῖ γὰρ ἄνδρας πόλεμος ἀγρεύειν νέους.   (Sophocles, frag. 554)

ἀγρεύω, ἀγρεύσω, ἤγρευσα, ἤγρευκα, ——, ——
    catch by hunting, hunt down

16.   τὰ μὲν διδακτὰ μανθάνω, τὰ δ᾽ εὑρετὰ
       ζητῶ, τὰ δ᾽ εὐκτὰ παρὰ θεῶν ᾐτησάμην.   (Sophocles, frag. 843)

διδακτός, διδακτή, διδακτόν that can be taught,   ζητέω seek (for)
    teachable   εὐκτός, εὐκτή, εὐκτόν that can be prayed for
εὑρετός, εὑρετή, εὑρετόν that can be discovered,   αἰτέω, αἰτήσω, ᾔτησα, ᾔτηκα, ᾔτημαι, ᾐτήθην
    discoverable   ask; *middle,* ask for oneself

17.   ἐλευθέρᾱ γὰρ γλῶςςα τῶν ἐλευθέρων.   (Sophocles, frag. 927a)

γλῶςςα, γλώςςης, ἡ tongue

18.   χρόνος δ᾽ ἀμαυροῖ πάντα κεἰς† λήθην ἄγει.   (Sophocles, frag. 984)

χρόνος, χρόνου, ὁ time   †κεἰς = καὶ εἰς
ἀμαυρόω make dark, darken   λήθη, λήθης, ἡ forgetfulness; oblivion

19. When counseling the Persian king Xerxes not to undertake the battle of Salamis, Artemisia
raises a concern.

       . . . τοῖςι μὲν χρηςτοῖςι τῶν ἀνθρώπων κακοὶ δοῦλοι φιλέουςι γίνεςθαι, τοῖςι δὲ κακοῖςι
       χρηςτοί.   (Herodotus, *Histories* VIII.68.6)

γίνεςθαι (Ionic) = Attic γίγνεςθαι

20. Iphigenia explains why she prefers seawater for a purification rite.

       θάλαςςα κλύζει πάντα τἀνθρώπων κακά.   (Euripides, *Iphigenia Among the Taurians* 1193)

κλύζω, κλύςω, ἔκλυςα, ——, κέκλυςμαι,
    ἐκλύςθην wash, wash away

Fragments from tragedies of Euripides

21.   ςὺν μῡρίοιςι τὰ καλὰ γίγνεται πόνοις.   (Euripides, frag. 236N)

μῡρίος, μῡρίᾱ, μῡρίον countless, myriad

22.   οὗτοι νόμιϲμα λευκὸϲ ἄργυροϲ μόνον
       καὶ χρῦϲόϲ ἐϲτιν, ἀλλὰ κἀρετὴ βροτοῖϲ
       νόμιϲμα κεῖται πᾶϲιν . . .   (Euripides, frag. 546N)

νόμιϲμα, νομίϲματοϲ, τό coin(age)   χρῦϲόϲ, χρῦϲοῦ, ὁ gold
λευκόϲ, λευκή, λευκόν white, bright, brilliant   κεῖμαι, κείϲομαι, ——, ——, ——, —— lie; be
ἄργυροϲ, ἀργύρου, ὁ silver   fixed; κεῖται = 3rd sing. pres. mid. indic.

23. A fragment from an unidentified tragedy

       οὐκ ἀξιῶ μῑκρῶν ϲε, μεγάλα δ᾽ οὐκ ἔχω.   (Tragica Adespota 31)

μῑκρόϲ, μῑκρά, μῑκρόν small, little

24. A bird arrives with an urgent question.

       ποῦ ποῦ ᾽ϲτι, ποῦ ποῦ ποῦ ᾽ϲτι, ποῦ ποῦ ποῦ ᾽ϲτι, ποῦ
       ποῦ Πειϲέταιρόϲ ἐϲτιν ἄρχων;   (Aristophanes, Birds 1122–23)

Πειϲέταιροϲ, Πειϲεταίρου, ὁ Peisetaerus (king
    of Cloudcuckooland)

25. Speaking to Lysistrata, Myrrhine pretends to be angry with her husband, Kinesias.

       φιλῶ, φιλῶ ᾽γω τοῦτον. ἀλλ᾽ οὐ βούλεται
       ὑπ᾽ ἐμοῦ φιλεῖϲθαι.   (Aristophanes, Lysistrata 870–71)

26. Chremylus reacts when the blind god Wealth seems uncertain about his own power.

       νὴ τὸν Δί᾽ ἀλλὰ καὶ λέγουϲι πάντεϲ ὡϲ
       δειλότατον ἐϲθ᾽ ὁ Πλοῦτοϲ.   (Aristophanes, Wealth 202–3)

δειλότατοϲ, δειλοτάτη, δειλότατον most cowardly   Πλοῦτοϲ, Πλούτου, ὁ (the god) Wealth

27. Chremylus invites Wealth into his home and explains why.

                          ἡ γὰρ οἰκίᾱ
       αὕτη ᾽ϲτὶν ἣν δεῖ χρημάτων ϲε τήμερον
       μεϲτὴν ποιῆϲαι καὶ δικαίωϲ κἀδίκωϲ.   (Aristophanes, Wealth 231–33)

τήμερον (adv.) today   μεϲτόϲ, μεϲτή, μεϲτόν full

28. A fragment from a comedy of Aristophanes

θύειν με μέλλει, καὶ κελεύει βῆ λέγειν. (Aristophanes, frag. 642K)

θύω, θύσω, ἔθῡσα, τέθυκα, τέθυμαι, ἐτύθην
  sacrifice

κελεύω, κελεύσω, ἐκέλευσα, κεκέλευκα,
  κεκέλευσμαι, ἐκελεύσθην order, command
βῆ (interj.) baa (the cry of sheep)

29. The ephor (magistrate) Sthenelaidas identifies one Spartan asset in the coming war with Athens.

ἄλλοις μὲν γὰρ χρήματά ἐστι πολλὰ καὶ νῆες καὶ ἵπποι, ἡμῖν δὲ ξύμμαχοι ἀγαθοί.
(Thucydides, *Peloponnesian War* I.86.3)

ναῦς, νεώς, ἡ ship; νῆες = *nom. pl.*

ἵππος, ἵππου, ὁ or ἡ horse; mare

30. The historian describes Attica.

ὥσπερ δὲ ἡ γῆ, οὕτω καὶ ἡ περὶ τὴν χώρᾱν θάλαττα παμφορωτάτη ἐστίν.
(Xenophon, *Concerning Levies* 1.3.4–5)

παμφορώτατος, παμφορωτάτη, παμφορώτατον
  very productive in all things

31. How the Persian king Cambyses determines the correct course of action

. . . μέτρον δὲ αὐτῷ οὐχ ἡ ψῡχὴ ἀλλ᾽ ὁ νόμος ἐστίν. (Xenophon, *Cyropaedia* I.3.18)

μέτρον, μέτρου, τό measure; standard

32. While seeking a definition of the holy, Socrates poses a question.

ἆρα τὸ ὅσιον ὅτι ὅσιόν ἐστιν φιλεῖται ὑπὸ τῶν θεῶν ἢ ὅτι φιλεῖται ὅσιόν ἐστιν;
(Plato, *Euthyphro* 9e11–12)

ὅσιος, ὁσίᾱ, ὅσιον holy

33. Socrates speaks to Ion, a reciter of and self-proclaimed expert on Homeric poetry.

. . . παντὶ δῆλον ὅτι τέχνῃ καὶ ἐπιστήμῃ περὶ Ὁμήρου λέγειν ἀδύνατος εἶ. (Plato, *Ion* 532c6)

ἐπιστήμη, ἐπιστήμης, ἡ knowledge
Ὅμηρος, Ὁμήρου, ὁ Homer

ἀδύνατος, ἀδύνατον unable (+ infin.)

34. A Platonic definition

> Τύχη φορὰ ἐξ ἀδήλου εἰς ἄδηλον . . .   ([Plato], *Definitions* 411b11)

φορά, φορᾶς, ἡ bringing, bearing

35. Aeschines speaks to the Athenian people and defends his conduct on an embassy to Philip of Macedon.

> ἡ μὲν τύχη καὶ Φίλιππος ἦcαν τῶν ἔργων κύριοι, ἐγὼ δὲ τῆc εἰc ὑμᾶc εὐνοίαc καὶ τῶν λόγων.   (Aeschines, *Concerning the False Embassy* 118.3)

Φίλιπποc, Φιλίππου, ὁ Philip (king of Macedon)   εὔνοια, εὐνοίαc, ἡ goodwill
κύριοc, κῡρίου, ὁ lord, master

36. After a brief discussion the philosopher draws a conclusion.

> ὅτι μὲν οὖν ὕπνου κοινωνεῖ τὰ ζῷα πάντα φανερὸν ἐκ τούτων.   (Aristotle, *About Sleep and Wakefulness* 454b23)

ὕπνοc, ὕπνου, ὁ sleep   φανερόc, φανερά, φανερόν clear, obvious
κοινωνέω have a share (in), partake (of) (+ gen.)

37. The philosopher offers an opinion about courage.

> . . . δεῖ δ’ οὐ δι’ ἀνάγκην ἀνδρεῖον εἶναι,[†] ἀλλ’ ὅτι καλόν.   (Aristotle, *Nicomachean Ethics* 1116b3–4)

[†]εἶναι, *supply* ἄνδρα   ἀνδρεῖοc, ἀνδρείᾱ, ἀνδρεῖον manly; courageous

38. The philosopher remarks on a characteristic of a morally good person.

> . . . ὡc δὲ πρὸc ἑαυτὸν ἔχει ὁ cπουδαῖοc, καὶ πρὸc τὸν φίλον (ἕτεροc γὰρ αὐτὸc ὁ φίλοc ἐcτίν) . . .   (Aristotle, *Nicomachean Ethics* 1170b5–7)

ἑαυτόν, *masc. sing. acc. of reflexive pron.*, himself   ἕτεροc, ἑτέρᾱ, ἕτερον (the) other (of two);
cπουδαῖοc, cπουδαίᾱ, cπουδαῖον serious, ear-   another
nest; (morally) good

Fragments and proverbial expressions from comedies of Menander

39. Ἥλιε, σε γὰρ δεῖ προσκυνεῖν πρῶτον θεῶν,
δι' ὃν θεωρεῖν ἔςτι τοὺς ἄλλους θεούς.   (Menander, frag. 609)

ἥλιος, ἡλίου, ὁ sun
προσκυνέω fall down and worship, do reverence to

πρῶτος, πρώτη, πρῶτον first
θεωρέω look at, behold

40. ἀνὴρ δίκαιος πλοῦτον οὐκ ἔχει ποτέ.   (Menander, *Sententiae* 62)

πλοῦτος, πλούτου, ὁ wealth

41. γνώμης γὰρ ἐςθλῆς ἔργα χρηςτὰ γίγνεται.   (Menander, *Sententiae* 170)

ἐςθλός, ἐςθλή, ἐςθλόν good

42. ἔστιν Δίκης ὀφθαλμός, ὃς τὰ πάνθ' ὁρᾷ.   (Menander, *Sententiae* 225)

ὀφθαλμός, ὀφθαλμοῦ, ὁ eye

43. εὑρεῖν τὸ δίκαιον πανταχῶς οὐ ῥᾴδιον.   (Menander, *Sententiae* 257)

εὑρίςκω, εὑρήςω, ηὗρον, ηὕρηκα, ηὕρημαι,
ηὑρέθην find

πανταχῶς (adv.) in all ways, altogether

44. ἡ γλῶςςα πολλοὺς εἰς ὄλεθρον ἤγαγεν.   (Menander, *Sententiae* 289)

γλῶςςα, γλώςςης, ἡ tongue

ὄλεθρος, ὀλέθρου, ὁ destruction, ruin

45. πονηρός ἐςτι πᾶς ἀχάριςτος ἄνθρωπος.   (Menander, *Sententiae* 456)

ἀχάριςτος, ἀχάριςτον ungrateful

46. μήτηρ ἀπάντων γαῖα καὶ κοινὴ τροφός.   (Menander, *Sententiae* 511)

μήτηρ, μητρός, ἡ mother

τροφός, τροφοῦ, ἡ nurse

47. πολλῶν ὁ καιρὸς γίγνεται διδάςκαλος.   (Menander, *Sententiae* 630)

καιρός, καιροῦ, ὁ critical time; opportunity

48.   πενίᾱν φέρειν οὐ παντός, ἀλλ᾽ ἀνδρὸς σοφοῦ.   (Menander, *Sententiae* 633)

πενίᾱ, πενίᾱς, ἡ poverty   φέρω, οἴσω, ἤνεγκα/ἤνεγκον, ἐνήνοχα,
                                            ἐνήνεγμαι, ἠνέχθην bear, endure

49.   πολλοὺς ὁ πόλεμος δι᾽ ὀλίγους ἀπώλεσεν.   (Menander, *Sententiae* 670)

ἀπόλλῡμι (ἀπο- + ὄλλῡμι), ἀπολῶ, ἀπώλεσα/
   ἀπωλόμην, ἀπολώλεκα/ἀπόλωλα, ——,
   —— destroy

50.   πάντη γάρ ἐστι πάντα τε βλέπει θεός.   (Menander, *Sententiae* 688)

πάντη (adv.) everywhere   βλέπω, ——, ἔβλεψα, ——, ——, —— see,
                                      look (at)

51.   coφίᾱ γάρ ἐcτι καὶ μαθεῖν ἃ μὴ νοεῖc.   (Menander, *Sententiae* 706)

νοέω think; perceive; apprehend

52.   τύχη τέχνην ὤρθωcεν, οὐ τέχνη τύχην.   (Menander, *Sententiae* 740)

ὀρθόω, ὀρθώcω, ὤρθωcα, ——, ——, ὠρθώθην
   set straight

53.   ὑπὸ τῆc ἀνάγκηc πολλὰ γίγνεται κακά.   (Menander, *Sententiae* 786)

54. A proverb from the philosopher Bion

     οἱ ἀγαθοὶ οἰκέται ἐλεύθεροι, οἱ δὲ πονηροὶ ἐλεύθεροι δοῦλοι πολλῶν ἐπιθῡμιῶν.
                                            (Bion, frag. 11)

οἰκέτηc, οἰκέτου, ὁ house slave   ἐπιθῡμίᾱ, ἐπιθῡμίᾱc, ἡ desire

55. The biographer quotes the tyrant Periander.

     μελέτη τὸ πᾶν.   (Diogenes Laertius, *Lives of the Philosophers* I.99)

μελέτη, μελέτηc, ὁ care, attention, practice

56. The biographer records some reasoning of the Cynic philosopher Diogenes.

τῶν θεῶν ἐcτι πάντα· φίλοι δὲ οἱ cοφοὶ τοῖc θεοῖc· κοινὰ δὲ τὰ τῶν φίλων. πάντ’ ἄρα ἐcτὶ
τῶν cοφῶν.   (Diogenes Laertius, *Lives of the Philosophers* VI.37)

ἄρα (particle) (so) then, therefore

57. An epitaph

Δοῦλοc Ἐπίκτητος γενόμην, καὶ cῶμ’ ἀνάπηρος,
    καὶ πενίην Ἶρος, καὶ φίλος ἀθανάτοιc.   (*Greek Anthology* VII.676)

Ἐπίκτητος, Ἐπικτήτου, ὁ Epictetus
γενόμην (Epic) = Attic ἐγενόμην
ἀνάπηρος, ἀνάπηρον maimed, mutilated

πενίᾱ, πενίᾱc, ἡ poverty; πενίην (Epic) = Attic
    πενίᾱν
Ἶρος, Ἴρου, ὁ Irus (a name given by the suitors to
    the Ithacan beggar because he carried messages)

58. An elegiac couplet about the king of the gods

Ζεὺc κύκνος, ταῦρος, cάτυρος, χρῡcὸc δι’ ἔρωτα
    Λήδηc, Εὐρώπης, Ἀντιόπης, Δανάης.   (*Greek Anthology* IX.48)

κύκνος, κύκνου, ὁ swan
ταῦρος, ταύρου, ὁ bull
cάτυρος, cατύρου, ὁ satyr
χρῡcόc, χρῡcοῦ, ὁ gold

Λήδη, Λήδηc, ἡ Leda
Εὐρώπη, Εὐρώπης, ἡ Europa
Ἀντιόπη, Ἀντιόπης, ἡ Antiope
Δανάη, Δανάης, ἡ Danaë

59. After defeating the Titans and imprisoning them in Tartarus, the Olympians begin their
reign.

αὐτοὶ δὲ διακληροῦνται περὶ τῆc ἀρχῆc, καὶ λαγχάνει Ζεὺc μὲν τὴν ἐν οὐρανῷ
δυναcτείᾱν, Ποcειδῶν δὲ τὴν ἐν θαλάccῃ, Πλούτων δὲ τὴν ἐν Ἅιδου.
                                                                               (Pseudo-Apollodorus, *The Library* I.7.6)

διακληρόω (δια- + κληρόω) assign by lot; *middle,*
    draw lots
λαγχάνω, λήξομαι, ἔλαχον, εἴληχα, εἴλημμαι,
    ἐλήχθην obtain (by lot), get possession of

δυναcτείᾱ, δυναcτείᾱc, ἡ power, lordship,
    sovereignty
Πλούτων, Πλούτωνος, ὁ Pluto (Hades)

Proverbs from Aesop

60.   **δῶρα καὶ θεοὺς ἔπεισεν.**   (Aesop, *Proverbs* 154)

δῶρον, δώρου, τό gift

61.   **ἄνευ χαλκοῦ Φοῖβος οὐ μαντεύεται.**   (Aesop, *Proverbs* 180)

χαλκός, χαλκοῦ, ὁ bronze   μαντεύομαι, μαντεύσομαι, ἐμαντευσάμην, ——,
                                           μεμάντευμαι, —— prophesy

Longer Readings

1. Solon, frag. 15

Solon contrasts rich and poor.

> πολλοὶ γὰρ πλουτέουϲι κακοί, ἀγαθοὶ δὲ πένονται·
> ἀλλ’ ἡμεῖϲ αὐτοῖϲ οὐ διαμειψόμεθα
> τῆϲ ἀρετῆϲ τὸν πλοῦτον, ἐπεὶ τὸ μὲν ἔμπεδον αἰεί,
> χρήματα δ’ ἀνθρώπων ἄλλοτε ἄλλοϲ ἔχει.

πλουτέω be rich
πένομαι, ——, ——, ——, ——, —— be poor
διαμείβω (δια- + ἀμείβω), διαμείψω, διήμειψα,
    ——, ——, —— *active or middle,* take (something, acc.) in exchange for (something, gen.) with (someone, dat.)

πλοῦτος, πλούτου, ὁ wealth
ἐπεί (conj.) since, because
ἔμπεδος, ἔμπεδον lasting
ἄλλοτε (adv.) at another time

Solon (634?–554? B.C.E.), the greatest Athenian statesman of the sixth century B.C.E., who reformed the Athenian constitution for the benefit of the people, wrote a number of poems in elegiac couplets and other meters, substantial fragments of which survive. These include lines concerning his own reforms and moralizing exhortations toward righteousness.

2. Aeschylus, *Agamemnon* 1085–88

The captured Cassandra cries out.

> Κα.   ὤπολλον, ὤπολλον·
>   ἀγυιᾶτ’, Ἀπόλλων ἐμόc·†
>   ἆ, ποῖ ποτ’ ἤγαγέc με; πρὸc ποίᾱν cτέγην;
> Χο.   πρὸc τὴν Ἀτρειδῶν·

Κα. = Cassandra
ἀγυιάτηc, ἀγυιάτου, ὁ Aguieus (epithet for
   Apollo as guardian of roads)
†Ἀπόλλων ἐμόc, *nominative for vocative*
ἆ (interj.) ah!

ποῖοc, ποίᾱ, ποῖον (interrog. adj.)
   what sort of
cτέγη, cτέγηc, ἡ roof; house
Χο. = Chorus

The Athenian **Aeschylus** (525?–456? B.C.E.) fought against the Persians at the Battle of Marathon and wrote perhaps ninety tragedies, more than a dozen of which are known to have won prizes in the competitions honoring the god Dionysus. Seven plays by Aeschylus survive, including the *Oresteia*, three dramas that were performed in a single day's competition along with a fourth, a satyr play. Tragedy combined choral songs with the enactment of a dramatic story first by only one actor. Aeschylus added a second actor and focused his plays on the power of Zeus and divine justice. The high art of Aeschylean tragedy is especially notable for the poet's elaborate diction and sustained use of vivid and concrete imagery to convey mood and meaning.

The *Agamemnon* is the first play in the *Oresteia,* a trilogy about both the destruction of the house of Atreus and the coming of divine justice to Athens. Victorious Agamemnon returns home to Argos after the Trojan War and is greeted by his wife, Clytaemnestra, who harbors hatred for her husband because of the killing of their daughter, Iphigenia, a sacrifice demanded by Artemis before the Greek fleet could sail for Troy. In her husband's absence, Clytaemnestra has taken Aegisthus, her husband's cousin, as her lover. After a long scene between husband and wife, Clytaemnestra follows Agamemnon and his Trojan war prize Cassandra into the palace and murders them.

3. Euripides, *Heracleidae* 329–32

The Chorus of citizens of Marathon comments on Demophon's decision to harbor Iolaus and the fugitive children of Heracles.

> ἀεί ποθ᾿† ἥδε γαῖα τοῖс ἀμηχάνοιс
> cὺν τῷ δικαίῳ βούλεται† προcωφελεῖν.
> τοιγὰρ πόνουc δὴ μῡρίουc ὑπὲρ φίλων
> ἤνεγκε, καὶ νῦν τόνδ᾿ ἀγῶν᾿ ὁρῶ πέλαc.

†ἀεί ποθ᾿ from always
ἀμήχανοc, ἀμήχανον without resource, helpless
†βούλεται, *here*, has been wanting
προcωφελέω (προc- + ὠφελέω) help, be of
   assistance (to) (+ dat.)

τοιγάρ (particle) therefore, accordingly
μῡρίοc, μῡρίᾱ, μῡρίον countless, myriad
φέρω, οἴcω, ἤνεγκα/ἤνεγκον, ἐνήνοχα,
   ἐνήνεγμαι, ἠνέχθην bear, endure
πέλαc (adv.) near, close by

Euripides (480?–406 b.c.e.) produced more than ninety plays, the first of which was performed in 455, the year after Aeschylus's death, and the last posthumously in 405. In 408 he moved north to Macedonia and never returned to his native city. The nineteen plays of Euripides that survive display a wider variety of themes and innovations in form than the surviving plays of either Sophocles or Aeschylus. The plots of many of Euripides' plays do not end with a tragic action or death, but instead, often through the use of divine intervention, represent the narrow avoidance of tragic experiences. Even in the plays based on more common sources (such as the stories about the characters of the Homeric epics), Euripides often dramatized domestic aspects or favored more fantastic plots. Euripides associated with many of the philosophers and sophists who spent time in Athens—including Anaxagoras, Antiphon, Prodicus, Gorgias, and, above all, Socrates—and the thought and writings of these rational thinkers are in part responsible for the tone and themes of his plays.

The *Heracleidae* (Children of Hercules) was probably produced in 430 b.c.e. near the beginning of the Peloponnesian War. Fleeing King Eurystheus of Tiryns, Hercules' old friend Iolaus and Hercules' children are given refuge in Athens by its king, Demophon. Eurystheus, in pursuit of Hercules' children, arrives with his army and is defeated by the Athenians after Hercules' daughter Macaria is sacrificed to Persephone in accordance with an oracle. In the course of the defeat, Iolaus (magically made young) captures Eurystheus, whose life is spared in the closing scene of the play.

4. Aristophanes, *Lysistrata* 15–19

Calonice reassures Lysistrata, who frets about the arrival of women she has called to an important secret meeting.

> Λυ.   . . . εὕδουσι κοὐχ ἥκουσιν. Κα. ἀλλ᾽, ὦ φιλτάτη,
> ἥξουσι· χαλεπή τοι γυναικῶν ἔξοδος.
> ἡ μὲν γὰρ ἡμῶν περὶ τὸν ἄνδρ᾽ ἐκύπτασεν,[†]
> ἡ δ᾽ οἰκέτην ἤγειρεν,[†] ἡ δὲ παιδίον
> κατέκλινεν,[†] ἡ δ᾽ ἔλουσεν,[†] ἡ δ᾽ ἐψώμισεν.[†]

Λυ. = Lysistrata
εὕδω, εὑδήσω,——, ——, ——, —— sleep
Κα. = Calonice
φίλτατος, φιλτάτη, φίλτατον dearest
γυνή, γυναικός, ἡ woman; wife
ἔξοδος, ἐξόδου, ἡ going out, exit
κυπτάζω, ——, ἐκύπτασα, ——, ——, —— poke
   about, potter about
[†]*gnomic aorists used to describe imagined events*
οἰκέτης, οἰκέτου, ὁ house slave

ἐγείρω, ἐγερῶ, ἤγειρα, ἐγρήγορα, ἐγήγερμαι,
   ἠγέρθην awaken, rouse
παιδίον, παιδίου, τό (little) child
κατακλίνω (κατα- + κλίνω), κατακλινῶ,
   κατέκλῖνα, ——, κατακέκλιμαι, κατεκλίνην/
   κατεκλίθην make lie down, put to sleep
λούω, λούσομαι, ἔλουσα, ——, λέλουμαι, ——
   wash
ψωμίζω, ψωμιῶ, ἐψώμισα, ——, ——, —— feed
   (tidbits to)

Aristophanes (448?–385? B.C.E.) is the only writer of Attic Old Comedy whose plays have survived, and, according to tradition, was its greatest exponent. Old Comedy is characterized by outrageous plots, pointed political satire, frequent allusions to and borrowings from tragedy, and regular disruptions of the dramatic illusion by direct addresses to the audience. Aristophanes' comedies have all these characteristics and are also marked by an astonishing creative imagination, a liberal use of wordplay, and irreverent humor that shows no regard for conventional taste or behavior. In lampooning the most important men and the most conventional ideas of the day, Aristophanes exercised nearly unlimited freedom of expression, making fun not just of men but even of the gods themselves.

The *Lysistrata* was produced in 411, probably in January for the Lenaean festival. It is named from its extraordinary protagonist, Lysistrata ("dissolver of armies"), who executes her plot to compel the women of the city-states of Greece to go on sexual strike in order to persuade their husbands to stop the war between Athens and Sparta, which has engulfed the Greek world and is already, at the time of the production of the play, two decades old. In the course of a series of verbal and physical fights that make up the bulk of the play, both men and women lament the political and domestic difficulties of their lives. There are two choruses in the play, one of old men and one of old women, who eventually unite before the reconciliation that closes the play.

5. Xenophon, *Anabasis* I.3.9

The Spartan general Clearchus speaks to his Greek soldiers while pretending to go along with their plan to desert Cyrus, who hired them for an expedition.

> Ἄνδρες στρατιῶται, τὰ μὲν δὴ Κύρου δῆλον ὅτι οὕτως ἔχει πρὸς ἡμᾶς ὥσπερ τὰ ἡμέτερα πρὸς ἐκεῖνον· οὔτε γὰρ ἡμεῖς ἐκείνου ἔτι στρατιῶται, ἐπεί γε οὐ συνεπόμεθα αὐτῷ, οὔτε ἐκεῖνος ἔτι ἡμῖν μισθοδότης.

στρατιώτης, στρατιώτου, ὁ soldier
Κῦρος, Κύρου, ὁ Cyrus (younger son of the Persian king Darius)
ἔτι (adv.) still; *after a negative,* any longer
ἐπεί (conj.) since, because

συνέπομαι (συν- + ἕπομαι), συνέψομαι, συνεσπόμην, ——, ——, —— follow along with; comply with (+ dat.)
μισθοδότης, μισθοδότου, ὁ paymaster (one who pays wages)

As a young man, **Xenophon** (429–354 B.C.E.) was a follower of Socrates, but in 401, soon after the Athenian democracy was suspended and then precariously restored following Sparta's victory in the Peloponnesian War, Xenophon left the city to become a mercenary in the army of the Persian Cyrus, who was warring against his brother for rule of the Persian Empire. Although he returned to Athens for a time after Cyrus was killed, Xenophon was exiled in 399, perhaps because of his association with Socrates, and he spent some time in the service of the Spartan king Agesilaus. He and his family lived in Sparta and Corinth, but he was eventually able to return to Athens for the last years of his life. Xenophon was a prolific writer on various subjects and wrote in a plain, appealing style, often employing the dialogue form. His works include several featuring the figure of Socrates, and Xenophon is, along with Plato, an important source of information concerning Socratic thought.

After the death of their leader, Cyrus, and following the murder of most of their commanders (including Clearchus), ten thousand Greek mercenaries were led, chiefly by Xenophon, through Mesopotamia toward the Black Sea and eventually out of Persia and back to their Greek homeland. The *Anabasis* (Journey Upland) is Xenophon's vivid account in eight books of these events. He records the many hardships suffered by his men as they traveled through rough terrain, engaging in battles with hostile inhabitants, running short of food, and often sinking into despair. The *Anabasis* includes exciting battle narratives and many rousing speeches by soldiers and commanders.

6. Greek Anthology Appendix, Epigram 6

A drinking song

> ὑγιαίνειν μὲν ἄριστον ἀνδρὶ θνητῷ,
> δεύτερον δὲ φυὰν καλὸν γενέσθαι,
> τὸ δὲ τρίτον πλουτεῖν ἀδόλως,
> τέταρτον δὲ ἡβᾶν μετὰ τῶν φίλων.

ὑγιαίνω, ὑγιανῶ, ὑγίᾱνα, ——, ——, —— be
  healthy
ἄριστος, ἀρίστη, ἄριστον best
δεύτερος, δευτέρᾱ, δεύτερον second
φυή, φυῆς, ἡ stature; φυάν (Doric) = Attic φυήν

τρίτος, τρίτη, τρίτον third
πλουτέω be rich
ἀδόλως (adv.) without fraud, without deceit
τέταρτος, τετάρτη, τέταρτον fourth
ἡβάω be in the prime of youth

The **Greek Anthology** (< ἀνθολόγιον, "garland") is the name given to a wide-ranging collection of short poems whose authors lived and wrote across a number of centuries. Many poems belonging to the whole period of Greek literature (including both pagan and Christian periods) survive only in its pages; these include epigrams, ecphrases, erotic poems, drinking poems, epitaphs, oracles, and even "figure poems," in which poems are written in the shapes of various objects. The original collection on which several other later collections were based is often called the *Garland* of Meleager. It was compiled in the first century B.C.E. The most important of the later expanded collections based on Meleager's original include the *Palatine Anthology* (a work arranged in fifteen books); an important collection compiled in the tenth century C.E. by Constantine Cephalas that made use of the *Palatine Anthology;* and finally an abridged collection produced by Maximus Planudes in the fourteenth century C.E. (often called the *Planudean Anthology*). The name *Greek Anthology* today is most often applied to a work that combines the works preserved in both the Palatine and Planudean anthologies. The *Greek Anthology Appendix* is the name given to the fifteenth book of the *Palatine Anthology*.

§72. About Meter

Introduction to Quantitative Meter

Unlike English poetry, whose rhythms are the result of variously arranged stressed and unstressed syllables, Greek poetry finds its rhythms in patterns of long and short syllables, and the meters of Greek poetry are said to be **quantitative**. The quantity of each syllable in a word is either **long** ($^-$) or **short** ($^\smile$), terms (and marks) that indicate the *quantity* of time for which that syllable is to be held when the line is recited. As with whole and half notes in music, one long syllable is usually equivalent to two short syllables. When one marks the long and short syllables in lines of poetry, one is said to **scan** those lines, and both the process and product of scanning are called **scansion**.

A Greek word has as many syllables as it has vowels and diphthongs (§2, p. 10). The quantity (long or short) of each syllable is determined by the length of the vowel or diphthong in it. A syllable is *long* if it contains:

1. a long vowel or diphthong (**long by nature**)
2. a short vowel followed by two or more consonants or the double consonants ζ, ξ, or ψ, *not necessarily in the same word* (**long by position**)

A syllable is *short* if it contains a short vowel followed by one consonant or by no consonant.

OBSERVATIONS

1. Even a diphthong that counts as *short* for purposes of accent is *long* for purposes of scansion (i.e., final -αι or -οι).
2. When a syllable contains a short vowel followed by two consonants, the first of which is a mute (γ, κ, χ, β, π, φ, δ, τ, θ) and the second of which is a liquid (λ, ρ) or a nasal (μ, ν), the syllable *may be either long or short*. For example, the first syllable of ὅπλον may be *long* or *short*.[1]
3. When one scans a line of poetry, word endings are not considered for determining whether a syllable is long by position. In the phrase δοῦλος γίγνεται, for example, the last syllable of δοῦλος is *long* (omicron followed by two consonants, sigma and gamma).
4. The *last syllable* in every line of poetry *counts as long even if it is short*.

---

1. A syllable that ends in a consonant is called **closed** and is long (ὅπ/λον). A syllable that ends in a vowel is called **open** and, if it contains a short vowel, is short (ὅ/πλον).

The smallest unit of rhythm in a line of Greek poetry is called a **foot**, and various feet are identified by different combinations of long and short syllables. For example:

dactyl	− ˘ ˘
spondee	− −
iamb	˘ −

A unit of rhythm sometimes equivalent to a foot but more often made up of two feet of the same type is called a **metron** (μέτρον, "measure"). For dactyls and spondees, the foot is equivalent to the metron:

− ˘ ˘	dactylic metron
− −	spondaic metron

For iambs two feet are required for a metron:

x − ˘ −	iambic metron

OBSERVATION

In any metrical scheme "x" marks a syllable that *may* be long *or* short. Such a syllable is called **anceps** ("two-headed").

Iambic Trimeter

Each Greek metrical scheme or **meter** is composed of specific combinations of feet or metra. One important meter used often in Greek comedy and tragedy is called **iambic trimeter**. In this scheme each line contains *three* iambic metra:

$$\text{x} \; − \; ˘ \; − \; | \; \text{x} \; \| \; − \; ˘ \; \| \; − \; | \; \text{x} \overset{\frown}{} − \; ˘ \; \text{x}$$

$$1 \qquad\qquad 2 \qquad 3$$

OBSERVATIONS

1. A vertical line (|) is used to mark the divisions between feet or metra.

2. A double vertical line (‖) is used to mark a **caesura**, a word ending within a foot or metron. While there may be additional caesurae in a line of iambic trimeter verse, the word ending after the anceps in the second metron is commonly the **principal** or **main caesura**, a key pausing point when the line is recited, often coinciding with a pause in sense and sometimes marked by punctuation. Somewhat less commonly, the principal caesura falls after the short syllable in the second metron. Although two possible caesurae are included in the general scheme presented above, only *one* principal caesura is marked for each iambic trimeter line.

3. The curved link (⌢) between the anceps in the third metron and the first long in that metron is called **Porson's Bridge**. An early-nineteenth-century scholar named Richard Porson observed that the anceps in the third metron in iambic trimeter lines in tragedy is *never* a long syllable at the end of a word. The avoidance of a word's ending at a particular point in a metrical scheme is called a **bridge**.

4. The last syllable in every iambic trimeter line may be long or short (anceps), but even a short syllable was probably held for as long as a long syllable and is marked long.

5. Sometimes in iambic trimeter lines **resolution** occurs. Resolution is the replacement of a long syllable (¯) with two short syllables (˘ ˘). Because an anceps syllable may be long, it is possible that any anceps syllable may appear as a short syllable, a long syllable, or two short syllables that are equivalent to the resolution of a long syllable.

When scanning a line of Greek verse, one marks the long and short syllables with the appopriate symbols *above* the words. Divisions between feet and principal caesura(e) are marked through the line.

$$\bar{\ }\ \bar{\ }\ \breve{\ }\ \bar{\ }\ |\ \bar{\ }\ \bar{\ }\ \breve{\ }\ \bar{\ }\ \|\ \breve{\ }\ \bar{\ }\ \breve{\ }\ \bar{\ }$$
σοὶ μὲν γαμεῖ | σθαι || μόρσιμον, | γαμεῖν δ' ἐμοί.

$$\bar{\ }\ \bar{\ }\ \breve{\ }\ \breve{\ }\ \breve{\ }\ \bar{\ }\ \ \breve{\ }\ \breve{\ }\ \breve{\ }\ \bar{\ }\ \breve{\ }\ \bar{\ }\ \breve{\ }\ \bar{\ }$$
πολλοὺς ὁ πόλε | μος || δι' ὀλίγους | ἀπώλεσεν.

$$\breve{\ }\ \breve{\ }\ \bar{\ }\ \breve{\ }\ \bar{\ }\ \ \bar{\ }\ \breve{\ }\ \breve{\ }\ \bar{\ }\ \breve{\ }\ \bar{\ }\ \breve{\ }\ \bar{\ }$$
ὑπὸ τῆς ἀνάγ | κης || πολλὰ γίγ | νεται κακά

$$\bar{\ }\ \bar{\ }\ \breve{\ }\ \bar{\ }\ \bar{\ }\ \ \bar{\ }\ \breve{\ }\ \breve{\ }\ \bar{\ }\ \breve{\ }\ \bar{\ }\ \breve{\ }\ \bar{\ }$$
οὐκ ἀξιῶ | μῑκρῶν σε || μεγά | λα δ' οὐκ ἔχω.

$$\breve{\ }\ \bar{\ }\ \breve{\ }\ \bar{\ }\ \ \bar{\ }\ \ \bar{\ }\ \breve{\ }\ \breve{\ }\ \bar{\ }\ \breve{\ }\ \bar{\ }\ \breve{\ }\ \bar{\ }$$
γαμεῖν ὁ μέλ | λων || εἰς μετάνοι | αν ἔρχεται.

OBSERVATIONS

1. In each of the first three lines and in the fifth line, the principal caesura falls after the first long syllable of the second metron. In the fourth line, the principal caesura falls after the first short syllable in the second metron.

2. In the second line, two short syllables appear at the end of the first metron (πόλε-), a resolution of a long syllable. Two short syllables also appear as the second element of the second metron (δι' ὀ-), a resolution of a long syllable. Multiple resolutions in a single line of iambic trimeter verse are more common in comedy than in tragedy.

3. The third line begins with two short syllables (ὑπό), a resolution of a long syllable in the first position. In the fourth line, the second metron ends with two short syllables (μεγά-), a resolution of a long syllable.

4. In the last line, *one short* syllable has been replaced by *two short syllables* (μετά-). This form of resolution is rare in tragedy but occurs commonly in Aristophanes and other comic writers.

Elegiac Couplet and Dactylic Hexameter

An important metrical scheme used in amatory and funeral epigrams and in lyric poetry generally is called the **elegiac couplet**, which comprises two lines with slightly different schemes. Unlike iambic trimeter, the elegiac couplet employs dactyls and spondees. The first line of each couplet is called **dactylic hexameter** because it contains six feet. The second line is called **dactylic pentameter** because it contains five feet, one foot of which is split into two halves.

Dactylic Hexameter

$$- \overset{1}{\smile\smile} \mid - \| \overset{2}{\smile\smile} \mid - \| \overset{3}{\smile\smile} \mid - \| \overset{4}{\smile\smile} \mid - \overset{5}{\smile\smile} \mid \overset{6}{- -}$$

Dactylic Pentameter

$$- \overline{\smile\smile} \mid - \overline{\smile\smile} \mid - \| - \quad \smile\smile \mid - \quad \smile\smile \mid -$$

$$ 1 2 2\tfrac{1}{2} 3\tfrac{1}{2} 4\tfrac{1}{2} 5$$

Ζεὺς κύκ | νος, ταῦ | ρος, ‖ σάτυ | ρος, χρῡ | σὸς δι' ἔ | ρωτα

Λήδης, | Εὐρώ | πης, ‖ Ἀντιό | πης, Δανά | ης.

πολλοὶ | γὰρ πλου | τέουσι κα | κοί, ‖ ἀγα | θοὶ δὲ πέ | νονται·

ἀλλ' ἡ | μεῖς αὐ | τοῖς ‖ οὐ δια | μειψόμε | θα

OBSERVATIONS

1. Each of the first five feet in a dactylic hexameter line may be a dactyl ($- \smile \smile$) or a spondee ($- -$). The fifth foot, however, is rarely a spondee. The sixth foot is always treated as a spondee, even if the last syllable is short.

2. The principal caesura in a dactylic hexameter line is often where a word ends within the third foot, either after the long first syllable (called a **strong caesura**) or after the first short syllable (called a **weak caesura**). It is also possible to have balancing principal caesurae in the second and fourth feet. In the first couplet, the principal caesura in the dactylic hexameter line is strong and falls in the third foot. In the second couplet, the principal caesura in the dactylic hexameter line is strong and falls in the fourth foot even though there is no balancing caesura in the second foot.

3. The dactylic pentameter line is always indented several spaces. It is made up of two segments of two and a half feet each. Each segment is called a **hemiepes** ($- \smile \smile - \smile \smile -$). The principal caesura in the dactylic pentameter line occurs after the first hemiepes. In the first two feet of the first hemiepes, dactyls or spondees may appear, but in the second hemiepes, the feet are almost always dactyls. The last syllable in the pentameter line always counts as long, even if it is short.

4. In the first line of the second couplet, the antepenult and penult of πλουτέουσι (-εου) are pronounced and scanned as a single long syllable. The pronunciation of two successive vowels or diphthongs in separate syllables as a single, long syllable is called **synizesis** (συνίζησις, "sitting together").

The dactylic hexameter line (without alternation with the dactylic pentameter line) is the meter of epic poetry. Thus, every line of Homer's *Iliad* and *Odyssey* is a dactylic hexameter.

Μῆνιν ἄ | ειδε, θε | ά, ‖ Πη | ληιά | δεω, Ἀχι | λῆος (*Iliad* I.1)

Ἄνδρα μοι | ἔννεπε, | Μοῦσα, ‖ πο | λύτροπον, ‖‖ ὃς μάλα | πολλά (*Odyssey* i.1)

1. In the first line the principal caesura is strong and falls in the third foot. In the second line the principal caesura is weak and falls in the third foot.

2. A second prominent pause in the second line is not a caesura, but a *diaeresis*. A **diaeresis** is a pause when the end of a word and the end of a foot coincide and is marked with three vertical lines (‖|). A diaeresis at the end of the fourth foot, as in the second line, is common in epic poetry.

3. In the first line synizesis occurs at the beginning of the fifth foot: -εω is pronounced and scanned as a single long syllable.

4. In the second line the syllable μοι counts as *short* for purposes of scansion. In epic and sometimes in elegiac poetry, a long vowel or diphthong that ends a word may *count as short* when the next word begins with a vowel or diphthong. The shortening of a long vowel or diphthong at the end of a word for purposes of scansion is called **epic correption**.

Although there are many other meters in Greek poetry, the iambic trimeter, the elegiac couplet, and the dactylic hexameter are among the most common. Since scansion allows for greater appreciation of poetic readings, students are encouraged to scan any readings marked "IT" (iambic trimeter), "EC" (elegiac couplet), or "DH" (dactylic hexameter).

☞   DRILL 72 MAY NOW BE DONE.

CHAPTER 7

Vocabulary

→ νοῦς, νοῦ, ὁ mind; sense; thought
πλοῦτος, πλούτου, ὁ wealth

→ γένος, γένους, τό race, descent; family; sort, kind

→ γυνή, γυναικός, ἡ woman; wife

→ Δημοσθένης, Δημοσθένους, ὁ Demosthenes

→ δύναμις, δυνάμεως, ἡ power; ability

→ Ἑλλάς, Ἑλλάδος, ἡ Hellas, Greece

→ ἔπος, ἔπους, τό word; pl., lines (of verse), epic poetry; ὡς ἔπος εἰπεῖν, so to speak; practically

→ μήτηρ, μητρός, ἡ mother

→ πάθος, πάθους, τό experience; suffering; passion

→ πατήρ, πατρός, ὁ father

→ πόλις, πόλεως, ἡ city

→ πρᾶγμα, πράγματος, τό deed; matter, thing; pl., affairs; troubles

→ Σωκράτης, Σωκράτους, ὁ Socrates

→ ὕβρις, ὕβρεως, ἡ insolence; (wanton) violence

→ φύσις, φύσεως, ἡ nature

→ ἀποπέμπω, ἀποπέμψω, ἀπέπεμψα, ἀποπέπομφα, ἀποπέπεμμαι, ἀπεπέμφθην send away; middle, send away from oneself

→ διαλέγομαι, διαλέξομαι, ——, ——, διείλεγμαι, διελέχθην talk (with), converse (with) (+ dat.); discuss (with) (+ dat.)

→ ζηλόω, ζηλώσω, ἐζήλωσα, ἐζήλωκα, ——, —— emulate; envy; passive, be deemed fortunate

→ πάρειμι, παρέσομαι, ——, ——, ——, —— be present, be near; be ready

→ πάσχω, πείσομαι, ἔπαθον, πέπονθα, ——, —— suffer; experience

→ πράττω, πράξω, ἔπρᾱξα, πέπρᾱχα (trans.)/πέπρᾱγα (intrans.), πέπρᾱγμαι, ἐπράχθην do; bring about; practice; manage; intrans, fare

→ προσέχω, προσέξω, προσέσχον, προσέσχηκα, ——, —— hold to; turn to, apply; νοῦν/γνώμην προσέχειν, to pay attention

→ χαίρω, χαιρήσω, ——, κεχάρηκα, ——, ἐχάρην rejoice (in), enjoy

→ ἕκαστος, ἑκάστη, ἕκαστον each (of several)

→ ἀληθής, ἀληθές true, real; truthful
σαφής, σαφές clear, plain; certain, sure
ψευδής, ψευδές false

→ ὄντως (adv.) really, actually

→ οὐδέ/μηδέ (conj.) and not, nor; (adv.) not even
οὐδέποτε/μηδέποτε (conj.) and not ever, nor ever; (adv.) never

→ ποθέν (enclitic adv.) from somewhere

→ ποι (enclitic adv.) to somewhere

→ που (enclitic adv.) somewhere; I suppose
τότε (adv.) then, at that time

Vocabulary Notes

→ **νοῦς, νοῦ, ὁ** means the "mind" as the seat of the intellect but may also convey the idea of rational thought or "sense." **νοῦς** is also used of the product of mind, "thought," "purpose." In Attic prose **νοῦς** is a *contracted* second-declension noun formed from the stem **νο-** and the second-declension masculine/feminine endings. Forms of the *uncontracted* noun **νόος, νόου, ὁ** appear regularly in Homer, in most other Greek dialects, and occasionally in Attic poetry. The declension of **νοῦς** follows the rules for contraction presented with omicron-contracted verbs. *All* forms have a circumflex. Plural forms of **νοῦς** occur rarely in Attic Greek and are not included in this textbook.

		Singular
Nom.	νοῦς	(< νόος)
Gen.	νοῦ	(< νόου)
Dat.	νῷ	(< νόῳ)
Acc.	νοῦν	(< νόον)
Voc.	νοῦ	(< νόε)

When an omicron contracts with the diphthong ῳ, the diphthong absorbs the omicron (o + ῳ > ῳ). MEMORIZE THIS ADDITIONAL RULE OF ATTIC CONTRACTION.

→ **γένος, γένους, τό** means "race" or "descent" in an abstract, remote way. It may also refer to one's immediate "tribe" or "family" or to an "offspring" of a man or god. **γένος** is also used as a general word for "sort" or "kind."

→ **γυνή, γυναικός, ἡ** is an *irregular* third-declension noun that means "woman" or "wife." MEMORIZE THE FOLLOWING DECLENSION, PAYING PARTICULAR ATTENTION TO ACCENTS:

	Singular	*Plural*
Nom.	γυνή	γυναῖκες
Gen.	γυναικός	γυναικῶν
Dat.	γυναικί	γυναιξί(ν)
Acc.	γυναῖκα	γυναῖκας
Voc.	γύναι	γυναῖκες

With the exception of the vocative singular, the accentual pattern of **γυνή** is similar to the one for third-declension nouns with monosyllabic nominative singulars (cf. the declension of **φρήν** and §52, Observation 2, p. 122). The vocative singular form is the stem with the kappa dropped and has a recessive accent. The double consonant **ξ** of the dative plural form results from the combination of the kappa of the stem and the sigma of the ending: *γυναικσί(ν) > **γυναιξί(ν)**.

→ **Δημοσθένης, Δημοσθένους, ὁ**, "Demosthenes," is the name of an Athenian general who participated in several battles in the Peloponnesian War and died in 413 B.C.E. **Δημοσθένης** is also the name of one of Athens's most famous orators and statesmen in the fourth century B.C.E. This latter Demosthenes was involved in a variety of political struggles, in particular with the city's response to the increasing power of Macedon and its king, Philip II. Written versions of many of Demosthenes' speeches, political and legal, have survived, in part because even in antiquity Demosthenes' plain style and effective mode of argument served as models for later writers, both Greek and Roman.

→ **δύναμις, δυνάμεως, ἡ** is a general word for "power" or "authority" (of a man, a god, a city). Both **παρὰ δύναμιν**, "contrary to (one's) power" and **ὑπὲρ δύναμιν**, "beyond (one's) power" may be contrasted with **κατὰ δύναμιν**, "according to (one's) power."

→ Ἑλλάς, Ἑλλάδος, ἡ, "Hellas," "Greece," was originally a name applied to a small area of Greece only, but it came to be used for the whole country of Greece from the Peloponnesus to Thessaly, all the lands inhabited by Ἕλληνες.

→ ἔπος, ἔπους, τό is derived from the same root as the verb εἶπον and means "word" or "utterance"; its uses overlap with those of λόγος. Thus, ἔπος appears in contrast with ἔργον or πρᾶγμα. In the plural, ἔπη may mean "words," but it often refers to the genre or to some works of "epic poetry." The plural also means "lines (of verse)." The idiom ὡς ἔπος εἰπεῖν means "so to speak," "almost," or "practically" and qualifies an apparent exaggeration.

> οὗτός γε ὁ νόμος ἐστὶν ἅπασιν ὡς ἔπος εἰπεῖν τοῖς ἀνθρώποις.
> Practically all humans have *this* custom.

→ The third-declension nouns μήτηρ, μητρός, ἡ, "mother," and πατήρ, πατρός, ὁ, "father," have irregular declensions that are similar to but not identical with the declension of ἀνήρ (p. 149).

MEMORIZE THE FOLLOWING DECLENSION, PAYING PARTICULAR ATTENTION TO ACCENTS:

Stems				Singular	Plural
long-vowel grade:	μητηρ-		Nom.	μήτηρ	μητέρες
short-vowel grade:	μητερ-		Gen.	μητρός	μητέρων
zero grade:	μητρ-		Dat.	μητρί	μητράσι(ν)
			Acc.	μητέρα	μητέρας
			Voc.	μῆτερ	μητέρες

The long-vowel grade of the stem appears in the nominative singular *only*. The zero-grade of the stem appears in the genitive singular, dative singular, and dative plural. In the dative plural an alpha is added: cf. ἀνδράσι(ν). All other forms have the short-vowel grade of the stem.

The declension of πατήρ is identical with the declension of μήτηρ except for a difference in accent on the nominative singular (πατήρ) and vocative singular (πάτερ).

→ πάθος, πάθους, τό is a noun derived from the root of the verb πάσχω (παθ-). Its basic meaning is *that which happens* to a person or thing or *that which is experienced passively*. Thus, πάθος means "experience" in general or a particular experience that one undergoes. When the experience is a bad one, πάθος is translated "suffering" or "misfortune." When πάθος refers to an internal experience, it means "passion" or "emotion."

→ πόλις, πόλεως, ἡ means "city" in the narrow geographical sense of an urban settlement, but it also describes the community of citizens taken as a whole, bound together by law, custom, and kinship, and encompassing the surrounding territory in which its citizens live ("city-state," "state"). Thus πόλις is used of places such as Athens or Sparta or of the community of Athenians or Spartans.

→ πρᾶγμα, πράγματος, τό is a noun derived from the root of the verb πράττω (πρᾱκ-). In the singular it means a concrete "deed" or "act," but it is frequently used of any "thing," "occurrence," or "affair." When πρᾶγμα is opposed to λόγος, it conveys the sense of "(concrete) reality." In the plural, πράγματα may be translated "circumstances" or "affairs." When these circumstances or affairs are understood to be bad, πράγματα means "troubles."

→ Σωκράτης, Σωκράτους, ὁ, "Socrates," was an Athenian citizen who was charged with corrupting the youth of Athens and worshiping gods different from those of the state religion. He was tried and put to death in 399 B.C.E. at the age of seventy. Although Socrates himself did not compose any written works and did not consider himself a teacher, he spent his time conversing with his fellow Athenians about the moral life of man. His follower Plato (429–347 B.C.E.) wrote approximately thirty-six works that present the character and thought of Socrates.

→ ὕβρις, ὕβρεως, ἡ has both abstract and concrete meanings. In the singular ὕβρις is either the abstract idea of "insolence" or a concrete act of "(wanton) violence," particularly but not exclusively referring to a crime against one's person (rape, beating, etc.). Beginning with its uses in Homer, ὕβρις is often caused by excessive pride in physical strength or any other kind of power. The plural of ὕβρις may be translated "acts of violence." An Objective Genitive expressing the object of an act of ὕβρις is translated with the English preposition "against."

→ φύσις, φύσεως, ἡ is related to the verb φύω, which means "produce" or "grow." Thus, φύσις is sometimes similar to γένος in meaning "birth" or "origin." More important is the meaning "nature," referring either to the outward appearance or the inner makeup or temperament of a person or thing. This "nature" is the result of birth and growth. φύσις is also the word for "nature" as the regular order of the world. In philosophy φύσις means "nature" in the sense of an essential power or elemental substance.

Compound Verbs

Ancient Greek owes its very large and highly nuanced vocabulary in part to its capacity to form *compounds*. A **compound** is a word composed of a *root word* and one or more than one *prefix* or *suffix*. For example, the compound adjective ἀθάνατος, ἀθάνατον, "immortal," is made from a root word meaning "death" (θάνατος) and the alpha privative ("not") .

Other parts of speech (adverbs, nouns) may form compounds, but perhaps most numerous and most important are *compound verbs*. A **compound verb** is composed of a root verb and one or more than one prefix, many of which are identical with prepositions. One may compare the principal parts of the root verb πέμπω, "send," and the compound verb ἀποπέμπω, "send away."

πέμπω, πέμψω, ἔπεμψα, πέπομφα, πέπεμμαι, ἐπέμφθην
ἀποπέμπω, ἀποπέμψω, ἀπέπεμψα, ἀποπέπομφα, ἀποπέπεμμαι, ἀπεπέμφθην

When a compound verb form contains a past indicative augment, the augment appears *between* the prefix and the root verb. If a prefix (other than περι- or προ-) ends in a vowel, elision occurs, and the final vowel of the prefix is dropped before the augment. Thus, in principal parts 3 and 6 of ἀποπέμπω the prefix ἀπο- appears as ἀπ- and is immediately followed by the past indicative augment, -ε-: ἀπέπεμψα, ἀπεπέμφθην.

When an unaugmented form is required, the past indicative augment is removed and the final vowel of the prefix is restored. For example, the aorist active infinitive of ἀποπέμπω is ἀποπέμψαι, which is formed from the unaugmented first aorist stem, ἀποπεμψ-.

WHEN A COMPOUND VERB FORMED FROM A VERB ALREADY PRESENTED IN THIS BOOK APPEARS IN A READING, ITS PRINCIPAL PARTS ARE NOT SUPPLIED, BUT THE PREFIX AND THE SIMPLE VERB ARE GIVEN. Principal parts are provided for compound verbs formed from verbs not yet introduced.

Accents on Compound Verb Forms

Finite compound verb forms have recessive accents except that *the accent may not recede beyond a past indicative augment*. For example, the third person singular aorist active indicative of προσέχω, προσέξω, προσέσχον, προσέσχηκα, ——, ——, "hold to" or "turn to," "apply," is προσέσχε: the re-

cessive accent does not recede to the antepenult. Memorize this exception to the rules for
recessive accent.

The accents on all forms of the participles of compound verbs remain the same as the accents on
the participles of the uncompounded verbs.

Uncompounded Participles	*Compounded Participles*
πέμποντες	ἀποπέμποντες
ὤν	παρών
ἐχόμενον	προσεχόμενον
λεχθεῖσα	διαλεχθεῖσα

→ διαλέγομαι, διαλέξομαι, ——, ——, διείλεγμαι, διελέχθην is a compound passive-in-the-aorist deponent. It is composed of the prefix δια- ("one with another") and middle and passive forms of λέγω.
When διαλέγομαι means "converse (with)," "talk (with)," or "discuss (with)," it often takes a Dative
of Reference to indicate the person *with whom* one is talking. When διαλέγομαι means "discuss," it
also takes an Accusative, Direct Object. διαλέγομαι is also used with prepositional phrases (e.g.,
περί + genitive instead of an Accusative, Direct Object).

οὕτω τῷ δήμῳ τῶν Ἀθηναίων διελέγετο. (Dative of Reference)
In this way he was conversing with the people of the Athenians.

ταῦτα διελέχθημεν τοῖς ἄρχουσιν. (Accusative, Direct Object; Dative of Reference)
We discussed these things with the commanders.

→ ζηλόω, ζηλώσω, ἐζήλωσα, ἐζήλωκα, ——, —— is an omicron-contracted verb that does *not* exhibit
reduplication in principal part 4. It has active and passive forms only. When it means "vie with," "emulate," or "envy," ζηλόω takes an Accusative, Direct Object. The grounds for admiration or envy may
be expressed by a Genitive of Cause (§80), ἐπί + dative, or a causal clause introduced by ὅτι. In the
passive ζηλόω means "be deemed fortunate."

σὲ τοῦ βίου ζηλῶ.
I envy you for/because of your life.

αὐτοὺς ἐζήλουν ὅτι καλὰς παῖδας εἶχον.
They were envying them because they had beautiful (female) children.

→ πάρειμι, παρέσομαι, ——, ——, ——, —— is a compound verb composed of the prefix παρα- ("beside," "by") and the verb εἰμί. Unlike εἰμί, πάρειμι has no enclitic forms and has a recessive accent in
the present active indicative. In the imperfect tense the accent may not recede past the past indicative augment (e.g., παρῆτε, not *πάρητε). The third person singular future middle indicative has an
irregular acute accent on the penult: παρέσται. The present active infinitive, παρεῖναι, has a persistent accent on the penult. The accent on the present active participle (παρών, παροῦσα, παρόν) does
not recede to the prefix. Memorize these exceptions to the rules of accent. πάρειμι means
"be near" (a person) or "be present (at)" (a place, an event). When its subject is a thing (power, ships),
πάρειμι may mean "be ready" (i.e., for use). It often takes a Dative with a Compound Verb (§82), but
it also appears with prepositional phrases and may be used absolutely. When it is used as an attributive participle or as a neuter substantive, it means "present" as opposed to past or future.

| (ἐν) μάχῃ παρῆν. | I was present at (in) the battle. |
| τὰ παρόντα πράγματα λέξω. | I shall recount the present matters. |

→ πάσχω, πείσομαι, ἔπαθον, πέπονθα, ——, —— is a partial deponent. Other than in the future tense, πάσχω does not occur in the middle voice, and it does not occur in the passive voice. Its basic meaning is "suffer" (have something done to one) or, more generally, "experience." When πάσχω is used as the virtual passive of ποιέω with the meaning "be treated," it is accompanied by a Genitive of Personal Agent.

κακὰ (κακῶς) πάσχομεν ὑπ' ἐκείνων.
We are suffering bad things (badly) at the hands of those men.
We are being treated badly by those men.

→ The basic meaning of πράττω, πράξω, ἔπρᾱξα, πέπρᾱχα (trans.)/πέπρᾱγα (intrans.), πέπρᾱγμαι, ἐπρᾱχθην is "do," and it emphasizes *doing* as a *process* rather than what is accomplished by doing. In this sense, πράττω contrasts with ποιέω, which emphasizes what is *created* by doing, and it is often paired with λέγω. When used transitively πράττω means "bring about" or "accomplish" (peace, friendship, a task), "practice" (justice, excellence), or "manage," "transact," or "do" (business, the affairs of the Athenians).

τοῖς ἔργοις εἰρήνην ἐπράττετε.	You (pl.) were bringing about peace by your deeds.
ἆρα δίκαια ἢ ἄδικα πράττεις;	Are you practicing just things or unjust things?
οὗτος τὰ κοινὰ εὖ πράξει.	This man will manage public affairs well.

When πράττω is used intransitively, it is accompanied by an adverb and is translated "fare."

εὖ πράττομεν. We are faring well.

Forms made from the fourth principal part πέπρᾱχα are used transitively ("have/has done"), and forms made from the fourth principal part πέπρᾱγα are used intransitively ("have/has fared"). πράττω appears often in the active and passive voice; it occurs rarely in the middle voice. Forms using the early Attic or Ionic stem πρᾱσσ- occur frequently in Attic poetry and in the work of Thucydides. Be prepared to recognize these forms when they occur in readings.

→ προσέχω, προσέξω, προσέσχον, προσέσχηκα, ——, —— is a compound verb composed of the prefix προσ- ("toward") and the verb ἔχω. προσέχω has the basic meaning "hold (Acc., D.O.) to (Dat. with a Compound Verb [§82])." When the direct object of προσέχω is νοῦν, "mind," or γνώμην, "judgment," this idiomatic expression is translated "pay attention." προσέχω occurs rarely in the middle and passive voices.

τοῖς λόγοις αὐτοῦ προσεῖχες τὸν νοῦν/τὴν γνώμην; Were you paying attention to his words?

Sometimes προσέχω meaning "attend to" takes a Dative with a Compound Verb alone or appears with a prepositional phrase introduced by πρός.

→ χαίρω, χαιρήσω, ——, κεχάρηκα, ——, ἐχάρην has mainly active voice forms and meanings for the tenses formed from the first, second, and fourth principal parts. χαίρω is also a passive-in-the-aorist deponent and therefore has a sixth principal part but no third principal part. χαίρω often takes a Dative of Cause (§81) or a supplementary participle (§76).

πάντες οἱ Ἀθηναῖοι τῇ τῶν βαρβάρων **νίκῃ** ἔχαιρον.   (Dative of Cause)
All the Athenians were rejoicing in (because of) the victory over the foreigners.

οὐ χαιρήσεις τοὺς τοῦ ἄρχοντος λόγους **ἀκούων**.   (supplementary participle)
You will not enjoy hearing the words of the commander.

→ ἕκαστος, ἑκάστη, ἕκαστον, "each," occurs mostly in the singular and is placed before or after an article-noun phrase. When it occurs in the plural, it may be translated "all (and each individually)" or "each (and every)." When a singular form of ἕκαστος is the subject of a verb, the verb is usually singular, but it is *sometimes plural* to emphasize that a plural subject is performing a verb, but each subject is doing so individually. When used in apposition to another noun, ἕκαστος emphasizes each individual of a group.

τοὺς νόμους κατὰ τὸ ἀγαθὸν **ἑκάστη** ἡ ἀρχὴ ποιεῖ.
Each rule makes laws according to the good.

εἰς Ἀθήνᾱς ἦλθον **ἕκαστος**. (pl. verb with sing. form of ἕκαστος)
They each went to Athens.

τούτοις τοῖς ἀνδράσιν, **ἑκάστῳ** αὐτῶν, ἦσαν πολλοὶ υἱοί. (sing. form in apposition to pl.)
These men, each (and every) one of them, had many sons.

→ ἀληθής, ἀληθές is a compound adjective composed of the alpha privative ("not") and the root of the noun λήθη, λήθης, ἡ, "forgetfulness." ἀληθής means "true," "real," or "genuine," and it may be used of a variety of things, feelings, events, or personal qualities (opinions, arguments, pleasure, pain, excellence). When ἀληθής is used of people, it means "truthful." It has a regularly formed adverb, ἀληθῶς (< ἀληθέως), which is often preceded by the proclitic particle ὡς (which is not translated) in the phrase ὡς ἀληθῶς, "truly," "really."

→ The adverb ὄντως, "really," "actually," has as its stem ὀντ-, the masculine and neuter stem of the present active participle of εἰμί. To this stem the adverbial suffix -ως is added. ὄντως most often modifies verbs or adjectives and indicates their truth or actuality. It has a function opposite to that of ὡς ἔπος εἰπεῖν, "so to speak," "practically," which indicates an exaggeration.

→ οὐδέ/μηδέ may be a conjunction or an adverb. As a conjunction οὐδέ/μηδέ connects two or more clauses and means "and not" or "nor." In Attic prose οὐδέ/μηδέ occurs most often after a preceding negative.[1] In Attic poetry, however, and occasionally in prose as well, it is used with *no* preceding negative. As an adverb οὐδέ means "not even" and ordinarily emphasizes the word immediately following it.

οὐ τῆς πόλεως ἔργον ποιοῦμεν **οὐδὲ** τῶν ἀγαθῶν ἀνθρώπων. (conj.)
We are not doing a work of the city and (we are) not (doing a work) of good men.

οὐδὲ τοῦθ᾽ ἕξουσιν εἰπεῖν, ὅτι δικαίως τοῦτον τὸν ποιητὴν ἐτίμων. (adv.)
Not even this thing will they be able to say, that they were honoring this poet justly.

---

1. The usual means of joining a negative clause to a preceding positive one is καὶ οὐ/μή .

➤ Like πότε and πῶς, the interrogative adverbs πόθεν, ποῖ, and ποῦ have corresponding enclitic forms that are indefinite.

Interrogative Adverb		Indefinite Adverb	
πότε	when	ποτέ	at some time
πῶς	how	πως	somehow
πόθεν	from where	ποθέν	from somewhere
ποῖ	to where	ποι	to somewhere
ποῦ	where	που	somewhere

➤ The indefinite adverb που is a monosyllabic enclitic. In addition to the meanings "somewhere," "anywhere," που may also be translated "perhaps," "I suppose," when it limits or qualifies an assertion. It may also strengthen a negative: "surely ... (not) ...," "I (don't) suppose."

καλῶς ἐπολέμησας. οὕτω που δόξαν ἔσχες.
You made war nobly. In this way, I suppose, you got glory.

καλῶς ἐπολέμησας. οὐ γάρ πού σ' εἶχεν ὁ φόβος.
You made war nobly. For surely fear was not holding you.
                     For I don't suppose fear was holding you.

Derivatives and Cognates

	Derivatives	*Cognates*
γένος	**geno**cide, gene, **genea**logy	genus
γυνή	**gyne**cocracy, andro**gyn**ous	queen, **ban**shee
δύναμις	**dynam**ic, **dynam**ite	
Ἑλλάς	**Hell**ene	
ἔπος	**ep**ic, **epop**ee	voice, vowel, in**vo**ke
μήτηρ	**metro**polis	**matri**lineal, **mater**nal, mother, material, matter
νοῦς	**no**esis	
πάθος	sym**pathy**, **path**etic	nepenthe
πατήρ	**patri**arch, **patri**ot	**pater**nal, **patr**on, goom**bah**
πλοῦτος	**pluto**cracy	flow, fly, flee, **plu**vial
πόλις	metro**polis**, **poli**tical, police	
πράττω	**prac**tical, **prag**matic	
ὕβρις	hubris	
ψευδής	**pseud**onym	

§73. Participles 1

A **participle** is a *verbal adjective,* an adjective that is derived from a verb and retains the properties of *tense* and *voice.* In the English phrases "the galloping horse" and "the stolen letter," *galloping* is a present participle and *stolen* is a past participle. English has only two participles, but Attic Greek has many more and makes much greater use of them than English does. In Greek there are present, future, aorist, and perfect participles.

Present Active Participle

Like any adjective in Greek, a participle declines in all three genders. The present active participle has endings borrowed from third-declension nouns for its masculine and neuter forms and endings borrowed from first-declension short-alpha nouns for its feminine forms. To form the present active participle of an omega verb:

1. take the **present stem** by removing the -ω from the **first** principal part
2. add the following endings:

	M.	F.	N.
Nom./Voc.	-ων	-ουσα	-ον
Gen.	-οντος	-ουσης	-οντος

Thus, the declension of the present active participle of παύω is:

Present Stem: παυ-

	M.	F.	N.
Singular			
Nom./Voc.	παύων	παύουσα	παῦον
Gen.	παύοντος	παυούσης	παύοντος
Dat.	παύοντι	παυούσῃ	παύοντι
Acc.	παύοντα	παύουσαν	παῦον
Plural			
Nom./Voc.	παύοντες	παύουσαι	παύοντα
Gen.	παυόντων	παυουσῶν	παυόντων
Dat.	παύουσι(ν)	παυούσαις	παύουσι(ν)
Acc.	παύοντας	παυούσᾱς	παύοντα

OBSERVATIONS
_____

1. The accent on the present active participle is *persistent* and *acute on the final syllable of the present stem.* Final -αι counts as short for purposes of accent. As with first-declension *nouns,* the accent shifts to the ultima in the feminine plural genitive and is a circumflex.

2. All the endings in the declension of the present active participle in the masculine are identical with the endings of a third-declension noun such as ἄρχων, ἄρχοντος, ὁ, which is in origin the present active participle of ἄρχω, "rule" (i.e., "ruling man"). The masculine/neuter plural

dative **παύουσι(ν)**—*παύοντσι(ν) > *παύονσσι(ν) > *παύονσι(ν) > **παύουσι(ν)**—is identical with the third person plural present active indicative. Context usually makes clear which form occurs in a particular sentence.

3. All the endings in the declension of the present active participle in the feminine are identical with the endings of a short-alpha first-declension noun such as **δόξα, δόξης, ἡ.**

4. The endings in the declension of the present active participle in the neuter are identical with the endings of a third-declension noun such as **ἄρχων, ἄρχοντος, ὁ** except in the nominative/vocative and accusative singular (**-ον**) and plural (**-α**). In the neuter singular nominative/vocative and accusative, there is a circumflex on the diphthong of the present stem (**παυ-**) in accordance with the rules for the possibilities of accent.

5. A present active participle may be translated with the English participle ending in "-ing." Thus, **παύων, παύουσα, παῦον** means "stopping" (trans.).

The present active participle of **εἰμί** is identical with the *endings* for the present active participle of omega verbs (the accent is persistent on the first syllable). The present active participle of contracted verbs is formed in the same way as the present active participle of other omega verbs, but contraction occurs according to regular rules.

	M.	F.	N.	M.	F.	N.
Singular						
Nom./Voc.	ὤν	οὖσα	ὄν	ποιῶν	ποιοῦσα	ποιοῦν
Gen.	ὄντος	οὔσης	ὄντος	ποιοῦντος	ποιούσης	ποιοῦντος
Dat.	ὄντι	οὔσῃ	ὄντι	ποιοῦντι	ποιούσῃ	ποιοῦντι
Acc.	ὄντα	οὖσαν	ὄν	ποιοῦντα	ποιοῦσαν	ποιοῦν
Plural						
Nom./Voc.	ὄντες	οὖσαι	ὄντα	ποιοῦντες	ποιοῦσαι	ποιοῦντα
Gen.	ὄντων	οὐσῶν	ὄντων	ποιούντων	ποιουσῶν	ποιούντων
Dat.	οὖσι(ν)	οὔσαις	οὖσι(ν)	ποιοῦσι(ν)	ποιούσαις	ποιοῦσι(ν)
Acc.	ὄντας	οὔσᾱς	ὄντα	ποιοῦντας	ποιούσᾱς	ποιοῦντα

	M.	F.	N.	M.	F.	N.
Singular						
Nom./Voc.	νῑκῶν	νῑκῶσα	νῑκῶν	δηλῶν	δηλοῦσα	δηλοῦν
Gen.	νῑκῶντος	νῑκώσης	νῑκῶντος	δηλοῦντος	δηλούσης	δηλοῦντος
Dat.	νῑκῶντι	νῑκώσῃ	νῑκῶντι	δηλοῦντι	δηλούσῃ	δηλοῦντι
Acc.	νῑκῶντα	νῑκῶσαν	νῑκῶν	δηλοῦντα	δηλοῦσαν	δηλοῦν
Plural						
Nom./Voc.	νῑκῶντες	νῑκῶσαι	νῑκῶντα	δηλοῦντες	δηλοῦσαι	δηλοῦντα
Gen.	νῑκώντων	νῑκωσῶν	νῑκώντων	δηλούντων	δηλουσῶν	δηλούντων
Dat.	νῑκῶσι(ν)	νῑκώσαις	νῑκῶσι(ν)	δηλοῦσι(ν)	δηλούσαις	δηλοῦσι(ν)
Acc.	νῑκῶντας	νῑκώσᾱς	νῑκῶντα	δηλοῦντας	δηλούσᾱς	δηλοῦντα

OBSERVATIONS

1. The declension of the present active participle of epsilon-contracted verbs follows regular rules of contraction (ε + ω > ω; ε + ο > ου; ε + ου > ου). The accent on the present active participle is determined by where the accent would fall on an uncontracted form. For example: **ποιῶν < ποιέων; ποιοῦντος < ποιέοντος.**

2. The declension of the present active participle of alpha-contracted verbs follows regular rules of contraction (α + ω > ω; α + o > ω; α + ου > ω). The accent on the present active participle is determined by where the accent would fall on an uncontracted form. For example: **νῑκῶν** < **νῑκάων**; **νῑκῶντος** < **νῑκάοντος**.

3. The declension of the present active participle of omicron-contracted verbs follows regular rules of contraction (o + ω > ω; o + o > ου; o + ου > ου). The accent on the present active participle is determined by where the accent would fall on an uncontracted form. For example: **δηλῶν** < **δηλόων**; **δηλοῦντος** < **δηλόοντος**. As a result of contraction, the declensions of the present active participle of epsilon-contracted verbs and omicron-contracted verbs are identical.

Present Middle/Passive Participle

To form the present middle/passive participle of an omega verb:

1. take the **present stem** by removing the **-ω** from the **first** principal part
2. add the following endings:

	M.	F.	N.
Nom.	-όμενος	-ομένη	-όμενον
Gen.	-ομένου	-ομένης	-ομένου

Thus, the declension of the present middle/passive participle of **παύω** is:

Present Stem: **παυ-**

	M.	F.	N.
Singular			
Nom.	παυόμενος	παυομένη	παυόμενον
Gen.	παυομένου	παυομένης	παυομένου
Dat.	παυομένῳ	παυομένῃ	παυομένῳ
Acc.	παυόμενον	παυομένην	παυόμενον
Voc.	παυόμενε	παυομένη	παυόμενον
Plural			
Nom./Voc.	παυόμενοι	παυόμεναι	παυόμενα
Gen.	παυομένων	παυομένων	παυομένων
Dat.	παυομένοις	παυομέναις	παυομένοις
Acc.	παυομένους	παυομένᾱς	παυόμενα

OBSERVATIONS

1. The accent on the present middle/passive participle is *persistent* and *acute on the first syllable of the ending*. Final **-οι** and **-αι** count as *short* for purposes of accent. As with other first-second-declension adjectives, the accent on the feminine plural genitive of the present middle/passive participle *does not* appear as a circumflex on the ultima.

2. All the endings in the declension of the present middle/passive participle are identical with the endings used for first-second-declension adjectives such as **καλός, καλή, καλόν**.

3. The same form may function as either the present middle or the present passive participle. Thus, **παυόμενος, παυομένη, παυόμενον** may mean "stopping" (intrans.) (middle) or "being stopped" (passive).

The present middle/passive participle of contracted verbs is formed in the same way as the present middle/passive participle of other omega verbs, but contraction occurs according to regular rules.

ποιούμενος, ποιουμένη, ποιούμενον (< ποιεόμενος, ποιεομένη, ποιεόμενον)
νῑκώμενος, νῑκωμένη, νῑκώμενον (< νῑκαόμενος, νῑκαομένη, νῑκαόμενον)
δηλούμενος, δηλουμένη, δηλούμενον (< δηλοόμενος, δηλοομένη, δηλοόμενον)

☞ DRILL 73A MAY NOW BE DONE.

First Aorist Active Participle

The first aorist active participle has endings borrowed from third-declension nouns for its masculine and neuter forms and endings borrowed from first-declension short-alpha nouns for its feminine forms. To form the first aorist active participle of an omega verb:

1. take the **unaugmented aorist active and middle stem** by removing the -α and the augment from the **third** principal part
2. add the following endings:

	M.	F.	N.
Nom./Voc.	-ᾱς	-ᾶσα	-αν
Gen.	-αντος	-ᾱσης	-αντος

Thus, the declension of the first aorist active participle of **παύω** is:

Unaugmented Aorist Active/Middle Stem: **παυσ-**

	M.	F.	N.
Singular			
Nom./Voc.	παύσᾱς	παύσᾱσα	παῦσαν
Gen.	παύσαντος	παυσάσης	παύσαντος
Dat.	παύσαντι	παυσάσῃ	παύσαντι
Acc.	παύσαντα	παύσᾱσαν	παῦσαν
Plural			
Nom./Voc.	παύσαντες	παύσᾱσαι	παύσαντα
Gen.	παυσάντων	παυσᾱσῶν	παυσάντων
Dat.	παύσᾱσι(ν)	παυσάσαις	παύσᾱσι(ν)
Acc.	παύσαντας	παυσάσᾱς	παύσαντα

OBSERVATIONS

1. The accent on the first aorist active participle is *persistent* and *acute on the final syllable of the aorist stem*. Final -αι counts as *short* for purposes of accent. As with first-declension *nouns*, the accent shifts to the ultima in the feminine plural genitive and is a circumflex.

2. In the masculine and neuter the first aorist active participle has third-declension endings. When the dative plural ending -σι(ν) was added to a stem ending in -αντ, the following sound changes produced the Attic Greek dative plural ending -ᾱσι(ν):

$$*παύσαντσι(ν) > *παύσανσσι(ν) > *παύσανσι(ν) > παύσᾱσι(ν).$$

The tau assimilated to the following sigma and was then dropped. The nu before the sigma was also dropped, and the vowel before it was lengthened (-ᾱ-) because of compensatory lengthening.

3. All the endings in the declension of the first aorist active participle in the feminine are identical with the endings of short-alpha first-declension nouns such as δόξα, δόξης, ἡ.

4. An aorist active participle always has simple aspect and has no exact equivalent in English. Although it does not express the simple aspect of an aorist participle, the translation "having _____ed" may be used. Thus, παύσᾱς, παύσᾱσα, παῦσαν may be translated "having stopped."

First Aorist Middle Participle

To form the first aorist middle participle of an omega verb:

1. take the **unaugmented aorist active and middle stem** by removing the -α and the augment from the **third** principal part
2. add the following endings:

	M.	F.	N.
Nom.	-άμενος	-αμένη	-άμενον
Gen.	-αμένου	-αμένης	-αμένου

Thus, the declension of the first aorist middle participle of παύω is:

Unaugmented Aorist Active/Middle Stem: παυσ-

	M.	F.	N.
Singular			
Nom.	παυσάμενος	παυσαμένη	παυσάμενον
Gen.	παυσαμένου	παυσαμένης	παυσαμένου
Dat.	παυσαμένῳ	παυσαμένῃ	παυσαμένῳ
Acc.	παυσάμενον	παυσαμένην	παυσάμενον
Voc.	παυσάμενε	παυσαμένη	παυσάμενον
Plural			
Nom./Voc.	παυσάμενοι	παυσάμεναι	παυσάμενα
Gen.	παυσαμένων	παυσαμένων	παυσαμένων
Dat.	παυσαμένοις	παυσαμέναις	παυσαμένοις
Acc.	παυσαμένους	παυσαμένᾱς	παυσάμενα

OBSERVATIONS

1. The accent on the first aorist middle participle is *persistent on the first syllable of the ending*. Final -οι and -αι count as *short* for purposes of accent. As with other first-second-declension ad-

jectives, the accent on the feminine plural genitive form of the first aorist middle participle *does not* appear as a circumflex on the ultima.

2. All the endings in the declension of the first aorist middle participle are identical with the endings used for first-second-declension adjectives such as καλός, καλή, καλόν.

3. An aorist middle participle always has simple aspect and has no exact equivalent in English. Although it does not express the simple aspect of an aorist participle, the translation "having _____ed" may be used. Thus, παυσάμενος, παυσαμένη, παυσάμενον may be translated "having stopped" (intrans.).

Second Aorist Active Participle

To form the second aorist active participle of an omega verb:

1. take the **unaugmented aorist active and middle stem** by removing the **-ον** and the augment from the **third** principal part
2. add the following endings:

	M.	F.	N.
Nom./Voc.	-ών	-οῦσα	-όν
Gen.	-όντος	-ούσης	-όντος

Thus, the declension of the second aorist active participle of ἄγω is:

Unaugmented Aorist Active/Middle Stem: ἀγαγ-

	M.	F.	N.
Singular			
Nom./Voc.	ἀγαγών	ἀγαγοῦσα	ἀγαγόν
Gen.	ἀγαγόντος	ἀγαγούσης	ἀγαγόντος
Dat.	ἀγαγόντι	ἀγαγούσῃ	ἀγαγόντι
Acc.	ἀγαγόντα	ἀγαγοῦσαν	ἀγαγόν
Plural			
Nom./Voc.	ἀγαγόντες	ἀγαγοῦσαι	ἀγαγόντα
Gen.	ἀγαγόντων	ἀγαγουσῶν	ἀγαγόντων
Dat.	ἀγαγοῦσι(ν)	ἀγαγούσαις	ἀγαγοῦσι(ν)
Acc.	ἀγαγόντας	ἀγαγούσᾱς	ἀγαγόντα

OBSERVATIONS

1. The accent on the second aorist active participle is *persistent* and *acute on the first syllable of the ending*. Final -αι counts as short for purposes of accent. As with first-declension *nouns*, the accent shifts to the ultima in the feminine plural genitive and is a circumflex.

2. All the endings in the declension of the second aorist active participle in the masculine are identical with the endings of third-declension nouns such as ἄρχων, ἄρχοντος, ὁ. The endings in the declension of the second aorist active participle in the neuter are identical with the endings of third-declension nouns such as ἄρχων, ἄρχοντος, ὁ except in the nominative/vocative and accusative singular (-ον) and plural (-α).

3. All the endings in the declension of the second aorist active participle in the feminine are identical with the endings of short-alpha first-declension nouns such as δόξα, δόξης, ἡ.

4. The second aorist active participle of εἶπον is εἰπών, εἰποῦσα, εἰπόν because there is no un-augmented aorist active stem.

Second Aorist Middle Participle

To form the second aorist middle participle of an omega verb:

1. take the **unaugmented aorist active and middle stem** by removing the **-ον** and the augment from the **third** principal part
2. add the following endings:

	M.	F.	N.
Nom.	-όμενος	-ομένη	-όμενον
Gen.	-ομένου	-ομένης	-ομένου

Thus, the declension of the second aorist middle participle of ἄγω is:

Unaugmented Aorist Active/Middle Stem: ἀγαγ-

	M.	F.	N.
Singular			
Nom.	ἀγαγόμενος	ἀγαγομένη	ἀγαγόμενον
Gen.	ἀγαγομένου	ἀγαγομένης	ἀγαγομένου
Dat.	ἀγαγομένῳ	ἀγαγομένῃ	ἀγαγομένῳ
Acc.	ἀγαγόμενον	ἀγαγομένην	ἀγαγόμενον
Voc.	ἀγαγόμενε	ἀγαγομένη	ἀγαγόμενον
Plural			
Nom./Voc.	ἀγαγόμενοι	ἀγαγόμεναι	ἀγαγόμενα
Gen.	ἀγαγομένων	ἀγαγομένων	ἀγαγομένων
Dat.	ἀγαγομένοις	ἀγαγομέναις	ἀγαγομένοις
Acc.	ἀγαγομένους	ἀγαγομένᾱς	ἀγαγόμενα

OBSERVATIONS

1. The accent on the second aorist middle participle is *persistent on the first syllable of the ending.* Final -οι and -αι count as *short* for purposes of accent. As with other first-second-declension adjectives, the accent on the feminine plural genitive form of the second aorist middle participle *does not* appear as a circumflex on the ultima.

2. All the endings in the declension of the second aorist middle participle are identical with the endings used for first-second-declension adjectives such as καλός, καλή, καλόν.

Aorist Passive Participle

To form the aorist passive participle of an omega verb:

1. take the **unaugmented aorist passive stem** by removing the -ην and the augment from the **sixth** principal part
2. add the following endings:

	M.	F.	N.
Nom./Voc.	-είς	-εῖσα	-έν
Gen.	-έντος	-είσης	-έντος

Thus, the declension of the aorist passive participle of παύω is:

Unaugmented Aorist Passive Stem: παυθ-

	M.	F.	N.
Singular			
Nom./Voc.	παυθείς	παυθεῖσα	παυθέν
Gen.	παυθέντος	παυθείσης	παυθέντος
Dat.	παυθέντι	παυθείσῃ	παυθέντι
Acc.	παυθέντα	παυθεῖσαν	παυθέν
Plural			
Nom./Voc.	παυθέντες	παυθεῖσαι	παυθέντα
Gen.	παυθέντων	παυθεισῶν	παυθέντων
Dat.	παυθεῖσι(ν)	παυθείσαις	παυθεῖσι(ν)
Acc.	παυθέντας	παυθείσᾱς	παυθέντα

OBSERVATIONS

1. The accent on the aorist passive participle is *persistent* and *acute on the first syllable of the ending*. Final -αι counts as *short* for purposes of accent. As with first-declension *nouns*, the accent shifts to the ultima in the feminine plural genitive and is a circumflex.

2. In the masculine and neuter the aorist passive participle has third-declension endings. When the dative plural ending -σι(ν) was added to a stem ending in -εντ, the following sound changes produced the Attic Greek dative plural ending -εισι(ν):

*παυθέντσι(ν) > *παυθένσσι(ν) > *παυθένσι(ν) > παυθεῖσι(ν).

The tau assimilated to the following sigma and was then dropped. The nu before the sigma was also dropped, and the vowel before it was lengthened to produce a spurious diphthong (-ει-) because of compensatory lengthening.

3. All the endings in the declension of the aorist passive participle in the feminine are identical with the endings of short-alpha first-declension nouns such as δόξα, δόξης, ἡ.

4. An aorist passive participle always has simple aspect and has no exact equivalent in English. Although it does not express the simple aspect of an aorist participle, the translation "having been _____ed" may be used. Thus παυθείς, παυθεῖσα, παυθέν may be translated "having been stopped."

Summary of Present and Aorist Participle Endings

		M.	F.	N.
Present Active	Nom./Voc.	-ων	-ουσα	-ον
	Gen.	-οντος	-ουσης	-οντος
Present Middle/Passive	Nom.	-όμενος	-ομένη	-όμενον
	Gen.	-ομένου	-ομένης	-ομένου
First Aorist Active	Nom./Voc.	-ᾱς	-ᾱσα	-αν
	Gen.	-αντος	-ᾱσης	-αντος
First Aorist Middle	Nom.	-άμενος	-αμένη	-άμενον
	Gen.	-αμένου	-αμένης	-αμένου
Second Aorist Active	Nom./Voc.	-ών	-οῦσα	-όν
	Gen.	-όντος	-ούσης	-όντος
Second Aorist Middle	Nom.	-όμενος	-ομένη	-όμενον
	Gen.	-ομένου	-ομένης	-ομένου
Aorist Passive	Nom./Voc.	-είς	-εῖσα	-έν
	Gen.	-έντος	-είσης	-έντος

Summary of Dative Plural Endings for Present and Aorist Participles

Present Active	*-οντσι(ν) > -ουσι(ν)
1st Aorist Active	*-αντσι(ν) > -ᾱσι(ν)
2nd Aorist Active	*-όντσι(ν) > -οῦσι(ν)
Aorist Passive	*-έντσι(ν) > -εῖσι(ν)

☛ DRILL 73B MAY NOW BE DONE.

§74. Synopsis 3: Present, Imperfect, Future, and Aorist Indicative; Present, Future, and Aorist Infinitives; Present and Aorist Participles

Here is a model synopsis for ἄγω in the first person plural with participles in the masculine plural nominative. It includes the forms of the present and aorist active, middle, and passive participles.

Principal Parts: ἄγω, ἄξω, ἤγαγον, ἦχα, ἦγμαι, ἤχθην
Person and Number: **1st pl.**
Gender, Number, and Case: **Masc. Pl. Nom.**

	Active	Middle	Passive
Indicative			
Present	ἄγομεν we are leading	ἀγόμεθα we are carrying away	ἀγόμεθα we are being led
Imperfect	ἤγομεν we were leading	ἠγόμεθα we were carrying away	ἠγόμεθα we were being led
Future	ἄξομεν we shall lead	ἀξόμεθα we shall carry away	ἀχθησόμεθα we shall be led
Aorist	ἠγάγομεν we led	ἠγαγόμεθα we carried away	ἤχθημεν we were led
Infinitives			
Present	ἄγειν to be leading	ἄγεσθαι to be carrying away	ἄγεσθαι to be being led
Future	ἄξειν to be about to lead	ἄξεσθαι to be about to carry away	ἀχθήσεσθαι to be about to be led
Aorist	ἀγαγεῖν to lead (once)	ἀγαγέσθαι to carry away (once)	ἀχθῆναι to be led (once)
Participles			
Present	ἄγοντες	ἀγόμενοι	ἀγόμενοι
Aorist	ἀγαγόντες	ἀγαγόμενοι	ἀχθέντες

OBSERVATION

In a synopsis basic English translations should be given for indicative and infinitive forms.

☛ DRILL 73–74 MAY NOW BE DONE.

§75. The Attributive and Substantive Uses of the Participle

Like any adjective, a participle may describe or modify a noun. When a participle appears in the attributive position, it functions as an attributive adjective. Even without an article a participle may function as an attributive adjective. A participle with or without an article may also stand alone as a substantive. For example:

ὁ εὖ λέγων ῥήτωρ
the speaking well orator (subj.)/the orator (subj.) speaking well
the orator (subj.) who is speaking well

οἱ Λακεδαιμόνιοι οἱ τοῦτο εἰπόντες
the Spartans (subj.) having said this thing
the Spartans (subj.) who said this thing

ἐν ταῖς νήσοις ταῖς ὑπὸ τῶν Ἀθηναίων ἀρχθείσαις
on the islands (having been) ruled by the Athenians
on the islands that were ruled by the Athenians

πολίτην τοῖς νόμοις πειθόμενον
a citizen (d.o.) obeying the laws
a citizen (d.o) who is obeying the laws

(τὰ) λεγόμενα
(the) things (subj. or d.o.) being said
(the) things (subj. or d.o.) that are being said

τῷ θέλοντι
for the man being willing
for the man who is willing

τῶν τοὺς νεᾱνίᾱς πεῑσᾱσῶν
of the women having persuaded the young men
of the women who persuaded the young men

<hr/>

OBSERVATIONS

1. Each of the participles in the first three phrases is in the attributive position: λέγων is masculine singular nominative modifying ῥήτωρ; εἰπόντες is masculine plural nominative modifying Λακεδαιμόνιοι; ἀρχθείσαις is feminine plural dative modifying νήσοις. In the fourth phrase πειθόμενον is masculine singular accusative modifying πολίτην, and although it is not in the attributive position, it is the equivalent of an attributive adjective.

2. The participles in the last three phrases are used substantively, and the words "things," "man," and "women" are supplied in the English translations.

3. Since both participles and relative clauses function as adjectives, an attributive or substantive participle may be translated with a relative clause introduced by a form of the English relative pronoun, as in the second translations. The relative clause translation ("who _____ed") represents especially well the simple aspect of an aorist participle and is to be preferred to the translation "having _____ed."

The action of a present attributive or substantive participle is usually *simultaneous with* the action of the main verb in a sentence, and the action of an aorist participle is usually *prior to* the action of the main verb. For example:

οἱ νεᾱνίαι οἱ ὑπὸ τοῦ ποιητοῦ διδασκόμενοι εὖ ποιοῦσιν.
The young men *being taught* by the poet are doing well.
The young men *who are being taught* by the poet are doing well.

οἱ νεᾱνίαι οἱ ὑπὸ τοῦ ποιητοῦ *διδασκόμενοι* εὖ ἐποίουν.
The young men *being taught* by the poet were doing well.
The young men *who were being taught* by the poet were doing well.

ὁ δῆμος *τοὺς ἀδικήσαντας* τῑμᾶν οὐκ ἐθέλει.
The people are refusing to honor *the men who did wrong.*

ὁ δῆμος *τοὺς ἀδικήσαντας* τῑμᾶν οὐκ ἠθέλησεν.
The people refused to honor *the men who had done wrong.*

OBSERVATIONS

1. In the first sentence the action of the attributive participle, διδασκόμενοι, is occurring in the present *at the same time* as the action of the main verb, ποιοῦσιν.

2. In the second sentence the action of the attributive participle, διδασκόμενοι, was occurring in the past *at the same time* as the action of the main verb, ἐποίουν.

3. When an attributive or substantive participle in the present tense is translated into English with a relative clause, care must be taken to indicate the simultaneous time of the participle, as in the second translations.

4. In the third sentence the action of the substantive participle, ἀδικήσαντας, occurred in the past *prior to* the action of the main verb, ἐθέλει.

5. In the fourth sentence the action of the substantive participle, ἀδικήσαντας, occurred in the past *prior to* the action of the main verb, ἠθέλησεν.

6. When an attributive or substantive participle in the aorist tense is translated into English with a relative clause, care must be taken to indicate the prior time of the participle.

Common Substantives of Participles

Neuter participles of certain verbs form common substantives with idiomatic meanings:

τὸ ὄν	existence; reality (subj. or d.o.) ("the thing being")
τὰ ὄντα	existence; reality (subj. or d.o.) ("the things being")
τῷ ὄντι	in reality; really ("in respect to the thing being")
τὸ δέον	the necessary thing (subj. or d.o.)
τὰ δέοντα	the necessary things (subj. or d.o.)
τὸ μέλλον	the future (subj. or d.o.) ("the thing about to be")
τὰ μέλλοντα	the future (subj. or d.o.) ("the things about to be")
τὸ παρόν	the present (subj. or d.o.) ("the thing being present")
τὰ παρόντα	the present (subj. or d.o.) ("the things being present")
(πάρειμι, παρέσομαι, ——, ——, ——, —— be present, be near; be ready)	

OBSERVATION

The neuter substantives formed from the impersonal verb δεῖ do not follow the rules of Attic contraction.

The Participle as Predicate Adjective

A participle without an article is occasionally used as a predicate adjective.

δίκαιός ἐστι καὶ εὖ ἔχων οὗτος ὁ λόγος ὁ περὶ τῆς ψῡχῆς.
This speech about the soul is just and good (holding well).

☛ DRILL 75 MAY NOW BE DONE.

§76. The Supplementary Participle

Participles not in the attributive position may appear with certain verbs to extend their meanings. A participle so used is called a **Supplementary Participle**. For example:

λέγων περὶ πολέμου παύσομαι.
Speaking about war I (masc.) shall stop.
I shall stop *speaking* about war.

ἀδικεῖς τῑμᾶν τοὺς θεοὺς οὐκ ἐθέλουσα.
You (fem.) do wrong *(in) refusing* to honor the gods.

εὖ γ’ ἐποίησας πέμψᾱς μ’ εἰς Ἀθήνᾱς.
You (masc.) did well *(in) sending* me *(once)* to Athens.

τὸν Γοργίᾱν παύσω λέγοντα περὶ ἀρετῆς.
I shall stop Gorgias *(from) speaking* about virtue.

OBSERVATIONS

1. A supplementary participle agrees either with the subject of a verb used intransitively, as in the first three sentences, or with the object of a transitive verb, as in the fourth sentence.
2. Sometimes English words ("in," "from") are added to the translations of supplementary participles for clarity.
3. In addition to the verbs used in these sentences (**παύω, ἀδικέω,** and **ποιέω**), **νῑκάω** meaning "prevail (over)" and **ἄρχω** in the middle voice meaning "begin" may also take supplementary participles. Other verbs that take supplementary participles are identified in the vocabulary notes.

☛ DRILL 76 MAY NOW BE DONE.

§77. Noun Morphology: Third Declension, σ-Stems

Two groups of third-declension nouns, one of men's names and one of neuter nouns, are identified by having **-ους** as the genitive singular ending. The stems of these nouns ended in sigma, but when regular third-declension case endings were added, the sigma of the stem became intervocalic and was lost. Contractions occurred, some of which are identical with the contractions that occur in epsilon-contracted verbs.

	Σωκράτης, Σωκράτους, ὁ Socrates stem = Σωκρατεσ-		γένος, γένους, τό race, descent; family; sort, kind stem = γενεσ-		
	Singular		*Singular*	*Plural*	
Nom.	Σωκράτης		γένος	γένη	(< *γένεσα)
Gen.	Σωκράτους	(< *Σωκράτεσος)	γένους (< *γένεσος)	γενῶν	(< *γενέσων)
Dat.	Σωκράτει	(< *Σωκράτεσι)	γένει (< *γένεσι)	γένεσι(ν)	(< *γένεσσι[ν])
Acc.	Σωκράτη	(< *Σωκράτεσα)	γένος	γένη	(< *γένεσα)
Voc.	Σώκρατες		γένος	γένη	(< *γένεσα)

MEMORIZE EACH SET OF ENDINGS, PROCEEDING DOWN THE SINGULAR COLUMN AND THEN DOWN THE PLURAL COLUMN. BE PREPARED TO RECITE THE ENDINGS QUICKLY.

OBSERVATIONS

1. Proper nouns such as Σωκράτης have no plural forms. The nominative singular of nouns such as Σωκράτης is the long-vowel grade of the stem. The vocative singular is the short-vowel grade of the stem and has a *recessive* accent on the first syllable of the stem.

2. In the genitive singular of Σωκράτης, regular Attic contraction (ε + ο > ου) produced the ending -ους. In the dative singular the epsilon of the stem combined with the ending iota to produce the spurious diphthong -ει. In the accusative singular epsilon and alpha contracted regularly to produce eta (ε + α > η). MEMORIZE THIS ADDITIONAL RULE OF ATTIC CONTRACTION.

3. As with all neuter nouns, the nominative and vocative of γένος (both singular and plural) are identical with the accusative forms. The genitive singular reflects regular Attic contraction (ε + ο > ου), and the dative singular ends in a spurious diphthong (ε + ι > ει). The nominative, vocative, and accusative plural reflect regular Attic contraction (ε + α > η). In the genitive plural of γένος, regular Attic contraction (ε + ω > ω) produced the ending -ων.

4. The accent on σ-stem third-declension nouns is persistent and is given by the nominative singular. The accent on the genitive plural follows the regular rules of Attic contraction.

5. For nouns such as Σωκράτης the first-declension accusative singular ending -ην is also used in Attic Greek (by analogy with such first-declension accusative singular forms as Ἀτρείδην). For example, the accusative singular of Σωκράτης may be Σωκράτη or Σωκράτην.

§78. Noun Morphology: Third Declension, ι-Stems

One group of third-declension nouns is identified by having -ις as the nominative singular ending and -εως as the genitive singular ending. The stems of these nouns ended in -ι or -ηι (= η + consonantal ι). In Attic Greek, however, changes were made both to the stem and to the endings, and the resulting declension has several peculiarities.

πόλις, πόλεως, ἡ city				
	Singular		*Plural*	
Nom.	πόλις		πόλεις	(< πόληες)
Gen.	πόλεως	(< πόληος)	πόλεων	(< πολίων)
Dat.	πόλει	(< *πόλιϊ)	πόλεσι(ν)	(< πόλισι[ν])
Acc.	πόλιν		πόλεις	(< *πόλενς)²
Voc.	πόλι		πόλεις	(< πόληες)

MEMORIZE EACH SET OF ENDINGS, PROCEEDING DOWN THE SINGULAR COLUMN AND THEN DOWN THE PLURAL COLUMN. BE PREPARED TO RECITE THE ENDINGS QUICKLY.

OBSERVATIONS

1. In the nominative, accusative, and vocative singular, the stem of **πόλις** is **πολι-**. The ending **-ν** is used for the accusative singular, and the vocative singular is identical with the stem.

2. In the genitive singular the stem was **ποληι-**, but the iota was dropped before the third-declension ending **-ος**, and the *length* of the final two vowels was *exchanged*: **-ηο- > -εω-**. This exchange of length is called **quantitative metathesis**. Against the rules for the possibilities of accent, the accent on the resulting form (**πόλεως**) *remains* the accent on the form *prior* to quantitative metathesis (**πόληος**). MEMORIZE THIS EXCEPTION TO THE RULES FOR THE POSSIBILITIES OF ACCENT.

3. In the dative singular and in all the plural forms, the stem was **πολι-**, but original iota was replaced by an eta that was shortened to an epsilon. In the dative singular, nominative, accusative, and vocative plural, this replacement resulted in spurious diphthongs.

dat. sing.   πόλεϊ > **πόλει**
nom./voc. pl.   πόληες > πόλεες (ε + ε > ει) > **πόλεις**
acc. pl.   πόλενς > **πόλεις** (by loss of ν and compensatory lengthening)

4. The irregular accent on the genitive plural **πόλεων** is modeled on the irregular accent on the genitive *singular*. MEMORIZE THIS EXCEPTION TO THE RULES FOR THE POSSIBILITIES OF ACCENT.

☛ DRILL 77–78 MAY NOW BE DONE.

§79. Third-Declension Adjectives 1: -ης, -ες

Several groups of adjectives use endings borrowed from third-declension nouns and are called **third-declension adjectives**. Most groups of third-declension adjectives have two forms in the nominative singular, a masculine/feminine form and a neuter form. One group of third-declension adjectives is identified by the nominative singular endings **-ης, -ες**. The stem of these adjectives is the neuter nominative singular. For example: **ἀληθής, ἀληθές** (masculine/feminine singular nominative, neuter singular nominative; stem = **ἀληθεσ-**). When regular third-declen-

2. The ending **-νς** is equivalent to the ordinary accusative plural ending **-ας** because both ν and α are derived from the IE semi-consonant *ṇ.

sion endings were added, the -σ of the stem became intervocalic and was lost, and contractions occurred.

		M./F.	N.	
ἀληθής, ἀληθές true, real				
stem = ἀληθεσ-				
		M./F.	N.	
Singular				
Nom.		ἀληθής	ἀληθές	
Gen.		ἀληθοῦς	ἀληθοῦς	(< *ἀληθέσος)
Dat.		ἀληθεῖ	ἀληθεῖ	(< *ἀληθέσι)
Acc.		ἀληθῆ	ἀληθές	(< *ἀληθέσα [m./f.])
Voc.		ἀληθές	ἀληθές	
Plural				
Nom./Voc.		ἀληθεῖς	ἀληθῆ	(< *ἀληθέσες [m./f.], *ἀληθέσα [n.])
Gen.		ἀληθῶν	ἀληθῶν	(< *ἀληθέσων)
Dat.		ἀληθέσι(ν)	ἀληθέσι(ν)	(< *ἀληθέσσι[ν])
Acc.		ἀληθεῖς	ἀληθῆ	(< *ἀληθέσα [n.])

MEMORIZE EACH SET OF ENDINGS, PROCEEDING DOWN THE SINGULAR COLUMN AND THEN DOWN THE PLURAL COLUMN. BE PREPARED TO RECITE THE ENDINGS QUICKLY.

OBSERVATIONS

1. The masculine/feminine singular nominative of adjectives such as ἀληθής is the long-vowel grade of the stem. The masculine/feminine and neuter singular vocatives are identical with the stem.

2. In the genitive singular, regular Attic contraction (ε + ο > ου) produced the ending -ους. In the dative singular the epsilon of the stem combined with the ending iota to produce the spurious diphthong -ει. In the masculine/feminine singular accusative, regular Attic contraction (ε + α > η) produced the ending -η.

3. In the masculine/feminine plural nominative and vocative, regular Attic contraction (ε + ε > ει) produced the ending -εις. In the neuter plural nominative, vocative, and accusative, regular Attic contraction (ε + α > η) produced the ending -η. In the genitive plural, regular Attic contraction (ε + ω > ω) produced the ending -ων.

The masculine/feminine plural accusative (ἀληθεῖς) is borrowed from the masculine/feminine plural nominative. This form replaces the expected *ἀληθῆς (< *ἀληθέας).

4. The accent on third-declension adjectives is persistent and is given by the neuter singular nominative form. The accents throughout the declension follow the rules of Attic contraction.

Adverbs

Adverbs are formed from third-declension adjectives in the same way as they are formed from first-second-declension adjectives. The ending -ως is added to the stem of the adjective. For a third-declension adjective identified by the nominative singular endings -ης, -ες, the accent is determined by the accent given in the neuter singular nominative form. The rules for the possibilities of accent are observed. For example:

Adjective	*Stem*	*Adverb*
ἀληθής, ἀληθές	ἀληθέσ-	ἀληθῶς (<*ἀληθέσως) truly, really

☛ DRILL 79 MAY NOW BE DONE.

§80. Genitive of Cause

A noun in the genitive case with no preposition may express the cause for the action of a verb. A genitive so used is called a **Genitive of Cause**. For example:

> τῶν ὑμετέρων ἔργων χάριν ἔχομεν πάντες.
> We all have gratitude *for/because of* your (pl.) *deeds*.
>
> αὐτὴν ζηλοῖ τῆς καλῆς δόξης.
> He envies her *for/because of* her fine *reputation*.
> (ζηλόω, ζηλώσω, ἐζήλωσα, ἐζήλωκα, ——, —— emulate; envy)

The syntax of each italicized word (ἔργων, δόξης) is **Genitive of Cause**.

OBSERVATIONS

1. The Genitive of Cause is an extension of the source and separation function ("from") of the genitive case.
2. Certain prepositional phrases may express ideas equivalent to the Genitive of Cause (e.g., διὰ τὰ ὑμέτερα ἔργα, ἐπὶ τῇ καλῇ δόξῃ).

§81. Dative of Cause

A noun in the dative case with no preposition may express the cause for the action of a verb. A dative so used is called a **Dative of Cause**. For example:

> ἀπ' Ἀθηνῶν φόβῳ ἤλθομεν.
> *Because of fear* we went away from Athens.
>
> λέγω ὡς ὕβρει καὶ οὐκ ἀνάγκῃ ἐπολεμήσατε.
> I say that *because of insolence* and not *because of necessity* you (pl.) made war.
> (ὕβρις, ὕβρεως, ἡ insolence)

The syntax of each italicized word (φόβῳ, ὕβρει, ἀνάγκῃ) is **Dative of Cause**.

OBSERVATIONS

1. The Dative of Cause is an extension of the Dative of Means.

2. Certain prepositional phrases may express ideas equivalent to the Dative of Cause (e.g., ἐκ φόβου, δι᾽ ὕβριν).

§82. Dative with a Compound Verb

Many compound verbs appear with a dative that is connected in sense with the meaning of their prefixes. Such a dative is called a **Dative with a Compound Verb.** For example:

αὐτῷ παρῆν.   I was near *him.*
(πάρειμι, παρέσομαι, ——, ——, ——, —— be present, be near; be ready)

τῷ πολέμῳ προσείχομεν τὴν γνώμην.   We were paying attention *to the war.*
(προσέχω, προσέξω, προσέσχον, προσέσχηκα, ——, —— hold to; turn to, apply; γνώμην προσέχειν to pay attention)

The syntax of each italicized word (αὐτῷ, πολέμῳ) is **Dative with a Compound Verb.**

OBSERVATIONS

1. When a prefix is compounded with a transitive verb, the resulting compound verb may take both an Accusative, Direct Object and a Dative with a Compound Verb, as in the second sentence.

2. A Dative with a Compound Verb replaces a prepositional phrase that has an equivalent meaning. For example, the idea expressed by the dative τῷ πολέμῳ in the second sentence might also be conveyed by πρὸς τὸν πόλεμον. Many compound verbs that take a Dative with a Compound Verb are also found with corresponding prepositional phrases.

3. When prefixes related to the following prepositions are used to form compound verbs, the resulting compound verbs *may* take a Dative with a Compound Verb:

ἐν	περί
ἐπί	πρός
σύν	ὑπό
παρά	

☛ DRILL 80–82 MAY NOW BE DONE.

Short Readings

1. An iambic fragment attributed to the poet Archilochus

> ὦ Ζεῦ, πάτερ Ζεῦ, σὸν μὲν οὐρανοῦ κράτος,
>   σὺ δ' ἔργ' ἐπ'† ἀνθρώπων ὁρᾷς†
> λεωργὰ καὶ θεμιστά, σοὶ δὲ θηρίων
>   ὕβρις τε καὶ δίκη μέλει.

(Archilochus, frag. 177)

κράτος, κράτους, τό might, power; rule
†ἐφοράω (ἐπι- + ὁράω) oversee; ἐπ'... ὁρᾷς =
     ἐφορᾷς
λεωργός, λεωργόν audacious; villainous

θεμιστός, θεμιστή, θεμιστόν lawful
θηρίον, θηρίου, τό wild animal, beast
μέλω, μελήσω, ἐμέλησα, μεμέληκα, ——, ——
     be an object of care

2. A fragment from an elegy of the Athenian lawgiver Solon

> πάντῃ δ' ἀθανάτων† ἀφανὴς νόος ἀνθρώποισιν.

(Solon, frag. 17)
DH

πάντῃ (adv.) in every way
†*The first alpha of* ἀθανάτων *here scans long.*

ἀφανής, ἀφανές unclear, not obvious; hidden

3. A line from the poetry of Theognis

> ἐλπὶς ἐν ἀνθρώποις μούνη θεὸς ἐσθλὴ ἔνεστιν.

(Theognis, *Elegies* I.1135)
DH

μούνη (Ionic) = Attic μόνη
ἐσθλός, ἐσθλή, ἐσθλόν good

ἔνειμι (ἐν- + εἰμί) be in

4. A couplet from the poetry of Theognis

> ἐχθρὸν μὲν χαλεπὸν καὶ δυσμενεῖ ἐξαπατῆσαι,
>   Κύρνε, φίλον δὲ φίλῳ ῥάδιον ἐξαπατᾶν.

(Theognis, *Elegies* I.1219–20)
EC

δυσμενής, δυσμενές hostile
ἐξαπατάω (ἐξ- + ἀπατάω) deceive

Κύρνος, Κύρνου, ὁ Cyrnus (one of the
     addressees of the poem)

5. A fragment from a play of the early comic poet Epicharmus

> νοῦς ὁρῇ καὶ νοῦς ἀκούει· τἆλλα κωφὰ καὶ τυφλά.

(Epicharmus, frag. 214)

ὁρῇ (Ionic) = Attic ὁρᾷ
κωφός, κωφή, κωφόν deaf

τυφλός, τυφλή, τυφλόν blind

6. A fragment from a poem by the lyric poet Simonides

ἀνάγκᾳ
δ' οὐδὲ θεοὶ μάχονται.

(Simonides, frag. 37.29–30)

ἀνάγκᾳ (Doric) = Attic ἀνάγκη

μάχομαι, μαχοῦμαι, ἐμαχεσάμην, ——,
μεμάχημαι, —— fight against (+ dat.)

Fragments from the works of the philosopher Heraclitus

7.   αἰὼν παῖς ἐστι παίζων, πεσσεύων· παιδὸς ἡ βασιληίη.   (Heraclitus, frag. 52)

αἰών, αἰῶνος, ὁ time; life
παίζω, παίξω, ἔπαισα/ἔπαιξα, πέπαικα,
  πέπαισμαι, —— play

πεσσεύω, ——, ——, ——, ——, —— play at
  draughts (a game similar to checkers)
βασιλείᾱ, βασιλείᾱς, ἡ kingship; dominion;
  βασιληίη (Ionic) = Attic βασιλείᾱ

8.   ἦθος ἀνθρώπῳ δαίμων.   (Heraclitus, frag. 119)

ἦθος, ἤθους, τό custom, habit; character

9.   φύσις κρύπτεσθαι φιλεῖ.   (Heraclitus, frag. 123)

κρύπτω, κρύψω, ἔκρυψα, ——, κέκρυμμαι,
  ἐκρύφθην hide, conceal; *middle,* conceal oneself

10. After killing his mother, Orestes expresses sorrow.

ἀλγῶ μὲν ἔργα καὶ πάθος γένος τε πᾶν,
ἄζηλα νίκης τῆσδ' ἔχων† μιάσματα.

(Aeschylus, *Libation Bearers* 1016–17)
IT

ἀλγέω suffer; grieve (for)
ἄζηλος, ἄζηλον unenvied, unenviable
†ἔχων because I have

μίασμα, μιάσματος, τό defilement, stain, taint of
  guilt

Fragments from tragedies of Aeschylus

11.   τό τοι κακὸν ποδῶκες ἔρχεται βροτοῖς
     καὶ τἀμπλάκημα τῷ περῶντι τὴν θέμιν.   (Aeschylus, frag. 22)
IT

ποδώκης, ποδῶκες swift of foot, swift-footed
ἀμπλάκημα, ἀμπλακήματος, τό error, fault

περάω pass through, go beyond
θέμις, θέμιτος, ἡ (customary) law; right

12.   ἁπλᾶ γάρ ἐστι τῆς ἀληθείᾱς ἔπη.   (Aeschylus, frag. 176)
                                                                                    IT

ἁπλοῦς, ἁπλῆ, ἁπλοῦν simple; ἁπλᾶ = *neut. pl. nom.*

13. A line from the *Penelope*, in which Odysseus lies to his wife

       ἐγὼ γένος μέν εἰμι Κρὴς ἀρχέστατον.   (Aeschylus, frag. 187)
                                                                                    IT

Κρής, Κρητός, ὁ Cretan   ἀρχέστατος, ἀρχεστάτη, ἀρχέστατον most
                                                 ancient

14.   πολλοῖς γάρ ἐστι κέρδος ἡ σῑγὴ βροτῶν.   (Aeschylus, frag. 188)
                                                                                    IT

κέρδος, κέρδους, τό profit, gain   σῑγή, σῑγῆς, ἡ silence

15.   τῷ πονοῦντι δ᾽ ἐκ θεῶν
          ὀφείλεται τέκνωμα τοῦ πόνου κλέος.   (Aeschylus, frag. 315)
                                                                                    IT

πονέω work hard, toil   τέκνωμα, τεκνώματος, τό offspring, child
ὀφείλω, ὀφειλήσω, ὠφείλησα, ὠφείληκα, ——,   κλέος, κλέους, τό fame, glory
—— owe

16.   κάτοπτρον εἴδους χαλκός ἐστ᾽, οἶνος δὲ νοῦ.   (Aeschylus, frag. 393)
                                                                                    IT

κάτοπτρον, κατόπτρου, τό mirror   χαλκός, χαλκοῦ, ὁ bronze
εἶδος, εἴδους, τό form, appearance   οἶνος, οἴνου, ὁ wine

17.   οὐκ ἀνδρὸς ὅρκοι πίστις, ἀλλ᾽ ὅρκων ἀνήρ.   (Aeschylus, frag. 394)
                                                                                    IT

ὅρκος, ὅρκου, ὁ oath   πίστις, πίστεως, ἡ that which gives confidence;
                                                 guarantee; proof

18. φιλεῖ δὲ τῷ κάμνοντι συσπεύδειν θεός. (Aeschylus, frag. 395)
IT

κάμνω, καμοῦμαι, ἔκαμον, κέκμηκα, ——, —— σῠσπεύδω (συν- + σπεύδω), ——, ——, ——,
toil, labor, work hard ——, —— assist eagerly

19. κακοὶ γὰρ εὖ πράσσοντες οὐκ ἀνασχετοί. (Aeschylus, frag. 398)
IT

ἀνασχετός, ἀνασχετόν endurable

20. Electra explains why she attacks her mother, Clytaemnestra, so outspokenly.

αἰσχροῖς γὰρ αἰσχρὰ πράγματ' ἐκδιδάσκεται. (Sophocles, *Electra* 621)
IT

ἐκδιδάσκω (ἐκ- + διδάσκω) teach thoroughly

21. An angry Oedipus insults the seer Teiresias.

... τυφλὸς τά τ' ὦτα τόν τε νοῦν τά τ' ὄμματ' εἶ. (Sophocles, *Oedipus Tyrannus* 371)
IT

τυφλός, τυφλή, τυφλόν blind ὄμμα, ὄμματος, τό eye
οὖς, ὠτός, τό ear

Fragments from tragedies of Sophocles

22. καὶ γὰρ δικαίᾱ γλῶσσ' ἔχει κράτος μέγα. (Sophocles, frag. 80)
IT

γλῶσσα, γλώσσης, ἡ tongue κράτος, κράτους, τό strength, power

23. ἀρετῆς βέβαιαι δ' εἰσὶν αἱ κτήσεις μόναι. (Sophocles, frag. 201d)
IT

βέβαιος, βεβαίᾱ, βέβαιον sure, certain; steadfast κτῆσις, κτήσεως, ἡ acquisition; possession

24. οὐκ ἔστι τοῖς μὴ δρῶσι σύμμαχος τύχη. (Sophocles, frag. 407)
IT

δράω, δράσω, ἔδρᾱσα, δέδρᾱκα, δέδρᾱμαι,
ἐδράσθην do, act

25. Addressed to Odysseus

> ὦ πάντα πράσσων, ὡς† ὁ Σίσυφος πολὺς
> ἔνδηλος ἐν σοὶ πάντα χὠ μητρὸς πατήρ.† (Sophocles, frag. 567)
> IT

†ὡς, here (exclam. adv.) how
Σίσυφος, Σισύφου, ὁ Sisyphus (a notorious trickster)

ἔνδηλος, ἔνδηλον manifest, clear
†πατήρ, refers to Autolycus (Odysseus's maternal grandfather and a notorious trickster)

26. φιλάργυρον μὲν πᾶν τὸ βάρβαρον γένος. (Sophocles, frag. 587)
IT

φιλάργυρος, φιλάργυρον silver-loving, money-loving

27. ὅρκους ἐγὼ γυναικὸς εἰς ὕδωρ γράφω. (Sophocles, frag. 811)
IT

ὅρκος, ὅρκου, ὁ oath
ὕδωρ, ὕδατος, τό water

γράφω, γράψω, ἔγραψα, γέγραφα, γέγραμμαι, ἐγράφην write

28. οὐκ ἐξάγουσι καρπὸν οἱ ψευδεῖς λόγοι. (Sophocles, frag. 834)
IT

ἐξάγω (ἐκ- + ἄγω) lead out, bring forth
καρπός, καρποῦ, ὁ fruit

29. οὐκ ἔστ' ἀπ' ἔργων μὴ καλῶν ἔπη καλά. (Sophocles, frag. 839)
IT

30. Α. ἐσθλοῦ γὰρ ἀνδρὸς τοὺς πονοῦντας ὠφελεῖν.
    Β. ἀλλ' ἡ φρόνησις ἀγαθὴ θεὸς μέγας. (Sophocles, frag. 922)
IT

ἐσθλός, ἐσθλή, ἐσθλόν good
πονέω work hard, toil; suffer
ὠφελέω help, aid

φρόνησις, φρονήσεως, ἡ intelligence, understanding

31. πολλῶν πόνων δεῖ τῷ καλῶς τῑμωμένῳ·
     μῑκροῦ δ᾽ ἀγῶνος οὐ μέγ᾽ ἔρχεται κλέος.   (Sophocles, frag. 938)

IT

μῑκρός, μῑκρά, μῑκρόν small   κλέος, κλέους, τό fame; glory

32. ἐλπὶς γὰρ ἡ βόσκουσα τοὺς πολλοὺς βροτῶν.   (Sophocles, frag. 948)

IT

βόσκω, βοσκήσω, ——, ——, ——, ἐβοσκήθην feed,
    nourish

33. The sophist Protagoras's doctrine of relative truth

   πάντων χρημάτων μέτρον ἄνθρωπος, τῶν μὲν ὄντων, ὡς ἔστιν, τῶν δὲ οὐκ ὄντων, ὡς οὐκ
   ἔστιν.   (Protagoras, frag. 1)

μέτρον, μέτρου, τό measure; standard

34. The seer Teiresias explains to Cadmus why he predicts Pentheus's downfall.

                μαντικῇ μὲν οὐ λέγω,
     τοῖς πράγμασιν δέ· μῶρα γὰρ μῶρος λέγει.   (Euripides, *Bacchae* 368–69)

IT

μαντική, μαντικῆς, ἡ (art of) prophecy   μῶρος, μώρᾱ, μῶρον dull; stupid, foolish

35. The Chorus sings of Bacchus.

     ὁ δαίμων ὁ Διὸς παῖς
     χαίρει μὲν θαλίαισιν,
     φιλεῖ δ᾽ ὀλβοδότειραν Εἰ-
     ρήνᾱν, κουροτρόφον θεάν.   (Euripides, Bacchae 417–20)

θαλίᾱ, θαλίᾱς, ἡ abundance; *pl.*, festivities, feasts   κουροτρόφος, κουροτρόφον rearing boys
ὀλβοδότειρα, ὀλβοδοτείρᾱς, ἡ wealth-giver   θεά, θεᾶς, ἡ goddess
Εἰρήνᾱν (Doric) = Attic Εἰρήνην

36. Dionysus speaks ambiguously to King Pentheus, who, dressed as a woman, is about to die.

     δεινὸς σὺ δεινὸς κἀπὶ δείν᾽ ἔρχῃ πάθη.   (Euripides, *Bacchae* 971)

IT

37. Aphrodite makes an admission.

> ἔνεστι γὰρ δὴ κἀν θεῶν γένει τόδε·
> τῑμώμενοι χαίρουσιν ἀνθρώπων ὕπο.
> (Euripides, *Hippolytus* 7–8)
> IT

ἔνειμι (ἐν- + εἰμί) be in

38. After Iphigenia agrees to be sacrificed to allow the Greeks to sail for Troy, Achilles praises her nobility.

> ζηλῶ δὲ σοῦ μὲν Ἑλλάδ', Ἑλλάδος δὲ σέ.
> εὖ γὰρ τόδ' εἶπας ἀξίως τε πατρίδος.
> (Euripides, *Iphigenia at Aulis*, 1406–7)
> IT

ἀξίως (adv.) worthily; in a manner worthy (+ gen.)   πατρίς, πατρίδος, ἡ homeland

39. An enslaved Andromache addresses her dead husband, Hector.

> σὲ δ', ὦ φίλ' Ἕκτορ, εἶχον ἄνδρ' ἀρκοῦντά μοι
> ξυνέσει γένει πλούτῳ τε κἀνδρείᾳ μέγαν·
> (Euripides, *Trojan Women* 673–74)
> IT

ἀρκέω be sufficient   ἀνδρείᾱ, ἀνδρείᾱς, ἡ manliness; courage
ξύνεσις, ξυνέσεως, ἡ intelligence; sagacity

Fragments from tragedies of Euripides

40. ἄδικον ὁ πλοῦτος, πολλὰ δ' οὐκ ὀρθῶς ποεῖ.   (Euripides, frag. 55N)
     IT

41. φεῦ φεῦ, τὰ μεγάλα μεγάλα καὶ πάσχει κακά.   (Euripides, frag. 80N)
     IT

φεῦ (interj.) alas! oh!

42. πρὸς τὴν ἀνάγκην πάντα τἄλλ' ἐστ' ἀσθενῆ.   (Euripides, frag. 299N)
     IT

ἀσθενής, ἀσθενές weak

43. πόνος γάρ, ὡς λέγουσιν, εὐκλείας πατήρ.   (Euripides, frag. 474N)
                                                                                      IT

εὔκλεια, εὐκλείας, ἡ good repute, glory

44. μεγάλη τυραννὶς ἀνδρὶ τέκνα καὶ γυνή.   (Euripides, frag. 543N)
                                                                                      IT

τυραννίς, τυραννίδος, ἡ monarchy; tyranny

45. καὶ τῶν παλαιῶν πόλλ' ἔπη καλῶς ἔχει·
      λόγοι γὰρ ἐσθλοὶ φάρμακον φόβου βροτοῖς.   (Euripides, frag. 1065N)
                                                                                      IT

παλαιός, παλαιά, παλαιόν old, ancient   ἐσθλός, ἐσθλή, ἐσθλόν good
                                                   φάρμακον, φαρμάκου, τό drug; remedy

46. In a speech to his men the general Nicias promises the survival of Athens and her citizens.

      ἄνδρες γὰρ πόλις, καὶ οὐ τείχη οὐδὲ νῆες ἀνδρῶν κεναί.
                                            (Thucydides, *Peloponnesian War* VII.77.7)

τεῖχος, τείχους, τό (city) wall   κενός, κενή, κενόν empty
ναῦς, νεώς, ἡ ship; νῆες = *nom. pl.*

47. A fragment from the works of Isocrates

      τῷ γὰρ πάθει τοῦ σώματος καὶ τὸ νοερὸν τῆς ψῡχῆς συνομολογεῖν ἀνέχεται.
                                                          (Isocrates, frag. 32)

νοερός, νοερά, νοερόν intellectual   ἀνέχω (ἀνα- + ἔχω) hold up; *middle,* endure
συνομολογέω (συν- + ὁμολογέω) agree (with),
    concede (to)

48. The historian reports a rhetorical question asked by Socrates in a discussion about the existence of the gods.

      οὐ γὰρ πάνυ σοι κατάδηλον ὅτι παρὰ τἆλλα ζῷα ὥσπερ θεοὶ ἄνθρωποι βιοτεύουσι;
                                                (Xenophon, *Memorabilia* I.4.14)

πάνυ (adv.) altogether, (very) much, exceedingly   βιοτεύω, βιοτεύσω, ——, ——, ——, —— live
κατάδηλος, κατάδηλον very clear

49. Part of an argument developed by Socrates about the nature of the like and the unlike

ἀδικοῦντας δὲ καὶ ἀδικουμένους ἀδύνατόν που φίλους εἶναι.   (Plato, *Lysis* 214c2–3)

ἀδύνατος, ἀδύνατον impossible

50. Socrates denies a commonly held opinion.

. . . οὐκ ἐπ᾽ ὠφελίᾳ ὁ ἔρως τῷ ἐρῶντι καὶ τῷ ἐρωμένῳ
ἐκ θεῶν ἐπιπέμπεται . . .   (Plato, *Phaedrus* 245b5–6)

ὠφελίᾱ, ὠφελίᾱς, ἡ benefit, advantage   ἐράω love, desire
                                               ἐπιπέμπω (ἐπι- + πέμπω) send upon or to

51. The sophist Protagoras explains his assertion that boldness and courage are not the same.

θάρσος μὲν γὰρ καὶ ἀπὸ τέχνης γίγνεται ἀνθρώποις καὶ ἀπὸ θῡμοῦ γε καὶ ἀπὸ μανίᾱς,
ὥσπερ ἡ δύναμις, ἀνδρείᾱ δὲ ἀπὸ φύσεως καὶ εὐτροφίᾱς τῶν ψῡχῶν γίγνεται.

                                                                       (Plato, *Protagoras* 351a7–b2)

θάρσος, θάρσους, τό boldness   ἀνδρείᾱ, ἀνδρείᾱς, ἡ manliness; courage
θῡμός, θῡμοῦ, ὁ spirit, heart; passion, anger   εὐτροφίᾱ, εὐτροφίᾱς, ἡ good nurture
μανίᾱ, μανίᾱς, ἡ madness

52. Socrates suggests the fate of virtue in an oligarchy, in which men value money above all things.

ἀσκεῖται δὴ τὸ ἀεὶ τῑμώμενον, ἀμελεῖται δὲ τὸ ἀτῑμαζόμενον.   (Plato, *Republic* 551a4)

ἀσκέω exercise, practice; cultivate   ἀτῑμάζω, ἀτῑμάσω, ἠτίμασα, ἠτίμακα, ἠτίμασμαι,
ἀμελέω have no care for; overlook   ἠτῑμάσθην hold in no honor

Some Platonic definitions

53.   Θεὸς ζῷον ἀθάνατον, αὔταρκες πρὸς εὐδαιμονίᾱν· οὐσίᾱ ἀίδιος,
      τῆς τἀγαθοῦ φύσεως αἰτίᾱ.   ([Plato], *Definitions* 411a4)

αὐτάρκης, αὔταρκες sufficient in oneself, self-   οὐσίᾱ, οὐσίᾱς, ἡ substance; (stable) being
   sufficient   ἀίδιος, ἀίδιον everlasting
εὐδαιμονίᾱ, εὐδαιμονίᾱς, ἡ happiness

54.   Ἀφοβίᾱ ἕξις καθ᾽ ἣν ἀνέμπτωτοί ἐσμεν εἰς φόβους.   ([Plato], *Definitions* 413a4)

ἀφοβίᾱ, ἀφοβίᾱς, ἡ fearlessness   ἀνέμπτωτος, ἀνέμπτωτον not falling into, not
ἕξις, ἕξεως, ἡ state, condition   susceptible

55. Ἀπάθεια ἕξις καθ' ἣν ἀνέμπτωτοί ἐσμεν εἰς πάθη.   ([Plato], *Definitions* 413a5)

ἀπάθεια, ἀπαθείας, ἡ insensibility; apathy; free-   ἀνέμπτωτος, ἀνέμπτωτον not falling into, not
dom from emotion   susceptible
ἕξις, ἕξεως, ἡ state, condition

56. Φόβος ἔκπληξις ψυχῆς ἐπὶ κακοῦ προσδοκίᾳ.   ([Plato], *Definitions* 415e5)

ἔκπληξις, ἐκπλήξεως, ἡ panic, consternation
προσδοκίᾱ, προσδοκίᾱς, ἡ anticipation, expectation

Fragments from comedies of Philemon

57. ἐχθροὺς ποιοῦσι τοὺς φίλους αἱ συγκρίσεις.   (Philemon, frag. 22)
                                                                                                IT

σύγκρισις, συγκρίσεως, ἡ comparison

58. γαμεῖν ὁ μέλλων εἰς μετάνοιαν ἔρχεται.   (Philemon, frag. 167)
                                                                                                IT

γαμέω marry (of a man)   μετάνοια, μετανοίᾱς, ἡ change of mind; regret

Fragments and proverbial expressions from comedies of Menander

59. πλοῦτος δὲ πολλῶν ἐπικάλυμμ' ἐστὶν κακῶν.   (Menander, frag. 90)
                                                                                                IT

ἐπικάλυμμα, ἐπικαλύμματος, τό veil, covering

60.   ... καὶ φύσει
        πως εὐαγωγόν ἐστι πᾶς ἀνὴρ ἐρῶν.   (Menander, frag. 352)
                                                                                                IT

εὐαγωγός, εὐαγωγόν easily led   ἐράω love, desire

61. ὁ νοῦς γὰρ ἡμῶν ἐστιν ἐν ἑκάστῳ θεός.   (Menander, frag. 762)
                                                                                                IT

62.　ἀνὴρ γὰρ ἄνδρα καὶ πόλις σῴζει πόλιν.　　(Menander, *Sententiae* 31)
IT

σῴζω, σώσω, ἔσωσα, σέσωκα, σέσω(σ)μαι,
ἐσώθην save, preserve

63.　δυσπαρακολούθητον δὲ πρᾶγμ' ἐσθ' ἡ τύχη.　　(Menander, *Sententiae* 202)
IT

δυσπαρακολούθητος, δυσπαρακολούθητον hard
to follow, hard to understand

64.　ἡ φύσις ἑκάστου τοῦ γένους ἐστὶν πατρίς.　　(Menander, *Sententiae* 295)
IT

πατρίς, πατρίδος, ἡ homeland

65.　ὁ λόγος ἰᾱτρὸς τοῦ κατὰ ψῡχὴν πάθους.　　(Menander, *Sententiae* 587)
IT

ἰᾱτρός, ἰᾱτροῦ, ὁ doctor, healer

66.　ὁ μὴ γαμῶν ἄνθρωπος οὐκ ἔχει κακά.　　(Menander, *Sententiae* 591)
IT

γαμέω marry (of a man)

67.　φῶς ἐστι τῷ νῷ πρὸς θεὸν βλέπειν ἀεί.　　(Menander, *Sententiae* 819)
IT

φῶς, φωτός, τό (day)light　　　　βλέπω, ——, ἔβλεψα, ——, ——, —— see, look

68.　χαίρειν προσήκει τοῖς παθῶν ἐλευθέροις.　　(Menander, *Sententiae* 838)
IT

προσήκει (προσ- + ἥκει) (impersonal verb) it belongs (to)

69.　ὡς† τῶν ἐχόντων πάντες ἄνθρωποι φίλοι.　　(Menander, *Sententiae* 854)
IT

†ὡς, *here* (exclam. adv.) how

70. A couplet from an elegiac poem to the poet Anacreon attributed to Antipater of Sidon

> ὦ τὸ φίλον στέρξᾱς, φίλε, βάρβιτον, ὦ σὺν ἀοιδᾷ
>   πάντα διαπλώσᾱς καὶ σὺν ἔρωτι βίον . . .

(Greek Anthology VII.23b)
EC

στέργω, στέρξω, ἔστερξα, ——, ——, —— love
βάρβιτον, βαρβίτου, τό lyre
ἀοιδή, ἀοιδῆς, ἡ song; ἀοιδᾷ = ἀοιδῇ

διαπλώω, ——, διέπλωσα, ——, ——, —— sail through

71. An epigram beneath a statue of Solon

> ἡ Μήδων ἄδικον παύσᾱσ᾽ ὕβριν, ἥδε Σόλωνα
>   τόνδε τεκνοῖ Σαλαμὶς θεσμοθέτην ἱερόν.

(Diogenes Laertius, Lives of the Philosophers I.62)
EC

Μῆδοι, Μήδων, οἱ (the) Medes
Σόλων, Σόλωνος, ὁ Solon (legendary Athenian lawgiver)
τεκνόω beget (children); *present*, be parent of

Σαλαμίς, Σαλαμῖνος, ἡ Salamis (an island near Athens)
θεσμοθέτης, θεσμοθέτου, ὁ lawgiver
ἱερός, ἱερά, ἱερόν sacred, holy

Proverbs from Aesop

72. Πατὴρ μὲν ὁ θρέψᾱς, οὐ μὴν δὲ ὁ γεννήσᾱς.   (Aesop, Proverbs 19)

τρέφω, θρέψω, ἔθρεψα, τέτροφα, τέθραμμαι, ἐτράφην nourish; raise

μήν (particle) indeed, truly
γεννάω beget

73. Ὕβρις ἔρωτα λύει.   (Aesop, Proverbs 166)

λύω, λύσω, ἔλῡσα, λέλυκα, λέλυμαι, ἐλύθην loosen, free; destroy

Longer Readings

1. Aeschylus, *Eumenides* 143–46

Waking from a charmed sleep, one Fury complains to the others that Apollo has stopped their pursuit of Orestes.

ἰοὺ ἰοὺ πόπαξ· ἐπάθομεν, φίλαι·
ἦ† πολλὰ δὴ παθοῦσα καὶ μάτην ἐγώ·
ἐπάθομεν πάθος δυσακές, ὦ πόποι,
ἄφερτον κακόν·

ἰού (interj.) oh! alas!
πόπαξ (interj.) *cry of anger or distress*
†ἦ, *here* (particle) in truth, surely
μάτην (adv.) in vain

δυσακής, δυσακές hard to heal, without cure
ὦ (interj.) oh!
πόποι (interj.) *cry of anger or distress*
ἄφερτος, ἄφερτον insufferable, intolerable

The *Eumenides* is the third play of the trilogy *Oresteia*. Pursued by the spirit of his murdered mother and the Furies, who are seeking vengeance for the matricide, Orestes has fled to Athens. A trial is staged by Athena with Apollo acting as Orestes' defender and the Furies serving as the prosecutors. The vote by the jury of Athenians is a tie, and Athena casts the deciding vote for Orestes' acquittal. The Furies are reconciled to the decision, renamed the Eumenides ("The Well-Disposed Ones"), and given a role in preserving justice in Athens.

2. Plato, *Symposium* 189d3–e2

The comic poet Aristophanes begins his explanation of the nature of Eros.

> ἐγὼ οὖν πειράσομαι ὑμῖν εἰσηγήσασθαι τὴν δύναμιν αὐτοῦ, ὑμεῖς δὲ τῶν ἄλλων
> διδάσκαλοι ἔσεσθε. δεῖ δὲ πρῶτον ὑμᾶς μαθεῖν τὴν ἀνθρωπίνην φύσιν καὶ τὰ παθήματα
> αὐτῆς. ἡ γὰρ πάλαι ἡμῶν φύσις οὐχ αὐτὴ ἦν ἥπερ νῦν, ἀλλ᾽ ἀλλοία. πρῶτον μὲν γὰρ τρία
> ἦν τὰ γένη τὰ τῶν ἀνθρώπων, οὐχ ὥσπερ νῦν δύο, ἄρρεν καὶ θῆλυ, ἀλλὰ καὶ τρίτον
> προσῆν . . .

πειράομαι, πειράσομαι, ἐπειρασάμην,
  ——, πεπείραμαι, ἐπειράθην try
εἰσηγέομαι (εἰσ- + ἡγέομαι), εἰσηγήσομαι,
  εἰσηγησάμην, ——, ——, —— relate, narrate,
  explain
πρῶτον (adv.) first
ἀνθρώπινος, ἀνθρωπίνη, ἀνθρώπινον human
πάθημα, παθήματος, τό experience, suffering
πάλαι (adv.) long ago

ἀλλοῖος, ἀλλοία, ἀλλοῖον of another sort,
  different
τρεῖς, τρία three; τρία = *neut. pl. nom.*
δύο two; δύο = *neut. dual nom.*
ἄρρην, ἄρρεν male; ἄρρεν = *neut. sing. nom.*
θῆλυς, θήλεια, θῆλυ female; θῆλυ = *neut. sing.*
  nom.
τρίτος, τρίτη, τρίτον third
πρόσειμι (προσ- + εἰμί) be present as well

Plato (429?–347 B.C.E.), born into a wealthy Athenian family, was the founder of the Academy (his philosophical school that survived his death by several centuries), the teacher of Aristotle, and the most important figure in Western philosophy. His philosophical works were written in dialogue form, in which his teacher Socrates is most often the chief protagonist. Thirty-six works are included in the manuscripts of Plato, although the authenticity of as many as ten of these has been called into question. Some of these dialogues are dramatic and are presented as direct conversations, often beginning in the middle of a discussion. Others are narrated, either by Socrates himself or by a third party, and recount earlier conversations. The dialogue form presents Socrates' means of teaching through dialectic—conversation and the careful posing of questions—and seems to be Plato's literary response to Socrates' contention that knowledge cannot be transmitted through writing. Through these dialogues Plato's Socrates tackles nearly every philosophical issue, including questions of ontology, psychology, morality, politics, literature, and the nature of the human soul. Often the philosophical issue under discussion is shaped by the dramatic context in which it is presented. Plato's prose style is among the richest and most varied in Greek literature and contains passages of both immense clarity and obscurity, even within the same dialogue.

In the **Symposium**, Apollodorus, a follower of Socrates, recounts to a group of businessmen the story of a banquet that took place two days after the tragic poet Agathon won a victory with his tragedy at the Lenaean festival in 416 B.C.E. Most of the dialogue comprises six speeches about Eros made by participants at the banquet, the last three of whom are Aristophanes (the comic poet), Agathon, and Socrates. The dialogue closes with the intrusion of the drunken general Alcibiades, who also gives a speech—not about Eros, but about Socrates.

3. Menander, frag. 68 (IT)

A character considers a particular danger and how it is to be avoided.

τὰ πατρῷα μὲν ποιεῖ καιρός ποτε
ἀλλότρια, σῴζει δ' αὐτὰ που τὰ σώματα.
βίου δ' ἔνεστιν ἀσφάλει' ἐν ταῖς τέχναις.

πατρῷος, πατρῴα, πατρῷον of or belonging
    to the father; *neut. pl. subst.*, father's goods,
    inheritance
καιρός, καιροῦ, ὁ (right) moment, critical time;
    opportunity
ἀλλότριος, ἀλλοτρίᾱ, ἀλλότριον of or belonging
    to another, another's

σῴζω, σώσω, ἔσωσα, σέσωκα, σέσω(σ)μαι,
    ἐσώθην save, preserve
ἔνειμι (ἐν- + εἰμί) be in
ἀσφάλεια, ἀσφαλείᾱς, ἡ security, safety

Menander (343?–291? B.C.E.) is the only poet of Attic New Comedy of whom whole plays have survived, in addition to numerous long and shorter fragments. Menander's plays were written and produced at a time when Athens was no longer prominent, and the political and military spheres were in the control of the Macedonians, who then ruled all of mainland Greece. Menander's plays are written in an unadorned style and present stock characters in realistic and conventional situations: young lovers thwarted by other characters (parents, older rivals, braggart soldiers, parasites), aided by clever slaves, and united at the close of the play. To the extent that there is a chorus, it sings songs that are unrelated to the plot and that function as nothing more than interludes. Although more than a hundred plays are ascribed to Menander, before the discovery in the twentieth century of the larger fragments and even whole plays, all that survived were much smaller fragments, many of which were proverbial utterances collected and presented under the title *Sententiae* (Maxims).

CHAPTER 8

Vocabulary

ἡδονή, ἡδονῆς, ἡ pleasure
λύπη, λύπης, ἡ pain
στρατιώτης, στρατιώτου, ὁ soldier
σωτηρίᾱ, σωτηρίᾱς, ἡ safety

κίνδῡνος, κινδύνου, ὁ danger
→ στρατηγός, στρατηγοῦ, ὁ general
στρατός, στρατοῦ, ὁ army

→ πλῆθος, πλήθους, τό great number, multitude
→ τεῖχος, τείχους, τό wall

→ ——, ἀλλήλων (reciprocal pronoun) one another, each other

→ ——, ἐρῶ, ——, εἴρηκα, εἴρημαι, ἐρρήθην say, tell (of), speak (of)
→ ζάω, ζήσω, ——, ——, ——, —— be alive, live
→ θνῄσκω, θανοῦμαι, ἔθανον, τέθνηκα, ——, —— die; *perfect*, be dead
    → ἀποθνῄσκω, ἀποθανοῦμαι, ἀπέθανον, τέθνηκα, ——, —— die; *perfect*, be dead
→ κτείνω, κτενῶ, ἔκτεινα, ——, ——, —— kill
    → ἀποκτείνω, ἀποκτενῶ, ἀπέκτεινα, ἀπέκτονα, ——, —— kill

→ μάχομαι, μαχοῦμαι, ἐμαχεσάμην, ——, μεμάχημαι, —— fight (against) (+ dat.)
→ οἴομαι/οἶμαι, οἰήσομαι, ——, ——, ——, ᾠήθην think, suppose, believe
→ *φάσκω, ——, ——, ——, ——, —— say, assert
→ φημί, φήσω, ἔφησα, ——, ——, —— say, assert (§87)
→ χρή, χρῆσται, ——, ——, ——, —— (impersonal verb) it is necessary, ought

→ ἐναντίος, ἐναντίᾱ, ἐναντίον facing, opposite; opposing, contrary (to) (+ gen. or dat.)
→ ἴσος, ἴση, ἴσον equal; fair
μακρός, μακρά, μακρόν large, great; long, tall
→ (σ)μῑκρός, (σ)μῑκρά, (σ)μῑκρόν small
παλαιός, παλαιά, παλαιόν old, ancient

ἔτι (adv.) still, yet; οὐκέτι/μηκέτι (adv.) no longer
→ ἴσως (adv.) equally; perhaps
→ πάνυ (adv.) altogether; very (much), exceedingly; *in answers,* by all means, certainly; οὐ πάνυ, not at all
→ πρό (prep. + gen.) before, in front of

Vocabulary Notes

→ στρατηγός, στρατηγοῦ, ὁ is a compound noun formed from the noun στρατός, "army," and the suffix -ηγος, which is derived from the verb ἄγω. Thus, στρατηγός first means "one who leads the army," "general," "commander," but it may also be applied more generally to any leader. In Athens, ten στρατηγοί were elected annually to oversee both the army and the navy.

→ πλῆθος, πλήθους, τό means a "great amount," "great number," or "multitude" (especially of people). With the article and a Partitive Genitive, πλῆθος may also mean "the greater part" or "the main body."

τὸ πλῆθος ψῦχῆς	the greater part (subj./d.o.) of a soul
τὸ πλῆθος τοῦ στρατοῦ	the main body (subj./d.o.) of the army

→ τεῖχος, τείχους, τό, "wall," is most commonly used of a wall around a town or city as opposed to the wall of an individual building. It appears regularly in both the singular and the plural. τὰ μακρὰ τείχη, "the long walls," most often refer to the walls that extended from the city of Athens, located atop a hill, down to its two harbors, Peiraeus and Phalerum.

→ ——, ἀλλήλων, "one another," "each other," is called a **reciprocal pronoun** because it is used to refer to a reciprocal or mutual relation between two or more than two individuals or things. The blank at the beginning of the vocabulary entry indicates that this word has no nominative forms. It uses the plural endings of a first-second-declension adjective and may occur in any gender in the genitive, dative, and accusative plural.

ἀγῶνας πρὸς ἀλλήλους ἐποίησαν.	They made contests against one another.
γίγνεται πολλὰ ἐξ ἀλλήλων.	Many things arise from one another.

Verbs with Contracted Futures

An omega verb in Attic Greek may have a second principal part whose stem ends in -ε. Such a verb is said to have a **Contracted Future**, and its forms in the future tense are contracted *in the same way as* the present tense forms of epsilon-contracted verbs.[1] Verbs with contracted futures are easily recognized by the accent on their second principal parts.

κτείνω, κτενῶ, ἔκτεινα, ——, ——, —— kill
θνήσκω, θανοῦμαι, ἔθανον, τέθνηκα, ——, —— die; *perfect,* be dead

The accent on the second principal part of κτείνω—κτενῶ—is a circumflex on the ultima. This accent results from the contraction of the epsilon at the end of the stem with the ending (κτενε- + -ω > κτενῶ); the accent indicates that κτείνω has a contracted future. θνήσκω is a partial deponent. Its second principal part—θανοῦμαι—has a circumflex on the penult because of the contraction of the epsilon at the end of the stem with the ending (θανε + -ομαι > θανοῦμαι). Other verbs with contracted futures are identified in the vocabulary notes.

---

1. A Contracted Future is often called an Attic Future because it is common in the Attic dialect, but both Ionic and the dialect of Homer have some verbs with contracted futures.

➤ The verb ——, ἐρῶ, ——, εἴρηκα, εἴρημαι, ἐρρήθην, "say," "tell (of)," "speak (of)," lacks the first and third principal parts, but the tenses formed from these principal parts are supplied by the verb λέγω. The accent on the second principal part indicates that this verb has a contracted future. The unaugmented stem from the sixth principal part is ῥηθ- with *one rho only*. The root of this verb is the same as that of the noun ῥήτωρ.

——, ἐρῶ often introduces an indirect statement (ὅτι/ὡς and a finite verb or a Subject Accusative and an infinitive [§88]), and, like other verbs meaning "say," "tell," "speak of," it may take an Accusative, Direct Object and a Dative of Indirect Object.

➤ ζάω, ζήσω, ——, ——, ——, ——, "be alive," "live," is an *irregular* contracted verb that has active voice forms only. In Attic Greek the present and imperfect tenses of ζάω are conjugated as if the stem were ζη- (< *ζα-). These conjugations employ the following regular rules of contraction:

$$η + ω = ω \qquad η + ε = η$$
$$η + o = ω \qquad η + ει = η$$
$$η + ου = ω \qquad η + η = η$$

MEMORIZE THESE RULES OF ATTIC CONTRACTION.

Present Active Indicative		Imperfect Active Indicative	
Singular			
1 ζῶ	(< *ζήω)	1 ἔζων	(< *ἔζηον)
2 ζῇς	(< *ζήεις)	2 ἔζης	(< *ἔζηες)
3 ζῇ	(< *ζήει)	3 ἔζη	(< *ἔζηε)
Plural			
1 ζῶμεν	(< *ζήομεν)	1 ἐζῶμεν	(< *ἐζήομεν)
2 ζῆτε	(< *ζήετε)	2 ἐζῆτε	(< *ἐζήετε)
3 ζῶσι(ν)	(< *ζήουσι[ν])	3 ἔζων	(< *ἔζηον)

Present Active Infinitive: ζῆν (< *ζήεεν)
Present Active Participle: ζῶν, ζῶσα, ζῶν (< *ζήων, *ζήουσα, *ζῆον)

MEMORIZE THESE IRREGULAR CONJUGATIONS AND FORMS.

ζάω is used of humans, animals, and plants, and it may also be used to describe a manner of living.

οὗτος ζῇ ἀλλ᾽ οὐκ εὖ ζῇ.   This man is alive, but he is not living well.

➤ θνῄσκω, θανοῦμαι, ἔθανον, τέθνηκα, ——, ——, "die," is derived from the same root as the noun θάνατος and the adjective θνητός. The first and fourth principal parts use the long-vowel grade θνη-, and the second and third principal parts use the zero grade θαν- (< PIE *thn̥). The first principal part is formed from θνη- with the addition of the suffix -ισκω. This suffix is called an **inchoative** suffix and indicates that an action is *beginning* or *becoming*.[2] Thus, the original meaning of θνῄσκω is "begin

---

2. There are also present and imperfect forms of θνῄσκω *without* the iota subscript (e.g., θνήσκει), which were formed by the addition of the suffix -σκω, also an inchoative suffix. Although these forms are rarer in modern printed texts than forms with the iota subscript, they are found in many ancient manuscripts and inscriptions. Since the suffix -σκω is known to be an older suffix than -ισκω, the forms without an iota subscript have an earlier origin than those with an iota subscript.

to die" or "become dead." The form and accent on principal part 2 of θνῄσκω indicate that it is a partial deponent and has a contracted future. The reduplication in principal part 4 reflects the dissimilation of aspirates (cf. πεφίληκα).

θνῄσκω has irregular plural forms in the perfect active indicative, and it has an irregular perfect active infinitive. These irregular forms use the stem τεθνα-. MEMORIZE THESE IRREGULAR FORMS:

	Singular	*Plural*
1	τέθνηκα	τέθναμεν
2	τέθνηκας	τέθνατε
3	τέθνηκε(ν)	τεθνᾶσι(ν) (< *τεθνάᾱσι[ν])

Perfect Active Infinitive: τεθνάναι

In Attic Greek the rare plural pluperfect forms are most often irregular (e.g., ἐτέθνασαν).

With the exception of the perfect, forms of the verb θνῄσκω are rare in prose, and forms of the compound verb ἀποθνῄσκω are used instead. Other than in the future tense, θνῄσκω has no middle or passive forms.

θνῄσκω is an intransitive verb that often appears with a prepositional phrase expressing cause or agency. In the perfect θνῄσκω means "have/has died" or "be dead."

ἔθανον ὑπὸ τῶν ἐχθρῶν.	They died at the hands of their enemies.
οὗτοι νῦν τεθνᾶσιν.	These men have now died/are now dead.

➤ ἀποθνῄσκω, ἀποθανοῦμαι, ἀπέθανον, τέθνηκα, ——, ——, "die," is a compound verb composed of the prefix ἀπο- and the verb θνῄσκω. The meaning of ἀποθνῄσκω does not differ from that of θνῄσκω, but in all tenses *except* the perfect the forms of the compound verb rather than those of the simple verb appear in Attic prose. ἀποθνῄσκω does not have perfect active forms of its own but uses the forms of the uncompounded verb θνῄσκω. The fourth principal part of ἀποθνῄσκω, τέθνηκα, is also the fourth principal part of θνῄσκω.

➤ κτείνω, κτενῶ, ἔκτεινα, ——, ——, ——, "kill," has a contracted future. It has active forms only. κτείνω appears often in poetry and prose, but in prose the forms of the compound verb ἀποκτείνω are more common than the forms of κτείνω.

➤ ἀποκτείνω, ἀποκτενῶ, ἀπέκτεινα, ἀπέκτονα, ——, ——, "kill," is a compound verb composed of the prefix ἀπο- and the verb κτείνω. The meaning of ἀποκτείνω does not differ from that of κτείνω, but the forms of the compound verb appear in prose more often than those of the simple verb. In Attic Greek ἀποκτείνω appears in the active voice *only*. Forms of θνῄσκω or ἀποθνῄσκω may be used as the passive forms of κτείνω or ἀποκτείνω (e.g., ἀπέθανε may be translated "he died" or, sometimes, "he was killed").

➤ μάχομαι, μαχοῦμαι, ἐμαχεσάμην, ——, μεμάχημαι, ——, "fight (against)," is a middle deponent that has a contracted future. It is intransitive and is often accompanied by either a Dative of Reference or πρός + acc. to indicate the person against whom one is fighting. Although μάχομαι is usually used of individuals or groups in combat, it may also mean "quarrel (with)."

βαρβάροις/πρὸς βαρβάρους μάχονται.	They are fighting against foreigners.

➤ οἴομαι/οἶμαι, οἰήσομαι, ——, ——, ——, ᾠήθην is a passive-in-the-aorist deponent. All forms made from its first two principal parts are middle. Its aorist forms are passive, made from the sixth principal part, with middle meanings. In the first person singular present indicative, both οἴομαι and οἶμαι appear, but the shortened form οἶμαι, which uses a personal ending with no thematic vowel before it, is much more common. In the first person singular imperfect indicative, the shortened form ᾤμην is much more common than ᾠόμην. No other shortened forms regularly appear.

οἴομαι/οἶμαι means "think," "suppose," "believe," and most often introduces an indirect statement with a Subject Accusative and an infinitive (§88), rarely with ὅτι/ὡς and a finite verb.

οἴεται τὸν ξένον εὖ λέγειν.	He thinks that the stranger is speaking well.

In answers to questions οἴομαι/οἶμαι indicates assent.

A. ἆρ᾽ εἶ ἀγαθὸς πολίτης;	Are you a good citizen?
B. οἶμαι ἔγωγε.	I, at least, think (so).

→ The verb *φάσκω, ——, ——, ——, ——, ——, "say," "assert," has an asterisk before the first principal part because the form φάσκω (first person singular present active indicative) does not occur in the Greek literature that survives. φάσκω was formed from φα-, the short-vowel grade stem of φημί, with the addition of the suffix -σκω. This suffix is called an **inchoative** suffix and indicates that an action is *beginning* or *becoming*. In Attic Greek φάσκω sometimes appears in the present active infinitive and in the imperfect active indicative, but it is most frequent in all forms of the present active participle. φάσκω introduces an indirect statement with a Subject Accusative and an infinitive (§88). It has the same meanings as φημί: "say," "assert."

→ The athematic verb φημί, φήσω, ἔφησα, ——, ——, —— "say," "assert," may accompany a direct quotation or may introduce an indirect statement with a Subject Accusative and an infinitive (§88). For the forms of φημί see §87. When φημί is negated and introduces an indirect statement, it means "deny that . . ." or "say that . . . not."

οὔ φησι θεὸν εἶναι τὸν Δία.	He denies that Zeus is a god.
	He says that Zeus is not a god.

In dialogue φημί may mean "say yes" and οὔ φημι may mean "say no."

ἆρα φὴς θεὸν εἶναι τὸν Δία;	Do you assert that Zeus is a god?
φημί/οὔ φημι.	I say yes/I say no.

→ χρή, χρῆσται, ——, ——, ——, —— is in origin a neuter noun ("necessity," "compulsion"), but it is treated as a third person singular form of an impersonal verb. χρή occurs with a Subject Infinitive that often has a Subject Accusative. It may be translated "it is necessary (for)" or the Subject Accusative of the Subject Infinitive may be translated as the subject of the verb "ought." The infinitive is negated with μή or οὐ.

χρὴ ἡμᾶς τοῦτο ποιεῖν.	It is necessary for us to do this thing.
	We ought to do this thing.
χρὴ ἡμᾶς τοῦτο μὴ/οὐ ποιεῖν.	We ought not to do this thing.

Sometimes χρή is used to indicate a necessity that stems from a subjective, moral obligation or a sense of propriety, in contrast to δεῖ, which may indicate an objective or external *need*, but this distinction is not always maintained.

Other forms of χρή are in origin combinations of χρή and forms of the verb εἰμί.

Imperfect Active Indicative	χρῆν	(< χρή + ἦν)
	ἐχρῆν	(< ἐ- + χρῆν)
Future Active Indicative	χρῆσται	(< χρή + ἔσται)
Present Active Infinitive	χρῆναι	(< χρή + εἶναι)
Present Active Participle	χρεών	(< χρή + ὄν)

MEMORIZE THESE FORMS.

When the imperfect active indicative is followed by an aorist infinitive, it expresses an obligation in the past. When it is followed by a present infinitive, it may express *either* an obligation in the past *or* an obligation in the past that has continued into the present and is *not being fulfilled*. Context usually makes clear whether the statement refers to past or present obligation.

χρῆν τοῦτο ποιῆσαι.
It was necessary to have done this thing. (obligation in the past)

χρῆν τοῦτο ποιεῖν.
It was necessary to have done this thing. (obligation in the past)
It was (and still is) necessary to be doing this thing. (obligation starting in the past and continuing into the present)

→ ἐναντίος, ἐναντίᾱ, ἐναντίον means "facing"; "opposite," "opposing," "contrary," and is often accompanied by a noun or pronoun in the *genitive* or *dative* case. The sense may be neutral or hostile.

ἐναντία τούτων λέξω.
I shall say things opposite from/contrary to these things.

ἡμῖν σύμμαχοι οὐκ εἰσὶν οἱ τῶν Ἀθηναίων ἐναντίοι.
The men opposing the Athenians are not allies to us.

τῷ ἀγαθῷ ἐναντίον τὸ κακόν.
The bad thing is opposite/contrary to the good thing.

The regularly formed adverb ἐναντίως means "in opposition," "conversely." The adverb also appears with words in the genitive or dative case.

→ ἴσος, ἴση, ἴσον is used to describe a size, number, or quality and means "equal" or "even." It is often accompanied by a Dative of Reference to indicate what a thing is equal *to*. When used of plains or land, it may mean "level." When ἴσος describes a person, it means "fair," "impartial," or it may indicate that people are of the same class or rank. Although in Attic Greek the iota of ἴσος is short, in all other dialects it is long.

→ (σ)μῑκρός, (σ)μῑκρά, (σ)μῑκρόν, "small," is spelled both with and without the initial sigma. Forms with the initial sigma occur roughly as often as forms without.

→ Although ἴσως, the regularly formed adverb of the adjective ἴσος, occasionally means "equally," it much more commonly means "perhaps" or "probably."

→ πάνυ is an irregularly formed adverb of πᾶς and sometimes means "altogether." When πάνυ modifies an adjective or a verb, it is translated "very (much)" or "exceedingly." πάνυ or πάνυ γε is also used as a strong affirmative answer ("by all means," "certainly"). οὐ πάνυ is used as a strong negative ("not at all").

→ The preposition πρό is always followed by the genitive case. It means "before" or "in front of" in space or time. πρό also means "before" in the sense of "ahead of," "more than."

πρὸ τῆς μάχης	before the battle
πρὸ τοῦ τείχους	in front of the wall
πρὸ πάντων ἄρχειν βούλεται.	He wants to rule before/more than all things.

The phrases πρὸ τούτου and πρὸ τοῦ both mean "before this."[3]

Derivatives and Cognates

	Derivatives	*Cognates*
ἡδονή	**hedon**ist	sweet, as**suade**, per**suade**, suave
ἴσος		**iso**sceles
μακρός	**macro**economics, **macro**n	**m**eager, **em**aciate, para**mecium**
παλαιός	**paleo**graphy, **Paleo**lithic	**tele**phone
πλῆθος		**ple**thora, com**plete**, fill, **ple**bs
(σ)μῑκρός	**micro**organism	
στρατός	**strat**agem	**str**ain, **str**ew
σωτηρίᾱ		**soter**iology
τεῖχος		**fig**ure, **fic**tion, **dairy**, la**dy**
φημί	pro**phet**, dys**phasia**	**fa**ble, **fa**te, **ban**ish, sym**phony**, blas**pheme**

---

3. In the expression πρὸ τοῦ, the article τοῦ is used as a demonstrative pronoun (= τούτου).

§83. Perfect and Pluperfect Active Indicative of Omega Verbs; Perfect Active Infinitive of Omega Verbs

The perfect indicative has *present* time with *completed* aspect. The pluperfect indicative has *past* time with *completed* aspect (§24).

I have (now) stopped   perfect (present completed)
I had (then) stopped   pluperfect (past completed)

Perfect and Pluperfect Active Indicative

To form the perfect active indicative of an omega verb:

1. take the **perfect active stem** by removing the -α from the **fourth** principal part
2. add the following perfect active indicative endings:

Person	Singular	Plural
1	-α	-αμεν
2	-ας	-ατε
3	-ε(ν)	-ᾱσι(ν)

MEMORIZE THESE ENDINGS, DOWN THE SINGULAR AND THEN DOWN THE PLURAL, AND BE PREPARED TO RECITE THEM QUICKLY.

To form the pluperfect active indicative of an omega verb:

1. take the **perfect active stem** by removing the -α from the **fourth** principal part
2. add the past indicative augment or lengthen the initial vowel of the stem
3. add the following pluperfect active indicative endings:

Person	Singular	Plural
1	-η	-εμεν
2	-ης	-ετε
3	-ει(ν)	-εσαν

MEMORIZE THESE ENDINGS, DOWN THE SINGULAR AND THEN DOWN THE PLURAL, AND BE PREPARED TO RECITE THEM QUICKLY.

Thus, the perfect and pluperfect active indicative conjugations of παύω are:

Perfect Active Stem: πεπαυκ-		Augmented Perfect Active Stem: ἐπεπαυκ-	
Singular		*Singular*	
1 πέπαυκα	I have stopped (trans.)	ἐπεπαύκη	I had stopped (trans.)
2 πέπαυκας	you have stopped (trans.)	ἐπεπαύκης	you had stopped (trans.)
3 πέπαυκε(ν)	he, she, it has stopped (trans.)	ἐπεπαύκει(ν)	he, she, it had stopped (trans.)
Plural		*Plural*	
1 πεπαύκαμεν	we have stopped (trans.)	ἐπεπαύκεμεν	we had stopped (trans.)
2 πεπαύκατε	you (pl.) have stopped (trans.)	ἐπεπαύκετε	you (pl.) had stopped (trans.)
3 πεπαύκᾱσι(ν)	they have stopped (trans.)	ἐπεπαύκεσαν	they had stopped (trans.)

OBSERVATIONS

1. The accent on finite verb forms is *recessive*.

2. The endings of the third person singular and third person plural perfect active indicative have a movable nu. The third person plural ending -ᾱσι(ν) was produced by regular sound change from the original ending *-αντσι(ν): *-αντσι(ν) > *-ανσσι(ν) > *-ανσι(ν) > -ᾱσι(ν).

3. The ending of the third person singular pluperfect active indicative has a movable nu. The third person singular ending -ει is a spurious diphthong formed from contraction: *-εε(ν) > -ει(ν).

4. Some verbs whose stems begin with vowels have fourth principal parts that begin with a long vowel because of reduplication, e.g., ἠθέληκα, ἦχα. The stems from such verbs *cannot* be augmented, and the perfect and pluperfect active forms of such verbs are distinguished by *endings only*, e.g., ἦχε(ν), perfect; ἤχει(ν), pluperfect.

5. Many verbs whose fourth principal parts begin with *short* vowels or diphthongs do not have a lengthened initial vowel in their pluperfect forms, and the perfect and pluperfect active forms of these verbs are distinguished by *endings only*. The initial short vowels or diphthongs in the fourth principal parts of the following verbs are not lengthened in the pluperfect tense:

ἀποκτείνω (ἀπέκτονα)   ἔχω (ἔσχηκα)
ἔρχομαι (ἐλήλυθα)   ζηλόω (ἐζήλωκα)
——, ἐρῶ (εἴρηκα)   ὁράω (ἑώρᾱκα/ἑόρᾱκα)

Pluperfect forms of all these verbs are rare.

Perfect Active Infinitive

To form the perfect active infinitive of an omega verb:

1. take the **perfect active stem** by removing the -α from the **fourth** principal part
2. add the perfect active infinitive ending -έναι.

For example:

Perfect Active Stem	Perfect Active Infinitive	Translation
πεπαυκ-	πεπαυκέναι	to have stopped (trans.)

OBSERVATIONS

1. The accent on the perfect active infinitive is *persistent on the penult*. Final -αι counts as *short* for purposes of accent.

2. The perfect active infinitive *does not always indicate present time but always indicates completed aspect*.

☛ DRILL 83 MAY NOW BE DONE.

§84. Perfect and Pluperfect Middle/Passive Indicative of Omega Verbs; Perfect Middle/Passive Infinitive of Omega Verbs

Perfect and Pluperfect Middle/Passive Indicative

In the perfect and pluperfect tenses, the middle and passive forms of omega verbs are identical. To form the perfect middle/passive indicative of an omega verb:

1. take the **perfect middle/passive stem** by removing the -μαι from the **fifth** principal part
2. add the primary middle/passive personal endings.

Thus, the perfect middle/passive indicative conjugation of παύω is:

Perfect Middle/Passive Stem: πεπαυ-

Primary Middle/ Passive Personal Endings		Middle Translation	Passive Translation
Singular			
1 -μαι	πέπαυμαι	I have stopped (intrans.)	I have been stopped
2 -σαι	πέπαυσαι	you have stopped (intrans.)	you have been stopped
3 -ται	πέπαυται	he, she, it has stopped (intrans.)	he, she, it has been stopped
Plural			
1 -μεθα	πεπαύμεθα	we have stopped (intrans.)	we have been stopped
2 -σθε	πέπαυσθε	you (pl.) have stopped (intrans.)	you (pl.) have been stopped
3 -νται	πέπαυνται	they have stopped (intrans.)	they have been stopped

OBSERVATIONS

1. In forms of the perfect middle/passive there are *no* thematic vowels between the stem and the endings: the endings are added directly to the stem. The accent on finite verb forms is *recessive*. The diphthong -αι counts as *short* for purposes of accent.

2. Context usually makes clear whether a form in a particular sentence is middle or passive.

3. Like the perfect active, the perfect middle/passive indicative tense has *present* time with *completed* aspect.

To form the pluperfect middle/passive indicative of an omega verb:

1. take the **perfect middle/passive stem** by removing the -μαι from the **fifth** principal part
2. add the past indicative augment or lengthen the initial vowel of the stem
3. add the secondary middle/passive personal endings.

Thus, the pluperfect middle/passive indicative conjugation of παύω is:

Augmented Perfect Middle/Passive Stem: ἐπεπαυ-

Secondary Middle/Passive Personal Endings		Middle Translation	Passive Translation
Singular			
1 -μην	ἐπεπαύμην	I had stopped (intrans.)	I had been stopped
2 -σο	ἐπέπαυσο	you had stopped (intrans.)	you had been stopped
3 -το	ἐπέπαυτο	he, she, it had stopped (intrans.)	he, she, it had been stopped
Plural			
1 -μεθα	ἐπεπαύμεθα	we had stopped (intrans.)	we had been stopped
2 -σθε	ἐπέπαυσθε	you (pl.) had stopped (intrans.)	you (pl.) had been stopped
3 -ντο	ἐπέπαυντο	they had stopped (intrans.)	they had been stopped

OBSERVATIONS

1. In forms of the pluperfect middle/passive there are *no* thematic vowels between the stem and the endings: the endings are added directly to the stem. The accent on finite verb forms is *recessive*.

2. Context usually makes clear whether a form in a particular sentence is middle or passive.

3. Like the pluperfect active, the pluperfect middle/passive indicative tense has *past* time with *completed* aspect.

4. The endings of the first person and second person plural in the perfect and pluperfect middle/passive indicative are identical (-μεθα, -σθε). When a verb has a perfect middle/passive stem that begins with a long vowel and *cannot* be augmented, the first person and second person plural forms are identical in these two tenses. Context usually makes clear which form occurs in a particular sentence.

> ἠδικήμεθα we have been wronged (perfect) *or* we had been wronged (pluperfect)

5. Many verbs whose fifth principal parts begin with *short* vowels or diphthongs do not have a lengthened initial vowel in their pluperfect forms. The initial short vowels or diphthongs in the fifth principal parts of the following verbs are not lengthened in the pluperfect tense:

> διαλέγομαι (διείλεγμαι)
> ———, ἐρῶ (εἴρημαι)
> ἔχω (-έσχημαι)
> ὁράω (ἑώραμαι)

Pluperfect forms of all these verbs are rare.

Perfect and Pluperfect Middle/Passive Indicative of Verbs with Consonant Stems

Some verbs have perfect middle/passive stems that end not in a vowel or diphthong but in a labial (π, β, φ), a dental (τ, δ, θ), or a palatal (κ, γ, χ) consonant. These verbs are said to have **consonant stems**. When the primary and secondary middle/passive endings were added to these stems, certain regular changes occurred, which produced conjugations that differ slightly from the patterns presented above. For example:

ὁράω, ὄψομαι, εἶδον, ἑώρᾱκα/ἑόρᾱκα, ἑώρᾱμαι/ὦμμαι, ὤφθην
(perfect middle/passive stem from ὦμμαι ends in a *labial:* ὠπ-)

πείθω, πείσω, ἔπεισα, πέπεικα, πέπεισμαι, ἐπείσθην
(perfect middle/passive stem ends in a *dental:* πεπειθ-)

ἄρχω, ἄρξω, ἦρξα, ἦρχα, ἦργμαι, ἤρχθην
(perfect middle/passive stem ends in a *palatal:* ἠρχ-)

OBSERVATION

When the fifth principal part of a verb ends in -μμαι, its perfect middle/passive stem ends in a labial (π, β, or φ). When the fifth principal part of a verb ends in -σμαι, its stem ends in a dental (τ, δ, or θ). When the fifth principal part of a verb ends in -γμαι, its stem ends in a palatal (κ, γ, or χ).[4]

	Stem Ending in a Labial		Stem Ending in a Dental		Stem Ending in a Palatal	
Perfect Middle/Passive Indicative						
Singular						
1	ὦμμαι	(<*ὦπμαι)	πέπεισμαι	(<*πέπειθμαι)	ἦργμαι	(<*ἦρχμαι)
2	ὦψαι	(<*ὦπσαι)	πέπεισαι	(<*πέπειθσαι)	ἦρξαι	(<*ἦρχσαι)
3	ὦπται	(<*ὦπται)	πέπεισται	(<*πέπειθται)	ἦρκται	(<*ἦρχται)
Plural						
1	ὦμμεθα	(<*ὦπμεθα)	πεπείσμεθα	(<*πεπείθμεθα)	ἦργμεθα	(<*ἦρχμεθα)
2	ὦφθε	(<*ὦπσθε)	πέπεισθε	(<*πέπειθσθε)	ἦρχθε	(<*ἦρχσθε)
3	—		—		—	
Pluperfect Middle/Passive Indicative						
Singular						
1	ὤμμην	(<*ὤπμην)	ἐπεπείσμην	(<*ἐπεπείθμην)	ἤργμην	(<*ἤρχμην)
2	ὦψο	(<*ὦπσο)	ἐπέπεισο	(<*ἐπέπειθσο)	ἦρξο	(<*ἦρχσο)
3	ὦπτο	(<*ὦπτο)	ἐπέπειστο	(<*ἐπέπειθτο)	ἦρκτο	(<*ἦρχτο)
Plural						
1	ὤμμεθα	(<*ὤπμεθα)	ἐπεπείσμεθα	(<*ἐπεπείθμεθα)	ἤργμεθα	(<*ἤρχμεθα)
2	ὦφθε	(<*ὦπσθε)	ἐπέπεισθε	(<*ἐπέπειθσθε)	ἦρχθε	(<*ἦρχσθε)
3	—		—		—	

OBSERVATIONS

1. In Attic Greek there is no third person plural perfect or pluperfect middle/passive indicative of verbs with consonant stems. A periphrastic form using a participle and a form of εἰμί is used instead (Part 2, §110).

2. For a consonant stem ending in a labial, the following sound changes occurred:

4. Although each of these endings indicates that a consonant stem ends in a labial, dental, or palatal, one cannot determine the specific consonant at the end of a root from the fifth principal part alone since the changes that produced the first person singular form (the fifth principal part) occurred for any consonant of each class.

In the first person singular and plural the labial assimilated to the mu of -μαι, -μην, or -μεθα (π, β, φ > μ).

In the second person singular the labial and the sigma were replaced with the double consonant psi (π, β, φ + σ > ψ).

In the third person singular the labial assimilated to the tau of -ται or -το by becoming voiceless and unaspirated (β, φ > π; original π unchanged).

In the second person plural the sigma of -σθε was lost, and the labial was aspirated (π, β > φ; original φ unchanged).

3. For a consonant stem ending in a dental, the following sound changes occurred:

In the first person singular, third person singular, and first person plural, the dental became a sigma (τ, δ, θ > σ).

In the second person singular and plural the dental was dropped.

4. For a consonant stem ending in a palatal, the following sound changes occurred:

In the first person singular and plural the palatal became voiced (κ, χ > γ; original γ unchanged).

In the second person singular the palatal and the sigma were replaced by the double consonant xi (κ, γ, χ + σ > ξ).

In the third person singular the palatal assimilated to the tau of -ται or -το by becoming voiceless and unaspirated (γ, χ > κ; original κ unchanged).

In the second person plural the sigma of -σθε was lost, and the palatal was aspirated (κ, γ > χ; original χ unchanged).

5. The perfect and pluperfect middle/passive conjugations of πέμπω differ slightly from other consonant stems ending in labials because its perfect middle/passive stem is πεπεμπ-. All the changes described above for a consonant stem ending in a labial occurred; however, wherever three mus might be expected (e.g., *πέπεμμμαι, *ἐπεπέμμμην), one mu was dropped (πέπεμμαι, ἐπεπέμμην). Here are the perfect and pluperfect middle/passive conjugations of πέμπω:

	Perfect	Pluperfect
Singular		
1	πέπεμμαι	ἐπεπέμμην
2	πέπεμψαι	ἐπέπεμψο
3	πέπεμπται	ἐπέπεμπτο
Plural		
1	πεπέμμεθα	ἐπεπέμμεθα
2	πέπεμφθε	ἐπέπεμφθε
3	—	—

Perfect Middle/Passive Infinitive

To form the perfect middle/passive infinitive of an omega verb:

1. take the **perfect middle/passive stem** by removing the -μαι from the **fifth** principal part
2. add the perfect middle/passive infinitive ending -σθαι.

For example:

Perfect Middle/ Passive Stem	Perfect Middle/ Passive Infinitive	Middle Translation	Passive Translation
πεπαυ-	πεπαῦσθαι	to have stopped (intrans.)	to have been stopped
ὠπ-	ὦφθαι	—	to have been seen
πεπεμπ-	πεπέμφθαι	—	to have been sent
πεπειθ-	πεπεῖσθαι	to have obeyed	to have been persuaded
ἠρχ-	ἦρχθαι	to have begun	to have been ruled

OBSERVATIONS

1. The accent on the perfect middle/passive infinitive of omega verbs is *persistent on the penult.* The final diphthong -αι counts as *short* for purposes of accent.

2. A perfect middle/passive infinitive *does not always indicate present time but always indicates completed aspect.*

3. When the perfect middle/passive infinitive ending -σθαι was added to a consonant stem, the same changes occurred that occurred with the addition of the second person plural ending -σθε.

§85. Synopsis 4: All Indicative Tenses; All Infinitives; Present and Aorist Participles

Here is a model synopsis for **διδάσκω** in the third person singular with participles in the masculine singular accusative. It includes the forms of the perfect and pluperfect active and middle/passive indicative and the perfect active and the perfect middle/passive infinitives.

Principal Parts: διδάσκω, διδάξω, ἐδίδαξα, δεδίδαχα, δεδίδαγμαι, ἐδιδάχθην
Person and Number: **3rd sing.**
Gender, Number, and Case: **Masc. Sing. Acc.**

	Active	*Middle*	*Passive*
Indicative			
Present	διδάσκει he is teaching	διδάσκεται he is causing to be taught	διδάσκεται he is being taught
Imperfect	ἐδίδασκε(ν) he was teaching	ἐδιδάσκετο he was causing to be taught	ἐδιδάσκετο he was being taught
Future	διδάξει he will teach	διδάξεται he will cause to be taught	διδαχθήσεται he will be taught
Aorist	ἐδίδαξε(ν) he taught	ἐδιδάξατο he caused to be taught	ἐδιδάχθη he was taught
Perfect	δεδίδαχε(ν) he has taught	δεδίδακται he has caused to be taught	δεδίδακται he has been taught
Pluperfect	ἐδεδιδάχει(ν) he had taught	ἐδεδίδακτο he had caused to be taught	ἐδεδίδακτο he had been taught
Infinitives			
Present	διδάσκειν to be teaching	διδάσκεσθαι to be causing to be taught	διδάσκεσθαι to be being taught
Future	διδάξειν to be about to teach	διδάξεσθαι to be about to cause to be taught	διδαχθήσεσθαι to be about to be taught
Aorist	διδάξαι to teach (once)	διδάξασθαι to cause to be taught (once)	διδαχθῆναι to be taught (once)
Perfect	δεδιδαχέναι to have taught	δεδιδάχθαι to have caused to be taught	δεδιδάχθαι to have been taught
Participles			
Present	διδάσκοντα	διδασκόμενον	διδασκόμενον
Aorist	διδάξαντα	διδαξάμενον	διδαχθέντα

OBSERVATION

In a synopsis basic English translations should be given for indicative and infinitive forms.

☛ DRILL 84–85 MAY NOW BE DONE.

§86. Dative of Agent

A noun or pronoun indicating the person *by whom* an action reported *in the perfect or pluperfect passive* has/had been done is regularly expressed by the dative case *with no preposition*. A noun so used is called a **Dative of Agent**. For example:

ὁ δῆμος ἐκείνῳ τῷ *ῥήτορι* πέπεισται.   The people have been persuaded *by* that *rhetor*.
ταῦτα τῷ *ἄρχοντι* ἐπέπρᾱκτο.   These things had been done *by* the *commander*.

The syntax of each italicized word (ῥήτορι, ἄρχοντι) is **Dative of Agent**.

OBSERVATION

The Dative of Agent that appears with the perfect or pluperfect passive tense is an extension of the referential function of the dative case. The person *with reference to whom* an action has/had been completed is understood to include the person *by whom* an action has/had been done.

☛ DRILL 83–86 MAY NOW BE DONE.

§87. The Verb φημί

A -μι verb or athematic verb has been defined as a verb whose endings are attached directly to the stem with no intervening thematic vowels (§26, footnote 8). The -μι verb φημί, φήσω, ἔφησα, ——, ——, ——, "say," "assert," has active voice forms only and follows regular rules for the conjugation of -μι verbs in the present and imperfect tenses.

Each -μι verb has both a long-vowel grade and a short-vowel grade of the present stem.[5] Thus, for φημί:

Long-vowel grade: φη-   (used in the *singular only* of the present and imperfect active indicative)
Short-vowel grade: φα-   (used wherever φη- is not used)

The personal endings for the present and imperfect active indicative conjugations of -μι verbs are similar to but *not* identical with those of omega verbs and must be memorized:

5. These two stems are not easily seen in the irregular conjugations of εἰμί.

Personal Endings for Athematic Verbs		
Present Active Indicative		**Imperfect Active Indicative**
Singular		
1	-μι	1	-ν
2	-ς	2	-ς
3	-σι(ν)	3	—
Plural		
1	-μεν	1	-μεν
2	-τε	2	-τε
3	-ᾱσι(ν)	3	-σαν

Thus, the conjugations of **φημί** in the present and imperfect active indicative are:

	Present Active Indicative	**Imperfect Active Indicative**
Singular		
1	φημί	ἔφην
2	φής	ἔφης/ἔφησθα
3	φησί(ν)	ἔφη
Plural		
1	φαμέν	ἔφαμεν
2	φατέ	ἔφατε
3	φᾱσί(ν)	ἔφασαν

OBSERVATIONS
___

1. In all forms of the present active indicative *except* the second person singular, **φημί** is a *disyllabic enclitic* (cf. **εἰμί**). When an enclitic form of **φημί** appears first in a sentence, it is accented on the ultima. The second person singular form **φής** is *not* enclitic and is formed irregularly. MEMORIZE THIS IRREGULAR FORM.

2. In the third person plural present active indicative, the -**α** of the stem contracts with the **ᾱ**- of the ending: *φαᾱσι(ν) > φᾱσί(ν).

3. The imperfect active indicative forms of **φημί** have the past indicative augment. They are *not* enclitic and have regular recessive accents. The alternate second person singular **ἔφησθα** uses an alternate second person singular ending, -**σθα**. MEMORIZE THIS IRREGULAR FORM.

4. There is no personal ending for the third person singular of the imperfect active indicative: the form is made up of the long-vowel grade of the stem with the past indicative augment.

To form the present active infinitive of a -**μι** verb:

1. take the short-vowel grade of the stem
2. add the athematic present active infinitive ending -**ναι**.

Short-Vowel Grade Stem: **φα**-	
Present Active Infinitive: **φάναι**	to be saying/to be asserting

The accent on the present active infinitive is *persistent on the penult*.

φημί has a regularly formed present active participle derived from the short-vowel grade of the stem (φα-).[6] In Attic Greek, however, the participle **φάσκων, φάσκουσα, *φάσκον** (< ***φάσκω, ——, ——, ——, ——, ——,** "say," "assert") is used instead.

☛ DRILL 87 MAY NOW BE DONE.

§88. Indirect Statement 2

In addition to ὅτι/ὡς and a finite verb, indirect speech or perception may also be expressed in Greek by a *Subject Accusative* and verb in the *infinitive*.[7] In this type of indirect statement there is no conjunction meaning "that" in Greek, but "that" should be supplied in an English translation. The infinitive, like the finite verb after ὅτι/ὡς, represents the tense (and often the aspect) of the verb in the original direct statement or perception and has time relative to the introductory verb of saying or perceiving:

present infinitive	=	time simultaneous with introductory verb
future infinitive	=	time subsequent to introductory verb
aorist infinitive	=	time prior to introductory verb
perfect infinitive	=	time simultaneous with introductory verb (completed aspect)

One verb that regularly introduces the accusative/infinitive construction is φημί.

6. Forms of this participle (φάς, φᾶσα, φάν) appear chiefly in Homer, Pindar, Herodotus and late Greek.

7. A similar construction appears in English sentences such as "I believe *him to be* an honorable man" (i.e., "I believe *that he is* an honorable man").

direct statement:	ἡ μάχη παύεται. The battle is being stopped.
indirect statements:	φὴς τὴν μάχην παύεσθαι. You say that the battle *is being stopped*.
	ἔφησθα τὴν μάχην παύεσθαι. You were saying that the battle *was being stopped*.
	φήσεις τὴν μάχην παύεσθαι. You will say that the battle *is being stopped*.
direct statement:	ἡ μάχη ἐπαύθη. The battle was stopped.
indirect statements:	φὴς τὴν μάχην παυθῆναι. You say that the battle *was stopped*.
	ἔφησθα τὴν μάχην παυθῆναι. You were saying that the battle *had been stopped*.
	φήσεις τὴν μάχην παυθῆναι. You will say that the battle *was stopped*.
direct statement:	ἡ μάχη παυθήσεται. The battle will be stopped.
indirect statements:	φὴς τὴν μάχην παυθήσεσθαι. You say that the battle *will be stopped*.
	ἔφησθα τὴν μάχην παυθήσεσθαι. You were saying that the battle *would be stopped*.
	φήσεις τὴν μάχην παυθήσεσθαι. You will say that the battle *will be stopped*.
direct statement:	ἡ μάχη οὐ πέπαυται. The battle has not been stopped.
indirect statements:	φὴς τὴν μάχην οὐ πεπαῦσθαι. You say that the battle *has not been stopped*.
	ἔφησθα τὴν μάχην οὐ πεπαῦσθαι. You were saying that the battle *had not been stopped*.
	φήσεις τὴν μάχην οὐ πεπαῦσθαι. You will say that the battle *has not been stopped*.

OBSERVATIONS

1. In each indirect statement the syntax of **μάχην** is Subject Accusative (of an infinitive in an indirect statement).

2. The infinitives in these indirect statements are not translated as infinitives but as finite verbs that reflect the relation in time of the infinitives to the introductory verbs of saying. Particularly when the introductory verbs are in past time, care must be taken to give the Greek infinitives correct English translations to indicate relative time.

3. Unlike other infinitives, which are negated with **μή**, an infinitive in an indirect statement is negated with **οὐ**, reflecting the negation of the verb in the direct statement.

When the infinitive in an indirect statement is a copulative verb, a Predicate Accusative or an Accusative, Predicate Adjective often appears. The verb **εἶναι** *may be omitted* from an indirect statement with a Predicate Accusative or an Accusative, Predicate Adjective.

> **οἱ πολλοί φᾶσι μοῖραν σώματος εἶναι τὸν θάνατον.**
> The majority say that *death* is the *fate* of the body.
>
> **ἆρ' ἔφης Γοργίαν εἶναι τῇ ἀληθείᾳ δεινόν;**
> Were you saying that *Gorgias* was truly *clever?*
>
> **φημὶ ἀθάνατον τὴν ψῡχήν.**
> I assert that the *soul is immortal.*

OBSERVATIONS

1. The syntax of **θάνατον**, **Γοργίαν**, and **ψῡχήν** is Subject Accusative. The syntax of **μοῖραν** is Predicate Accusative, and the syntax of **δεινόν** and **ἀθάνατον** is Accusative, Predicate Adjective.

2. In the third sentence the infinitive **εἶναι** has been omitted from a sentence with a Subject Accusative and an Accusative, Predicate Adjective. An appropriate form of "to be" is added in an English translation of such a sentence.

When the subject of an indirect statement with a verb in the infinitive is the same as the subject of the introductory verb, that subject is *not expressed* in Greek, but it should be supplied in an English translation.

> **Γοργίᾱς φησὶ εὖ διδάσκειν.**   Gorgias says *that he* is teaching well.
> **Γοργίᾱς φησὶ δεινὸς εἶναι.**   Gorgias says *that he* is clever.

OBSERVATIONS

1. These indirect statements *have no expressed Subjects Accusative,* but they have verbs in the infinitive (**διδάσκειν, εἶναι**).

2. In the second sentence a Predicate Adjective (**δεινός**) appears in the nominative case to agree with the expressed subject of the introductory verb (**Γοργίᾱς**).

☛ DRILL 88 MAY NOW BE DONE.

§89. Indirect Statement 3

In addition to ὅτι/ὡς and a finite verb and Subject Accusative with a verb in the infinitive, indirect speech or perception may also be expressed in Greek by a Subject Accusative and a *supplementary participle* agreeing in gender, number, and case with the Subject Accusative. In this type of indirect statement there is no conjunction meaning "that" in Greek, but "that" should be supplied in an English translation. The participle represents the tense (and often the aspect) of the verb in the original direct statement or perception and has time relative to the introductory verb of saying or perceiving:

present participle	=	time simultaneous with introductory verb
future[8] participle	=	time subsequent to introductory verb
aorist participle	=	time prior to introductory verb
perfect[9] participle	=	time simultaneous with introductory verb (completed aspect)

Two verbs that regularly introduce the accusative/supplementary participle construction are ἀκούω and ὁράω.

direct statement:	αἱ γυναῖκες εὖ πράττουσιν. The women are faring well.
indirect statements:	ἀκούω τὰς γυναῖκας εὖ πρᾱττούσᾱς. I hear that the women *are faring* well.
	ἤκουσα τὰς γυναῖκας εὖ πρᾱττούσᾱς. I heard that the women *were faring* well.
	ἀκούσομαι τὰς γυναῖκας εὖ πρᾱττούσᾱς. I shall hear that the women *are faring* well.
direct statement:	αἱ γυναῖκες εὖ ἔπρᾱξαν. The women fared well.
indirect statements:	ὁρῶ τὰς γυναῖκας εὖ πρᾱξᾱσᾱς. I see that the women *fared* well.
	εἶδον τὰς γυναῖκας εὖ πρᾱξᾱσᾱς. I saw that the women *had fared* well.
	ὄψομαι τὰς γυναῖκας εὖ πρᾱξᾱσᾱς. I shall see that the women *fared* well.

OBSERVATIONS

1. In each indirect statement the syntax of γυναῖκας is Subject Accusative (of a supplementary participle in an indirect statement).

8. For the formation of the future participle see Part 2, §110.
9. For the formation of the perfect participle see Part 2, §110.

2. The participles in these indirect statements are not translated as participles but as finite verbs that reflect the relation in time of the participles to the introductory verbs of perceiving. Particularly when the introductory verbs are in the past time, care must be taken to give the Greek participles correct English translations to indicate relative time.

A supplementary participle in an indirect statement is negated by **οὐ**.

ἠκούομεν ὑμᾶς οὐκ ἀποπεμπομένους εἰς μάχην οὐδὲ τοὺς υἱούς.
We were hearing that you (pl.) were not being sent away to battle nor (were) your sons.

When the supplementary participle in an indirect statement is a copulative verb, a Predicate Accusative or an Accusative, Predicate Adjective often appears.

ὁρῶ ἄνδρα νῦν ὄντα τὸν σὸν παῖδα.	I see that your *child* is now a *man*.
ἠκούσαμεν σοφὸν ὄντα τοῦτον τὸν ποιητήν.	We heard that this *poet* was *wise*.

OBSERVATIONS
_____

1. The syntax of **παῖδα** and **ποιητήν** is Subject Accusative. The syntax of **ἄνδρα** is Predicate Accusative, and the syntax of **σοφόν** is Accusative, Predicate Adjective.

2. A form of **ὤν, οὖσα, ὄν** *may be omitted* from an indirect statement with a supplementary participle. An appropriate form of "to be" is supplied in translation. For example: **ἤκουσα σοφὸν πάντα ποιητήν** ("I heard that every poet *was* wise").

When the subject of an indirect statement with a supplementary participle is *the same as* the subject of the introductory verb, that subject is *not expressed* in Greek, and the participle is in the *nominative* case to agree with the subject. When the participle is a copulative verb, a Predicate Nominative or a Predicate Adjective in the Nominative Case often appears.

ὁ δοῦλος ἤκουσεν εἰς μάχην πεμπόμενος.
The slave heard *that he was being sent* to battle.

ὁρῶμεν ἐχθροὶ ὄντες.
We see *that we are enemies*.

ὁρᾷ καλὴ οὖσα.
She sees *that she is beautiful*.

OBSERVATIONS
_____

1. These indirect statements *have no expressed Subjects Accusative*, but they have supplementary participles (**πεμπόμενος, ὄντες, οὖσα**).

2. In the second sentence the syntax of **ἐχθροί** is Predicate Nominative. In the third sentence the syntax of **καλή** is Nominative, Predicate Adjective.

A Note on Indirect Statement

Although some verbs in Greek introduce only one type of indirect statement, many verbs may introduce more than one type. Below is a table indicating the constructions taken by the verbs that have appeared thus far.[10]

	ὅτι/ὡς and a Finite Verb	Subject Accusative and an Infinitive	Subject Accusative and a Supplementary Participle
ἀκούω	x	x	x
δῆλόν ἐστι(ν)	x		
δηλόω	x	x	x
——, ἐρῶ	x	x	
λέγω	x	x	
μανθάνω	x		x
οἴομαι/οἶμαι		x	
ὁράω	x		x
πείθω	x	x	x
φάσκω		x	
φημί		x	

OBSERVATIONS
___

1. Verbs of perceiving such as ἀκούω and ὁράω most often introduce an indirect statement with a Subject Accusative and a supplementary participle. This construction indicates a *direct physical perception*. When these verbs introduce an indirect statement with ὅτι/ὡς and a finite verb, the perception is rather an intellectual observation.

2. λέγω and ——, ἐρῶ most often introduce an indirect statment with ὅτι/ὡς and a finite verb, but they may introduce an indirect statement with a Subject Accusative and an infinitive, particularly in definitions or other statements of equivalency.

☛ DRILL 89 MAY NOW BE DONE.

§90. Personal Constructions

Sometimes the subject of an indirect statement is the subject of a verb of saying or perceiving in the passive voice and is in the nominative case. An infinitive completes the meaning. For example:

ὁ Πρίαμος λέγεται πάντας τοὺς υἱοὺς εἰς μάχην πέμπειν/πέμψαι.
Priam is said to be *sending/to have sent* all his sons into battle.

Such a sentence is called a **Personal Construction of Indirect Statement** because the verb (λέγεται) has as its subject the *person* performing the action of the infinitive.

___
10. When a verb that takes indirect statement is introduced, its vocabulary note indicates what construction(s) of indirect statement it employs. See also the appendix "Verbs Introducing Indirect Statement."

1. The Personal Construction is considered a variety of indirect statement even though it has a subject in the nominative case and does *not* have a noun clause that is the subject or object of a verb of saying or perceiving.

2. The infinitive in the Personal Construction shows relative time to the verb of saying or perceiving. However, it is translated with the English word "to." The English conjunction "that" is not used in the translation of a Personal Construction.

The Personal Construction may be contrasted with an impersonal construction:

λέγεται τὸν Πρίαμον πάντας τοὺς υἱοὺς εἰς μάχην πέμπειν/πέμψαι.
That *Priam is sending/sent* all his sons into battle is (being) said.
It is said that *Priam is sending/sent* all his sons into battle.

In this sentence an indirect statement with a Subject Accusative (τὸν Πρίαμον) and an infinitive (πέμπειν/πέμψαι) is the subject of λέγεται, and the verb of saying or perceiving does not have a personal subject. Instead, the subject is the entire indirect statement. In the second translation the pronoun "it" is an expletive standing in place of and anticipating the actual subject, the indirect statement.

Another Personal Construction of Indirect Statement appears with certain adjectives and uses either a supplementary participle or an indirect statement with ὅτι/ὡς and a finite verb. For example:

δῆλος εἶ ἐκεῖνο τὸ αἰσχρὸν ἔργον πράξας.
You are clear having done that shameful deed.
It is clear that you did that shameful deed.

δῆλός ἐστιν ὅτι ἐκεῖνο τὸ αἰσχρὸν ἔργον ἔπραξεν.
He is clear that he did that shameful deed.
It is clear that he did that shameful deed.

1. In the first sentence the supplementary participle (πράξας) is nominative to agree with the subject of the sentence. The second translation is to be preferred because it more clearly expresses an indirect statement.

2. The second sentence is a variety of binary construction (§70), in which the subject of the indirect statement, "he," is first expressed as the subject of the main verb (ἐστιν). The second translation is to be preferred.

A Personal Construction may also be used instead of a Subject Accusative and Subject Infinitive with certain predicate adjectives.

δίκαιός εἰμι τόδε λέγειν.
I am just (i.e., justified) to say (in saying) this thing.
It is just that I say this thing.

This Personal Construction may be contrasted with an impersonal construction.

δίκαιόν ἐστιν ἐμὲ τόδε λέγειν.
For me to say this thing is just.
It is just for me to say this thing.

☛ DRILL 90 MAY NOW BE DONE.

§91. Articular Infinitive

When an article is followed by an infinitive, a substantive called an *Articular Infinitive* is formed.
An **Articular Infinitive** is a neuter singular noun comprising a neuter singular form of the article
and any tense and any voice of the infinitive. For example:

Nom.	τὸ ἀδικεῖν	(the) to do wrong; doing wrong	τὸ τετῑμῆσθαι	(the) to have been honored; having been honored
Gen.	τοῦ ἀδικεῖν	of (the) doing wrong	τοῦ τετῑμῆσθαι	of (the) having been honored
Dat.	τῷ ἀδικεῖν	for, by (the) doing wrong	τῷ τετῑμῆσθαι	for, by (the) having been honored
Acc.	τὸ ἀδικεῖν	(the) doing wrong (d.o.)	τὸ τετῑμῆσθαι	(the) having been honored (d.o.)

OBSERVATIONS

---

1. The Articular Infinitive has no vocative case and no plural forms.
2. Since it is a verbal noun, the Articular Infinitive may be translated with the English infinitive
or with the other verbal noun of English, the gerund. The gerund is particularly useful in translating the genitive and dative case forms of the Articular Infinitive. Although the article is
present in Greek, "the" is not included in English translations of Articular Infinitives.
3. The particular *tense* of an Articular Infinitive usually indicates *aspect only*. Thus, τῷ πέμπειν
means "by sending (repeatedly)," but τῷ πέμψαι means "by sending" (once).

The Articular Infinitive is a noun and has the syntax of a noun, but it retains the verbal properties
of tense and voice, and it functions as a verb in having expressed subjects and objects and being
modified by adverbs. Like Subject and Object Infinitives, the Articular Infinitive is negated by μή.

καλὸν τὸ τοῖς παισὶ τὴν τῆς ἀρετῆς ὁδὸν δηλοῦν.
A noble thing is *to show/showing* children the path of virtue.
Showing children the path of virtue is a noble thing.

πολλὰ καὶ δεινὰ ἠκούσαμεν περὶ τοῦ τοὺς πολεμίους ἐν τῇ γῇ ὀφθῆναι.
We heard many and terrible things about *the* enemies' *being seen (once)* in the land.

τῷ εὖ λέγειν τὸν δῆμον πείθειν εἶχον.

By speaking well I was able to persuade the people.

ὑπὲρ τοῦ μὴ ψῡχὴν ἄδικοι γενέσθαι οἱ νεᾱνίαι τὸ δίκαιον μανθάνουσιν.

On behalf of (i.e., for the purpose of) *not becoming* unjust in soul, the young men are learning the just thing.

OBSERVATIONS

1. In the first sentence the Articular Infinitive (τὸ . . . δηλοῦν) contains both an Accusative, Direct Object (ὁδόν) and a Dative of Indirect Object (παισί). The Articular Infinitive is nominative, the subject of a nominal sentence.

2. In the second sentence the Articular Infinitive (τοῦ . . . ὀφθῆναι) is genitive, object of the preposition περί, and contains a Subject Accusative and a prepositional phrase. When translating the Subject Accusative of an Articular Infinitive, care must be taken to use the English possessive form before the gerund ("the enem<u>ies'</u> being seen").

3. In the third sentence the Articular Infinitive (τῷ . . . λέγειν) is modified by the adverb εὖ. The syntax of this Articular Infinitive is Dative of Means.

4. In the fourth sentence the Articular Infinitive (τοῦ . . . γενέσθαι) is negated by μή and is genitive, object of the preposition ὑπέρ. This construction frequently, as here, expresses an idea of *purpose*. The Articular Infinitive also contains a Predicate Adjective in the Nominative Case, ἄδικοι. This adjective is nominative because it refers to νεᾱνίαι, the subject of the main verb of the sentence.

☞ DRILL 91 MAY NOW BE DONE.

Short Readings

1. A fragment from a comedy of Epicharmus

οὐ μετανοεῖν ἀλλὰ προνοεῖν χρὴ τὸν ἄνδρα τὸν σοφόν. (Epicharmus, frag. 280)

μετανοέω (μετα- + νοέω) perceive afterward   προνοέω (προ- + νοέω) perceive beforehand

2. A fragment from the works of the philosopher Xenophanes

. . . ἐξ ἀρχῆς καθ' Ὅμηρον ἐπεὶ μεμαθήκᾱσι πάντες . . . (Xenophanes, frag. 10)

DH

Ὅμηρος, Ὁμήρου, ὁ Homer
ἐπεί (conj.) since, because

3. A fragment from the works of the philosopher Heraclitus

μάχεςθαι χρὴ τὸν δῆμον ὑπὲρ τοῦ νόμου ὅκωςπερ τείχεος. (Heraclitus, frag. 44)

ὅκωςπερ (Ionic) = Attic ὥςπερ   τείχεος (Ionic) = Attic τείχους

4. Ajax concludes a speech to his wife, Tecmessa, and the Chorus with a forceful expression of his own viewpoint.

ἀλλ' ἢ καλῶς ζῆν ἢ καλῶς τεθνηκέναι
τὸν εὐγενῆ χρή. πάντ' ἀκήκοας λόγον. (Sophocles, Ajax 479–80)

IT

τεθνηκέναι = τεθνάναι   εὐγενής, εὐγενές well-born, noble

5. The Chorus accounts for the murder of Agamemnon.

δόλος ἦν ὁ φράςᾱς, ἔρος ὁ κτείνᾱς,
δεινὰν δεινῶς προφυτεύςαντες
μορφάν, εἴτ' οὖν θεὸς εἴτε βροτῶν
ἦν ὁ ταῦτα πράςςων. (Sophocles, Electra 197–200)

δόλος, δόλου, ὁ deceit, treachery
φράζω, φράςω, ἔφραςα, πέφρακα, πέφραςμαι,
 ἐφράςθην show; advise
ἔρος = ἔρως
δεινάν (Doric) = Attic δεινήν

προφυτεύω (προ- + φυτεύω), προφυτεύςω,
 προυφύτευςα, ——, ——, —— produce, give
 birth to
μορφή, μορφῆς, ἡ form; μορφάν (Doric) = Attic
 μορφήν
εἴτε . . . εἴτε . . . whether . . . or (if) . . .

6. Electra begins an attack on her mother, Clytaemnestra.

> λέξω δέ σοι
> ὡς οὐ δίκῃ γ’ ἔκτεινας, ἀλλά σ’ ἔσπασεν
> πειθὼ κακοῦ πρὸς ἀνδρός, ᾧ τανῦν ξύνει.

(Sophocles, *Electra* 560–62)

IT

σπάω, σπάσω, ἔσπασα, ἔσπακα, ἔσπασμαι,
　ἐσπάσθην draw; carry away
πειθώ, πειθοῦς, ἡ persuasion

τανῦν (adv.) now, presently
ξύνειμι (ξυν- + εἰμί) be with; live with

7. Oedipus asks Creon what Apollo's oracle said about the murderers of Laius.

> Οι.　οἱ δ’ εἰσὶ ποῦ γῆς; ποῦ τόδ’ εὑρεθήσεται
> 　　ἴχνος παλαιᾶς δυστέκμαρτον αἰτίας;
> Κρ.　ἐν τῇδ’ ἔφασκε γῇ. τὸ δὲ ζητούμενον
> 　　ἁλωτόν, ἐκφεύγει δὲ τἀμελούμενον.

(Sophocles, *Oedipus Tyrannus* 108–11)

IT

Οι. = Oedipus
εὑρίσκω, εὑρήσω, ηὖρον, ηὕρηκα, ηὕρημαι,
　ηὑρέθην find
ἴχνος, ἴχνους, τό track, footstep; trace
δυστέκμαρτος, δυστέκμαρτον hard to conjecture
Κρ. = Creon

ζητέω, ζητήσω, ἐζήτησα, ἐζήτηκα, ——, ——
　seek (for)
ἁλωτός, ἁλωτόν able to be caught
ἐκφεύγω (ἐκ- + φεύγω), ἐκφεύξομαι, ἐξέφυγον,
　ἐκπέφευγα, ——, —— escape
ἀμελέω have no care for; overlook

Fragments from tragedies of Sophocles

8.　　　τὸ χρύσεον δὲ τᾶς Δίκᾱς
> δέδορκεν ὄμμα, τὸν δ’ ἄδικον ἀμείβεται.

(Sophocles, frag. 12)

IT

χρύσεος, χρῡσέᾱ, χρύσεον golden
τᾶς Δίκᾱς (Doric) = Attic τῆς Δίκης
δέρκομαι, ——, ἔδρακον, δέδορκα, ——,
　ἐδέρχθην see clearly; *perfect with present meaning*

ὄμμα, ὄμματος, τό eye
ἀμείβω, ἀμείψω, ἤμειψα, ——, ——, ἠμείφθην
　change; *middle*, answer; repay

9.　　θνητὴν δὲ φύσιν χρὴ θνητὰ φρονεῖν . . .

(Sophocles, frag. 590)

φρονέω think

10.   οἴμοι, πέπρᾱκται τοῦ θεοῦ τὸ θέσφατον.   (Sophocles, frag. 885a)
IT

οἴμοι (interj.) alas! woe is me!   θέσφατος, θέσφατον spoken by a god, decreed; *neut. subst.*, decree, oracle

11.   χαίρειν ἐπ᾽ αἰσχραῖς ἡδοναῖς οὐ χρή ποτε.   (Sophocles, frag. 926)
IT

12.   οὐ γὰρ θέμις ζῆν πλὴν θεοῖς ἄνευ κακῶν.   (Sophocles, frag. 946)
IT

θέμις, θέμιτος, ἡ (customary) law; right   πλήν (conj.) except

13.   θανόντι κείνῳ συνθανεῖν ἔρως μ᾽ ἔχει.   (Sophocles, frag. 953)
IT

κείνῳ = ἐκείνῳ   συνθνήσκω (συν- + θνήσκω) die with

14. Ion explains to his long-lost father why he prefers to remain a priest in the temple of Apollo.

ἴση γὰρ ἡ χάρις,
μεγάλοισι χαίρειν σμῑκρὰ θ᾽ ἡδέως ἔχειν.   (Euripides, *Ion* 646–47)
IT

ἡδέως (adv.) gladly

15. When Hector refuses to go to battle with Rhesus, Rhesus responds.

μόνος μάχεσθαι πολεμίοις, Ἕκτορ, θέλω.   (Euripides, *Rhesus* 488)
IT

Fragments from tragedies of Euripides

16.   οἴμοι, θανοῦμαι διὰ τὸ χρήσιμον φρενῶν,
ὃ τοῖσιν ἄλλοις γίγνεται σωτηρίᾱ.   (Euripides, frag. 58N)
IT

οἴμοι (interj.) alas! woe is me!   χρήσιμος, χρησίμη, χρήσιμον useful; *neut. subst.*, excellence

17.   τήν τοι Δίκην λέγουσι παῖδ᾽ εἶναι Διός
      ἐγγύς τε ναίειν τῆς βροτῶν ἁμαρτίᾱς.   (Euripides, frag. 151N)
                                                                              IT

ἐγγύς (prep. + gen.) near to   ἁμαρτίᾱ, ἁμαρτίᾱς, ἡ error
ναίω, ——, ——, ——, ——, —— dwell

18.   τεθνᾶσι παῖδες οὐκ ἐμοὶ μόνῃ βροτῶν
      οὐδ᾽ ἀνδρὸς ἐστερήμεθ᾽, ἀλλὰ μῡρίαι
      τὸν αὐτὸν ἐξήντλησαν ὡς ἐγὼ βίον.   (Euripides, frag. 454N)
                                                                              IT

στερέω, στερήσω, ἐστέρησα, ——, ἐστέρημαι,   μῡρίος, μῡρίᾱ, μῡρίον countless, myriad
   ἐστερήθην deprive, bereave; rob   ἐξαντλέω (ἐξ- + ἀντλέω) endure to the end

19.   ὦ πάτερ, ἐχρῆν μὲν οὓς λόγους λέγω,
      τούτους λέγειν σε·   (Euripides, frag. 953N)
                                                                              IT

20.   ἀνδρῶν τάδ᾽ ἐστὶν ἐνδίκων τε καὶ σοφῶν,
      κἀν τοῖς κακοῖσι μὴ τεθῡμῶσθαι θεοῖς.   (Euripides, frag. 1078N)
                                                                              IT

ἔνδικος, ἔνδικον upright, just   θῡμόομαι, θῡμώσομαι, ἐθῡμωσάμην, ——,
                                                    τεθῡμωμαι, ἐθῡμώθην be angry (at) (+ dat.);
                                                    perfect with present meaning

21. The general Nicias begins an address to his men before a battle near Syracuse on Sicily.

   Ἄνδρες στρατιῶται Ἀθηναίων τε καὶ τῶν ἄλλων ξυμμάχων, ὁ μὲν ἀγὼν ὁ μέλλων
   ὁμοίως κοινὸς ἅπᾱσιν ἔσται περί τε σωτηρίᾱς καὶ πατρίδος.   (Thucydides, *Peloponnesian War*
   VII.61.1)

ὁμοίως (adv.) similarly   πατρίς, πατρίδος, ἡ homeland

22. The Neoplatonic philosopher Syrianus reports a comment of the orator Isocrates.

> καὶ γὰρ Ἰσοκράτης ἔργον ἔφασκεν εἶναι ῥητορικῆc τὰ μὲν cμῑκρὰ μεγάλωc εἰπεῖν, τὰ δὲ μέγαλα cμῑκρῶc· καὶ μὲν καινὰ παλαιῶc, τὰ δὲ παλαιὰ καινῶc. (Isocrates, frag. 2)

Ἰσοκράτης, Ἰσοκράτους, ὁ Isocrates
ῥητορική, ῥητορικῆc, ἡ (art of) rhetoric

καινόc, καινή, καινόν new

23. In a speech written by the orator for Euphiletus, who is defending himself on a charge of murder, Euphiletus repeats what he said to the victim, Eratosthenes, when he caught him in his bedroom with his wife.

> Οὐκ ἐγώ cε ἀποκτενῶ ἀλλ᾽ ὁ τῆc πόλεωc νόμοc. (Lysias, *Speech in Defense of the Murder of Eratosthenes* 26)

24. A fragment from the works of the orator

> ἡ γὰρ γλῶττα νοῦν οὔτε πολὺν οὔτε μῑκρὸν ἔχει, ὁ δὲ νοῦc, ᾧ μὲν πολύ, πολύc, ᾧ δὲ μῑκρόν, μῑκρόc. (Lysias, frag. 429.2–4)

γλῶττα, γλώττης, ἡ tongue

25. In a speech to the assembled Greek generals, Xenophon reminds them of something that they all know.

> . . . οὔτε πλῆθόc ἐcτιν οὔτε ἰcχὺc ἡ ἐν τῷ πολέμῳ τὰc νίκᾱc ποιοῦcα. (Xenophon, *Anabasis* III.1.42)

ἰcχύc, ἰcχύοc, ἡ strength, might

26. While visiting his grandfather, the king of the Medes, the Persian Cyrus takes special delight in learning to ride horses.

> ἐν Πέρcαιc γὰρ διὰ τὸ χαλεπὸν εἶναι καὶ τρέφειν ἵππους καὶ ἱππεύειν ἐν ὀρεινῇ οὔcῃ τῇ χώρᾳ καὶ ἰδεῖν ἵππον πάνυ cπάνιον ἦν. (Xenophon, *Cyropaedia* I.3.3)

Πέρcαι, Περcῶν, οἱ (the) Persians
τρέφω, θρέψω, ἔθρεψα, τέτροφα, τέθραμμαι, ἐτράφην nourish; raise
ἵππος, ἵππου, ὁ *or* ἡ horse; mare

ἱππεύω, ἱππεύcω, ἵππευcα, ἵππευκα, —, — be a horseman, ride
ὀρεινόc, ὀρεινή, ὀρεινόν mountainous
cπάνιος, cπανίᾱ, cπάνιον rare

27. Socrates cautions an ambitious Euthydemus.

> . . . πολλοὶ δὲ διὰ δόξαν καὶ πολῑτικὴν δύναμιν μεγάλα κακὰ πεπόνθᾱσιν.
>
> (Xenophon, Memorabilia IV.2.35)

πολῑτικός, πολῑτική, πολῑτικόν of or belonging to
  a citizen or state; political

28. Socrates asks Euthyphro a question about the gods.

> Cω. Οὐκοῦν ἅπερ καλὰ ἡγοῦνται ἕκαστοι καὶ ἀγαθὰ καὶ δίκαια, ταῦτα καὶ φιλοῦcιν, τὰ
> δὲ ἐναντία τούτων μῑcοῦcιν;
> Εὐ. Πάνυ γε.
>
> (Plato, Euthyphro 7e6–8)

οὐκοῦν (particle) *introduces a question expecting*
  the answer yes, therefore, accordingly
ἡγέομαι, ἡγήcομαι, ἡγηcάμην, ——, ἥγημαι,
  ἡγήθην regard, believe

μῑcέω hate
Εὐ. = Euthyphro

29. Socrates corrects those who claim that like is friendly to like.

> τοῦτο τοίνυν αἰνίττονται, ὡς ἐμοὶ δοκοῦcιν, ὦ ἑταῖρε, οἱ τὸ ὅμοιον τῷ ὁμοίῳ φίλον
> λέγοντες, ὡc ὁ ἀγαθὸc τῷ ἀγαθῷ μόνοc μόνῳ φίλοc, ὁ δὲ κακὸc οὔτε ἀγαθῷ οὔτε κακῷ
> οὐδέποτε εἰc ἀληθῆ φιλίᾱν ἔρχεται.
>
> (Plato, Lysis 214d3–d7)

τοίνυν (particle) accordingly, therefore
αἰνίττομαι, αἰνίξομαι, ἠνιξάμην, ——, ——,
  —— speak darkly, riddle; hint (at)

δοκέω, δόξω, ἔδοξα, ——, δέδογμαι, —— seem
ὅμοιος, ὁμοίᾱ, ὅμοιον similar, like
φιλίᾱ, φιλίᾱc, ἡ friendship

30. Phaedrus responds to Socrates' suggestion that a speaker must know the truth about his topic
in order to speak well.

> Οὑτωcὶ περὶ τούτου ἀκήκοα, ὦ φίλε Cώκρατες, οὐκ εἶναι ἀνάγκην τῷ μέλλοντι ῥήτορι
> ἔcεcθαι τὰ τῷ ὄντι δίκαια μανθάνειν, ἀλλὰ τὰ δόξαντ᾿ ἂν πλήθει, οἵπερ† δικάcουcιν, οὐδὲ
> τὰ ὄντωc ἀγαθὰ ἢ καλά, ἀλλ᾿ ὅcα δόξει· ἐκ γὰρ τούτων εἶναι τὸ πείθειν, ἀλλ᾿ οὐκ ἐκ τῆc
> ἀληθείᾱc.
>
> (Plato, Phaedrus 259e7–260a4)

οὑτωcί = *emphatic form of* οὕτωc
δοκέω, δόξω, ἔδοξα, ——, δέδογμαι, —— seem;
  seem good; τὰ δόξαντ᾿ ἄν, the things that
  would seem (good) (ἄν *adds potential force*)

†οἵπερ, antecedent is people (*implied by* πλήθει)
δικάζω, δικάcω, ἐδίκαcα, ——, δεδίκαcμαι,
  ἐδικάcθην judge
ὅcος, ὅcη, ὅcον (rel. adj.) (as many) as

31. Socrates is reluctant to accept a commonly held notion.

   τοῖς γὰρ φάσκουϲι λῦπῶν εἶναι παῦλαν πάϲαϲ τὰϲ ἡδονὰϲ οὐ πάνυ πωϲ πείθομαι...

(Plato, Philebus 51a3–4)

παῦλα, παύληϲ, ἡ pause; cessation

32. A question posed by Socrates and its answer are reported.

   "...ταὐτόν ϲοι δοκεῖ εἶναι τὸ γενέϲθαι καὶ τὸ εἶναι, ἢ ἄλλο;"
   "Ἄλλο νὴ Δί'," ἔφη ὁ Πρόδικοϲ.

(Plato, Protagoras 340b4–6)

δοκέω, δόξω, ἔδοξα, ——, δέδογμαι, —— seem

Πρόδικοϲ, Προδίκου, ὁ Prodicus (a philosopher and participant in the dialogue)

33. Socrates attempts to explain to Protagoras what that sophist believes is a contradiction in a poem of Simonides.

   οὐ γὰρ τοῦτο ὁ Πίττακοϲ ἔλεγεν τὸ χαλεπόν, γενέϲθαι ἐϲθλόν, ὥϲπερ ὁ Ϲιμωνίδηϲ,
   ἀλλὰ τὸ ἔμμεναι. ἔϲτιν δὲ οὐ ταὐτόν, ὦ Πρωταγόρᾱ, ὥϲ φηϲιν Πρόδικοϲ ὅδε, τὸ εἶναι καὶ
   τὸ γενέϲθαι.

(Plato, Protagoras 340c3–7)

Πίττακοϲ, Πιττάκου, ὁ Pittacus (of Mytilene) (often included among the Seven Sages)
ἐϲθλόϲ, ἐϲθλή, ἐϲθλόν good
Ϲιμωνίδηϲ, Ϲιμωνίδου, ὁ Simonides (a Greek lyric poet)
ἔμμεναι (Epic) = Attic εἶναι

Πρωταγόρᾱϲ, Πρωταγόρου, ὁ Protagoras (a sophist)
Πρόδικοϲ, Προδίκου, ὁ Prodicus (a philosopher and participant in the dialogue); Πρόδικοϲ ὅδε, Prodicus here

34. Eryximachus gives his opinion about a dangerous habit.

   ἐμοὶ γὰρ δὴ τοῦτό γε οἶμαι κατάδηλον γεγονέναι ἐκ τῆϲ ἰᾱτρικῆϲ, ὅτι χαλεπὸν τοῖϲ
   ἀνθρώποιϲ ἡ μέθη ἐϲτί...

(Plato, Symposium 176c8–d2)

κατάδηλοϲ, κατάδηλον very clear
ἰᾱτρική, ἰᾱτρικῆϲ, ἡ (art of) medicine

μέθη, μέθηϲ, ἡ drunkenness

35. A Platonic definition

   Δίκη ἀμφιϲβήτηϲιϲ περὶ τοῦ ἀδικεῖν ἢ μή.

([Plato], Definitions 413d10)

ἀμφιϲβήτηϲιϲ, ἀμφιϲβητήϲεωϲ, ἡ dispute, controversy

36. The philosopher reports a saying of Heraclitus.

    ... Ἡράκλειτος δὲ τὴν ἀρχὴν εἶναί φησι ψῡχήν, ...   (Aristotle, *Concerning the Soul* 405a25)

Ἡράκλειτος, Ἡρακλείτου, ὁ Heraclitus

37. The philosopher offers a definition.

    ἔστι δὲ ἡ ψῡχὴ τοῦ ζῶντος cώματος αἰτίᾱ καὶ ἀρχή.   (Aristotle, *Concerning the Soul* 415b8)

    Fragments from comedies of Philemon

38.   χαλεπὸν τὸ ποιεῖν, τὸ δὲ κελεῦcαι ῥᾴδιον.   (Philemon, frag. 27)
                                                   IT

κελεύω, κελεύcω, ἐκέλευcα, κεκέλευκα,
    κεκέλευcμαι, ἐκελεύcθην order

39.   οἱ γὰρ θεὸν cέβοντες ἐλπίδας καλὰc
    ἔχουcιν εἰc cωτηρίᾱν.   (Philemon, frag. 197)
                                                   IT

cέβω, ——, ——, ——, ——, —— worship, honor

    Fragments and proverbial expressions from comedies of Menander

40.   τὸ δ' ἐρᾶν ἐπιcκοτεῖ
    ἅπᾱcιν, ὡc ἔοικε, καὶ τοῖc εὐλόγωc
    καὶ τοῖc κακῶc ἔχουcιν.   (Menander, frag. 48)
                                                   IT

ἐράω love   ἔοικε(ν) (perf. act. impersonal verb) it is likely; it
ἐπιcκοτέω throw a shadow over; blind (+ dat.)   seems
                                            εὐλόγωc (adv.) with good reason, reasonably

41.   γυνὴ δικαίᾱ τοῦ βίου cωτηρίᾱ.   (Menander, *Sententiae* 149)
                                                   IT

42.   ζῆν αἰcχρὸν οἷc ζῆν ἐφθόνηcεν ἡ τύχη.   (Menander, *Sententiae* 280)
                                                   IT

φθονέω begrudge

43.   τὸ γὰρ θανεῖν οὐκ αἰσχρόν, ἀλλ’ αἰσχρῶς θανεῖν.   (Menander, *Sententiae* 742)

IT

44.   χαίρειν ἐπ’ αἰσχροῖς οὐδέποτε χρὴ πράγμασιν.   (Menander, *Sententiae* 833)

IT

45. The biographer reports a saying of Solon.

ἔλεγε δὲ τὸν μὲν λόγον εἴδωλον εἶναι τῶν ἔργων.

(Diogenes Laertius, *Lives of the Philosophers* I.58)

εἴδωλον, εἰδώλου, τό image

Longer Readings

1. Sophocles, *Philoctetes* 260–65 (IT)

Philoctetes introduces himself to Neoptolemus, Achilles' son, who has come with Odysseus to
bring him back to the Greek army at Troy.

> ὦ τέκνον, ὦ παῖ πατρὸς ἐξ Ἀχιλλέως,
> ὅδ᾽ εἴμ᾽ ἐγώ† σοι κεῖνος, ὃν κλύεις ἴcωc
> τῶν Ἡρακλείων ὄντα δεσπότην ὅπλων,
> ὁ τοῦ Ποίαντος παῖc Φιλοκτήτης, ὃν οἱ
> διccοὶ cτρατηγοὶ χὠ Κεφαλλήνων ἄναξ
> ἔρρῑψαν αἰcχρῶc ὧδ᾽† ἔρημον, . . .

Ἀχιλλεύc, Ἀχιλλέωc, ὁ Achilles	δίccοc, δίccη, δίccον twofold, double
†ὅδ᾽ εἴμ᾽ ἐγώ, here I am	Κεφαλλήν, Κεφαλλῆνος, ὁ Cephallenian (a man
κεῖνοc = ἐκεῖνοc	from Cephallenia)
κλύω, ——, ——, ——, ——, —— hear	ἄναξ, ἄνακτοc, ὁ lord, master
Ἡράκλειοc, Ἡρακλείᾱ, Ἡράκλειον of or belong-	ῥίπτω, ῥίψω, ἔρρῑψα, ἔρρῑφα, ἔρρῑμμαι, ἐρρίφην/
ing to Hercules	ἐρρίφθην throw, hurl, cast away
Ποίᾱc, Ποίαντοc, ὁ Poeas	†ὧδε, *here*, hither, to this place
Φιλοκτήτηc, Φιλοκτήτου, ὁ Philoctetes	ἔρημοc, ἔρημον alone, deserted

Sophocles (496–406 B.C.E.) was born into a wealthy Athenian family and participated in many aspects of public life, including holding the office of general more than once. He may have written as many as 125 tragedies,
but only 7 complete plays and a large number of fragments from the lost plays survive. Sophocles is credited
with adding a third actor to tragedy, and he integrated the chorus more closely with the events of his plays. A
master of irony and plain but ambiguous language, Sophocles is praised in Aristotle's *Poetics* particularly for his
perfectly worked plots. Among the surviving plays, three concern the Theban Oedipus, while others reinterpret
or extend stories from the Homeric epics. Sophocles competed in many dramatic competitions and won many
first and second prizes.

The ***Philoctetes*** was probably produced in 409 B.C.E. It presents the tormented Greek hero Philoctetes, aban-
doned on the island of Lemnos by Agamemnon and the other Greek leaders of the expedition to Troy because
of a never-healing wound in his foot. When the Greeks learn, in the last year of the war, that Troy cannot be
captured without the bow of Heracles, which Philoctetes possesses, an embassy is sent to Lemnos to bring
Philoctetes and the bow to Troy. The clever speaker Odysseus, accompanied by Neoptolemus, the son of dead
Achilles, manages to gain the bow by trickery, but Neoptolemus, in sympathy for Philoctetes, gives it back and
offers to help him return to his home. Heracles miraculously appears, however, and promises Philoctetes that at
Troy he will be healed and the bow will guarantee a Greek victory.

2. Isocrates, *Nicocles* 7–8

Nicocles, king of Salamis in eastern Cyprus, praises the power of speech.

διὰ τούτου† τούς τ' ἀνοήτους παιδεύομεν καὶ φρονίμους δοκιμάζομεν· τὸ γὰρ λέγειν
ὡς δεῖ τοῦ φρονεῖν εὖ μέγιστον cημεῖον ποιούμεθα, καὶ λόγος ἀληθὴς καὶ νόμιμος
καὶ δίκαιος ψῡχῆς ἀγαθῆς καὶ πιστῆς εἴδωλόν ἐστιν. μετὰ τούτου καὶ περὶ τῶν
ἀμφιcβητηcίμων ἀγωνιζόμεθα καὶ περὶ τῶν ἀγνοουμένων σκοπούμεθα.

†τούτου, *supply* λόγου
ἀνόητοc, ἀνόητον not understanding, senseless,
  foolish
παιδεύω, παιδεύcω, ἐπαίδευcα, πεπαίδευκα,
  πεπαίδευμαι, ἐπαιδεύθην educate
φρόνιμοc, φρόνιμον sensible, prudent; intelligent
δοκιμάζω, δοκιμάcω, ἐδοκίμαcα, ———,
  δεδοκίμαcμαι, ἐδοκιμάcθην test, examine
φρονέω think
μέγιcτοc, μεγίcτη, μέγιcτον greatest

cημεῖον, cημείου, τό mark, sign
νόμιμοc, νόμιμον customary, lawful
πιcτόc, πιcτή, πιcτόν trustworthy, faithful
εἴδωλον, εἰδώλου, τό image
ἀμφιcβητήcιμοc, ἀμφιcβητήcιμον disputable,
  disputed
ἀγωνίζομαι, ἀγωνιοῦμαι, ἠγωνιcάμην, ———,
  ἠγώνιcμαι, ἠγωνίcθην contend (for a prize)
ἀγνοέω (ἀ- + νοέω) not know
cκοπέω *active or middle,* examine, consider

A contemporary of Plato, the long-lived Athenian **Isocrates** (436?–338 B.C.E.) was a writer of speeches, a teacher of rhetoric, the founder of an influential school, a lecturer on education, and a passionate proponent of Athens during its decline from greatness in the fifth and fourth centuries. Isocrates was well acquainted with Socrates and with many sophists teaching in Athens during his youth. Isocrates was greatly influenced by the latter and eventually himself founded a school of rhetoric. Twenty-one of his speeches and nine of his letters survive. The six forensic speeches were all written early in his career, but for most of his life he eschewed any direct role in legal matters or politics and devoted himself to writing speeches for others and giving speeches on grand themes (Athenian greatness, the best political system, the nature of education). Isocrates' prose style is noted for its consistent, almost repetitive, use of balanced, extended prose periods.

    The **Nicocles** is a speech written by Isocrates for delivery by Nicocles to his subjects. The speech makes the case for monarchy as the best form of government and outlines the duties and advantages of the subjects of a monarchy.

3. Xenophon, *Cynegeticus* 13.1

In the midst of a treatise on the value of hunting, Xenophon makes a remark about sophists.

> θαυμάζω δὲ τῶν σοφιστῶν καλουμένων, ὅτι φᾱcὶ μὲν ἐπ' ἀρετὴν ἄγειν οἱ πολλοὶ τοὺc
> νέουc, ἄγουcι δ' ἐπὶ τοὐναντίον· οὔτε γὰρ ἄνδρα που ἑωράκαμεν ὅντιν' οἱ νῦν cοφιcταὶ
> ἀγαθὸν ἐποίηcαν, οὔτε γράμματα παρέχονται ἐξ ὧν χρὴ ἀγαθοὺc γίγνεcθαι, ἀλλὰ περὶ
> μὲν τῶν ματαίων πολλὰ αὐτοῖc γέγραπται, ἀφ' ὧν τοῖc νέοιc αἱ μὲν ἡδοναὶ κεναί, ἀρετὴ
> δ' οὐκ ἔνι·

θαυμάζω, θαυμάcομαι, ἐθαύμαca, τεθαύμακα,
  ——, ἐθαυμάcθην wonder (at); be astonished
  (at) (+ gen.)
cοφιcτήc, cοφιcτοῦ, ὁ wise man; sophist
καλέω, καλῶ, ἐκάλεcα, κέκληκα, κέκλημαι,
  ἐκλήθην call
ὅcτιc, ἥτιc, ὅτι (indef. rel. pron.) who(ever),
  what(ever); ὅντινα = *masc. sing. acc.*

γράμμα, γράμματοc, τό letter (of the alphabet);
  pl., writings, treatises
παρέχω (παρα- + ἔχω) provide; *middle,* supply
μάταιοc, ματαίᾱ, μάταιον vain, empty; trifling
γράφω, γράψω, ἔγραψα, γέγραφα, γέγραμμαι,
  ἐγράφην write
κενόc, κενή, κενόν empty; to no purpose
ἔνειμι (ἐν- + εἰμί) be in; ἔνι = ἔνεcτι(ν)

The **Cynegeticus** (On Hunting) is a brief treatise offering instruction in the sport of hunting, particularly hares. It provides details about the necessary equipment, tracking, the training and management of dogs, and the setting of nets. The author also gives his views on the benefits of hunting for health and even moral development.

4. Plato, *Lysis* 214a5–b8

In a reported conversation about the origin of friendship, Socrates reminds Lysis of an idea of the poets.

> λέγουϲι δέ πωϲ ταῦτα, ὡϲ ἐγῷμαι, ὡδί—
> > αἰεί τοι τὸν ὅμοιον ἄγει θεὸϲ ὡϲ† τὸν ὅμοιον
>
> καὶ ποιεῖ γνώριμον· οὐκ ἐντετύχηκαϲ τούτοιϲ τοῖϲ ἔπεϲιν; "Ἔγωγ'," ἔφη.† "Οὐκοῦν καὶ
> τοῖϲ τῶν ϲοφωτάτων ϲυγγράμμαϲιν ἐντετύχηκαϲ ταῦτα αὐτὰ λέγουϲιν, ὅτι τὸ ὅμοιον τῷ
> ὁμοίῳ ἀνάγκη ἀεὶ φίλον εἶναι; εἰϲὶν δέ που οὗτοι οἱ περὶ φύϲεώϲ τε καὶ τοῦ ὅλου
> διαλεγόμενοι καὶ γράφοντεϲ." "Ἀληθῆ," ἔφη, "λέγειϲ." "Ἆρ' οὖν," ἦν† δ' ἐγώ, "εὖ
> λέγουϲιν;" "Ἴϲωϲ," ἔφη. "Ἴϲωϲ," ἦν† δ' ἐγώ, "τὸ ἥμιϲυ αὐτοῦ, ἴϲωϲ δὲ καὶ πᾶν . . ."

ὡδί = *emphatic form of* ὧδε
ὅμοιοϲ, ὁμοίᾱ, ὅμοιον similar, like; ὁμοῖον (Epic)
 = Attic ὅμοιον
†ὡϲ, *here* (prep. + acc.) to, toward
γνώριμοϲ, γνωρίμου, ὁ acquaintance, friend
ἐντυγχάνω (ἐν- + τυγχάνω), ἐντεύξομαι,
 ἐνέτυχον, ἐντετύχηκα, ——, —— meet with,
 come upon
†ἔφη, *subject is Lysis*
οὐκοῦν (particle) *introduces a question expecting
 the answer yes,* therefore, accordingly

ϲοφώτατοϲ, ϲοφωτάτη, ϲοφώτατον wisest
ϲύγγραμμα, ϲυγγράμματοϲ, τό writing; work
ὅλοϲ, ὅλη, ὅλον whole
γράφω, γράψω, ἔγραψα, γέγραφα, γέγραμμαι,
 ἐγράφην write
†ἦν, *here, 1st sing. imperf. act. indic. of the defective
 verb* ἠμί, ——, ——, ——, ——, —— say; ἦν
 δ' ἐγώ, I said
ἥμιϲυϲ, ἡμίϲεια, ἥμιϲυ half; ἥμιϲυ = *neut. sing. acc.*

The *Lysis* is a dialogue narrated by Socrates in which he recalls a conversation that he had with Hippothales (who has a crush on Lysis), Ctesippus, Lysis, and Menexenus about the nature of friendship and the definition of *friend*. In the course of the dialogue, several definitions of friendship are proposed and rejected.

CHAPTER 9

Vocabulary

ἀμαθίᾱ, ἀμαθίᾱς, ἡ ignorance; stupidity
ἀνδρείᾱ, ἀνδρείᾱς, ἡ manliness;
courage
δικαιοσύνη, δικαιοσύνης, ἡ justice
σωφροσύνη, σωφροσύνης, ἡ
moderation

→ τρόπος, τρόπου, ὁ way, manner; habit;
pl., character

→ τέλος, τέλους, τό end, purpose; power
φρόνησις, φρονήσεως, ἡ intelligence,
understanding

τίς, τί (interrog. pron./adj.) who, what;
which (§93)
τις, τι (indef. pron./adj.) someone,
something; anyone, anything; some,
any (§94)

→ διαφθείρω, διαφθερῶ, διέφθειρα,
διέφθαρκα/διέφθορα, διέφθαρμαι,
διεφθάρην destroy (utterly); corrupt,
ruin
→ ἕπομαι, ἕψομαι, ἑσπόμην, ——, ——,
—— follow (+ dat.)
→ λαμβάνω, λήψομαι, ἔλαβον, εἴληφα,
εἴλημμαι, ἐλήφθην take, seize;
understand; receive; *middle,* take hold
(of)(+ gen.)
  → δίκην λαμβάνειν, to exact
   punishment

→ ὑπολαμβάνω, ὑπολήψομαι,
ὑπέλαβον, ὑπείληφα, ὑπείλημμαι,
ὑπελήφθην take up, reply; suppose
→ μένω, μενῶ, ἔμεινα, μεμένηκα, ——,
—— remain, stay; *trans.,* await
→ οἶδα, εἴσομαι, ——, ——, ——, ——
know (§92)
→ φέρω, οἴσω, ἤνεγκα/ἤνεγκον, ἐνήνοχα,
ἐνήνεγμαι, ἠνέχθην bear, bring, carry;
endure; *middle,* carry away with oneself;
win
→ φεύγω, φεύξομαι, ἔφυγον, πέφευγα,
——, —— flee, avoid, escape

ἄθλιος, ἀθλίᾱ, ἄθλιον wretched,
miserable

ἀμαθής, ἀμαθές ignorant, foolish
εὐδαίμων, εὔδαιμον fortunate, happy
σώφρων, σῶφρον moderate, prudent

εἷς, μία, ἕν (numerical adj.) one (§95)
οὐδείς, οὐδεμία, οὐδέν/ μηδείς,
μηδεμία, μηδέν (adj./substantive) no,
not any; no one, nothing (§95)

ἄν (particle) *used in the apodoses of some
conditional sentences* (§96)
→ ἄρα (postpositive particle) (so) then,
therefore; after all
εἰ (conj.) if
ἐκεῖ (adv.) there
→ πω (enclitic adv.) yet
  → πώποτε (adv.) ever yet

Vocabulary Notes

→ τρόπος, τρόπου, ὁ first means "turn" or "direction." More common are the meanings "way," "manner," particularly in adverbial phrases such as τούτῳ τῷ τρόπῳ (§98) and τοῦτον τὸν τρόπον, "in this way" (§99). τρόπος also refers to a "way" or "habit" of a person; in the plural one's "habits" are virtually equivalent to one's "character."

→ τέλος, τέλους, τό, "end," "purpose," "power," is broadly used to refer to any consummation, result, or completion. One may speak of the "end" of toils, of a day, of one's life. τέλος frequently appears as an Adverbial Accusative (§99) with the meaning "finally" and in prepositional phrases such as ἐς/εἰς τέλος, "to the end," "in the long run," and διὰ τέλους, "through to the end," "completely." τέλος may also mean "power" or "office," and οἱ ἐν τέλει (ὄντες) are "the men who are in power/office." In philosophy τέλος often refers to the "purpose" of an action.

> τέλος ἁπάντων τῶν ἔργων τὸ ἀγαθόν.   The good is the purpose of all deeds.

→ διαφθείρω, διαφθερῶ, διέφθειρα, διέφθαρκα/διέφθορα, διέφθαρμαι, διεφθάρην, "destroy (utterly)"; "corrupt," "ruin," is a compound verb composed of the prefix δια- ("thoroughly") and the simple verb φθείρω. διαφθείρω has a contracted future. The form διέφθειρε(ν) may be third person singular imperfect *or* aorist active indicative. Context usually makes clear which form occurs in a particular sentence. Pluperfect forms of διαφθείρω are rare, and when they do occur, they have no augment. The perfect passive infinitive is διεφθάρθαι (no σ). διαφθείρω means "destroy" or "slay" in a physical sense (enemy soldiers, creations, ships) or metaphorical sense (hopes, mind). In a moral sense, it means "corrupt," "ruin" (young people, a woman, reputation). διαφθείρω has forms in the active and passive voices *only*.

> ἅπαντες οἱ στρατιῶται διεφθάρησαν.   All the soldiers were destroyed (slain).
> τὰς φρένας ἡ ἀρχὴ διέφθορεν.   Rule has ruined his wits.

→ The original stem of ἕπομαι, ἕψομαι, ἑσπόμην, ——, ——, —— was *σεπ-. When initial sigma was lost in Greek, it was replaced by a rough breathing in accordance with a regular sound change (e.g., *σέπομαι > ἕπομαι). ἕπομαι is an *intransitive* middle deponent. It may be used absolutely, but it usually appears with a Dative of Reference (translated into English as a direct object). ἕπομαι means "follow" both in a physical sense (follow a leader, follow other soldiers) and in a metaphorical one (follow an argument, obey a law). The imperfect tense of ἕπομαι has an irregular augment with the spurious diphthong εἱ-, produced by the addition of the past indicative augment to the original stem and the loss of intervocalic sigma. The rough breathing was borrowed by analogy from other tenses (e.g., *ἐσεπόμην > *εἱπόμην > εἱπόμην).

→ λαμβάνω, λήψομαι, ἔλαβον, εἴληφα, εἴλημμαι, ἐλήφθην is a partial deponent. Pluperfect forms do not have an augment and are rare in the middle/passive. It occurs in all three voices. λαμβάνω in the active voice means "grasp" in a variety of senses. It may mean "take," seize," "capture" (reins, money, a city, people). When the subject is an emotion, it often means "seize." When the direct object is a thought, speech, or idea, λαμβάνω may mean "understand" ("grasp" with one of the senses). It may also mean "receive" (things, people [i.e., into one's home]). In the middle voice λαμβάνω means "take hold of" (a hand, the truth, an opportunity, a place) and is followed by an Objective Genitive.

οἱ στρατιῶται τὴν πόλιν ἔλαβον.	The soldiers took the city.
φόβος αὐτὸν εἴληφεν.	Fear has seized him.
ταῦτα ἐν νῷ ἔλαβον.	I understood these things in (my) mind.
ἆρα ταῦτα παρὰ τοῦ στρατηγοῦ ἐλάβετε;	Did you (pl.) receive these things from the general?
νῦν τῆς ἀληθείας λαμβάνῃ, ὦ παῖ.	Now you are taking hold of the truth, child.

→ The idiom **δίκην λαμβάνειν**, "to exact punishment," literally means "to take justice." It frequently appears with a prepositional phrase expressing the person punished and often with a Genitive of Cause.

ταύτης τῆς ὕβρεως δίκην παρ' ἐκείνου ληψόμεθα.
For (Because of) this outrage we shall exact punishment from that man.

→ The compound verb **ὑπολαμβάνω** (ὑπο- + λαμβάνω), **ὑπολήψομαι, ὑπέλαβον, ὑπείληφα, ὑπείλημμαι, ὑπελήφθην**, "take up," "reply," "suppose," is a partial deponent. It has active and passive forms but middle forms only in the future. Pluperfect forms are rare and do not have an augment. The literal meaning of **ὑπολαμβάνω** is "take or hold up (from under)," and like **λαμβάνω** it may also mean "seize." In discourse **ὑπολαμβάνω** may mean "take up" or "reply." It often means "take up (an idea)" or "suppose" and is followed by a direct object or by an indirect statement with a Subject Accusative and an infinitive or **ὅτι/ὡς** and a finite verb.

→ **μένω, μενῶ, ἔμεινα, μεμένηκα, ——, ——,** "remain," "stay"; "await," has active voice forms only. It has a contracted future and a first aorist whose stem includes a spurious diphthong resulting from compensatory lengthening after the loss of a sigma (*ἔμενσα > ἔμεινα). **μένω** is almost always intransitive and appears with a variety of adverbial modifiers or with predicate adjectives.

ἐν τῇ νήσῳ ἐμένομεν.	We were remaining on the island.
ἐν τῇ πόλει μετὰ τῶν ἑταίρων ἔμεινα.	I stayed in the city with my companions.
καλὸς οὐκ ἀεὶ μενεῖς.	You will not always remain handsome.

When **μένω** is *transitive,* it means "await" or "expect" (an attack, a storm, a person) and takes an Accusative, Direct Object.

→ **οἶδα, εἴσομαι, ——, ——, ——, ——** has forms in the perfect, pluperfect, and future tenses *only.* For its forms see §92. The stems of **οἶδα** (οἰδ-, εἰσ-) are related to the aorist active stem of **ὁράω** (εἰδ-), and thus its original meaning was "I have seen (in the mind's eye)," from which **οἶδα** came to mean "know" in a general sense. It may also mean "be acquainted with," "be aware of." **οἶδα** often introduces an indirect statement with **ὅτι/ὡς** and a finite verb or with a Subject Accusative and a supplementary participle. Occasionally **οἶδα** may also introduce an indirect statement with a Subject Accusative and an infinitive.

οἶδ' ὅτι ταῦτα ἔπραξας.	I know that you did these things.
οἶδά σε ταῦτα πράξαντα.	I know that you did these things.

When **οἶδα** is followed by an infinitive, it regularly means "know how."

οἶδα ταῦτα πρᾶξαι.	I know how to do these things.

➔ φέρω, οἴσω, ἤνεγκα/ἤνεγκον, ἐνήνοχα, ἐνήνεγμαι, ἠνέχθην is based on three different stems: φερ-, οἰσ-, and ἐνεγκ-. φέρω has both a first and second aorist with no difference in meaning. It exhibits irregular reduplication in the fourth and fifth principal parts. Pluperfect forms do not occur. The initial short vowels in these principal parts are *not* lengthened in the pluperfect tense. Forms of φέρω occur in all three voices but less frequently in the middle voice. The basic meaning of φέρω is "bear," "bring," "carry," and it takes a variety of direct objects (weights, speeches, people, gifts). φέρω may also mean "endure" (pains, misfortunes, evils). When the direct object is a word, speech, or other utterance, φέρω may be translated "report" ("bring word"). When the subject of φέρω is a road or land, it may be used absolutely to mean "lead," "stretch."

τὰ χρήματα εἰς τοὺς στρατηγοὺς οἴσομεν.	We shall carry the money to the generals.
ταῦτα τὰ κακὰ χαλεπῶς ἔφερεν.	He was enduring these evils with difficulty.
οὐ μακρὰ ἦν ἡ ὁδὸς ἡ εἰς ἀγορὰν φέρουσα.	The road leading to the agora was not long.

In the middle voice, φέρω means "carry away with oneself" or, by extension, "win," "achieve" (honor, a prize, gratitude, happiness).

ἐπὶ τούτοις τὴν τοῦ δήμου χάριν ἠνέγκετο.
For these things he won the gratitude of the people.

➔ φεύγω, φεύξομαι, ἔφυγον, πέφευγα, ——, ——, "flee," "avoid," "escape," is a partial deponent. The reduplication in the fourth principal part reflects the dissimilation of aspirates (cf. πεφίληκα). Other than in the future tense, φεύγω does not occur in the middle or the passive voice. φεύγω is used intransitively with a variety of prepositional phrases, but it may also function as a transitive verb with a direct object.

ἐς τὴν τῶν βαρβάρων γῆν ἔφυγεν. (intrans. use)
He fled to the land of the foreigners.

βροτοὶ τὴν Διὸς δίκην οὐ φεύξονται. (trans. use)
Mortals will not escape the justice of Zeus.

In the present and imperfect tenses φεύγω often has conative force and refers only to the intention or attempt to flee.

τὴν Διὸς δίκην ἔφευγεν.   He was trying to escape the justice of Zeus.

➔ In the epic dialect of Homer an enclitic form of the Attic postpostive particle ἄρα marks a wide variety of connections, transitions, and consequences. In Attic Greek, however, ἄρα almost always has *inferential* force and marks conclusions drawn from logical thought, feeling, or impression. Thus, ἄρα is more subjective and more lively than οὖν, which marks conclusions drawn from facts real or assumed.

A. ἄλλοις μὲν τῶν θεῶν φίλος ὁ πόλεμος, ἄλλοις δὲ οὔ.
B. οὐκ ἄρα πάντες οἱ θεοὶ πολέμους καὶ μάχᾱς φιλοῦσιν.
A. To some of the gods war is dear, but to others (it is) not.
B. So then, not all the gods love wars and battles.

ἄρα may also indicate a new perception or surprise of recognition or realization, especially with imperfect tense forms of εἰμί, which are translated as present.

τοῦτ' ἄρ' ἦν ἀληθές.   This thing (which I thought was false) *is* true *after all*.

In questions ἄρα retains its inferential force but also adds feeling, often marking increased anxiety.

A. ἡ σὴ μήτηρ ἐτελεύτησεν.
B. πῶς ἄρα πράσσει ὁ πατήρ μου;
A. Your mother died.
B. How then is my father faring?

After the conjunction εἰ (and other words introducing protases [if-clauses of conditional sentences]), ἄρα suggests that the condition is improbable or undesirable: "if really," "if after all." When ἄρα appears in a protasis with negation, it often adds irony: "unless (perhaps)."

εἰ ἄρα ἐγένετο ὡς οὗτοι λέγουσιν, εὖ ἔχει.   If after all it happened as these men say, it is good.

→ The enclitic adverb πω means "up to this time," "yet." It combines with ποτέ to form πώποτε, a *non-enclitic* adverb meaning "ever yet" whose accent is on the antepenult. According to the regular rules of accent, the proclitic οὐ has an acute accent when followed by πω, and this combination may be written as one word or, rarely, two words: οὔπω or οὔ πω, "not yet." The compound adverbs οὐπώποτε and οὐδεπώποτε mean "not yet at any time," "never yet." μήπω, μηπώποτε, and μηδεπώποτε also occur.
    πω and its compounds most often appear in negative contexts:

λέγων οὐδὲ νῦν πω πέπαυται.
Not even now has he yet stopped speaking.

οὐδείς πω Ἑλλήνων ὑπὸ βαρβάρου οὐδενὸς ἐτεθνήκειν.
No one yet of the Greeks had died at the hands of any non-Greek.

Derivatives and Cognates

	Derivatives	*Cognates*
εἷς	**hen**diadys, hyp**hen**	same, seem, **sim**ple
ἕπομαι		**sequ**ence, **sec**ond, **seg**ue, **so**cial
μένω		re**main**, **man**sion, per**man**ent
τέλος	**tele**ology	cycle, culture
τίς		what, **qui**bble
τρόπος	**trope**, **troub**adour, con**trive**	en**trop**y, apo**trop**aic, **trop**ic
φέρω	am**phora**, phos**phorus**	bear, trans**fer**, **birth**, **bur**den
φεύγω		**fug**itive

§92. The Verb οἶδα

The irregular verb **οἶδα, εἴσομαι, ——, ——, ——, ——,** "know," is a partial deponent verb. Other than future middle forms, **οἶδα** has irregular forms in the perfect and pluperfect active only. MEMO-RIZE THE FOLLOWING IRREGULAR PERFECT AND PLUPERFECT CONJUGATIONS AND PERFECT ACTIVE INFINITIVE FORM:

	Perfect Active Indicative	Pluperfect Active Indicative
Singular		
1	οἶδα	ᾔδη/ᾔδειν
2	οἶσθα	ᾔδησθα/ᾔδεις
3	οἶδε(ν)	ᾔδει(ν)
Plural		
1	ἴσμεν	ᾖσμεν
2	ἴστε	ᾖστε
3	ἴσᾱσι(ν)	ᾖσαν/ᾔδεσαν

Perfect Active Infinitive: εἰδέναι

OBSERVATIONS

1. Originally **οἶδα** had three stems that began with the Greek letter digamma (ϝ):

e grade:[1]	ϝειδ-
o grade:	ϝοιδ-
zero grade:	ϝιδ-

The digamma was lost in many Greek dialects, including Attic and Ionic. The perfect active indicative conjugation uses the o grade of the stem (οἰδ-) in the *singular* and the zero grade of the stem (ἰδ-) in the plural. Certain endings of the perfect active indicative conjugation of **οἶδα** are regular: first singular -α, third singular -ε(ν), third plural -ᾱσι(ν). The second singular ending -σθα is also used in ἦσθα and ἔφησθα. In the plural a sigma gradually replaced the delta of the stem, first in the second person plural, where regular sound change brought about ἴστε (< *ἴδτε), then in the other forms by analogy with the second person plural.

2. The pluperfect active indicative conjugation uses the e grade of the stem, which is augmented by lengthening ει- to η-. Certain endings of the pluperfect active indicative conjugation of **οἶδα** are regular: first singular -η, third singular -ει(ν), third plural -εσαν. In all the plural forms *except* ᾔδεσαν, a sigma gradually replaced the delta of the stem, first in the second person plural, where regular sound change brought about ᾖστε (< *ᾖδτε), then in the other forms by analogy with the second person plural.

3. The perfect active infinitive uses the e grade of the stem (εἰδ-) and the perfect active infinitive ending -έναι. The accent is *persistent* on the penult.

4. The future middle conjugation uses the e grade of the stem (εἰδ-) throughout with the delta of the stem lost through regular sound change (*εἴδσομαι > *εἴσσομαι > εἴσομαι).

---

1. An **e grade** of a stem has an ε in it, an **o grade** of a stem has an o in it, and a **zero grade** of a stem has neither an ε nor an o. The zero grade of **οἶδα**, ϝιδ-, is used in the aorist active and middle conjugations of **ὁράω** (e.g., εἶδον < *ἔϝιδον; ἰδεῖν < *ϝιδεῖν).

οἶδα literally means "I have seen," but the completion of "seeing" was understood to result in "knowing." Therefore, the perfect active tense of **οἶδα** is always translated as if it were *present,* and the pluperfect active tense is translated as if it were *imperfect.*

ταῦτα ἴσμεν.	We know these things.
ἆρα τοῦτο ᾔδησθα;	Did you know (repeatedly) this thing?
εὖ εἰδέναι χρὴ τοὺς νόμους.	One ought to know well the laws.

☞ DRILL 92 MAY NOW BE DONE.

§93. The Interrogative Pronoun and Adjective τίς, τί

In the questions "Who are you?" and "What are you doing?" the words *who* and *what* are interrogative pronouns. An **interrogative pronoun** is a pronoun used to ask a question. In the questions "What island was ruled by that leader?" and "Which men were sent into battle?" *what* and *which* are interrogative adjectives. An **interrogative adjective** is an adjective used to ask a question. In Attic Greek the word τίς, τί may appear either as an interrogative pronoun—when it does not modify another word—or as an interrogative adjective—when it does modify another word.

Interrogative Pronoun/Adjective τίς, τί		
	M./F.	N.
Singular		
Nom.	τίς	τί
Gen.	τίνος/τοῦ	τίνος/τοῦ
Dat.	τίνι/τῷ	τίνι/τῷ
Acc.	τίνα	τί
Plural		
Nom.	τίνες	τίνα
Gen.	τίνων	τίνων
Dat.	τίσι(ν)	τίσι(ν)
Acc.	τίνας	τίνα

OBSERVATIONS

1. There are no vocative forms for τίς, τί.
2. The stem of the interrogative pronoun/adjective, τιν-, is found by dropping the ending -ος from the neuter singular genitive. τίς, τί has third-declension endings.
3. With the exception of the alternate forms τοῦ and τῷ, the accent on the interrogative pronoun/adjective is always an acute on the first syllable. Even when the monosyllabic forms τίς and τί are followed by another word, the accent *remains an acute.* For example:

τίς (τίς ἀνὴρ) τῶν πολῑτῶν λέγειν βούλεται;
Who (What man) of the citizens wants to speak?

MEMORIZE THIS EXCEPTION TO THE RULES OF ACCENT.

4. The alternate forms for the genitive and dative singular—τοῦ and τῷ, respectively—are identical with the genitive and dative singular masculine or neuter of the article. Context usually makes clear whether a form in a particular sentence is the interrogative pronoun/adjective or the article.

5. Translations of interrogative pronouns in Greek require mastery of the uses of the interrogative pronouns in English:

	Beings	*Things*
Subject	who	what
Possessive	whose/of whom	whose/of what
Object of verbs and prepositions	whom	what

These forms of the English interrogative pronoun may be singular or plural.

6. Forms of the interrogative adjective are translated "what" or "which."

An interrogative pronoun or adjective is usually placed at or near the beginning of a question. Sometimes it is placed immediately after an important element of a question.

τίνες εἰσὶν οἱ τούτου υἱοί;
Who are the sons of this man?

τίς οὖν ἡ τούτων αἰτίᾱ;
What therefore (is) the cause of these things?

οὗτος δὲ τίς ἐστιν;
But this man, who is he?
But who is this man?

πρὸς τίνος ῥήτορος ταῦτ' ἔμαθες;
From which orator did you learn these things?

περὶ τούτου τοῦ πρᾱ́γματος τίνι λόγῳ ῡ̔μᾶς πείσω;
About this affair by what speech shall I persuade you (pl.)?
By what speech shall I persuade you (pl.) about this affair?

OBSERVATION

When an interrogative pronoun occurs in a nominal sentence or a sentence with a copulative verb, it functions as a predicate nominative, and its gender and number are determined by the subject, as in the first three sentences.

☛ DRILL 93 MAY NOW BE DONE.

§94. The Enclitic Indefinite Pronoun and Adjective τις, τι

In the sentences "Someone is being wronged by this orator" and "That poet was saying something about the nature of war," *someone* and *something* are indefinite pronouns. An **indefinite pronoun** is a pronoun that does not define or specify the person or thing for which it stands. In the sentences "There is some fear in the hearts of the people" and "Do you have any opinion about the war?" *some* and *any* are indefinite adjectives. An **indefinite adjective** is an adjective that does not define or specify the person or thing that it modifies. In Attic Greek the word τις, τι may function either as an indefinite pronoun or as an indefinite adjective. Its forms are identical with those of the interrogative pronoun/adjective *except that the indefinite pronoun/adjective is enclitic in all its forms.*

	Indefinite Pronoun/Adjective τις, τι	
	M./F.	N.
Singular		
Nom.	τις	τι
Gen.	τινός/του	τινός/του
Dat.	τινί/τῳ	τινί/τῳ
Acc.	τινά	τι
Plural		
Nom.	τινές	τινά/ἄττα
Gen.	τινῶν	τινῶν
Dat.	τισί(ν)	τισί(ν)
Acc.	τινάς	τινά/ἄττα

OBSERVATIONS

1. There are no vocative forms for τις, τι.
2. The stem of the indefinite pronoun/adjective, τιν-, is found by dropping the ending -ος from the neuter singular genitive. τις, τι has third-declension endings.
3. All the forms of the indefinite pronoun/adjective are enclitic. When the genitive plural is accented, it receives a *circumflex* (not an acute) on its ultima. There is an *accented* alternate form for the *neuter plural nominative and accusative:* ἄττα. MEMORIZE THIS ALTERNATE FORM.
4. The pronoun τις, τι is translated "someone," "anyone," "something," "anything." Plural forms are translated "some men," "some people," "some things," etc.
5. The indefinite adjective τις, τι is translated "some" or "any."

τις, τι may be used to indicate uncertainty about who is performing an action.

θεός τις ἡμᾶς πολεμοῦντας παύσει.   Some god will stop us (from) quarreling.

When τις, τι appears with a form of ἕκαστος, πᾶς, or ἅπας, it is translated "one."

πάντα τινὰ ὑμῶν δεῖ παρεῖναι.   It is necessary for every one of you to be present.

τις, τι is used to emphasize the indefiniteness of a number or word, but it often cannot be translated.

πολλοί τινες   (some) many men (subj.)

☞ DRILL 93–94 MAY NOW BE DONE.

§95. The Adjectives εἷς, μία, ἕν and οὐδείς, οὐδεμία, οὐδέν/μηδείς, μηδεμία, μηδέν

The numerical adjective εἷς, μία, ἕν, "one," has third-declension endings in the masculine and neuter and first-declension short-alpha endings in the feminine. The compound adjective/substantive οὐδείς, οὐδεμία, οὐδέν/μηδείς, μηδεμία, μηδέν, "no," "not any"; "no one," "nothing"—composed of the word οὐδέ/μηδέ and the numerical adjective εἷς, μία, ἕν—also has third-declension endings in the masculine and neuter and first-declension short-alpha endings in the feminine. With rare exceptions these words occur in the singular *only*.[2] MEMORIZE THE FOLLOWING DECLENSIONS, PAYING PARTICULAR ATTENTION TO ACCENTS:

	M.	F.	N.
Nom.	εἷς	μία	ἕν
Gen.	ἑνός	μιᾶς	ἑνός
Dat.	ἑνί	μιᾷ	ἑνί
Acc.	ἕνα	μίαν	ἕν

	M.	F.	N.	M.	F.	N.
Nom.	οὐδείς	οὐδεμία	οὐδέν	μηδείς	μηδεμία	μηδέν
Gen.	οὐδενός	οὐδεμιᾶς	οὐδενός	μηδενός	μηδεμιᾶς	μηδενός
Dat.	οὐδενί	οὐδεμιᾷ	οὐδενί	μηδενί	μηδεμιᾷ	μηδενί
Acc.	οὐδένα	οὐδεμίαν	οὐδέν	μηδένα	μηδεμίαν	μηδέν

OBSERVATIONS

1. There are no vocative forms for εἷς, οὐδείς, and μηδείς.

2. The stem of εἷς in the masculine and neuter is ἑν- and is found by dropping the ending -ος from the neuter singular genitive.[3] The stem of εἷς in the feminine is μι-. The stems of οὐδείς/μηδείς are similar: οὐδεν-/μηδεν- in the masculine and neuter, οὐδεμι-/μηδεμι- in the feminine.

3. The accentual pattern in the masculine and neuter of εἷς and οὐδείς/μηδείς is similar to the pattern of third-declension nouns with monosyllabic nominative singulars *except* that the masculine singular nominative of εἷς has a circumflex (cf. the declension of φρήν and §52, Observation 2, p. 122). The accent on the feminine singular genitive and dative of εἷς and οὐδείς/μηδείς is a circumflex on the ultima.

Although εἷς and οὐδείς/μηδείς may be used as adjectives not in the attributive position, they are more often used substantively.

Used Substantively		*Used Adjectivally*	
ἕν	one; one thing (subj. or d.o.)	ἑνὶ λόγῳ	by one word
μία	one woman (subj.)	μία ὁδός	one way (subj.)
οὐδένα	no one (m.; d.o.)	οὐδεὶς λόγος	not any speech (subj.)
οὐδέν	nothing (subj. or d.o.)	οὐδενὸς νόμου	of no law

---

2. Occasionally the plural forms of οὐδείς appear.

3. An earlier form of εἷς was *ἕνς; the spurious diphthong in εἷς is the result of the loss of the nu and compensatory lengthening.

When a simple negative (οὐ or μή) follows a compound negative (οὐδείς, οὔτε, οὔποτε, etc.), the meaning of a sentence is positive.

οὐδεὶς οὐκ ἤκουσεν.   No one did not listen (i.e., Everyone listened).

When a compound negative follows a simple negative or another compound negative, the negation is *strengthened*.

οὐκ ἤκουσεν οὐδείς.   No one listened.
οὐδείς μοι οὐδὲν περὶ τούτου οὔποτ᾽ εἶπεν.   No one ever said anything to me about this thing.

OBSERVATION

───

The redundant negatives in these sentences are not translated into English. The emphasis achieved in Greek by redundant negatives may be represented in English only by italics or underlining.

☞ DRILL 95 MAY NOW BE DONE.

§96. Conditional Sentences 1

A **conditional sentence** is a complex sentence that includes a *condition* or conditional clause—a type of subordinate clause—and a main clause. For example:

> *If he is doing these things,* he is living well.
> *If he was doing these things,* he was living well.
> *If he does these things,* he will live well.
> *If he were doing these things,* he would be living well.

The italicized portion of each of these sentences states the condition that must occur in order for the main clause to occur. For example, *only* "if he does these things" will "he live well." The subordinate clause or "if-clause" of a conditional sentence is called a **protasis** (πρότασις, "proposition"). The main clause is called an **apodosis** (ἀπόδοσις, "giving back," "return"). Both in Greek and in English, the protasis may precede or follow the apodosis.

Protasis   **Apodosis**
If he is doing these things, he is living well.
Apodosis   **Protasis**
He is living well if he is doing these things.

There are three classes of conditional sentences in Greek: *simple* or *general, future,* and *contrary-to-fact.* **Simple** (or **General**) conditional sentences make statements of fact about present or past time (the first two sentences above are simple conditional sentences). **Future** conditional sentences make statements about the future (the third sentence above is a future conditional sentence). **Contrary-to-Fact** conditional sentences make statements that suppose that the actions of both the protasis and the apodosis *are not occurring now* or *did not occur in the past* (the fourth sentence above is a contrary-to-fact conditional sentence). The protases of many conditional sentences in Greek are introduced by the proclitic subordinating conjunction εἰ, "if." The protases of all types of conditional sentences are negated by μή, and the apodoses of all types of conditional sentences are negated by οὐ.

Simple Conditional Sentences

Simple conditional sentences are of two types: *present* or *past*. In a **Present Simple** conditional sentence, the verbs of both the protasis and the apodosis are in the *present indicative*.[4] In a **Past Simple** conditional sentence, the verbs of both the protasis and the apodosis are in *any past tense of the indicative*. For example:

> εἰ ταῦτα ποιεῖ, εὖ ζῇ. (Present Simple)
> If *he is doing* these things, *he is living* well.
>
> εἰ μή τις ταῦτα ἐποίει, οὐκ εὖ ἔζη. (Past Simple)
> If someone *was* not *doing* these things, *he was* not *living* well.
> Unless someone was doing these things, he was not living well.

OBSERVATIONS

1. Simple conditional sentences make simple factual statements about the present or the past in the indicative mood, the mood used to represent something as a fact. They may have a *particular* meaning, stating something about a particular moment in time, or a *general* meaning, making a general statement. Context usually makes clear whether a simple conditional sentence is particular or general.

2. When the protasis of a conditional sentence is negated, as in the second sentence, εἰ μή is translated "if . . . not" or "unless."

3. The syntax of, for example, ἐποίει is **imperfect indicative in the protasis of a Past Simple conditional sentence**.[5]

Future Conditional Sentences

One kind of **future conditional sentence** is called a **Future Most Vivid** because it imagines future events as vividly as possible in the indicative mood.[6] In a Future Most Vivid conditional sentence, the verbs of both the protasis and the apodosis are in the *future indicative*. For example:

> εἰ ταῦτα ποιήσει, εὖ ζήσει.
> If *he will do* these things, *he will live* well.
> If *he does* these things, *he will live* well.

---

4. Because the perfect indicative is also present in time, it sometimes appears in the protasis or apodosis of a Present Simple conditional sentence.

5. The syntax of a finite verb comprises tense, mood, reason for mood, and reason for tense.

6. For Future More Vivid conditional sentences see Part 2, §128. For Future Less Vivid conditional sentences see Part 2, §141.

1. A Future Most Vivid conditional sentence in Greek requires the future indicative in both the protasis and the apodosis because both events will occur in the future. The second translation above is to be preferred, however, since in English the *present tense* is commonly used in the protasis of such a conditional sentence. The English phrase "if he does" is understood to refer to future time because the verb in the main clause ("will live") clearly indicates future time.

2. The syntax of, for example, ζήσει is **future indicative in the apodosis of a Future Most Vivid conditional sentence.**

Contrary-to-Fact Conditional Sentences

Contrary-to-Fact conditional sentences are of two types: **present** or **past**. In a **Present Contrary-to-Fact** conditional sentence, the verbs of both the protasis and the apodosis are in the *imperfect indicative*. In a **Past Contrary-to-Fact** conditional sentence, the verbs of both the protasis and the apodosis are in the *aorist indicative*. The particle ἄν is added to the *apodosis* of contrary-to-fact conditional sentences to indicate that the indicative mood does *not* represent an action as factual. For example:

εἰ ταῦτα ἐποίει, εὖ ἂν ἔζη.
If *he were* (now) *doing* these things (but he is not), *he would* (now) *be living* well (but he is not).

εἰ ταῦτα ἐποίησεν, ὑπὸ τοῦ δήμου ἐτιμήθη ἄν.
If *he had done* these things (but he did not), *he would have been honored* by the people (but he was not).

1. In a Present Contrary-to-Fact conditional sentence, the verbs in the imperfect indicative report nonfactual or contrary-to-fact events *that are not occurring in the present*. The English words "were" (in the protasis) and "would" (in the apodosis) are regularly used to translate a Present Contrary-to-Fact conditional sentence.

2. In a Past Contrary-to-Fact conditional sentence, the verbs in the aorist indicative report nonfactual or contrary-to-fact events *that did not occur in the past*. The English words "had" (in the protasis) and "would have" (in the apodosis) are regularly used to translate a Past Contrary-to-Fact conditional sentence.

3. The particle ἄν is added to the apodosis of a Contrary-to-Fact conditional sentence and distinguishes a Contrary-to-Fact conditional sentence from a Past Simple Conditional sentence. If, however, the verb of the apodosis is an impersonal expression of *unfulfilled* necessity or possibility (ἔδει, χρῆν, etc.), ἄν may be omitted.

εἰ ταῦτα ἐποίει, ἔδει αὐτὸν τῑμᾶσθαι ὑπὸ πάντων.
If he were doing these things, it would be necessary for him to be honored by all men.

ἄν most often appears near the beginning of its clause but *not* first, and it may be repeated later in the same clause.

> εἰ ταῦτα ἐποίει, ὑπὸ πάντων ἂν διὰ τὴν ἀρετὴν ἂν ἐτῑμᾶτο.
> If he were doing these things, he would be being honored by all men on account of his excellence.

4. The syntax of, for example, ἐτῑμήθη is **aorist indicative in the apodosis of a Past Contrary-to-Fact conditional sentence.**

In addition to Present and Past Contrary-to-Fact conditional sentences, *mixed* contrary-to-fact conditional sentences occur. A **Mixed Contrary-to-Fact** conditional sentence combines the protasis of one contrary-to-fact conditional sentence with the apodosis of the other. In one mixed contrary-to-fact conditional sentence, the verb of the *protasis* is in the *aorist indicative,* and the verb of the *apodosis* is in the *imperfect indicative.* For example:

> εἰ ταῦτα ἐποίησεν, ἐκ τῆς χώρᾱς νῦν ἐπέμπετ᾽ ἄν.
> If he had done these things, now he would be being sent out from the land.

OBSERVATION

This type of Mixed-Contrary-to-Fact conditional sentence combines the protasis of a Past Contrary-to-Fact with the Apodosis of a Present Contrary-to-Fact. The verb of the protasis reports an event that *did not occur in the past,* and the verb of the apodosis reports an event *that is not occurring in the present.* The English words "had" (in the protasis) and "would" (in the apodosis) are regularly used to translate this Mixed Contrary-to-Fact conditional sentence.

When the adversative conjunction ἀλλά (sometimes accompanied by γε) appears at the beginning of the *apodosis* of a conditional sentence, it means "still," "yet," "at least."

> εἰ πολέμιοι οἱ Λακεδαιμόνιοι, ἀλλ᾽ ἄγουσιν τὴν εἰρήνην.
> If the Spartans (are) hostile, *still* they are keeping the peace.

When a sentence immediately *following* a Present or Past Contrary-to-Fact conditional sentence begins with νῦν δέ, the phrase emphasizes the *return to the factual from the contrafactual* and may be translated "but as it is."

> εἰ ἦν ποιητής, ἔπη καλὰ ἐποίουν ἄν. νῦν δ᾽ οὐκ ἐμοὶ αὕτη ἡ τέχνη.
> If I were a poet, I would be making beautiful lines of verse. But as it is, I do not have this skill.

Summary of Conditional Sentences

Name	Verbs in Greek	Verbs in English
Present Simple	Protasis: εἰ + Present Indicative	does[7]
	Apodosis: Present Indicative	does
Past Simple	Protasis: εἰ + Imperfect or Aorist Indicative	did
	Apodosis: Imperfect or Aorist Indicative	did
Future Most Vivid	Protasis: εἰ + Future Indicative	does
	Apodosis: Future Indicative	will do
Present Contrary-to-Fact	Protasis: εἰ + Imperfect Indicative	were doing
	Apodosis: Imperfect Indicative + ἄν	would be doing
Past Contrary-to-Fact	Protasis: εἰ + Aorist Indicative	had done
	Apodosis: Aorist Indicative + ἄν	would have done
Mixed Contrary-to-Fact	Protasis: εἰ + Aorist Indicative	had done
	Apodosis: Imperfect Indicative + ἄν	would be doing

☛ DRILL 96 MAY NOW BE DONE.

§97. Third-Declension Adjectives 2: -ων, -ον

One group of third-declension adjectives is identified by the nominative singular endings -ων, -ον. The stem of these adjectives is the neuter singular nominative form. For example:

εὐδαίμων, εὔδαιμον fortunate, happy
stem = εὐδαιμον-

	M./F.	N.
Singular		
Nom.	εὐδαίμων	εὔδαιμον
Gen.	εὐδαίμονος	εὐδαίμονος
Dat.	εὐδαίμονι	εὐδαίμονι
Acc.	εὐδαίμονα	εὔδαιμον
Voc.	εὔδαιμον	εὔδαιμον
Plural		
Nom./Voc.	εὐδαίμονες	εὐδαίμονα
Gen.	εὐδαιμόνων	εὐδαιμόνων
Dat.	εὐδαίμοσι(ν)	εὐδαίμοσι(ν)
Acc.	εὐδαίμονας	εὐδαίμονα

7. The model verb "to do" is used to indicate English translation formulas.

1. The masculine/feminine singular nominative of adjectives such as **εὐδαίμων** is the stem with the final vowel lengthened. The masculine/feminine and neuter singular vocative singular are identical with the stem.

2. When the dative plural ending -**σι(ν)** is added to a stem ending in nu, the nu is dropped: *εὐδαίμονσι(ν) > **εὐδαίμοσι(ν)**.

3. The accent on third-declension adjectives is *persistent* and is given by the neuter singular nominative form.

☞   DRILL 97 MAY NOW BE DONE.

§98. Dative of Manner

The *way in which* something occurs or is done may be expressed by the dative case, and a dative so used is called a **Dative of Manner**. For example:

> **τούτῳ τῷ τρόπῳ αὐτοὺς πείσω.**   (τρόπος, τρόπου, ὁ way, manner)
> *In* this *way/manner* I shall persuade them.
>
> **καὶ οἱ Ἀθηναῖοι καὶ οἱ Λακεδαιμόνιοι πολλοὺς κοινῇ ἔχουσι νόμους.**
> Both the Athenians and the Spartans have *in (a) common (way)* many laws.
> Both the Athenians and the Spartans have many laws *in common*.

The syntax of each italicized word (τρόπῳ, κοινῇ) is **Dative of Manner**.

The feminine singular dative of the adjective **κοινός, κοινή, κοινόν** functions as a Dative of Manner. One may assume an ellipsis of the noun ὁδῷ: **κοινῇ ὁδῷ**, "in a common way," "in common," "commonly." The feminine singular datives **ταύτῃ** and **τῇδε** may be used with a similar meaning ("in this way").

The feminine singular dative of a relative pronoun, with or without an expressed antecedent such as ὁδῷ, may be used in a similar way. For example:

> **ταῦτα πράττει (ὁδῷ) ᾗ πολλοὶ τῶν Ἀθηναίων.**
> He does these things *in the way in which* many of the Athenians (do).

§99. Adverbial Accusative

Certain nouns, pronouns, adjectives, and substantives formed with the article (in the neuter singular or plural) may function as *adverbs* when they appear in the accusative case. Such an accusative is called an **Adverbial Accusative**. For example:

οἱ βάρβαροι ἐν τῇ ἡμετέρᾳ ἐπολέμουν μὲν χώρᾳ, παύονται δὲ τὸ νῦν.
The non-Greeks were making war in our country, but they are stopping (*for*) *now*.

περὶ τούτων τὴν ἀλήθειαν οὐκ εἶπες. τοῦτον τὸν τρόπον πᾶς ὁ δῆμος ἠδικήθη.
About these things you did not speak the truth. *In* this *way* all the people were wronged.

The syntax of each italicized word or phrase (τὸ νῦν, τρόπον) is **Adverbial Accusative**.

OBSERVATION

___

Like the Accusative of Respect, the Adverbial Accusative derives from the capacity of the accusative case to express *extent*: τὸ νῦν = as far as now goes, (for) now.

Several pronouns and adjectives in the neuter singular or plural accusative form are commonly used as Adverbial Accusatives. MEMORIZE THESE COMMON ADVERBIAL ACCUSATIVES:

(τὸ) ἐναντίον	in opposition, conversely
μέγα	greatly, to a great extent
οὐδέν/μηδέν	not at all
(τὸ) (τὰ) νῦν	now; presently
(τὸ) πολύ	much, a lot
(τὰ) πολλά	many times, often; much, a lot
(σ)μῑκρόν	a little
τέλος	finally
τί	why; how
τι	in any way; at all

OBSERVATION

___

The parentheses around the articles indicate that the article is sometimes used with these and other similar Adverbial Accusatives.

☛ DRILL 98–99 MAY NOW BE DONE.

Short Readings

1. A fragment from a work of the archaic poet Archilochus

πόλλ' οἶδ' ἀλώπηξ, ἀλλ' ἐχῖνος ἓν μέγα. (Archilochus, frag. 201)

IT

ἀλώπηξ, ἀλώπεκος, ἡ fox

ἐχῖνος, ἐχίνου, ὁ hedgehog

Couplets from the poetry of Theognis

2. οὐδεὶς ἀνθρώπων οὔτ' ὄλβιος οὔτε πενιχρός
   οὔτε κακὸς νόσφιν δαίμονος οὔτ' ἀγαθός. (Theognis, *Elegies* I.165–66)

EC

ὄλβιος, ὀλβίᾱ, ὄλβιον happy, blessed, prosperous
πενιχρός, πενιχρά, πενιχρόν poor, needy

νόσφι(ν) (prep. + gen.) without, apart from

3. Ὤνθρωπ', εἰ γνώμης ἔλαχες μέρος ὥσπερ ἀνοίης
   καὶ σώφρων οὕτως ὥσπερ ἄφρων ἐγένου,
   πολλοῖσ' ἂν ζηλωτὸς ἐφαίνεο τῶνδε πολῑτῶν
   οὕτως ὥσπερ νῦν οὐδενὸς ἄξιος εἶ. (Theognis, *Elegies* I.452–55)

EC

λαγχάνω, λήξομαι, ἔλαχον, εἴληχα, εἴληγμαι,
   ἐλήχθην obtain (by lot)
μέρος, μέρους, τό part
ἄνοια, ἀνοίᾱς, ἡ lack of understanding, folly,
   stupidity; ἀνοίης (Epic) = Attic ἀνοίᾱς
ἄφρων, ἄφρον senseless, foolish

ζηλωτός, ζηλωτή, ζηλωτόν enviable
φαίνω, φανῶ, ἔφηνα, πέφηνα, πέφασμαι, ἐφάνην
   show; *middle*, appear; ἐφαίνεο (Epic) = Attic
   ἐφαίνου
ἄξιος, ἀξίᾱ, ἄξιον worth; worthy (+ gen.)

4. An epigram of Simonides

χαίρει τις Θεόδωρος ἐπεὶ θάνον· ἄλλος ἐπ' αὐτῷ
   χαιρήσει. θανάτῳ πάντες ὀφειλόμεθα. (Simonides, *Epigrams* X.105)

EC

Θεόδωρος, Θεοδώρου, ὁ Theodorus
ἐπεί (conj.) since, because
θάνον = ἔθανον

ὀφείλω, ὀφειλήσω, ὠφείλησα, ὠφείληκα, ——,
—— owe

Fragments from the works of Simonides

5.   πάντα γὰρ μίαν ἱκνεῖται δασπλῆτα Χάρυβδιν,
       αἱ μεγάλαι τ' ἀρεταὶ καὶ ὁ πλοῦτος.   (Simonides, frag. 17)

ἱκνέομαι, ἵξομαι, ἱκόμην, ——, ἷγμαι, —— come   Χάρυβδις, Χαρύβδεως, ἡ Charybdis (a danger-
   (to), arrive (at), reach   ous whirlpool off the coast of Sicily)
δασπλής, δασπλῆτος masc./fem. adj., horrible,
   frightful

6.   οὔτις ἄνευ θεῶν
       ἀρετὰν λάβεν, οὐ πόλις, οὐ βροτός.
       θεὸς ὁ πάμμητις . . .   (Simonides, frag. 21)

οὔτις = οὔ τις   πάμμητις, παμμήτιδος masc./fem. adj.,
ἀρετάν (Doric) = Attic ἀρετήν   all-knowing
λάβεν (Epic) = Attic ἔλαβεν

7. A fragment from the works of the philosopher Heraclitus

       ἓν τὸ σοφὸν μοῦνον λέγεσθαι οὐκ ἐθέλει καὶ ἐθέλει Ζηνὸς ὄνομα.   (Heraclitus, frag. 32)

μοῦνον (Ionic) = Attic μόνον   ὄνομα, ὀνόματος, τό name

8. The Chorus reflects after Agamemnon's murder.

       τί βροτοῖς ἄνευ Διὸς τελεῖται;
       τί τῶνδ' οὐ θεόκραντόν ἐστιν;   (Aeschylus, *Agamemnon* 1487–88)

τελέω complete, accomplish
θεόκραντος, θεόκραντον accomplished by the
   gods

9. Darius explains the Greek advantage to an uncomprehending Chorus.

       Δα. αὐτὴ γὰρ ἡ γῆ ξύμμαχος κείνοις πέλει.
       Χο. πῶς τοῦτ' ἔλεξας, τίνι τρόπῳ δὲ συμμαχεῖ;   (Aeschylus, *Persians* 792–93)
                                                                                              IT

Δα. = Darius (the Persian king)   Χο. = Chorus
κείνοις = ἐκείνοις   συμμαχέω be an ally
πέλω, ——, ——, ——, ——, —— be

10. On the verge of battle against Polynices, Eteocles considers the possibility of victory for his brother.

> εἰ δ' ἡ Διὸς παῖς παρθένος Δίκη παρῆν
> ἔργοις ἐκείνου καὶ φρεσίν, τάχ' ἂν τόδ᾿⁺ ἦν·

(Aeschylus, *Seven Against Thebes* 662–63)

IT

παρθένος, παρθένου, ἡ maiden
τάχα (adv.) perhaps

⁺τόδ', *refers to Polynices' victory over his brother*

11. A messenger reports a terrible occurrence during the battle for Thebes.

> Αγ.   ἄνδρες τεθνᾶσιν ἐκ χερῶν αὐτοκτόνων.
> Χο.   τίνες; τί δ' εἶπας; παραφρονῶ φόβῳ λόγου.

(Aeschylus, *Seven Against Thebes* 805–6)

IT

Αγ. = Messenger
χείρ, χειρός, ἡ hand; χερῶν = χειρῶν
αὐτοκτόνος, αὐτοκτόνον self-killing; slaying oneself

Χο. = Chorus
παραφρονέω (παρα- + φρονέω) be beside one-self; be out of one's mind

12. A fragment from a tragedy of Aeschylus

> . . . ἁπλῆ γὰρ οἶμος εἰς Ἅιδου φέρει.

(Aeschylus, frag. 239)

ἁπλοῦς, ἁπλῆ, ἁπλοῦν simple; single

οἶμος, οἴμου, ἡ way, road, path

13. Haemon expresses his displeasure at a decision of his father, Creon.

> εἰ μὴ πατὴρ ἦσθ', εἶπον ἄν σ' οὐκ εὖ φρονεῖν.

(Sophocles, *Antigone* 755)

IT

φρονέω think

14. Deianeira addresses her son in surprise at the words of her nurse.

> ὦ τέκνον, ὦ παῖ, κἀξ ἀγεννήτων ἄρα
> μῦθοι καλῶς πίπτουσιν· ἥδε γὰρ γυνὴ
> δούλη μέν, εἴρηκεν δ' ἐλεύθερον λόγον.

(Sophocles, *Trachiniae* 61–63)

IT

ἀγέννητος, ἀγέννητον low-born
μῦθος, μύθου, ὁ word, speech
πίπτω, πεσοῦμαι, ἔπεσον, πέπτωκα, ——, ——
  fall

δούλη, δούλης, ἡ (female) slave

Fragments from tragedies of Sophocles

15.   τοῦ ζῆν γὰρ οὐδεὶς ὡς ὁ γηράσκων ἐρᾷ.   (Sophocles, frag. 66)
                                                                                        IT

γηράσκω, γηράσω, ἐγήρᾱσα, γεγήρᾱκα, ——,   ἐράω love (+ gen.)
   —— grow old

16.   τὸν ἀίδᾱν γὰρ οὐδὲ γῆρας οἶδε φιλεῖν.   (Sophocles, frag. 298)
                                                                                        IT

ἀίδᾱν (Doric) = Attic Ἅιδην   γῆρας, γήραος, τό old age

17.   ὕβρις δέ τοι
         οὐπώποθ’ ἥβης εἰς τὸ σῶφρον ἵκετο
         ἀλλ’ ἐν νέοις ἀνθεῖ τε καὶ πάλιν φθίνει.   (Sophocles, frag. 786)
                                                                                        IT

ἥβη, ἥβης, ἡ young manhood, youth   πάλιν (adv.) again
ἱκνέομαι, ἵξομαι, ἱκόμην, ——, ἷγμαι, —— come   φθίνω, φθίσομαι, ἔφθισα, ——, ἔφθιμαι, ——
   (to), arrive (at), reach   decay, perish
ἀνθέω bloom

18.   οὐ γάρ τι βουλῆς ταὐτὸ καὶ δρόμου τέλος.   (Sophocles, frag. 856)
                                                                                        IT

δρόμος, δρόμου, ὁ race

19.   οἴκοι μένειν δεῖ τὸν καλῶς εὐδαίμονα.   (Sophocles, frag. 934)
                                                                                        IT

οἴκοι (adv.) at home

20.   νόμοις ἕπεσθαι τοῖσιν ἐγχώροις καλόν.   (Sophocles, frag. 937)
                                                                                        IT

ἔγχωρος, ἔγχωρον of or belonging to the country

21.   εἰ σῶμα δοῦλον,† ἀλλ' ὁ νοῦς ἐλεύθερος.   (Sophocles, frag. 940)

IT

†δοῦλος, δούλη, δοῦλον of or belonging to a slave

22.   εἰ δείν' ἔδρασας, δεινὰ καὶ παθεῖν σε δεῖ.   (Sophocles, frag. 956)

IT

δράω, δράσω, ἔδρασα, δέδρακα, δέδραμαι, ἐδράσθην do

23. Expelled from her family home, Electra explains to a peasant why she, a princess, is tending to her inferior.

ἐγώ σ' ἴσον θεοῖσιν ἡγοῦμαι φίλον·
ἐν τοῖς ἐμοῖς γὰρ οὐκ ἐνύβρισας κακοῖς.
μεγάλη δὲ θνητοῖς μοῖρα συμφορᾶς κακῆς
ἰᾱτρὸν εὑρεῖν, ὡς ἐγὼ σὲ λαμβάνω.   (Euripides, *Electra* 67–70)

IT

ἡγέομαι, ἡγήσομαι, ἡγησάμην, ——, ἥγημαι,
—— regard, believe, think
ἐνυβρίζω (ἐν- + ὑβρίζω), ἐνυβριῶ, ἐνύβρισα,
——, ——, —— mock, insult

ἰᾱτρός, ἰᾱτροῦ, ὁ doctor, healer
εὑρίσκω, εὑρήσω, ηὗρον, ηὕρηκα, ηὕρημαι,
ηὑρέθην find

24. Electra responds to a messenger's report of the killing of Aegisthus by Orestes.

ὦ θεοί, Δίκη τε πάνθ' ὁρῶσ' ἦλθες ποτέ.
ποίῳ τρόπῳ δὲ καὶ τίνι ῥυθμῷ φόνου
κτείνει Θυέστου παῖδα; βούλομαι μαθεῖν.   (Euripides, *Electra* 771–73)

IT

ποῖος, ποίᾱ, ποῖον what sort (of)
ῥυθμός, ῥυθμοῦ, ὁ rhythm; manner
φόνος, φόνου, ὁ murder

Θυέστης, Θυέστου, ὁ Thyestes (son of Pelops,
brother of Atreus, father of Aegisthus)

25. Iolaus, guardian of the children of Heracles, who has died and joined the gods, tells of his troubles.

ἐγὼ δὲ σὺν φεύγουσι συμφεύγω τέκνοις
καὶ σὺν κακῶς πράσσουσι συμπράσσω κακῶς ...   (Euripides, *Heracleidae* 26–27)

IT

συμφεύγω (συν- + φεύγω) flee together

συμπράσσω (συν- + πράσσω) fare together

26. Phaedra's nurse questions her.

τί φής; ἐρᾷς, ὦ τέκνον; ἀνθρώπων τίνος;   (Euripides, *Hippolytus* 350)
IT

ἐράω love (+ gen.)

27. The Chorus is moved to comment by Clytaemnestra's appeal on behalf of her daughter Iphigenia.

δεινὸν τὸ τίκτειν καὶ φέρει φίλτρον μέγα
πᾶσίν τε κοινόν ἐσθ' ὑπερκάμνειν τέκνων.   (Euripides, *Iphigenia at Aulis* 917–18)
IT

τίκτω, τέξομαι, ἔτεκον, τέτοκα, ——, ἐτέχθην   ὑπερκάμνω (ὑπερ- + κάμνω), ὑπερκαμοῦμαι,
  beget, give birth (to)   ——, ——, ——, —— suffer for, labor for
φίλτρον, φίλτρου, τό charm, spell   (+ gen.)

28. After Hector's description of Odysseus's wily tactics, Rhesus responds.

οὐδεὶς ἀνὴρ εὔψῡχος ἀξιοῖ λάθρᾳ
κτεῖναι τὸν ἐχθρόν . . .   (Euripides, *Rhesus* 510–11)
IT

εὔψῡχος, εὔψῡχον spirited, courageous   λάθρᾳ (adv.) secretly, stealthily

Fragments from tragedies of Euripides

29.   κακῆς ἀπ' ἀρχῆς γίγνεται τέλος κακόν.   (Euripides, frag. 32N)
IT

30.   νόσοι δὲ θνητῶν αἱ μέν εἰσ' αὐθαίρετοι,
      αἱ δ' ἐκ θεῶν πάρεισιν, ἀλλὰ τῷ νόμῳ
      ἰώμεθ' αὐτάς. ἀλλά σοι λέξαι θέλω,
      εἰ θεοί τι δρῶσιν αἰσχρόν, οὐκ εἰσὶν θεοί.   (Euripides, frag. 292.3–7N)
IT

νόσος, νόσου, ἡ sickness, disease   ἰάομαι cure, heal
αὐθαίρετος, αὐθαίρετον by one's own choice,   δράω, δράσω, ἔδρᾱσα, δέδρᾱκα, δέδρᾱμαι,
  voluntary   ἐδράσθην do

31.   ... κοὐκ ἐμὸς ὁ μῦθος, ἀλλ’ ἐμῆς μητρὸς πάρα,
       ὡς οὐρανός τε γαῖά τ’ ἦν μοφρὴ μία ...   (Euripides, frag. 484N)
                                                                                                IT

μῦθος, μύθου, ὁ word, speech; story   μορφή, μορφῆς, ἡ form

32.   πόλλ’ ἐλπίδες ψεύδουσι καὶ λόγοι βροτούς.   (Euripides, frag. 650N)
                                                                                                IT

ψεύδω, ψεύσω, ἔψευσα, ——, ἔψευσμαι, ἐψεύσθην deceive

33. The irreponsible Phidippides shows some concern for his befuddlcd father, Strepsiades.

       ὦ δαιμόνιε, τί χρῆμα πάσχεις, ὦ πάτερ;
       οὐκ εὖ φρονεῖς, μὰ τὸν Δία τὸν Ὀλύμπιον.   (Aristophanes, *Clouds* 816–17)
                                                                                                IT

δαιμόνιος, δαιμονίᾱ, δαιμόνιον miraculous, mar-   φρονέω think
   velous; *voc. masc. subst.*, good sir   Ὀλύμπιος, Ὀλυμπίᾱ, Ὀλύμπιον Olympian

34. Xenophon reports some things said by Socrates.

       ἔφη δὲ καὶ τὴν δικαιοσύνην καὶ τὴν ἄλλην πᾶσαν ἀρετὴν σοφίᾱν εἶναι. τά τε γὰρ δίκαια
       καὶ πάντα ὅσα ἀρετῇ πράττεται καλά τε καὶ ἀγαθὰ εἶναι.   (Xenophon, *Memorabilia* III.9.5)

ὅσος, ὅση, ὅσον (rel. adj.) (as many) as

35. At his trial Socrates imagines questions that might be put to him.

       "Ἀλλ’, ὦ Σώκρατες, τὸ σὸν τί ἐστι πρᾶγμα; πόθεν αἱ διαβολαί σοι αὗται γεγόνᾱσιν;"
                                                                            (Plato, *Apology* 20c4–6)

διαβολή, διαβολῆς, ἡ false accusation, slander

36. The Athenian Stranger begins to respond to a question about why there are different names for the four virtues, yet virtue is one.

> ἐρῶ γάρ σοι τὴν αἰτίαν, ὅτι τὸ μέν ἐστιν περὶ φόβον, οὗ καὶ τὰ θηρία μετέχει, τῆς ἀνδρείᾱς, καὶ τά γε τῶν παίδων ἤθη τῶν πάνυ νέων· ἄνευ λόγου καὶ φύσει γίγνεται ἀνδρείᾱ† ψῡχή, ἄνευ δὲ αὖ λόγου ψῡχὴ φρόνιμός τε καὶ νοῦν ἔχουσα οὔτ' ἐγένετο πώποτε οὔτ' ἔστιν οὐδ' αὖθίς ποτε γενήσεται ...
>
> (Plato, *Laws* 963e3–8)

θηρίον, θηρίου, τό wild animal, beast
μετέχω (μετα- + ἔχω) have a share (of), partake (of) (+ gen.)
ἦθος, ἤθους, τό custom, habit; *pl.,* character

†ἀνδρεῖος, ἀνδρείᾱ, ἀνδρεῖον manly; courageous
αὖ (adv.) again, in turn
φρόνιμος, φρόνιμον sensible, prudent; intelligent
αὖθις (adv.) again

37. Meno opens the dialogue that bears his name with this question.

> Ἔχεις μοι εἰπεῖν, ὦ Σώκρατες, ἆρα διδακτὸν ἡ ἀρετή; ἢ οὐ διδακτὸν ἀλλ' ἀσκητόν; ἢ οὔτε ἀσκητὸν οὔτε μαθητόν, ἀλλὰ φύσει παραγίγνεται τοῖς ἀνθρώποις ἢ ἄλλῳ τινὶ τρόπῳ;
>
> (Plato, *Meno* 70a1–4)

διδακτός, διδακτή, διδακτόν that can be taught, teachable
ἀσκητός, ἀσκητή, ἀσκητόν that can be acquired by practice

μαθητός, μαθητή, μαθητόν that can be learned, learnable
παραγίγνομαι (παρα- + γίγνομαι) be at hand (to), belong (to)

38. Part of a reported conversation between Socrates and Cebes, one of the visitors in his jail cell

> Τί οὖν; ἔφη,† Τῷ ζῆν ἐστί τι ἐναντίον, ὥσπερ τῷ ἐγρηγορέναι τὸ καθεύδειν;
> Πάνυ μὲν οὖν, ἔφη. ††
> Τί;
> Τὸ τεθνάναι, ἔφη. ††
>
> (Plato, *Phaedo* 71c1–c5)

†ἔφη, *subject is Socrates*
ἐγείρω, ἐγερῶ, ἤγειρα, ἐγρήγορα, ἐγήγερμαι, ἠγέρθην awaken, rouse; *perfect active,* be awake

καθεύδω (κατα- + εὕδω), καθευδήσω, ——, ——, ——, —— sleep
††ἔφη, *subject is Cebes*

39. Socrates explains why he and his companions deny the truth of an ugly story about Asclepius, the doctor reported to be a son of Apollo.

> ... εἰ μὲν θεοῦ ἦν, οὐκ ἦν, φήσομεν, αἰσχροκερδής· εἰ δ' αἰσχροκερδής, οὐκ ἦν θεοῦ.
>
> (Plato, *Republic* 408c3–4)

αἰσχροκερδής, αἰσχροκερδές shamefully desiring profit

40. Socrates gives an opinion about one kind of human being.

> **σμῑκρὰ δὲ φύσις οὐδὲν μέγα οὐδέποτε οὐδένα οὔτε ἰδιώτην οὔτε πόλιν δρᾷ.**
>
> (Plato, Republic 495b5–6)

ἰδιώτης, ἰδιώτου, ὁ private citizen

δράω, δράσω, ἔδρᾱσα, δέδρᾱκα, δέδρᾱμαι, ἐδράσθην do (something [acc.]) to or for (someone [acc.])

41. In his myth about the original, spherical human beings, whom the gods have split into two, Aristophanes reports what happened when two halves of an original human found each other.

> **... ἀπέθνῃσκον ὑπὸ λῑμοῦ καὶ τῆς ἄλλης ἀργίᾱς διὰ τὸ μηδὲν ἐθέλειν χωρὶς ἀλλήλων ποιεῖν.**
>
> (Plato, Symposium 191a8–9)

λῑμός, λῑμοῦ, ὁ hunger
ἀργίᾱ, ἀργίᾱς, ἡ rest from work, inactivity

χωρίς (prep. + gen.) apart from

Some Platonic definitions

42. **Σωφροσύνη μετριότης τῆς ψῡχῆς περὶ τὰς ἐν αὐτῇ κατὰ φύσιν γιγνομένᾱς ἐπιθῡμίᾱς τε καὶ ἡδονάς.**
([Plato], Definitions 411e6)

μετριότης, μετριότητος, ἡ middle condition

ἐπιθῡμίᾱ, ἐπιθῡμίᾱς, ἡ desire

43. **Ἀνδρείᾱ ἕξις ψῡχῆς ἀκίνητος ὑπὸ φόβου.**
([Plato], Definitions 412a3)

ἕξις, ἕξεως, ἡ state, condition

ἀκίνητος, ἀκίνητον unmoved; unmovable

44. **Σώφρων ὁ μετρίᾱς ἐπιθῡμίᾱς ἔχων.**
([Plato], Definitions 415d8)

μέτριος, μετρίᾱ, μέτριον moderate, temperate

ἐπιθῡμίᾱ, ἐπιθῡμίᾱς, ἡ desire

45. **Ὕβρις ἀδικίᾱ πρὸς ἀτῑμίᾱν φέρουσα.**
([Plato], Definitions 415e2)

ἀδικίᾱ, ἀδικίᾱς, ἡ injustice, wrongdoing

ἀτῑμίᾱ, ἀτῑμίᾱς, ἡ dishonor, disgrace

46.   The opening lines of the Metaphysics

πάντες ἄνθρωποι τοῦ εἰδέναι ὀρέγονται φύσει. σημεῖον δ᾽ ἡ τῶν αἰσθήσεων ἀγάπησις.

(Aristotle, *Metaphysics* 980a21-22)

ὀρέγω, ὀρέξω, ὤρεξα, ——, ——, ὠρέχθην
  reach; offer; *middle*, reach after, grasp at, desire
  (+ gen.)
σημεῖον, σημείου, τό sign; proof

αἴσθησις, αἰσθήσεως, ἡ perception (by the
  senses)
ἀγάπησις, ἀγαπήσεως, ἡ love

47. The philospher makes a comparison between city and individual.

ἀδύνατον δὲ καλῶς πράττειν τοῖς μὴ τὰ καλὰ πράττουσιν· οὐθὲν δὲ καλὸν ἔργον οὔτ᾽
ἀνδρὸς οὔτε πόλεως χωρὶς ἀρετῆς καὶ φρονήσεως· ἀνδρείᾱ δὲ πόλεως καὶ δικαιοσύνη
καὶ φρόνησις <καὶ σωφροσύνη> τὴν αὐτὴν ἔχει δύναμιν καὶ μορφὴν ὧν μετασχὼν
ἕκαστος τῶν ἀνθρώπων λέγεται <ἀνδρεῖος καὶ> δίκαιος καὶ φρόνιμος καὶ σώφρων.

(Aristotle, *Politics* 1323b31–37)

ἀδύνατος, ἀδύνατον impossible
οὐθέν = later Attic form of οὐδέν
χωρίς (prep. + gen.) apart from
μορφή, μορφῆς, ἡ form

μετέχω (μετα- + ἔχω) have a share (of), partake
  (of) (+ gen.); μετασχών, when partaking (of)
ἀνδρεῖος, ἀνδρείᾱ, ἀνδρεῖον manly; courageous
φρόνιμος, φρονίμη, φρόνιμον sensible, prudent;
  intelligent

Proverbial expressions from plays of Menander

48.   βίου δικαίου γίγνεται τέλος καλόν.   (Menander, *Sententiae* 108)

IT

49.   γυνὴ γὰρ οὐδὲν οἶδε πλὴν ὃ βούλεται.   (Menander, *Sententiae* 143)

IT

πλήν (conj.) except

50.   γυνὴ δὲ κολακεύει σε τοῦ λαβεῖν χάριν.   (Menander, *Sententiae* 167)

IT

κολακεύω, κολακεύσω, ἐκολάκευσα,
  κεκολάκευκα, ——, —— flatter

51.   καλὸν φέρουσι καρπὸν οἱ σεμνοὶ τρόποι.   (Menander, *Sententiae* 402)

IT

καρπός, καρποῦ, ὁ fruit   σεμνός, σεμνή, σεμνόν revered, august

52. καλὸν τὸ θνήσκειν οἷς ὕβριν τὸ ζῆν φέρει. (Menander, *Sententiae* 410)

IT

53. μένει δ' ἑκάστῳ τοῦθ' ὅπερ μέλλει παθεῖν.† (Menander, *Sententiae* 479)

IT

†παθεῖν, here, aor. infin. with μέλλει

54. οὐ χρὴ φέρειν τὰ πρόσθεν ἐν μνήμῃ κακά. (Menander, *Sententiae* 589)

IT

πρόσθεν (adv.) earlier μνήμη, μνήμης, ἡ memory

55. νόμων ἔχεσθαι πάντα δεῖ τὸν σώφρονα. (Menander, *Sententiae* 380M)

IT

56. An elegiac fragment from the works of Callimachus

ἦν ἄρ' ἔπος τόδ' ἀληθές, ὅτ' οὐ μόνον ὕδατος αἶσαν
ἀλλά τι καὶ λέσχης οἶνος ἔχειν ἐθέλει. (Callimachus, *Causes* frag. 178.15–16)

EC

ὕδωρ, ὕδατος, τό water; *the upsilon of* ὕδατος *here scans long.*
αἶσα, αἴσης, ἡ lot; portion; share

λέσχη, λέσχης, ἡ talking, conversation
οἶνος, οἴνου, ὁ wine

57. Plutarch reports a question posed to a Spartan woman by a woman from Attica and her reply.

"Διὰ τί ὑμεῖς ἄρχετε μόναι τῶν ἀνδρῶν αἱ Λάκαιναι;"
"'Ότι," ἔφη, "καὶ τίκτομεν μόναι ἄνδρας." (Plutarch, *Spartan Sayings* 240e7)

Λάκαινα *fem. adj.,* Laconian, Spartan; *fem. subst.,* Spartan woman

τίκτω, τέξομαι, ἔτεκον, τέτοκα, ——, ἐτέχθην beget, give birth to

58. A proverb from the school of Pythagoras

ἰσχὺς καὶ τεῖχος καὶ ὅπλον τοῦ σοφοῦ ἡ φρόνησις. (*Opinions of the Pythagoreans* 46)

ἰσχύς, ἰσχύος ἡ strength, might

Proverbs from Aesop

59.   **Καὶ τίς λέγει τῷ λέοντι ὅτι† Ὄζει τὸ στόμα σου;**   (Aesop, *Proverbs* 126)

λέων, λέοντος, ὁ lion   **ὄζω, ὀζήσω, ὤζησα, ὄδωδα, ——, ——** smell;
†**ὅτι**, *here, introduces a direct quotation and is not*   stink
   translated   **στόμα, στόματος, τό** mouth

60.   **Πάντα ὁ ἄνθρωπος καὶ οὐδὲν ὁ ἄνθρωπος.**   (Aesop, *Proverbs* 142)

61. The emperor explains why he does not mind being refuted.

   ζητῶ γὰρ τὴν ἀλήθειαν, ὑφ' ἧς οὐδεὶς πώποτε ἐβλάβη.   (Marcus Aurelius, *Meditations* VI.21.1)

ζητέω seek (for)   **βλάπτω, βλάψω, ἔβλαψα, βέβλαφα, βέβλαμμαι,**
                                                             ἐβλάβην/ἐβλάφθην harm, injure

62. An elegiac couplet attributed to the late Greek poet Rufinus

   εἰ μὲν ἐπ'† ἀμφοτέροισιν, Ἔρως, ἴσα τόξα τιταίνεις,
   εἶ θεός· εἰ δὲ ῥέπεις πρὸς μέρος, οὐ θεὸς εἶ.   (*Greek Anthology*, V.97)

                                                                                                    EC

†**ἐπί**, *here,* against   **ῥέπω, ῥέψω, ——, ——, ——, ——** incline
ἀμφότερος, ἀμφοτέρᾱ, ἀμφότερον both   **μέρος, μέρους, τό** part
τόξον, τόξου, τό *sing. or pl.,* bow
τιταίνω, ——, ἐτίτηνα, ——, ——, —— stretch,
   extend

Longer Readings

1. Theognis, *Elegies* I.833–36 (EC)

The poet explains who is responsible for the terrible state of things.

πάντα τάδ' ἐν κοράκεσσι καὶ ἐν φθόρῳ· οὐδέ τις ἡμῖν
  αἴτιος ἀθανάτων,[†] Κύρνε, θεῶν μακάρων,
ἀλλ' ἀνδρῶν τε βίη καὶ κέρδεα δειλὰ καὶ ὕβρις
  πολλῶν ἐξ ἀγαθῶν ἐς κακότητ' ἔβαλεν.

κόραξ, κόρακος, ὁ crow;
  κοράκεσσι (Ionic) = Attic κόραξι
φθόρος, φθόρου, ὁ destruction, ruin, perdition
αἴτιος, αἰτία, αἴτιον responsible, to blame
[†]*The first alpha of* ἀθανάτων *here scans long.*
Κύρνος, Κύρνου, ὁ Cyrnus (one of the addressees of the poem)
μάκαρ, μάκαρος *masc. adj.,* blessed, happy

βίᾱ, βίᾱς, ἡ force, violence;
  βίη (Ionic) = Attic βίᾱ
κέρδος, κέρδους, τό profit, gain;
  κέρδεα (Ionic) = Attic κέρδη
δειλός, δειλή, δειλόν craven, vile
κακότης, κακότητος, ἡ badness, baseness
βάλλω, βαλῶ, ἔβαλον, βέβληκα, βέβλημαι,
  ἐβλήθην throw; ἔβαλεν, *supply* ἡμᾶς

Little is known of **Theognis**, who lived in the second half of the 6th century B.C.E. He was a poet from Megara whose name is associated with approximately 1,400 elegiac lines (not clearly separated into discrete poems) that have a number of themes and addressees. Many couplets speak of the evils of hubris and the importance of moderation, honesty, and the other virtues.

2. Sophocles, *Antigone* 506–17 (IT)

Antigone and Creon argue after Antigone's failed attempt to bury her brother.

Αν.   …
       ἀλλ' ἡ τυραννὶς πολλά τ' ἄλλ' εὐδαιμονεῖ
       κἄξεστιν αὐτῇ δρᾶν λέγειν θ' ἃ βούλεται.
Κρ. σὺ τοῦτο μούνη τῶνδε Καδμείων ὁρᾷς.
Αν. ὁρῶσι χοὗτοι· σοὶ δ' ὑπίλλουσι στόμα.
Κρ. σὺ δ' οὐκ ἐπαιδῇ, τῶνδε χωρὶς εἰ φρονεῖς;   510
Αν. οὐδὲν γὰρ αἰσχρὸν τοὺς ὁμοσπλάγχνους σέβειν.
Κρ. οὔκουν ὅμαιμος χὠ καταντίον θανών;
Αν. ὅμαιμος ἐκ μιᾶς τε καὶ ταὐτοῦ πατρός.
Κρ. πῶς δῆτ' ἐκείνῳ δυσσεβῆ τῖμᾷς† χάριν;
Αν. οὐ μαρτυρήσει ταῦθ' ὁ κατθανὼν νέκυς.   515
Κρ. εἴ τοί σφε τῖμᾷς ἐξ ἴσου† τῷ δυσσεβεῖ.
Αν. οὐ γάρ τι δοῦλος, ἀλλ' ἀδελφὸς ὤλετο.

Αν. = Antigone
τυραννίς, τυραννίδος, ἡ monarchy; tyranny
εὐδαιμονέω be prosperous
ἔξεστι(ν) (ἐκ- + ἐστί[ν]) (impersonal verb) it is
   possible
δράω, δράσω, ἔδρᾱσα, δέδρᾱκα, δέδρᾱμαι,
   ἐδράσθην do
Κρ. = Creon
μούνη = μόνη
Καδμεῖοι, Καδμείων, οἱ Cadmeans (the people
   descended from Cadmus), Thebans
ὑπίλλω, ——, ——, ——, ——, —— keep shut
στόμα, στόματος, τό mouth
ἐπαιδέομαι (ἐπι- + αἰδέομαι), ——, ——, ——,
   ——, ἐπῃδέσθην be ashamed
χωρίς (prep. + gen.) apart from; differently from
φρονέω think
ὁμόσπλαγχνος, ὁμόσπλαγχνον born of the same
   mother

σέβω, ——, ——, ——, ——, —— worship,
   honor
οὔκουν *in emotional questions* = οὐ
ὅμαιμος, ὅμαιμον of the same blood
καταντίον (adv.) opposite, facing
δῆτα = *emphatic form of* δή
δυσσεβής, δυσσεβές irreverent, impious
†τῖμάω, *here,* bestow
μαρτυρέω bear witness to
καταθνῄσκω (κατα- + θνῄσκω) die; κατθανών =
   *καταθανών
νέκυς, νέκυος, ὁ corpse; dead person
σφε = *enclitic masc. sing. acc. of 3rd person personal
   pron.,* him
†ἐξ ἴσου, *here,* equally
ἀδελφός, ἀδελφοῦ, ὁ brother
ὄλλῡμι, ὀλῶ, ὤλεσα (trans.)/ὠλόμην (intrans.),
   ὀλώλεκα (trans.)/ὄλωλα (intrans.), ——, ——
   destroy; *middle or intrans.,* perish

The **Antigone** continues the tragic story of the family of Oedipus and dramatizes an irreconcilable conflict between the claims of the family and the rule of the city. After the defeat of the seven attackers of Thebes, including Polynices, one of the sons of Oedipus, the ruler, Creon, forbids his burial because he was an enemy of the city, but Polynices' sister Antigone defies Creon and buries her brother. She is then imprisoned by Creon, who is persuaded too late by the seer Teiresias to relent. Antigone has hanged herself, and Creon's son, who was to marry her, has taken his own life as well. When Creon's wife learns of these events, she too commits suicide, and Creon is left bereft.

3. Sophocles, frag. 941

On the power and complexity of Aphrodite (1T)

ὦ παῖδες, ἤ τοι Κύπρις οὐ Κύπρις μόνον,
ἀλλ' ἐστὶ πολλῶν ὀνομάτων ἐπώνυμος.
ἔστιν μὲν Ἅιδης, ἔστι δ' ἄφθιτος βίος,
ἔστιν δὲ λύσσα μανιάς, ἔστι δ' ἵμερος
ἄκρᾶτος, ἔστ' οἰμωγμός, ἐν κείνῃ τὸ πᾶν
σπουδαῖον, ἡσυχαῖον, ἐς βίᾶν ἄγον.
ἐντήκεται γὰρ πλευμόνων ὅσοις ἔνι
ψῡχή· τίς οὐχὶ τῆσδε τῆς θεοῦ πόρος;
εἰσέρχεται μὲν ἰχθύων πλωτῷ γένει,
χέρσου δ' ἔνεστιν ἐν τετρασκελεῖ γονῇ,
νωμᾷ δ' ἐν οἰωνοῖσι τοὐκείνης πτερόν.

Κύπρις, Κύπριδος, ἡ Cypris (a name for
   Aphrodite)
ὄνομα, ὀνόματος, τό name
ἐπώνυμος, ἐπώνυμον surnamed; named after
   (+ gen.)
ἄφθιτος, ἄφθιτον imperishable, undecaying
λύσσα, λύσσης, ἡ rage, fury
μανιάς, μανιάδος *fem. adj.*, frantic, insane
ἵμερος, ἱμέρου, ὁ longing, yearning
ἄκρᾶτος, ἄκρᾶτον unmixed, pure; absolute;
   uncontrolled
οἰμωγμός, οἰμωγμοῦ, ὁ wailing, lamentation
κείνῃ = ἐκείνῃ
σπουδαῖος, σπουδαίᾶ, σπουδαῖον serious, ear-
   nest; active, energetic
ἡσυχαῖος, ἡσυχαίᾶ, ἡσυχαῖον quiet, gentle,
   peaceful
βίᾱ, βίᾶς, ἡ force, violence

ἐντήκομαι (ἐν- + τήκομαι), ——, ——,
   ἐντέτηκα, ἐντέτημαι, —— melt in; sink in
   (+ gen.)
πλεύμων, πλεύμονος, ὁ *sing. or pl.*, lungs
ὅσος, ὅση, ὅσον (rel. adj.) (as many) as
ἔνειμι (ἐν- + εἰμί) be in; ἔνι = ἔνεστι(ν)
οὐχί = *emphatic form of* οὐκ
πόρος, πόρου, ὁ passage, pathway
εἰσέρχομαι (εἰσ- + ἔρχομαι) go into (+ dat.)
ἰχθῦς, ἰχθύος, ὁ fish
πλωτός, πλωτή, πλωτόν swimming
χέρσος, χέρσου, ἡ (dry) land
τετρασκελής, τετρασκελές four-legged
γονή, γονῆς, ἡ offspring; stock
νωμάω be the guiding power
οἰωνός, οἰωνοῦ, ὁ bird
πτερόν, πτεροῦ, τό wing

Although only 7 complete plays of Sophocles survive, the titles of approximately 125 are known, and several hundred lines from these other works are extant as fragments, most often quoted by ancient grammarians or later writers about literature. While many are brief, aphoristic utterances of one or two lines, longer fragments offer speeches and choral songs on a variety of themes. Many fragments can be placed in particular plays, and all the fragments have been collected and numbered in standard editions.

4. Euripides, *Bacchae* 464–68 (IT)

A disguised Dionysus, who has allowed himself to be captured, is questioned by Pentheus about his origins. He speaks of Tmolus, a region in Asia Minor.

Δι.   ἐντεῦθέν εἰμι, Λῡδίᾱ δέ μοι πατρίς.

Πε.   πόθεν† δὲ τελετὰς τάσδ' ἄγεις ἐς Ἑλλάδα;

Δι.   Διόνῡσος αὐτός μ' εἰσέβησ', ὁ τοῦ Διός.

Πε.   Ζεὺς δ' ἔστ' ἐκεῖ τις ὃς νέους τίκτει θεούς;

Δι.   οὔκ, ἀλλ' ὁ Σεμέλην ἐνθάδε ζεύξᾱς γάμοις.

ἐντεῦθεν (adv.) from there
Λῡδίᾱ, Λῡδίᾱς, ἡ Lydia (a country in Asia Minor)
πατρίς, πατρίδος, ἡ homeland
Πε. = Pentheus
†πόθεν, *here*, wherefore, why
τελετή, τελετῆς, ἡ (mystic) rite
εἰσβαίνω (εἰσ- + βαίνω), εἰσβήσομαι, εἰσέβησα, εἰσβέβηκα, ——, —— embark; *aorist*, cause to go

τίκτω, τέξομαι, ἔτεκον, τέτοκα, ——, ἐτέχθην beget, give birth to
Σεμέλη, Σεμέλης, ἡ Semele
ἐνθάδε (adv.) here
ζεύγνῡμι, ζεύξω, ἔζευξα, ——, ἔζευγμαι, ἐζύγην/ ἐζεύχθην yoke, join
γάμος, γάμου, ὁ *sing. or pl.,* marriage

The **Bacchae** was produced posthumously (along with the *Iphigenia at Aulis*) in 405 B.C.E. and won first prize at the City Dionysia. Although it is one of Euripides' last plays, it is remarkably traditional in form, with an old-fashioned chorus and a violent closing. The play presents the introduction of the Dionysian mysteries and the worship of Dionysus to Thebes, the city of the god's mother, Semele. Pentheus, ruler of Thebes and nephew of Semele, rejects the god's rites, which have disrupted his city and maddened the city's women, including Pentheus's mother, Agave. Dionysus, in human disguise, confronts and then seduces Pentheus into viewing the rites. When he is discovered, he is torn apart by the women, who have mistaken him for a beast. The play ends with Agave's realization that she is carrying in triumphal procession into the city not a beast's head but that of her own son.

5. Euripides, *Cyclops* 113–28 (1T)

On the island of the Cyclopes, Odysseus converses with Silenus, the companion of Dionysus.

ΟΔ. τίς δ' ἥδε χώρᾱ καὶ τίνες ναίουσί νιν;

Σι. Αἰτναῖος ὄχθος Σικελίᾱς ὑπέρτατος.

ΟΔ. τείχη δὲ ποῦ 'στι καὶ πόλεως πυργώματα; 115

Σι. οὐκ ἔστ'· ἔρημοι πρῶνες ἀνθρώπων, ξένε.

ΟΔ. τίνες δ' ἔχουσι γαῖαν; ἦ† θηρῶν γένος;

Σι. Κύκλωπες, ἄντρ' ἔχοντες, οὐ στέγᾱς δόμων.

ΟΔ. τίνος κλύοντες; ἢ δεδήμευται κράτος;

Σι. μονάδες· ἀκούει δ' οὐδὲν οὐδεὶς οὐδενός. 120

ΟΔ. σπείρουσι δ'—ἢ τῷ ζῶσι;—Δήμητρος στάχυν;

Σι. γάλακτι καὶ τῡροῖσι καὶ μήλων βορᾷ.

ΟΔ. Βρομίου δὲ πῶμ' ἔχουσιν, ἀμπέλου ῥοάς;

ΟΔ. = Odysseus

ναίω, ——, ——, ——, ——, —— dwell in, inhabit

νιν = *enclitic fem. sing. acc. of 3rd person personal pron.*, it

Σι. = Silenus

Αἰτναῖος, Αἰτναίᾱ, Αἰτναῖον of *or* belonging to Mount Aetna

ὄχθος, ὄχθου, ὁ hill

Σικελίᾱ, Σικελίᾱς, ἡ Sicily

ὑπέρτατος, ὑπερτάτη, ὑπέρτατον highest

πύργωμα, πυργώματος, τό walled city; *pl.*, battlements

ἔρημος, ἔρημον desolate, barren (+ gen.)

πρών, πρῶνος, ὁ headland

†ἦ, here (particle) *introduces a question*

θήρ, θηρός, ὁ wild beast

Κύκλωψ, Κύκλωπος, ὁ Cyclops ("Round Eye")

ἄντρον, ἄντρου, τό cave, cavern

στέγη, στέγης, ἡ roof

δόμος, δόμου, ὁ house

κλύω, ——, ——, ——, ——, —— hear, listen to; obey (+ gen.)

δημεύω, δημεύσω, ἐδήμευσα, ——, δεδήμευμαι, —— make public

κράτος, κράτους, τό might, power; rule

μονάς, μονάδος *masc./fem. adj.*, lone, solitary

σπείρω, σπερῶ, ἔσπειρα, ἔσπαρκα, ἔσπαρμαι, ἐσπάρην sow, plant

στάχῡς, στάχυος, ὁ (ear of) corn; στάχυν = *acc. sing.*

γάλα, γάλακτος, τό milk

τῡρός, τῡροῦ, ὁ cheese

μῆλον, μήλου, τό sheep

βορά, βορᾶς, ἡ meat

Βρόμιος, Βρομίου, ὁ Bromius (a name of Bacchus)

πῶμα, πώματος, τό drink

ἄμπελος, ἀμπέλου, ἡ vine

ῥοή, ῥοῆς, ἡ stream

The *Cyclops* is the only complete surviving example of a satyr play. The term **satyr play** makes reference to a mythical beast of the woods, perhaps similar to a goat or a horse. Satyrs, along with Silenus, their leader or father, represented animal desires and accompanying coarse behavior. When a tragedian competed in the dramatic festivals, he regularly offered three tragedies and one shorter, lighter piece that combined elements of both comedy and tragedy. The *Cyclops* reprises (with a number of notable changes of detail and emphasis) the story known from Homer's *Odyssey* of the hero's harrowing visit to the island of the uncivilized one-eyed shepherds, the Cyclopes.

Σι.   ἥκιστα· τοιγὰρ ἄχορον οἰκοῦσι χθόνα.

Οδ.   φιλόξενοι δὲ χὤσιοι περὶ ξένους;   125

Σι.   γλυκύτατά φᾶσι τὰ κρέα τοὺς ξένους φορεῖν.

Οδ.   τί φῄς; βορᾷ χαίρουσιν ἀνθρωποκτόνῳ;

Σι.   οὐδεὶς μολὼν δεῦρ' ὅστις οὐ κατεσφάγη.

ἥκιστα (adv.) least; not at all
τοιγάρ (particle) therefore, accordingly
ἄχορος, ἄχορον without the dance
οἰκέω inhabit, occupy
χθών, χθονός, ἡ earth, land
φιλόξενος, φιλόξενον loving strangers,
    hospitable
ὅσιος, ὁσίᾱ, ὅσιον holy; devout
γλυκύτατος, γλυκυτάτη, γλυκύτατον sweetest
κρέας, κρέως, τό flesh, meat; κρέα = acc. pl.
φορέω bear; have, possess

βορά, βορᾶς, ἡ meat
ἀνθρωπόκτονος, ἀνθρωπόκτονον furnished by
    slaughtered men
βλώσκω, μολοῦμαι, ἔμολον, μέμβλωκα, ——,
    —— go, come
δεῦρο (adv.) hither, to here
ὅστις, ἥτις, ὅτι (indef. rel. pron.) who(ever),
    what(ever)
κατασφάζω (κατα- + σφάζω), ——, κατέσφαξα,
    ——, ——, κατεσφάγην slaughter, murder

6. Euripides, *Helen* 255–61 (1T)

Helen addresses the Chorus of captive Greek women.

> Φίλαι γυναῖκες, τίνι πότμῳ συνεζύγην;
> γυνὴ γὰρ οὔθ᾽ Ἑλληνὶς οὔτε βάρβαρος
> τεῦχος νεοσσῶν λευκὸν ἐκλοχεύεται,
> ἐν ᾧ με Λήδαν φασὶν ἐκ Διὸς τεκεῖν.
> ἆρ᾽ ἡ τεκοῦσά μ᾽ ἔτεκεν ἀνθρώποις τέρας;
> τέρας γὰρ ὁ βίος καὶ τὰ πράγματ᾽ ἐστί μου,
> τὰ μὲν δι᾽ Ἥραν, τὰ δὲ τὸ κάλλος αἴτιον.

πότμος, πότμου, ὁ lot, (evil) destiny
συζεύγνῡμι (συν- + ζεύγνῡμι), συζεύξω, ——,
    ——, συνέζευγμαι, συνεζύγην yoke together
Ἑλληνίς, Ἑλληνίδος *fem. adj.*, Greek
τεῦχος, τεύχους, τό vessel; container
νεοσσός, νεοσσοῦ, ὁ young bird
λευκός, λευκή, λευκόν white
ἐκλοχεύω (ἐκ- + λοχεύω), ——, ——, ——,
    ——, —— *active or middle*, bring forth, give
    birth to

Λήδᾱ, Λήδᾱς, ἡ Leda (mother of Helen)
τίκτω, τέξομαι, ἔτεκον, τέτοκα, ——, ἐτέχθην
    beget, give birth to
τέρας, τέρατος, τό portent; monster
κάλλος, κάλλους, τό beauty
αἴτιος, αἰτίᾱ, αἴτιον reponsible, to blame

Produced immediately after the end of the failed Sicilian expedition, Athens' attempt to gain a foothold in the western Mediterranean, the **Helen** presents another view of the futility of war. The *Helen* is set in Egypt immediately after the Trojan War. In this version, Helen herself was never taken to Troy, but a phantom image of her was there, while she herself was placed under the protection of the Egyptian king Proteus. Teucer arrives in Egypt and informs the Egyptians, their king Theoclymenus (Proteus's successor), and Helen that Menelaus is dead. Although this appears to leave Theoclymenus free to marry Helen, Teucer's report soon proves false. Menelaus arrives, recognizes Helen, realizes that he has left behind a false Helen in a cave, and contrives to steal Helen away before Theoclymenus can force her to marry him. Through a trick in which they are aided by Theoclymenus's sister Theonoë, the two manage to escape, and at play's end Theoclymenus is prevented from taking his revenge on his sister by Castor and Polydeuces, Helen's half-brothers.

7. Aristophanes, *Frogs* 757–60 (IT)

Part of a conversation between two slaves in Hades

> Ξα.   τίς οὗτος οὔνδον ἐστὶ θόρυβος καὶ βοὴ
> χὠ λοιδορησμός; Αι. Αἰσχύλου κεὐρῑπίδου.
>
> Ξα.   ἆ. Αι. πρᾶγμα πρᾶγμα μέγα κεκίνηται μέγα
> ἐν τοῖς νεκροῖσι καὶ στάσις πολλὴ πάνυ.

Ξα. = Xanthias (slave of Dionysus)
ἔνδον (adv.) within
θόρυβος, θορύβου, ὁ uproar
βοή, βοῆς, ἡ shouting
λοιδορησμός, λοιδορησμοῦ, ὁ abuse
Αι. = Aiakos (a slave in the Underworld)

Αἰσχύλος, Αἰσχύλου, ὁ Aeschylus
ἆ (interj.) ah
κῑνέω move, set in motion
νεκρός, νεκροῦ, ὁ corpse
στάσις, στάσεως, ἡ sedition; discord

The *Frogs* was produced at the Lenaean festival in early 405 B.C.E., near the end of the Peloponnesian War and shortly after the deaths of both Euripides and Sophocles. It not only earned first prize in the comic contest but also, according to tradition, was awarded the singular honor of a second production later in the year. Accompanied by his unusual slave Xanthias, the god Dionysus, in despair about the inferior quality of tragic writers in Athens, makes his way to Hades' house in order to retrieve Euripides. The first half of the play describes Dionysus's journey, and the second half is taken up with a contest in the Underworld between Aeschylus and Euripides, the winner of which is to return with Dionysus to Athens. The play takes its name from a group of frogs who sing one choral song while Dionysus tries to row himself to the Underworld.

8. Xenophon, *Memorabilia* I.1.1–2

The historian summarizes the indictment brought against Socrates and begins his refutation of it.

> ἡ μὲν γὰρ γραφὴ κατ᾽ αὐτοῦ τοιάδε τις ἦν· ἀδικεῖ Σωκράτης οὓς μὲν ἡ πόλις νομίζει
> θεοὺς οὐ νομίζων, ἕτερα δὲ καινὰ δαιμόνια εἰσφέρων· ἀδικεῖ δὲ καὶ τοὺς νέους
> διαφθείρων.
>
> πρῶτον μὲν οὖν, ὡς οὐκ ἐνόμιζεν οὓς ἡ πόλις νομίζει θεούς, ποίῳ ποτ᾽ ἐχρήσαντο
> τεκμηρίῳ; θύων τε γὰρ φανερὸς ἦν πολλάκις μὲν οἴκοι, πολλάκις δὲ ἐπὶ τῶν κοινῶν τῆς
> πόλεως βωμῶν, καὶ μαντικῇ χρώμενος οὐκ ἀφανὴς ἦν.

γραφή, γραφῆς, ἡ indictment
τοιόσδε, τοιάδε, τοιόνδε such (as this),
   of such a sort (as this)
νομίζω, νομιῶ, ἐνόμισα, νενόμικα, νενόμισμαι,
   ἐνομίσθην believe (in)
ἕτερος, ἑτέρᾱ, ἕτερον (the) other (of two)
καινός, καινή, καινόν new
δαιμόνιον, δαιμονίου, τό (diminutive of δαίμων)
   divinity; god
εἰσφέρω (εἰσ- + φέρω) bring in, introduce
πρῶτον (adv.) first
ποῖος, ποίᾱ, ποῖον what sort (of)

χράομαι, χρήσομαι, ἐχρησάμην, ——, κέχρημαι,
   —— use (+ dat.)
τεκμήριον, τεκμηρίου, τό sure sign; proof
θύω, θύσω, ἔθῡσα, τέθυκα, τέθυμαι, ἐτύθην
   sacrifice
φανερός, φανερά, φανερόν visible, evident,
   conspicuous
οἴκοι (adv.) at home
βωμή, βωμῆς, ἡ altar
μαντική, μαντικῆς, ἡ (art of) prophecy
ἀφανής, ἀφανές unclear, not obvious

The **Memorabilia** (Recollections) is a work in four books (largely in narrated or reported dialogues) that presents and defends the moral philosophy of Socrates, who was tried and put to death in 399 B.C.E. on charges of impiety and corrupting the youth of Athens. Xenophon opens the *Memorabilia* with a brief but pointed refutation of those charges, but the greater portion of the work depicts Socrates conversing on many topics with a variety of his fellow citizens. Although some of the discourses may recall conversations heard by Xenophon himself, many were invented by the author in order to display what he believed were the essentials of Socratic thought.

9. Aristotle, *Categories* 65.20–66.3

The philosopher speaks about opposites.

> τῶν ὄντων τῶν μὲν ἔστι τι ἐναντίον, τῶν δὲ οὔ. χρῡσῷ μὲν γὰρ καὶ ἀνθρώπῳ καὶ ἱματίῳ καὶ τοῖς τοιούτοις οὐδέν ἐστιν ἐναντίον, ἀρετῇ δὲ καὶ ἀγαθῷ καὶ θερμῷ ἔστι τι ἐναντίον· ἀγαθῷ μὲν γὰρ ἐναντίον τὸ κακόν, ἀρετῇ δὲ κακίᾱ, θερμῷ δὲ ψῡχρόν. τῶν ἐναντίων τοίνυν αὐτῶν τὰ μὲν ἔχουσί† τι ἀνὰ μέσον, τὰ δὲ οὔ. ἀγαθοῦ μὲν γὰρ καὶ κακοῦ ἔστι τι ἀνὰ μέσον, κῑνήσεως καὶ ἠρεμίᾱς οὐδέν ἐστιν ἀνὰ μέσον· ἐξ ἀνάγκης γὰρ πάντα ἢ κῑνεῖται ἢ ἠρεμεῖ. καὶ ζωῆς καὶ θανάτου οὐδέν ἐστιν ἀνὰ μέσον· ἐξ ἀνάγκης γὰρ ὅπερ τῆς ζωῆς δεκτικόν ἐστιν ἢ ζῇ ἢ τέθνηκεν.

χρῡσός, χρῡσοῦ, ὁ gold
ἱμάτιον, ἱματίου, τό cloak
τοιοῦτος, τοιαύτη, τοιοῦτον/τοιοῦτο such,
    of such a sort
θερμός, θερμή, θερμόν warm
κακίᾱ, κακίᾱς, ἡ wickedness
ψῡχρός, ψῡχρά, ψῡχρόν cold
τοίνυν (particle) further
†ἔχουσι, *here, subject is neut. pl.*

ἀνά (prep. + acc.) through; in
μέσον, μέσου, τό middle
κίνησις, κῑνήσεως, ἡ motion
ἠρεμίᾱ, ἠρεμίᾱς, ἡ stillness, rest
κῑνέω move, set in motion
ἠρεμέω be still, be at rest
ζωή, ζωῆς, ἡ life
δεκτικός, δεκτική, δεκτικόν able to receive
    (+ gen.), capable (+ gen.)

The prolific and influential **Aristotle** (384–322 B.C.E.) was born in Stagira on the peninsula of Calcidice in Macedonia. His father was the court physician to Amyntas III, the father of Philip II. As a young man, Aristotle emigrated to Athens and became Plato's student at the Academy until the latter's death. He then spent the next several years in various locations doing biological research before becoming tutor to Philip's son Alexander (the Great) in 342. From there he returned first to his birthplace, then to Athens, where he founded his own school, the Lyceum. There he produced most of the writings that have survived. Aristotle addressed nearly every subject of philosophy and science (natural philosophy), but there is much controversy over the relation between what Aristotle wrote and what has survived under his name. The prevalent view is that most of the extant Aristotelian works are unrevised, unpolished lectures, often supplemented with notes by students, which were edited centuries after his death. Popular in antiquity but lost today are Aristotle's own dialogues, whose style was much admired.

The ***Categories*** is one of Aristotle's most influential and complex works on logic, the most important parts of which are his definition and discussion of "beings" and his definition and discussion of ten categories that can be used to classify, among other things, substances, quantity, relativity, and quality. In this work Aristotle is concerned to define both what may be spoken about accurately and the correct syntax that may be used when speaking about concepts and beings.

10. Demosthenes, *On the Crown* 299

After summarizing what he said and did to defend Athens from the Macedonians, the orator reveals why he thinks that he and the Athenians failed to defeat them.

ταῦτα προυβαλόμην ἐγὼ πρὸ τῆς Ἀττικῆς, ὅσον ἦν ἀνθρωπίνῳ λογισμῷ δυνατόν, καὶ
τούτοις ἐτείχισα τὴν χώραν, οὐχὶ τὸν κύκλον τοῦ Πειραῶς οὐδὲ τοῦ ἄστεως, οὐδέ γ᾽
ἡττήθην ἐγὼ τοῖς λογισμοῖς Φιλίππου, πολλοῦ γε καὶ δεῖ,† οὐδὲ ταῖς παρασκευαῖς, ἀλλ᾽
οἱ τῶν συμμάχων στρατηγοὶ καὶ αἱ δυνάμεις† τῇ τύχῃ. τίνες αἱ τούτων ἀπόδειξεις;
ἐναργεῖς καὶ φανεραί.

προβάλλω (προ- + βάλλω), προβαλῶ,
  προύβαλον, προβέβληκα, προβέβλημαι,
  προυβλήθην throw forward; (*middle*) put (before to protect)
Ἀττική, Ἀττικῆς, ἡ Attica (the peninsula of
  Greece controlled by Athens)
ὅσος, ὅση, ὅσον (rel. adj.) (as much) as
ἀνθρώπινος, ἀνθρωπίνη, ἀνθρώπινον human
λογισμός, λογισμοῦ, ὁ reason(ing)
δυνατός, δυνατή, δυνατόν possible
τειχίζω, τειχιῶ, ἐτείχισα, τετείχικα, ——, ——
  build a wall for, fortify with a wall
οὐχί = *emphatic form of* οὐκ
κύκλος, κύκλου, ὁ circle, wall going round

Πειραιεύς, Πειραιῶς, ὁ (the) Piraeus (the harbor
  of Athens joined to the city through long walls)
ἄστυ, ἄστεως, ἡ city
ἡττάομαι be defeated
Φίλιππος, Φιλίππου, ὁ Philip (king of Macedon)
†πολλοῦ ... δεῖ it lacks much; far from it
παρασκευή, παρασκευῆς, ἡ preparation;
  armament
†δυνάμεις, *here,* (armed) forces
ἀπόδειξις, ἀποδείξεως, ἡ proof
ἐναργής, ἐναργές manifest
φανερός, φανερά, φανερόν visible, evident,
  conspicuous

The Athenian **Demosthenes** (384?-322 B.C.E.) was even in antiquity considered the greatest of the Greek orators. His style is marked by clarity and the manipulation of ordinary language to make persuasive speeches before large, not necessarily educated, audiences. His reputation rests on his ability to be emotionally convincing both before the public assembly and in the private law courts, in which juries ranged in size from five hundred to a thousand and cast their ballots immediately after the orators finished speaking. His earliest speeches, written and delivered when he was only twenty years old, were part of his successful prosecution of the guardians who had lost his inheritance. Demosthenes became a successful speechwriter and eventually an important politician. His most famous speeches in the public arena were made in a losing effort to rally the Athenians against Philip II and the encroachment of the Macedonians into the rest of Greece. Of his orations, many of them polished and published by Demosthenes after they were given, sixty-one survive (not all considered genuine), as well as dozens of prologues of additional speeches and a few letters. Much information about the daily lives of Athenians in the fourth century B.C.E. and about Athenian law is preserved in his speeches.

Demosthenes' *On the Crown* is generally regarded as the orator's masterpiece. Ostensibly a defense of Ctesiphon, who was charged by Aeschines with having broken the law when he proposed the award of a civil crown to Demosthenes for public services, the speech justifies the award and praises and defends the rectitude of the failed policy of those Athenians who sought to resist Philip II of Macedon. By placing his own actions and those of his allies in the patriotic light of Athenian resistance to a tyrant, Demosthenes won Ctesiphon's acquittal although he was indeed guilty of the technicalities with which he had been charged. The speech represents the greatest of Demosthenes' triumphs over Aeschines, for decades his chief political and oratorical rival.

AUTHORS AND PASSAGES

This list includes the authors and passages appearing in the Short and Longer Readings of Part 1 of *Learn to Read Greek*. Citations are given by chapter and page number of the textbook (e.g., the citation "3.78" next to a reading indicates that the reading is to be found in Chapter 3 on page 78). Page numbers in boldface indicate that the reading is in a Longer Readings section. An "**A**" next to the page number indicates that a biography of the author appears with the passage, and a "**W**" indicates that a description of the work appears with the passage. (Biographies and descriptions of works appear only in the Longer Readings.)

Aeschines
   Concerning the False Embassy
      118.3 6.178
Aeschylus
   Agamemnon
      1085–88 **6.184 (A/W)**
      1487–88 9.292
   Eumenides
      143–46 **7.232 (W)**
      273–75 6.174
   Libation Bearers
      1016–17 7.221
   Persians
      792–93 9.292
   Prometheus Bound
      250–51 6.174
      1039 5.137
   Seven Against Thebes
      592 5.137
      596 5.137
      662–63 9.293
      805–6 9.293
   Suppliant Women
      1048–49 5.138
   frag. 13 6.174
   frag. 22 7.221
   frag. 146 6.174
   frag. 161 4.107
   frag. 176 7.222
   frag. 187 7.222
   frag. 188 7.222
   frag. 232 5.138
   frag. 239 9.293
   frag. 301 4.107
   frag. 315 7.222
   frag. 353 5.138
   frag. 385 5.138
   frag. 393 7.222

   frag. 394 7.222
   frag. 395 7.223
   frag. 396 5.138
   frag. 398 7.223
Aesop
   Proverbs
      1 5.145
      19 7.231
      30 3.84
      97 4.109
      126 9.301
      142 9.301
      143 5.145
      154 6.182
      166 7.231
      171 5.145
      180 6.182
Alcaeus
   frag. 333 5.137
Anacreon
   7.160 6.173
Archilochus
   frag. 177 7.220
   frag. 201 9.291
Aristophanes
   Birds
      375 5.140
      1122–23 6.176
   Clouds
      816–17 9.297
   Frogs
      757–60 **9.310 (W)**
   Knights
      1111 5.141
   Lysistrata
      15–19 **6.186 (A/W)**
      870–71 6.176

GREEK TO ENGLISH VOCABULARY

This Greek to English Vocabulary includes all the words from the vocabulary lists in Part 1 of *Learn to Read Greek*. Numbers in parentheses refer to chapter (e.g., 2) or section (e.g., §12) in which the vocabulary word is introduced. If only a chapter number is listed, the word or phrase appears in the chapter-opening vocabulary list; if the chapter number is followed by a dagger (†), the word or phrase appears in the vocabulary notes or in a section of the chapter.

ἀγαθός, ἀγαθή, ἀγαθόν good (2)

ἀγορά, ἀγορᾶς, ἡ agora, marketplace (1)

ἄγω, ἄξω, ἤγαγον, ἦχα, ἦγμαι, ἤχθην lead, bring; keep; *middle*, carry away with oneself; marry (5)

ἀγών, ἀγῶνος, ὁ contest; struggle (6)

ἄδηλος, ἄδηλον unclear (6)

ἀδικέω, ἀδικήσω, ἠδίκησα, ἠδίκηκα, ἠδίκημαι, ἠδικήθην (do) wrong (to); injure (4)

ἄδικος, ἄδικον unjust (2)

ἀεί (adv.) always (5)

ἀθάνατος, ἀθάνατον deathless, immortal (2)

Ἀθηνᾶ, Ἀθηνᾶς, ἡ Athena (§59)

Ἀθῆναι, Ἀθηνῶν, αἱ Athens (6)

Ἀθηναῖος, Ἀθηναίā, Ἀθηναῖον Athenian; *masc. pl. subst.*, Athenians (2)

ἄθλιος, ἀθλίā, ἄθλιον wretched, miserable (9)

Ἅιδης, Ἅιδου, ὁ Hades (2)

αἰεί (adv.) always (5)

αἰσχρός, αἰσχρά, αἰσχρόν disgraceful, shameful; ugly (3)

αἰτίā, αἰτίᾱς, ἡ cause; responsibility (2)

ἀκούω, ἀκούσομαι, ἤκουσα, ἀκήκοα, ——, ἠκούσθην listen (to), hear (of) (5); be spoken of (with adv.), be called (with pred. adj.)

Ἀλέξανδρος, Ἀλεξάνδρου, ὁ Alexander (1)

ἀλήθεια, ἀληθείᾱς, ἡ truth (2)

ἀληθής, ἀληθές true, real; truthful (7)

ἀλλά (conj.) but; *in narrative transitions and responses in dialogue*, but yet; well . . . (2)

ἀλλὰ γάρ but as a matter of fact (3†)

ἀλλὰ δή but indeed, and in particular (4†)

——, ἀλλήλων (reciprocal pronoun) one another, each other (8)

ἄλλος, ἄλλη, ἄλλο other, another; *in the attributive position*, the rest (of) (5)

ἀμαθής, ἀμαθές ignorant, foolish (9)

ἀμαθίā, ἀμαθίᾱς, ἡ ignorance; stupidity (9)

ἄν (particle) *used in the apodoses of some conditional sentences* (9)

ἀνάγκη, ἀνάγκης, ἡ necessity (5)

ἀνδρείā, ἀνδρείᾱς, ἡ manliness; courage (9)

ἄνευ (prep. + gen.) without (6)

ἀνήρ, ἀνδρός, ὁ man; husband (6)

ἄνθρωπος, ἀνθρώπου, ὁ or ἡ human being, man (1)

ἀξιόω, ἀξιώσω, ἠξίωσα, ἠξίωκα, ἠξίωμαι, ἠξιώθην think worthy; think (it) right; expect, require (4)

ἅπᾱς, ἅπᾱσα, ἅπαν (quite) all, every; whole (6)

ἀπό (prep. + gen.) (away) from (2)

ἀπὸ κοινοῦ, at public expense (3†)

ἀποθνῄσκω, ἀποθανοῦμαι, ἀπέθανον, τέθνηκα, ——, —— die; *perfect*, be dead (8)

ἀποκτείνω, ἀποκτενῶ, ἀπέκτεινα, ἀπέκτονα, ——, —— kill (8)

Ἀπόλλων, Ἀπόλλωνος, ὁ (voc. = Ἄπολλον) Apollo (§59)

ἀποπέμπω, ἀποπέμψω, ἀπέπεμψα, ἀποπέπομφα, ἀποπέπεμμαι, ἀπεπέμφθην send away; *middle*, send away from oneself (7)

ἆρα (interrog. particle) *introduces a question* (3)

ἄρα (postpositive particle) (so) then, therefore; after all (9)

ἀρετή, ἀρετῆς, ἡ excellence; valor; virtue (4)

Ἄρης, Ἄρεος/Ἄρεως, ὁ (voc. = Ἄρες) Ares (§59)

Ἄρτεμις, Ἀρτέμιδος, ἡ Artemis (§59)

ἀρχή, ἀρχῆς, ἡ beginning; (supreme) power, rule; empire (2)

    ἀρχὴν ποιεῖσθαι, to make a beginning, to begin (4†)

ἄρχω, ἄρξω, ἦρξα, ἦρχα, ἦργμαι, ἤρχθην rule (+ gen.); *middle*, begin (+ gen.) (3)

ἄρχων, ἄρχοντος, ὁ ruler, commander; archon, magistrate (5)

Ἀτρείδης, Ἀτρείδου, ὁ Atreides, son of Atreus (2)

αὐτός, αὐτή, αὐτό -self, very; same (6)

αὐτοῦ, αὐτῆς, αὐτοῦ him, her, it; them (6)

Ἀφροδίτη, Ἀφροδίτης, ἡ Aphrodite (§59)

βάρβαρος, βάρβαρον non-Greek, foreign; barbarous; *masc. pl. subst.*, foreigners; barbarians (5)

βίος, βίου, ὁ life; livelihood (4)

βουλή, βουλῆς, ἡ will; plan; council; advice (1)

    βουλὴν ποιεῖσθαι, to make a plan, to plan (4†)

βούλομαι, βουλήσομαι, ——, ——, βεβούλημαι, ἐβουλήθην want, wish (6)

βροτός, βροτοῦ, ὁ mortal (4)

γαῖα, γαίας, ἡ earth; land (3)

γάρ (postpositive conj.) *explanatory*, for; *confirming*, indeed, in fact (3)

γε (enclitic particle) *limiting*, at least, at any rate; *emphasizing*, indeed (5)

γένος, γένους, τό race, descent; family; sort, kind (7)

γῆ, γῆς, ἡ earth; land (3)

γίγνομαι, γενήσομαι, ἐγενόμην, γέγονα, γεγένημαι, —— become; happen; arise, be born (6)

γνώμη, γνώμης, ἡ judgment; spirit, inclination; opinion (1)

    γνώμην προσέχειν, to pay attention (7)

Γοργίας, Γοργίου, ὁ Gorgias (2)

γυνή, γυναικός, ἡ woman; wife (7)

δαίμων, δαίμονος, ὁ or ἡ divinity, divine power; spirit (5)

δέ (postpositive conj.) *adversative*, but; *connective*, and (3)

    μέν . . . , δέ . . . on the one hand . . . , on the other hand . . . ; . . . , but . . . (3)

δεῖ, δεήσει, ἐδέησε(ν), ——, ——, —— (impersonal verb) it is necessary, must; there is need (+ gen.) (5)

δεινός, δεινή, δεινόν fearsome, terrible; marvelous, strange; clever (2)

δεσπότης, δεσπότου, ὁ master, lord; absolute ruler (6)

δέχομαι, δέξομαι, ἐδεξάμην, ——, δέδεγμαι, —— accept, receive; welcome (6)

δή (postpositive particle) certainly, indeed, of course (4)

δῆλος, δήλη, δῆλον clear (6)

δηλόω, δηλώσω, ἐδήλωσα, δεδήλωκα, δεδήλωμαι, ἐδηλώθην show, make clear, reveal (4)

Δημήτηρ, Δημητρός, ἡ (voc. = Δήμητερ) Demeter (§59)

δῆμος, δήμου, ὁ (the) people (2)

Δημοσθένης, Δημοσθένους, ὁ Demosthenes (7)

διά (prep. + gen.) through; (prep. + acc.) on account of, because of (2)

    διὰ τέλους, through to the end, completely (9†)

διαλέγομαι, διαλέξομαι, ——, ——,
     διείλεγμαι, διελέχθην talk (with),
     converse (with) (+ dat.); discuss (with)
     (+ dat.) (7)

διαφθείρω, διαφθερῶ, διέφθειρα,
     διέφθαρκα/διέφθορα, διέφθαρμαι,
     διεφθάρην destroy (utterly); corrupt,
     ruin (9)

διδάσκαλος, διδασκάλου, ὁ teacher (5)

διδάσκω, διδάξω, ἐδίδαξα, δεδίδαχα,
     δεδίδαγμαι, ἐδιδάχθην teach;
     explain; *middle,* cause to be taught (3)

δίκαιος, δικαίᾱ, δίκαιον right, just (2)

δικαιοσύνη, δικαιοσύνης, ἡ justice (9)

δίκη, δίκης, ἡ justice (1)
     δίκην λαμβάνειν, to exact punishment
     (9)

Διόνῡσος, Διονῡσου, ὁ Dionysus (§59)

δόξα, δόξης, ἡ opinion, belief; reputation;
     glory; expectation (2)

δοῦλος, δούλου, ὁ slave (6)

δύναμις, δυνάμεως, ἡ power; ability (7)

δῶμα, δώματος, τό *sing. or pl.,* house,
     home (5)

ἐγώ, ἐμοῦ/μου I; me (6)

ἐθέλω/θέλω, ἐθελήσω, ἠθέλησα, ἠθέληκα,
     ——, —— be willing, wish (3)

εἰ (conj.) if (9)

εἰμί, ἔσομαι, ——, ——, ——, —— be;
     exist; *impersonal,* it is possible (5)

εἰρήνη, εἰρήνης, ἡ peace (1)
     ἐπὶ εἰρήνης, in (time of) peace (4†)

εἰς (prep. + acc.) to, toward; into; against;
     with a view to, regarding (1)
     εἰς/ἐς κοινόν, openly, publicly (3†)
     ἐς/εἰς τέλος, to the end, in the long
     run (9†)

εἷς, μία, ἕν (numerical adj.) one (9)

ἐκ (prep. + gen.) (out) from, out of; resulting
     from, in accordance with (1)
     ἐκ κοινοῦ, at public expense (3†)

ἕκαστος, ἑκάστη, ἕκαστον each (of several) (7)

ἐκεῖ (adv.) there (9)

ἐκεῖνος, ἐκείνη, ἐκεῖνο (demonstr. adj./
     pron.) that; *pl.,* those (4)

Ἕκτωρ, Ἕκτορος, ὁ Hector (5)

Ἑλένη, Ἑλένης, ἡ Helen (1)

ἐλευθερίᾱ, ἐλευθερίᾱς, ἡ freedom (6)

ἐλεύθερος, ἐλευθέρᾱ, ἐλεύθερον free (6)

Ἑλλάς, Ἑλλάδος, ἡ Hellas, Greece (7)

Ἕλλην, Ἕλληνος, ὁ Hellene, Greek (5)

ἐλπίς, ἐλπίδος, ἡ hope; expectation (5)

ἐμός, ἐμή, ἐμόν my (6)

ἐν (prep. + dat.) in, on; among, in the
     presence of (1)

ἐναντίος, ἐναντίᾱ, ἐναντίον facing,
     opposite; opposing, contrary (to)
     (+ gen. or dat.) (8)
     (τὸ) ἐναντίον, in opposition, conversely
     (9†)

ἐναντίως (adv.) in opposition, conversely
     (8†)

ἐξ (prep. + gen.) (out) from, out of; resulting
     from, in accordance with (1)

ἐπί (prep. + gen.) in, on, upon; (prep. + dat.)
     in, on; in addition to; for (i.e., because
     of); on condition of; (prep. + acc.) to;
     against; for (the purpose of) (4)
     ἐπὶ εἰρήνης, in (time of) peace (4†)
     ἐπὶ (τὸ) πολύ to a great extent; for the
     most part (4†)

ἕπομαι, ἕψομαι, ἑσπόμην, ——, ——, ——
     (+ dat.) follow (9)

ἔπος, ἔπους, τό word; *pl.,* lines (of verse),
     epic poetry (7)

Ἐρατώ, Ἐρατοῦς, ἡ Erato (§59)

ἔργον, ἔργου, τό task, work; deed (1)

Ἑρμῆς, Ἑρμοῦ, ὁ Hermes (4)

ἔρχομαι, ἐλεύσομαι, ἦλθον, ἐλήλυθα, ——,
     —— go, come (6)

——, ἐρῶ, ——, εἴρηκα, εἴρημαι, ἐρρήθην
     say, tell (of), speak (of) (8)

ἔρως, ἔρωτος, ὁ desire, passion, love (5)

Ἔρως, Ἔρωτος, ὁ (voc. = Ἔρως)
     Eros (§59)

ἐς (prep. + acc.) to, toward; into; against; with a view to, regarding (1)
Ἑστίᾱ, Ἑστίᾱς, ἡ Hestia (§59)
ἑταῖρος, ἑταίρου, ὁ companion (1)
ἔτι (adv.) still, yet (8)
εὖ (adv.) well (3)
εὐδαίμων, εὔδαιμον fortunate, happy (9)
Εὐρῑπίδης, Εὐρῑπίδου, ὁ Euripides (2)
Εὐτέρπη, Εὐτέρπης, ἡ Euterpe (§59)
ἐχθρός, ἐχθρά, ἐχθρόν hated, hateful; hostile; *masc. subst.,* enemy (2)
ἔχω, ἕξω/σχήσω, ἔσχον, ἔσχηκα, -έσχημαι, —— have, hold; inhabit, occupy; *intrans.,* be able (+ inf.); be (+ adv.); *middle,* hold on to, cling to (+ gen.) (4)

ζάω, ζήσω, ——, ——, ——, —— be alive, live (8)
Ζεύς, Διός, ὁ Zeus (5)
ζηλόω, ζηλώσω, ἐζήλωσα, ἐζήλωκα, ——, —— emulate; envy; *passive,* be deemed fortunate (7)
ζῷον, ζῴου, τό living being; animal (1)

ἤ (conj.) or (2)
    ἤ . . . ἤ . . . either . . . or . . . (2)
ἡδονή, ἡδονῆς, ἡ pleasure (8)
ἥκω, ἥξω, ——, ——, ——, —— have come; be present (5)
ἡμεῖς, ἡμῶν we; us (6)
ἡμέτερος, ἡμετέρᾱ, ἡμέτερον our (6)
Ἥρᾱ, Ἥρᾱς, ἡ Hera (§59)
Ἥφαιστος, Ἡφαίστου, ὁ Hephaestus (§59)

θάλαττα, θαλάττης, ἡ sea (2)
Θάλεια, Θαλείᾱς, ἡ Thalia (§59)
θάνατος, θανάτου, ὁ death (4)
θέλω/ἐθέλω, ἐθελήσω, ἠθέλησα, ἠθέληκα, ——, —— be willing, wish (3)
θεός, θεοῦ, ὁ or ἡ god; goddess (1)
θνῄσκω, θανοῦμαι, ἔθανον, τέθνηκα, ——, —— die; *perfect,* be dead (8)
θνητός, θνητή, θνητόν mortal (5)

ἴσος, ἴση, ἴσον equal, even; flat; fair, impartial (8)
ἴσως (adv.) equally; perhaps (8)

καί (conj.) and (1); (adv.) even, also (1)
    καὶ γάρ, for in fact (3†)
    καὶ δή and indeed, and in particular (4†)
    καὶ δὴ καί and in particular (4†)
    καί . . . καί . . . both . . . and . . . (1)
κακός, κακή, κακόν bad, evil (2)
Καλλιόπη, Καλλιόπης, ἡ Calliope (§59)
καλός, καλή, καλόν beautiful; noble; fine (2)
κατά (prep. + gen.) down from, beneath; against; (prep. + acc.) according to, in relation to; throughout (5)
κίνδῡνος, κινδύνου, ὁ danger (8)
Κλειώ, Κλειοῦς, ἡ Clio (§59)
κοινά, κοινῶν, τά public treasury; public affairs (3†)
κοινόν, κοινοῦ, τό state, government (3†)
κοινός, κοινή, κοινόν common (to), shared (with) (+ gen. or dat.); public (3)
    ἀπὸ κοινοῦ, at public expense (3†)
    εἰς/ἐς κοινόν, openly, publicly (3†)
    ἐκ κοινοῦ, at public expense (3†)
κτείνω, κτενῶ, ἔκτεινα, ——, ——, —— kill (8)

Λακεδαιμόνιος, Λακεδαιμονίᾱ, Λακεδαιμόνιον Lacedaemonian, Spartan; *masc. pl. subst.,* Lacedaemonians, Spartans (2)
λαμβάνω, λήψομαι, ἔλαβον, εἴληφα, εἴλημμαι, ἐλήφθην take, seize; understand; receive; *middle,* take hold (of) (+ gen.) (9)
    δίκην λαμβάνειν, to exact punishment (9)
λέγω, λέξω, ἔλεξα/εἶπον, ——, λέλεγμαι, ἐλέχθην say, speak; tell (of), recount (3)

λόγος, λόγου, ὁ word; speech; argument (1)
    λόγους ποιεῖσθαι, to make words, to speak (4†)
λύπη, λύπης, ἡ pain (8)

μά (particle + acc.) *used in oaths,* by (5)
μαθητής, μαθητοῦ, ὁ student (5)
μακρός, μακρά, μακρόν large, great; long, tall (8)
μανθάνω, μαθήσομαι, ἔμαθον, μεμάθηκα, ——, —— learn; understand (5)
μάχη, μάχης, ἡ battle (1)
μάχομαι, μαχοῦμαι, ἐμαχεσάμην, ——, μεμάχημαι, —— fight (against) (+ dat.) (8)
μέγας, μεγάλη, μέγα great, big (4)
    μέγα, greatly, to a great extent (9†)
μέλλω, μελλήσω, ἐμέλλησα, ——, ——, —— intend, be about, be likely (+ inf.) (3)
Μελπομένη, Μελπομένης, ἡ Melpomene (§59)
μέν (postpositive particle) on the one hand (3)
    μέν..., δέ... on the one hand..., on the other hand...;..., but... (3)
    μὲν οὖν (particle combination) *in affirmations,* certainly, by all means; *in corrections,* no, on the contrary; *in transitions to a new subject,* so then, therefore (6)
μένω, μενῶ, ἔμεινα, μεμένηκα, ——, —— remain, stay; *trans.,* await (9)
μετά (prep. + gen.) (along) with; with the aid of; in accordance with; (prep. + acc.) after (4)
μή (adv.) not (2)
    μὴ μόνον... ἀλλὰ καί... not only... but also... (2)
μηδέ (conj.) and not, nor; (adv.) not even (7)
μηδείς, μηδεμία, μηδέν (adj./substantive) no, not any; no one, nothing (9)
    μηδέν, not at all (9†)

μηδέποτε (conj.) and not ever, nor ever; (adv.) never (7)
μηδεπώποτε (adv.) not yet at any time, never yet (9†)
μηκέτι (adv.) no longer (8)
μήποτε (adv.) never (5)
μήπω (adv.) not yet (9†)
μηπώποτε (adv.) not yet at any time, never yet (9†)
μήτε... μήτε... neither... nor... (6)
μήτηρ, μητρός, ἡ mother (7)
μῑκρός, μῑκρά, μῑκρόν small (8)
    μῑκρόν, a little (9†)
μοῖρα, μοίρᾱς, ἡ fate (2)
μόνον (adv.) only (2)
μόνος, μόνη, μόνον only, alone (2)
Μοῦσα, Μούσης, ἡ Muse (§59)

νεᾱνίᾱς, νεᾱνίου, ὁ young man (2)
νέος, νέᾱ, νέον new; young (4)
νή (particle + acc.) *expresses strong affirmation,* (yes,) by (5)
νῆσος, νήσου, ἡ island (1)
νῑκάω, νῑκήσω, ἐνίκησα, νενίκηκα, νενίκημαι, ἐνῑκήθην conquer, defeat; prevail (over), win (4)
νίκη, νίκης, ἡ victory (4)
νόμος, νόμου, ὁ custom; law (1)
νοῦς, νοῦ, ὁ mind; sense; thought (7)
    νοῦν προσέχειν, to pay attention (7)
νῦν (adv.) now (3)
    (τὸ)(τὰ) νῦν, now; presently (9†)

ξένος, ξένου, ὁ host, guest, guest-friend; stranger, foreigner (3)
ξύν (prep. + dat.) (along) with; with the aid of; in accordance with (1)

ὁ, ἡ, τό (article) the (1)
ὅδε, ἥδε, τόδε (demonstr. adj./pron.) this; *pl.,* these (4)
ὁδός, ὁδοῦ, ἡ road, path; journey; way (1)

οἶδα, εἴσομαι, ——, ——, ——, ——
    know (9)

οἰκίᾱ, οἰκίᾱς, ἡ house (1)

οἴομαι/οἶμαι, οἰήσομαι, ——, ——, ——,
    ᾠήθην think, suppose, believe (8)

ὀλίγος, ὀλίγη, ὀλίγον little, small; *pl.,* few (4)

ὄντως (adv.) really, actually (7)

ὅπλον, ὅπλου, τό tool; *pl.,* arms, weapons (1)

ὁράω, ὄψομαι, εἶδον, ἑώρᾱκα/ἑόρᾱκα,
    ἑώρᾱμαι/ὦμμαι, ὤφθην see (6)

ὀρθός, ὀρθή, ὀρθόν straight; correct (6)

ὅς, ἥ, ὅ (relative pron.) who, whose, whom;
    which, that (5)

ὅτι (conj.) that; because (6)

οὐ, οὐκ, οὐχ (adv.) not (2)
    οὐ μόνον . . . ἀλλὰ καί . . . not only . . .
    but also . . . (2)
    οὐ πάνυ, not at all (8)

οὐδέ (conj.) and not, nor; (adv.) not
    even (7)

οὐδείς, οὐδεμία, οὐδέν (adj./substantive)
    no, not any; no one, nothing (9)
    οὐδέν, not at all (9†)

οὐδέποτε (conj.) and not ever, nor ever;
    (adv.) never (7)

οὐδεπώποτε (adv.) not yet at any time,
    never yet (9†)

οὐκέτι (adv.) no longer (8)

οὖν (postpositive conj.) then, therefore (6)

οὔποτε (adv.) never (5)

οὔπω (adv.) not yet (9†)

οὐπώποτε (adv.) not yet at any time, never
    yet (9†)

Οὐρανίᾱ, Οὐρανίᾱς, ἡ Urania (§59)

οὐρανός, οὐρανοῦ, ὁ sky, heaven (3)

οὔτε . . . οὔτε . . . neither . . . nor . . . (6)

οὗτος, αὕτη, τοῦτο (demonstr. adj./pron.)
    this; *pl.,* these (2)

οὕτω(ς) (adv.) in this way, thus, so (4)

πάθος, πάθους, τό experience; suffering;
    passion (7)

παῖς, παιδός, ὁ or ἡ child; slave (5)

παλαιός, παλαιά, παλαιόν old, ancient (8)

πάνυ (adv.) altogether; very (much),
    exceedingly; *in answers,* by all means,
    certainly (8)

παρά (prep. + gen.) from (the side of); by;
    (prep. + dat.) near; at (the house of);
    among; (prep. + acc.) to (the side of),
    beside; contrary to (5)

πάρειμι, παρέσομαι, ——, ——, ——, ——
    be present, be near; be ready (7)

πᾶς, πᾶσα, πᾶν all, every; whole (6)

πάσχω, πείσομαι, ἔπαθον, πέπονθα, ——,
    —— suffer; experience (7)

πατήρ, πατρός, ὁ father (7)

παύω, παύσω, ἔπαυσα, πέπαυκα, πέπαυμαι,
    ἐπαύθην stop (trans.); *middle,* stop
    (intrans.), cease (3)

πείθω, πείσω, ἔπεισα, πέπεικα, πέπεισμαι,
    ἐπείσθην persuade; *middle,* obey;
    heed; believe (+ dat.) (3)

πέμπω, πέμψω, ἔπεμψα, πέπομφα, πέπεμμαι,
    ἐπέμφθην send (3)

περ (enclitic particle) very, even (5)

περί (prep. + gen.) concerning, about;
    (prep. + dat.) around; (prep.+ acc.)
    around; concerning, about (1)
    περὶ πολλοῦ of much value (4†)

πλῆθος, πλήθους, τό great number,
    multitude (8)

πλοῦτος, πλούτου, ὁ wealth (7)

πόθεν (interrog. adv.) from where (6)

ποθέν (enclitic adv.) from somewhere (7)

ποῖ (interrog. adv.) to where (6)

ποι (enclitic adv.) to somewhere (7)

ποιέω, ποιήσω, ἐποίησα, πεποίηκα,
    πεποίημαι, ἐποιήθην make; do; *middle,*
    make; do; deem, consider (4)
    ἀρχὴν ποιεῖσθαι, to make a beginning,
    to begin (4)
    βουλὴν ποιεῖσθαι, to make a plan,
    to plan (4)
    λόγους ποιεῖσθαι, to make words,
    to speak (4)

ποιητής, ποιητοῦ, ὁ maker; poet (2)

πολεμέω, πολεμήσω, ἐπολέμησα, πεπολέμηκα,
———, ἐπολεμήθην make war (upon), be at
war (with) (+ dat.); quarrel; fight; *passive,*
be treated as an enemy, have war made
upon (oneself) (4)

πολέμιος, πολεμίᾱ, πολέμιον of an enemy,
hostile; *masc. subst.,* enemy (4)

πόλεμος, πολέμου, ὁ war (1)
    ἐπὶ πολέμου (engaged) in war (4†)

πόλις, πόλεως, ἡ city (7)

πολίτης, πολίτου, ὁ citizen (2)

πολλάκις (adv.) many times, often (3)

Πολύμνια, Πολυμνίᾱς, ἡ Polymnia (§59)

πολύς, πολλή, πολύ much, many (4)
    ἐπὶ (τὸ) πολύ to a great extent; for
    the most part (4†)
    περὶ πολλοῦ of much value (4†)
    (τὰ) πολλά, many times, often; much,
    a lot (9†)
    (τὸ) πολύ, much, a lot (9†)

πονηρός, πονηρά, πονηρόν worthless;
wicked (4)

πόνος, πόνου, ὁ labor, toil; distress,
suffering (3)

Ποσειδῶν, Ποσειδῶνος, ὁ (voc. =
Πόσειδον) Poseidon (§59)

πότε (interrog. adv.) when (3)

ποτέ (enclitic adv.) at some time, ever,
in the world† (5)
    ποτέ..., ποτέ... at one time..., at
    another time...; sometimes...,
    sometimes... (5)

ποῦ (interrog. adv.) where (6)

που (enclitic adv.) somewhere; I suppose (7)

πρᾶγμα, πρᾱγματος, τό deed; matter, thing;
pl., affairs; troubles (7)

πράττω, πράξω, ἔπρᾱξα, πέπρᾱχα (trans.)/
πέπρᾱγα (intrans.), πέπρᾱγμαι,
ἐπράχθην do; bring about; practice;
manage; *intrans.,* fare (7)

Πρίαμος, Πριάμου, ὁ Priam (1)

πρό (prep. + gen.) before, in front of (8)
    πρὸ τοῦ before this (8†)
    πρὸ τούτου before this (8†)

πρός (prep. + gen.) from; by; in the name of;
(prep. + dat.) near; in addition to;
(prep. + acc.) toward; against; in reply
to, in the face of, in relation to (3)

προσέχω, προσέξω, προσέσχον,
προσέσχηκα, ———, ——— hold to; turn
to, apply (7)
    νοῦν/γνώμην προσέχειν, to pay
    attention (7)

πω (enclitic adv.) yet (9)

πώποτε (adv.) ever yet (9)

πῶς (interrog. adv.) how (3)

πως (enclitic adv.) somehow (5)

ῥᾴδιος, ῥᾳδίᾱ, ῥᾴδιον easy (5)

ῥήτωρ, ῥήτορος, ὁ public speaker, orator;
rhetor (5)

σαφής, σαφές clear, plain; certain, sure (7)

σμῑκρός, σμῑκρά, σμῑκρόν small (8)
    σμῑκρόν, a little (9†)

σός, σή, σόν your (6)

σοφίᾱ, σοφίᾱς, ἡ wisdom (1)

σοφός, σοφή, σοφόν wise (2)

στρατηγός, στρατηγοῦ, ὁ general (8)

στρατιώτης, στρατιώτου, ὁ soldier (8)

στρατός, στρατοῦ, ὁ army (8)

σύ, σοῦ/σου you (6)

σύμμαχος, συμμάχου, ὁ ally (3)

συμφορά, συμφορᾶς, ἡ circumstance;
misfortune, disaster (1)

σύν (prep. + dat.) (along) with; with the
aid of; in accordance with (1)

Σωκράτης, Σωκράτους, ὁ Socrates (7)

σῶμα, σώματος, τό body (5)

σωτηρίᾱ, σωτηρίᾱς, ἡ safety (8)

σωφροσύνη, σωφροσύνης, ἡ moderation (9)

σώφρων, σῶφρον moderate, prudent (9)

τε (enclitic conj.) and (5)

τεῖχος, τείχους, τό wall (8)

τέκνον, τέκνου, τό child (1)

τελευτάω, τελευτήσω, ἐτελεύτησα, τετελεύτηκα, ——, ἐτελευτήθην accomplish, end, finish; die (4)

τέλος, τέλους, τό end, purpose; power (9)
   διὰ τέλους, through to the end, completely (9†)
   ἐν τέλει, in office, in power (9†)
   ἐς/εἰς τέλος, to the end, in the long run (9†)
   τέλος, finally (9†)

Τερψιχόρᾱ, Τερψιχόρᾱς, ἡ Terpsichore (§59)

τέχνη, τέχνης, ἡ skill, art (5)

τῑμάω, τῑμήσω, ἐτίμησα, τετίμηκα, τετίμημαι, ἐτιμήθην honor; middle, value, deem worthy (4)

τίς, τί (interrog. pron./adj.) who, what; which (9)
   τί, why; how (9†)

τις, τι (indef. pron./adj.) someone, something; anyone, anything; some, any (9)
   τι, in any way; at all (9†)

τοι (enclitic particle) surely, you know (5)

τότε (adv.) then, at that time (7)

τρόπος, τρόπου, ὁ way, manner; habit; pl., character (9)

τύχη, τύχης, ἡ chance, fortune (4)

ὕβρις, ὕβρεως, ἡ insolence; (wanton) violence (7)

υἱός, υἱοῦ, ὁ son (4)

ὑμεῖς, ὑμῶν you (pl.) (6)

ὑμέτερος, ὑμετέρᾱ, ὑμέτερον your (pl.) (6)

ὑπέρ (prep. + gen.) over; on behalf of; (prep. + acc.) beyond (6)

ὑπό (prep. + gen.) (from) under; by; at the hands of; (prep. + dat.) under; under the power of; (prep. + acc.) under; during (3)

ὑπολαμβάνω, ὑπολήψομαι, ὑπέλαβον, ὑπείληφα, ὑπείλημμαι, ὑπελήφθην take up, reply; suppose (9)

*φάσκω, ——, ——, ——, ——, —— say, assert (8)

φέρω, οἴσω, ἤνεγκα/ἤνεγκον, ἐνήνοχα, ἐνήνεγμαι, ἠνέχθην bear, bring, carry; endure; middle, carry away with oneself; win (9)

φεύγω, φεύξομαι, ἔφυγον, πέφευγα, ——, —— flee, avoid, escape (9)

φημί, φήσω, ἔφησα, ——, ——, —— say, assert (8)

φιλέω, φιλήσω, ἐφίλησα, πεφίληκα, πεφίλημαι, ἐφιλήθην love, like; regard with affection; approve of; kiss; be accustomed, be fond of (+ inf.) (4)

φίλος, φίλη, φίλον (be)loved, dear; loving, friendly; masc./fem. subst., friend; loved one (2)

φόβος, φόβου, ὁ fear (2)

Φοῖβος, Φοίβου, ὁ Phoebus (Apollo) (§59)

φρήν, φρενός, ἡ sing. or pl., heart, mind, wits (5)

φρόνησις, φρονήσεως, ἡ intelligence, understanding (9)

φύσις, φύσεως, ἡ nature (7)

χαίρω, χαιρήσω, ——, κεχάρηκα, ——, ἐχάρην rejoice (in), enjoy (7)

χαλεπός, χαλεπή, χαλεπόν severe, harsh; difficult (4)

χαλεπῶς (adv.) hardly, with difficulty (4†)

χάριν (prep. + preceding gen.) for the sake of (5)

χάρις, χάριτος, ἡ grace, favor, goodwill; delight; gratitude (5)

χρή, χρῆσται, ——, ——, ——, —— (impersonal verb) it is necessary, ought (8)

χρῆμα, χρήματος, τό thing, matter, affair; pl., goods, property, money (5)

χρηστός, χρηστή, χρηστόν useful;
    good (6)

χώρᾱ, χώρᾱς, ἡ land; country (1)

ψευδής, ψευδές false (7)

ψῡχή, ψῡχῆς, ἡ soul; life force (1)

ὦ (interj.) O (1)

ὧδε (adv.) in this way, so; in the following
    way (4)

ὡς (proclitic conj.) that; as (6)

    ὡς ἀληθῶς, (so) truly, really (7[†])

    ὡς ἔπος εἰπεῖν, so to speak (7[†])

ὥσπερ (conj.) just as (6)

ENGLISH TO GREEK VOCABULARY

This English to Greek Vocabulary includes all the words from the vocabulary lists in Part 1 of *Learn to Read Greek*. Numbers in parentheses refer to chapter (e.g., 2) or section (e.g., §12) in which the vocabulary word is introduced. If only a chapter number is listed, the word or phrase appears in the chapter-opening vocabulary list; if the chapter number is followed by a dagger (†), the word or phrase appears in the vocabulary notes or in a section of the chapter.

ability δύναμις, δυνάμεως, ἡ (7)

be able *intrans.*, ἔχω, ἕξω/σχήσω, ἔσχον, ἔσχηκα, -έσχημαι, —— (+ inf.) (4)

about περί (prep. + gen.) (1); περί (prep. + acc.) (1)

be about μέλλω, μελλήσω, ἐμέλλησα, ——, ——, —— (+ inf.) (3)

absolute ruler δεσπότης, δεσπότου, ὁ (6)

accept δέχομαι, δέξομαι, ἐδεξάμην, ——, δέδεγμαι, —— (6)

accomplish τελευτάω, τελευτήσω, ἐτελεύτησα, τετελεύτηκα, ——, ἐτελευτήθην (4)

according to κατά (prep. + acc.) (5)

be accustomed φιλέω, φιλήσω, ἐφίλησα, πεφίληκα, πεφίλημαι, ἐφιλήθην (+ inf.) (4)

actually ὄντως (adv.) (7)

advice βουλή, βουλῆς, ἡ (1)

affair χρῆμα, χρήματος, τό (5)

affairs πράγματα, πρᾱγμάτων, τά (7)

after μετά (prep. + acc.) (4)

after all ἄρα (postpositive particle) (9)

against εἰς, ἐς (prep. + acc.) (1); πρός (prep. + acc.) (3); ἐπί (prep. + acc.) (4); κατά (prep. + gen.) (5);

agora ἀγορά, ἀγορᾶς, ἡ (1)

Alexander Ἀλέξανδρος, Ἀλεξάνδρου, ὁ (1)

be alive ζάω, ζήσω, ——, ——, ——, —— (8)

all πᾶς, πᾶσα, πᾶν (6); ἅπᾱς, ἅπᾱσα, ἅπαν (6)

ally σύμμαχος, συμμάχου, ὁ (3)

alone μόνος, μόνη, μόνον (2)

(along) with σύν/ξύν (prep. + dat.) (1); μετά (prep. + gen.) (4)

a lot (τὸ) πολύ (9†); τὰ πολλά (9†)

also καί (adv.) (1)

altogether πάνυ (adv.)(8)

always ἀεί/αἰεί (adv.) (5)

among ἐν (prep. + dat.) (1); παρά (prep. + dat.) (5)

ancient παλαιός, παλαιά, παλαιόν (8)

and καί (conj.) (1); δέ (postpositive conj.) (3); τε (enclitic conj.) (5)

and in particular καὶ δή (4†); καὶ δὴ καί (4†)

and not οὐδέ/μηδέ (conj.) (7)

and not ever οὐδέποτε/μηδέποτε (conj.) (7)

animal ζῷον, ζῴου, τό (1)

another ἄλλος, ἄλλη, ἄλλο (5)

any τις, τι (indef. adj.) (9)

anyone τις, τι (indef. pron.) (9)

anything τις, τι (indef. pron.) (9)

Aphrodite Ἀφροδίτη, Ἀφροδίτης, ἡ (§59)

Apollo Ἀπόλλων, Ἀπόλλωνος, ὁ (voc. = Ἄπολλον) (§59)

apply προσέχω, προσέξω, προσέσχον, προσέσχηκα, ——, —— (7)

archon ἄρχων, ἄρχοντος, ὁ (5)

Ares Ἄρης, Ἄρεος/Ἄρεως, ὁ (voc. = Ἄρες) (§59)

argument λόγος, λόγου, ὁ (1)

arise γίγνομαι, γενήσομαι, ἐγενόμην, γέγονα, γεγένημαι, —— (6)

armed σὺν ὅπλοις (1)

arms ὅπλα, ὅπλων, τά (1)

army στρατός, στρατοῦ, ὁ (8)

around περί (prep. + dat.) (1); περί (prep. + acc.) (1)

art τέχνη, τέχνης, ἡ (5)

Artemis Ἄρτεμις, Ἀρτέμιδος, ἡ (§59)

as ὡς (proclitic conj.) (6)

(but) as a matter of fact ἀλλὰ γάρ (3[†])

assert *φάσκω, ——, ——, ——, ——, —— (8); φημί, φήσω, ἔφησα, ——, ——, —— (8)

at (the house of) παρά (prep. + dat.) (5)

at all τι (9[†])

at any rate γε (enclitic particle) (5)

at least γε (enclitic particle) (5)

at one time ... , at another time ... ποτέ ... , ποτέ ... (5)

at public expense ἀπὸ/ἐκ κοινοῦ (3[†])

at some time ποτέ (enclitic adv.) (5)

at that time τότε (adv.) (7)

at the hands of ὑπό (prep. + gen.) (3)

Athena Ἀθηνᾶ, Ἀθηνᾶς, ἡ (§59)

Athenian Ἀθηναῖος, Ἀθηναίᾱ, Ἀθηναῖον (2)

Athenians Ἀθηναῖοι, Ἀθηναίων, οἱ (2)

Athens Ἀθῆναι, Ἀθηνῶν, αἱ (6)

Atreides Ἀτρείδης, Ἀτρείδου, ὁ (2)

avoid φεύγω, φεύξομαι, ἔφυγον, πέφευγα, ——, —— (9)

await *trans.*, μένω, μενῶ, ἔμεινα, μεμένηκα, ——, —— (9)

(away) from ἀπό (prep. + gen.) (2)

bad κακός, κακή, κακόν (2)

barbarians βάρβαροι, βαρβάρων, οἱ (5)

barbarous βάρβαρος, βάρβαρον (5)

battle μάχη, μάχης, ἡ (1)

be *intrans.*, ἔχω, ἕξω/σχήσω, ἔσχον, ἔσχηκα, -έσχημαι, —— (+ adv.) (4); εἰμί, ἔσομαι, ——, ——, ——, —— (5)

be able *intrans.*, ἔχω, ἕξω/σχήσω, ἔσχον, ἔσχηκα, -έσχημαι, —— (+ inf.) (4)

be about μέλλω, μελλήσω, ἐμέλλησα, ——, ——, —— (+ inf.) (3)

be accustomed φιλέω, φιλήσω, ἐφίλησα, πεφίληκα, πεφίλημαι, ἐφιλήθην (+ inf.) (4)

be alive ζάω, ζήσω, ——, ——, ——, —— (8)

be at war (with) πολεμέω, πολεμήσω, ἐπολέμησα, πεπολέμηκα, ——, ἐπολεμήθην (+ dat.) (4)

be born γίγνομαι, γενήσομαι, ἐγενόμην, γέγονα, γεγένημαι, —— (6)

be called ἀκούω, ἀκούσομαι, ἤκουσα, ἀκήκοα, ——, ἠκούσθην (with pred. adj.) (5)

be dead *perfect*, θνῄσκω, θανοῦμαι, ἔθανον, τέθηνκα, ——, —— (8); *perfect*, ἀποθνῄσκω, ἀποθανοῦμαι, ἀπέθανον, τέθηνκα, ——, —— (8)

be deemed fortunate *passive*, ζηλόω, ζηλώσω, ἐζήλωσα, ἐζήλωκα, ——, —— (7)

be fond of φιλέω, φιλήσω, ἐφίλησα, πεφίληκα, πεφίλημαι, ἐφιλήθην (+ inf.) (4)

be likely μέλλω, μελλήσω, ἐμέλλησα, ——, ——, —— (+ inf.) (3)

be near πάρειμι, παρέσομαι, ——, ——, ——, —— (7)

be present ἥκω, ἥξω, ——, ——, ——, —— (5); πάρειμι, παρέσομαι, ——, ——, ——, —— (7)

be ready πάρειμι, παρέσομαι, ——, ——, ——, —— (7)

be spoken of ἀκούω, ἀκούσομαι, ἤκουσα, ἀκήκοα, ——, ἠκούσθην (with adv.) (5)

be treated as an enemy *passive*, πολεμέω, πολεμήσω, ἐπολέμησα, πεπολέμηκα, ——, ἐπολεμήθην (4)

be willing ἐθέλω/θέλω, ἐθελήσω, ἠθέλησα, ἠθέληκα, ——, —— (3)

bear φέρω, οἴσω, ἤνεγκα/ἤνεγκον, ἐνήνοχα, ἐνήνεγμαι, ἠνέχθην (9)

bearing arms σὺν ὅπλοις (1[†])

beautiful καλός, καλή, καλόν (2)

because ὅτι (conj.) (6)
because of διά (prep. + acc.) (2)
become γίγνομαι, γενήσομαι, ἐγενόμην, γέγονα, γεγένημαι, —— (6)
before πρό (prep. + gen.) (8)
before this πρὸ τοῦ (8†); πρὸ τούτου (8†)
begin *middle,* ἄρχω, ἄρξω, ἦρξα, ἦρχα, ἦργμαι, ἤρχθην (+ gen.) (3)
  to begin ἀρχὴν ποιεῖσθαι (4†)
beginning ἀρχή, ἀρχῆς, ἡ (2)
belief δόξα, δόξης, ἡ (2)
believe *middle,* πείθω, πείσω, ἔπεισα, πέπεικα, πέπεισμαι, ἐπείσθην (+ dat.) (3); οἴομαι/οἶμαι, οἰήσομαι, ——, ——, ——, ᾠήθην (8)
beloved φίλος, φίλη, φίλον (2)
beneath κατά (prep. + gen.) (5)
beside παρά (prep. + acc.) (5)
beyond ὑπέρ (prep. + acc.) (6)
big μέγας, μεγάλη, μέγα (4)
body σῶμα, σώματος, τό (5)
both ... and ... καί ... καί ... (1)
bring ἄγω, ἄξω, ἤγαγον, ἦχα, ἦγμαι, ἤχθην (5); φέρω, οἴσω, ἤνεγκα/ἤνεγκον, ἐνήνοχα, ἐνήνεγμαι, ἠνέχθην (9)
bring about πράττω, πράξω, ἔπρᾱξα, πέπρᾱχα (trans.)/πέπρᾱγα (intrans.), πέπρᾱγμαι, ἐπράχθην (7)
but ἀλλά (conj.) (2); δέ (postpositive conj.) (3)
but as a matter of fact ἀλλὰ γάρ (3†)
but yet *in narrative transitions and responses in dialogue,* ἀλλά (conj.) (2†)
by πρός (prep. + gen.) (3); ὑπό (prep. + gen.) (3); παρά (prep. + gen.) (5); *in oaths,* μά (particle + acc.) (5); *expressing strong affirmation,* νή (particle + acc.) (5)
by all means *in answers,* πάνυ (adv.) (8); *in affirmations,* μὲν οὖν (particle combination) (6†)

call λέγω, λέξω, ἔλεξα/εἶπον, ——, λέλεγμαι, ἐλέχθην (3†)
Calliope Καλλιόπη, Καλλιόπης, ἡ (§59)

carry φέρω, οἴσω, ἤνεγκα/ἤνεγκον, ἐνήνοχα, ἐνήνεγμαι, ἠνέχθην (9)
carry away with oneself *middle,* ἄγω, ἄξω, ἤγαγον, ἦχα, ἦγμαι, ἤχθην (5); *middle,* φέρω, οἴσω, ἤνεγκα/ἤνεγκον, ἐνήνοχα, ἐνήνεγμαι, ἠνέχθην (9)
cause αἰτίᾱ, αἰτίᾱς, ἡ (2)
cause to be taught *middle,* διδάσκω, διδάξω, ἐδίδαξα, δεδίδαχα, δεδίδαγμαι, ἐδιδάχθην (3)
cease *middle,* παύω, παύσω, ἔπαυσα, πέπαυκα, πέπαυμαι, ἐπαύθην (3)
certain σαφής, σαφές (7)
certainly δή (postpositive particle) (4); *in answers,* πάνυ (adv.) (8); *in affirmations,* μὲν οὖν (particle combination) (6†)
chance τύχη, τύχης, ἡ (4)
character τρόποι, τρόπων, οἱ (9)
child τέκνον, τέκνου, τό (1); παῖς, παιδός, ὁ or ἡ (5)
circumstance συμφορά, συμφορᾶς, ἡ (1)
citizen πολίτης, πολίτου, ὁ (2)
city πόλις, πόλεως, ἡ (7)
clear δῆλος, δήλη, δῆλον (6); σαφής, σαφές (7)
clever δεινός, δεινή, δεινόν (2)
cling to *middle,* ἔχω, ἕξω/σχήσω, ἔσχον, ἔσχηκα, -έσχημαι, —— (+ gen.) (4)
Clio Κλειώ, Κλειοῦς, ἡ (§59)
come ἔρχομαι, ἐλεύσομαι, ἦλθον, ἐλήλυθα, ——, —— (6)
have come ἥκω, ἥξω, ——, ——, ——, —— (5)
commander ἄρχων, ἄρχοντος, ὁ (5)
common (to) κοινός, κοινή, κοινόν (+ gen. or dat.) (3)
companion ἑταῖρος, ἑταίρου, ὁ (1)
completely διὰ τέλους (9†)
concerning περί (prep. + gen.) (1); περί (prep. + acc.) (1)
conquer νῑκάω, νῑκήσω, ἐνίκησα, νενίκηκα, νενίκημαι, ἐνῑκήθην (4)
consider *middle,* ποιέω, ποιήσω, ἐποίησα, πεποίηκα, πεποίημαι, ἐποιήθην (4)

contest ἀγών, ἀγῶνος, ὁ (6)

contrary (to) ἐναντίος, ἐναντίᾱ, ἐναντίον (+ gen. or dat.) (8)

contrary to παρά (prep. + acc.) (5)

converse (with) διαλέγομαι, διαλέξομαι, ——, ——, διείλεγμαι, διελέχθην (+ dat.) (7)

conversely ἐναντίως (adv.) (8†); (τὸ) ἐναντίον (9†)

correct ὀρθός, ὀρθή, ὀρθόν (6)

corrupt διαφθείρω, διαφθερῶ, διέφθειρα, διέφθαρκα/διέφθορα, διέφθαρμαι, διεφθάρην (9)

council βουλή, βουλῆς, ἡ (1)

country χώρᾱ, χώρᾱς, ἡ (1)

courage ἀνδρείᾱ, ἀνδρείᾱς, ἡ (9)

custom νόμος, νόμου, ὁ (1)

danger κίνδῡνος, κινδύνου, ὁ (8)

dear φίλος, φίλη, φίλον (2)

death θάνατος, θανάτου, ὁ (4)

deathless ἀθάνατος, ἀθάνατον (2)

deed ἔργον, ἔργου, τό (1); πρᾶγμα, πράγματος, τό (7)

deem *middle,* ποιέω, ποιήσω, ἐποίησα, πεποίηκα, πεποίημαι, ἐποιήθην (4)

deem worthy *middle,* τῑμάω, τῑμήσω, ἐτίμησα, τετίμηκα, τετίμημαι, ἐτῑμήθην (4)

defeat νῑκάω, νῑκήσω, ἐνίκησα, νενίκηκα, νενίκημαι, ἐνῑκήθην (4)

delight χάρις, χάριτος, ἡ (5)

Demeter Δημήτηρ, Δημητρός, ἡ (voc. = Δήμητερ) (§59)

Demosthenes Δημοσθένης, Δημοσθένους, ὁ (7)

descent γένος, γένους, τό (7)

desire ἔρως, ἔρωτος, ὁ (5)

destroy (utterly) διαφθείρω, διαφθερῶ, διέφθειρα, διέφθαρκα/διέφθορα, διέφθαρμαι, διεφθάρην (9)

die τελευτάω, τελευτήσω, ἐτελεύτησα, τετελεύτηκα, ——, ἐτελευτήθην (4); θνῄσκω, θανοῦμαι, ἔθανον, τέθνηκα, ——, —— (8); ἀποθνῄσκω, ἀποθανοῦμαι, ἀπέθανον, τέθνηκα, ——, —— (8)

　be dead *perfect,* θνῄσκω, θανοῦμαι, ἔθανον, τέθνηκα, ——, —— (8); *perfect,* ἀποθνῄσκω, ἀποθανοῦμαι, ἀπέθανον, τέθηνκα, ——, —— (8)

difficult χαλεπός, χαλεπή, χαλεπόν (4)

　with difficulty χαλεπῶς (adv.) (4†)

Dionysus Διόνῡσος, Διονύσου, ὁ (§59)

disaster συμφορά, συμφορᾶς, ἡ (1)

discuss (with) διαλέγομαι, διαλέξομαι, ——, ——, διείλεγμαι, διελέχθην (+ dat.) (7)

disgraceful αἰσχρός, αἰσχρά, αἰσχρόν (3)

distress πόνος, πόνου, ὁ (3)

divine power δαίμων, δαίμονος, ὁ or ἡ (5)

divinity δαίμων, δαίμονος, ὁ or ἡ (5)

do *active or middle,* ποιέω, ποιήσω, ἐποίησα, πεποίηκα, πεποίημαι, ἐποιήθην (4); πράττω, πράξω, ἔπρᾱξα, πέπρᾱχα (trans.)/πέπρᾱγα (intrans.), πέπρᾱγμαι, ἐπρᾱχθην (7)

(do) wrong (to) ἀδικέω, ἀδικήσω, ἠδίκησα, ἠδίκηκα, ἠδίκημαι, ἠδικήθην (4)

down from κατά (prep. + gen.) (5)

during ὑπό (prep. + acc.) (3)

each (of several) ἕκαστος, ἑκάστη, ἕκαστον (7)

each other ——, ἀλλήλων (reciprocal pronoun) (8)

earth γαῖα, γαίᾱς, ἡ (3); γῆ, γῆς, ἡ (3)

easy ῥᾴδιος, ῥᾳδίᾱ, ῥᾴδιον (5)

either . . . or . . . ἤ . . . ἤ . . . (2)

empire ἀρχή, ἀρχῆς, ἡ (2)

emulate ζηλόω, ζηλώσω, ἐζήλωσα, ἐζήλωκα, ——, —— (7)

end τελευτάω, τελευτήσω, ἐτελεύτησα, τετελεύτηκα, ——, ἐτελευτήθην (4); τέλος, τέλους, τό (9)

endure φέρω, οἴσω, ἤνεγκα/ἤνεγκον, ἐνήνοχα, ἐνήνεγμαι, ἠνέχθην (9)

enemy ἐχθρός, ἐχθροῦ, ὁ (2); πολέμιος, πολεμίου, ὁ (4)

of an enemy πολέμιος, πολεμία, πολέμιον (4)

be treated as an enemy *passive*, πολεμέω, πολεμήσω, ἐπολέμησα, πεπολέμηκα, ——, ἐπολεμήθην (4)

(engaged) in war ἐπὶ πολέμου (4†)

enjoy χαίρω, χαιρήσω, ——, κεχάρηκα, ——, ἐχάρην (7)

envy ζηλόω, ζηλώσω, ἐζήλωσα, ἐζήλωκα, ——, —— (7)

epic poetry ἔπη, ἐπῶν, τά (7)

equal ἴσος, ἴση, ἴσον (8)

equally ἴσως (adv.) (8)

Erato Ἐρατώ, Ἐρατοῦς, ἡ (§59)

Eros Ἔρως, Ἔρωτος, ὁ (voc. = Ἔρως) (§59)

escape φεύγω, φεύξομαι, ἔφυγον, πέφευγα, ——, —— (9)

Euripides Εὐρῑπίδης, Εὐρῑπίδου, ὁ (2)

Euterpe Εὐτέρπη, Εὐτέρπης, ἡ (§59)

even καί (adv.) (1); περ (enclitic particle) (5)

ever ποτέ (enclitic adv.) (5)

ever yet πώποτε (adv.) (9)

every πᾶς, πᾶσα, πᾶν (6); ἅπᾱς, ἅπᾱσα, ἅπαν (6)

evil κακός, κακή, κακόν (2)

to exact punishment δίκην λαμβάνειν (9)

exceedingly πάνυ (8)

excellence ἀρετή, ἀρετῆς, ἡ (4)

exist εἰμί, ἔσομαι, ——, ——, ——, —— (5)

expect ἀξιόω, ἀξιώσω, ἠξίωσα, ἠξίωκα, ἠξίωμαι, ἠξιώθην (4)

expectation δόξα, δόξης, ἡ (2); ἐλπίς, ἐλπίδος, ἡ (5)

experience πάθος, πάθους, τό (7); πάσχω, πείσομαι, ἔπαθον, πέπονθα, ——, —— (7)

explain διδάσκω, διδάξω, ἐδίδαξα, δεδίδαχα, δεδίδαγμαι, ἐδιδάχθην (3)

facing ἐναντίος, ἐναντίᾱ, ἐναντίον (+ gen. or dat.) (8)

fair ἴσος, ἴση, ἴσον (8)

false ψευδής, ψευδές (7)

family γένος, γένους, τό (7)

fare *intrans.*, πράττω, πράξω, ἔπρᾱξα, πέπρᾱχα (trans.)/πέπρᾱγα (intrans.), πέπρᾱγμαι, ἐπράχθην (7)

fate μοῖρα, μοίρᾱς, ἡ (2)

father πατήρ, πατρός, ὁ (7)

favor χάρις, χάριτος, ἡ (5)

fear φόβος, φόβου, ὁ (2)

fearsome δεινός, δεινή, δεινόν (2)

few ὀλίγοι, ὀλίγαι, ὀλίγα (4)

fight πολεμέω, πολεμήσω, ἐπολέμησα, πεπολέμηκα, ——, ἐπολεμήθην (4)

fight (against) μάχομαι, μαχοῦμαι, ἐμαχεσάμην, ——, μεμάχημαι, —— (+ dat.) (8)

finally τέλος (9†)

fine καλός, καλή, καλόν (2)

finish τελευτάω, τελευτήσω, ἐτελεύτησα, τετελεύτηκα, ——, ἐτελευτήθην (4)

flee φεύγω, φεύξομαι, ἔφυγον, πέφευγα, ——, —— (9)

follow ἕπομαι, ἕψομαι, ἑσπόμην, ——, ——, —— (+ dat.) (9)

be fond of φιλέω, φιλήσω, ἐφίλησα, πεφίληκα, πεφίλημαι, ἐφιλήθην (+ inf.) (4)

foolish ἀμαθής, ἀμαθές (9)

for *explanatory*, γάρ (postpositive conj.) (3); (i.e., *because of*) ἐπί (prep. + dat.) (4)

for (the purpose of) ἐπί (prep. + acc.) (4)

for in fact καὶ γάρ (3†)

for the most part ἐπὶ (τὸ) πολύ (4†)

for the sake of χάριν (prep. + preceding gen.) (5)

foreign βάρβαρος, βάρβαρον (5)

foreigner ξένος, ξένου, ὁ (3)

foreigners βάρβαροι, βαρβάρων, οἱ (5)
former ἐκεῖνος, ἐκείνη, ἐκεῖνο (4†)
fortunate εὐδαίμων, εὔδαιμον (9)
    be deemed fortunate *passive*, ζηλόω,
    ζηλώσω, ἐζήλωσα, ἐζήλωκα, ——, ——
    (7)
fortune τύχη, τύχης, ἡ (4)
free ἐλεύθερος, ἐλευθέρᾱ, ἐλεύθερον (6)
freedom ἐλευθερίᾱ, ἐλευθερίᾱς, ἡ (6)
friend φίλος, φίλου, ὁ (2); φίλη, φίλης, ἡ (2)
friendly φίλος, φίλη, φίλον (2)
from πρός (prep.) + gen. (3)
(away) from ἀπό (prep. + gen.) (2)
(out) from ἐκ, ἐξ (prep. + gen.) (1)
from (the side of) παρά (prep. + gen.) (5)
from somewhere ποθέν (enclitic adv.) (7)
from under ὑπό (prep. + gen.) (3)
from where πόθεν (interrog. adv.) (6)

general στρατηγός, στρατηγοῦ, ὁ (8)
get *simple aspect*, ἔχω, ἕξω/σχήσω, ἔσχον,
    ἔσχηκα, -έσχημαι, —— (4†)
glory δόξα, δόξης, ἡ (2)
go ἔρχομαι, ἐλεύσομαι, ἦλθον, ἐλήλυθα,
    ——, —— (6)
god θεός, θεοῦ, ὁ (1)
goddess θεός, θεοῦ, ἡ (1)
good ἀγαθός, ἀγαθή, ἀγαθόν (2); χρηστός,
    χρηστή, χρηστόν (6)
goods χρήματα, χρημάτων, τά (5)
goodwill χάρις, χάριτος, ἡ (5)
Gorgias Γοργίᾱς, Γοργίου, ὁ (2)
government κοινόν, κοινοῦ, τό (3†)
grace χάρις, χάριτος, ἡ (5)
gratitude χάρις, χάριτος, ἡ (5)
great μέγας, μεγάλη, μέγα (4); μακρός,
    μακρά, μακρόν (8)
great number πλῆθος, πλήθους, τό (8)
greatly μέγα (9†)
Greece Ἑλλάς, Ἑλλάδος, ἡ (7)
Greek Ἕλλην, Ἕλληνος, ὁ (5)
guest ξένος, ξένου, ὁ (3)
guest-friend ξένος, ξένου, ὁ (3)

habit τρόπος, τρόπου, ὁ (9)
Hades Ἅιδης, Ἅιδου, ὁ (2)
happen γίγνομαι, γενήσομαι, ἐγενόμην,
    γέγονα, γεγένημαι, —— (6)
happy εὐδαίμων, εὔδαιμον (9)
hardly χαλεπῶς (adv.) (4†)
harsh χαλεπός, χαλεπή, χαλεπόν (4)
hated ἐχθρός, ἐχθρά, ἐχθρόν (2)
hateful ἐχθρός, ἐχθρά, ἐχθρόν (2)
have ἔχω, ἕξω/σχήσω, ἔσχον, ἔσχηκα,
    -έσχημαι, —— (4)
have come ἥκω, ἥξω, ——, ——, ——, ——
    (5)
have war made upon one *passive*, πολεμέω,
    πολεμήσω, ἐπολέμησα, πεπολέμηκα,
    ——, ἐπολεμήθην (4)
hear (of) ἀκούω, ἀκούσομαι, ἤκουσα,
    ἀκήκοα, ——, ἠκούσθην (5)
heaven οὐρανός, οὐρανοῦ, ὁ (3)
Hector Ἕκτωρ, Ἕκτορος, ὁ (5)
heed *middle*, πείθω, πείσω, ἔπεισα, πέπεικα,
    πέπεισμαι, ἐπείσθην (+ dat.) (3)
Helen Ἑλένη, Ἑλένης, ἡ (1)
Hellas Ἑλλάς, Ἑλλάδος, ἡ (7)
Hellene Ἕλλην, Ἕλληνος, ὁ (5)
Hephaestus Ἥφαιστος, Ἡφαίστου, ὁ (§59)
her αὐτοῦ, αὐτῆς, αὐτοῦ (6)
Hera Ἥρᾱ, Ἥρᾱς, ἡ (§59)
Hermes Ἑρμῆς, Ἑρμοῦ, ὁ (4)
Hestia Ἑστίᾱ, Ἑστίᾱς, ἡ (§59)
him αὐτοῦ, αὐτῆς, αὐτοῦ (6)
hold ἔχω, ἕξω/σχήσω, ἔσχον, ἔσχηκα,
    -έσχημαι, —— (4)
hold on to *middle*, ἔχω, ἕξω/σχήσω, ἔσχον,
    ἔσχηκα, -έσχημαι, —— (+ gen.) (4)
hold to προσέχω, προσέξω, προσέσχον,
    προσέσχηκα, ——, —— (7)
home *sing. or pl.*, δῶμα, δώματος, τό (5)
honor τῑμάω, τῑμήσω, ἐτίμησα, τετίμηκα,
    τετίμημαι, ἐτῑμήθην (4)
hope ἐλπίς, ἐλπίδος, ἡ (5)
host ξένος, ξένου, ὁ (3)

hostile ἐχθρός, ἐχθρά, ἐχθρόν (2); πολέμιος, πολεμίᾱ, πολέμιον (4)

house οἰκίᾱ, οἰκίᾱς, ἡ (1); *sing. or pl.,* δῶμα, δώματος, τό (5)

how πῶς (interrog. adv.) (3); τί (9†)

how is it that πῶς (interrog. adv.) (3†)

human being ἄνθρωπος, ἀνθρώπου, ὁ or ἡ (1)

husband ἀνήρ, ἀνδρός, ὁ (6)

I ἐγώ, ἐμοῦ/μου (6)

I suppose που (enclitic adv.) (7)

if εἰ (conj.) (9)

ignorance ἀμαθίᾱ, ἀμαθίᾱς, ἡ (9)

ignorant ἀμαθής, ἀμαθές (9)

immortal ἀθάνατος, ἀθάνατον (2)

in ἐν (prep. + dat.) (1); ἐπί (prep. + gen.) (4); ἐπί (prep. + dat.) (4)

in accordance with ἐκ, ἐξ (prep. + gen.) (1); σύν/ξύν (prep. + dat.) (1); μετά (prep. + gen.) (4)

in addition to πρός (prep. + dat.) (3); ἐπί (prep. + dat.) (4)

in any way τι (9†)

in fact *confirming,* γάρ (postpositive conj.) (3)

in front of πρό (prep. + gen.) (8)

in office ἐν τέλει (9†)

in opposition ἐναντίως (adv.) (8†); (τὸ) ἐναντίον (9†)

and in particular καί δή (4†); καὶ δὴ καί (4†)

in power ἐν τέλει (9†)

in relation to πρός (prep. + acc.) (3); κατά (prep. + acc.) (5)

in reply to πρός (prep. + acc.) (3)

in the face of πρός (prep. + acc.) (3)

in the following way ὧδε (adv.) (4)

in the name of πρός (prep. + gen.) (3)

in the power of ἐν (prep. + dat.) (1†)

in the presence of ἐν (prep. + dat.) (1)

in the world ποτέ (enclitic adv.) (5†)

in this way οὕτω(ς) (adv.) (4); ὧδε (adv.) (4)

in (time of) peace ἐπὶ εἰρήνης (4†)

(engaged) in war ἐπὶ πολέμου (4†)

inclination γνώμη, γνώμης, ἡ (1)

indeed *confirming,* γάρ (postpositive conj.) (3); δή (postpositive particle) (4); *emphasizes,* γε (enclitic particle) (5)

injure ἀδικέω, ἀδικήσω, ἠδίκησα, ἠδίκηκα, ἠδίκημαι, ἠδικήθην (4)

insolence ὕβρις, ὕβρεως, ἡ (7)

intelligence φρόνησις, φρονήσεως, ἡ (9)

intend μέλλω, μελλήσω, ἐμέλλησα, ——, ——, —— (+ inf.) (3)

into εἰς, ἐς (prep. + acc.) (1)

island νῆσος, νήσου, ἡ (1)

it αὐτοῦ, αὐτῆς, αὐτοῦ (6)

it is necessary δεῖ, δεήσει, ἐδέησε(ν), ——, ——, —— (impersonal verb) (5); χρή, χρῆσται, ——, ——, ——, —— (impersonal verb) (8)

it is possible *used impersonally in 3rd person sing.,* εἰμί, ἔσομαι, ——, ——, ——, —— (5)

journey ὁδός, ὁδοῦ, ἡ (1)

judgment γνώμη, γνώμης, ἡ (1)

just δίκαιος, δικαίᾱ, δίκαιον (2)

just as ὥσπερ (conj.) (6)

justice δίκη, δίκης, ἡ (1); δικαιοσύνη, δικαιοσύνης, ἡ (9)

justly σὺν δίκη (1†)

keep ἄγω, ἄξω, ἤγαγον, ἦχα, ἦγμαι, ἤχθην (5)

kill κτείνω, κτενῶ, ἔκτεινα, ——, ——, —— (8); ἀποκτείνω, ἀποκτενῶ, ἀπέκτεινα, ἀπέκτονα, ——, —— (8)

kind γένος, γένους, τό (7)

know οἶδα, εἴσομαι, ——, ——, ——, —— (9)

labor πόνος, πόνου, ὁ (3)

Lacedaemonian Λακεδαιμόνιος, Λακεδαιμονίᾱ, Λακεδαιμόνιον (2)

Lacedaemonians Λακεδαιμόνιοι, Λακεδαιμονίων, οἱ (2)

land χώρᾱ, χώρᾱς, ἡ (1); γαῖα, γαίᾱς, ἡ (3); γῆ, γῆς, ἡ (3)

large μακρός, μακρά, μακρόν (8)

latter οὗτος, αὕτη, τοῦτο (4†)

law νόμος, νόμου, ὁ (1)

lead ἄγω, ἄξω, ἤγαγον, ἦχα, ἦγμαι, ἤχθην (5)

learn μανθάνω, μαθήσομαι, ἔμαθον, μεμάθηκα, ——, —— (5)

life βίος, βίου, ὁ (4)

life force ψῡχή, ψῡχῆς, ἡ (1)

like φιλέω, φιλήσω, ἐφίλησα, πεφίληκα, πεφίλημαι, ἐφιλήθην (4)

be likely μέλλω, μελλήσω, ἐμέλλησα, ——, ——, —— (+ inf.) (3)

lines (of verse) ἔπη, ἐπῶν, τά (7)

listen (to) ἀκούω, ἀκούσομαι, ἤκουσα, ἀκήκοα, ——, ἠκούσθην (5)

little ὀλίγος, ὀλίγη, ὀλίγον (4)

a little (σ)μῑκρόν (9†)

live ζάω, ζήσω, ——, ——, ——, —— (8)

livelihood βίος, βίου, ὁ (4)

living being ζῷον, ζῴου, τό (1)

long μακρός, μακρά, μακρόν (8)

lord δεσπότης, δεσπότου, ὁ (6)

love ἔρως, ἔρωτος, ὁ (5); φιλέω, φιλήσω, ἐφίλησα, πεφίληκα, πεφίλημαι, ἐφιλήθην (4)

loved φίλος, φίλη, φίλον (2)

loved one φίλος, φίλου, ὁ (2); φίλη, φίλης, ἡ (2)

loving φίλος, φίλη, φίλον (2)

magistrate ἄρχων, ἄρχοντος, ὁ (5)

majority *preceded by an article (whether modifying a noun or used substantively)*, πολύς, πολλή, πολύ (4†)

make *active or middle*, ποιέω, ποιήσω, ἐποίησα, πεποίηκα, πεποίημαι, ἐποιήθην (4)

    to make a beginning ἀρχὴν ποιεῖσθαι (4†)

    to make a plan βουλὴν ποιεῖσθαι (4†)

    to make words λόγους ποιεῖσθαι (4†)

make clear δηλόω, δηλώσω, ἐδήλωσα, δεδήλωκα, δεδήλωμαι, ἐδηλώθην (4)

make war (upon) πολεμέω, πολεμήσω, ἐπολέμησα, πεπολέμηκα, ——, ἐπολεμήθην (+ dat.) (4)

maker ποιητής, ποιητοῦ, ὁ (2)

man ἄνθρωπος, ἀνθρώπου, ὁ (1); ἀνήρ, ἀνδρός, ὁ (6)

manage *trans.*, πράττω, πράξω, ἔπρᾱξα, πέπρᾱχα (trans.)/πέπρᾱγα (intrans.), πέπρᾱγμαι, ἐπράχθην (7)

manner τρόπος, τρόπου, ὁ (9)

many πολύς, πολλή, πολύ (4)

many times πολλάκις (adv.) (3); (τὰ) πολλά (9†)

marketplace ἀγορά, ἀγορᾶς, ἡ (1)

marry *middle*, ἄγω, ἄξω, ἤγαγον, ἦχα, ἦγμαι, ἤχθην (5)

marvelous δεινός, δεινή, δεινόν (2)

master δεσπότης, δεσπότου, ὁ (6)

matter χρῆμα, χρήματος, τό (5); πρᾶγμα, πράγματος, τό (7)

me ἐγώ, ἐμοῦ/μου (6)

Melpomene Μελπομένη, Μελπομένης, ἡ (§59)

mind *sing. or pl.*, φρήν, φρενός, ἡ (5); νοῦς, νοῦ, ὁ (7)

miserable ἄθλιος, ἀθλίᾱ, ἄθλιον (9)

misfortune συμφορά, συμφορᾶς, ἡ (1)

moderate σώφρων, σῶφρον (9)

moderation σωφροσύνη, σωφροσύνης, ἡ (9)

money χρήματα, χρημάτων, τά (5)

mortal βροτός, βροτοῦ, ὁ (4); θνητός, θνητή, θνητόν (5)

mother μήτηρ, μητρός, ἡ (7)

much πολύς, πολλή, πολύ (4); (adv.) (τὸ) πολύ (9†); (τὰ) πολλά (9†)

of much value περὶ πολλοῦ (4†)

multitude πλῆθος, πλήθους, τό (8)

Muse Μοῦσα, Μούσης, ἡ (§59)

must δεῖ, δεήσει, ἐδέησε(ν), ——, ——, —— (impersonal verb) (5)

my ἐμός, ἐμή, ἐμόν (6)

nature φύσις, φύσεως, ἡ (7)

near πρός (prep. + dat.) (3); παρά (prep. + dat.) (5)

be near πάρειμι, παρέσομαι, ——, ——, ——, —— (7)

necessity ἀνάγκη, ἀνάγκης, ἡ (5)

neither ... nor ... οὔτε/μήτε ... οὔτε/ μήτε ... (6)

never οὔ ποτε, οὔποτε/μή ποτε, μήποτε (5); οὐδέποτε/μηδέποτε (adv.) (7)

new νέος, νέα, νέον (4)

no οὐδείς, οὐδεμία, οὐδέν/μηδείς, μηδεμία, μηδέν (9)

no, on the contrary *in corrections,* μὲν οὖν (particle combination) (6)

no longer οὐκέτι/μηκέτι (adv.) (8)

no one οὐδείς, οὐδεμία, οὐδέν/μηδείς, μηδεμία, μηδέν (9)

noble καλός, καλή, καλόν (2)

non-Greek βάρβαρος, βάρβαρον (5)

nor οὐδέ/μηδέ (conj.) (7)

nor ever οὐδέποτε/μηδέποτε (conj.) (7)

not οὐ, οὐκ, οὐχ (adv.) (2); μή (adv.) (2)

not any οὐδείς, οὐδεμία, οὐδέν/μηδείς, μηδεμία, μηδέν (adj.) (9)

not at all οὐ πάνυ (8); οὐδέν/μηδέν (9[†])

not even οὐδέ/μηδέ (adv.) (7)

not ever yet οὐπώποτε/μηπώποτε (9[†]); οὐδεπώποτε/μηδεπώποτε (9[†])

not only ... but also ... οὐ/μὴ μόνον ... ἀλλὰ καί ... (2)

not yet οὔπω/μήπω (adv.) (9[†])

not yet at any time οὐπώποτε/μηπώποτε (9[†]); οὐδεπώποτε/μηδεπώποτε (9[†])

nothing οὐδείς, οὐδεμία, οὐδέν/μηδείς, μηδεμία, μηδέν (9)

now νῦν (adv.) (3); (τὸ)(τὰ) νῦν (9[†])

O ὦ (interj.) (1)

obey *middle,* πείθω, πείσω, ἔπεισα, πέπεικα, πέπεισμαι, ἐπείσθην (+ dat.) (3)

occupy ἔχω, ἕξω/σχήσω, ἔσχον, ἔσχηκα, -ἔσχημαι, —— (4)

of an enemy πολέμιος, πολεμίᾱ, πολέμιον (4)

of course δή (postpositive particle) (4)

of much value περὶ πολλοῦ (4[†])

(political) office ἀρχή, ἀρχῆς, ἡ (2[†])

often πολλάκις (adv.) (3); (τὰ) πολλά (9[†])

old παλαιός, παλαιά, παλαιόν (8)

on ἐν (prep. + dat.) (1); ἐπί (prep. + gen.) (4); ἐπί (prep. + dat.) (4)

on account of διά (prep. + acc.) (2)

on behalf of ὑπέρ (prep. + gen.) (6)

on condition of ἐπί (prep. + dat.) (4)

no, on the contrary *in corrections,* μὲν οὖν (particle combination) (6)

on the one hand μέν (postpositive particle) (3)

on the one hand ..., on the other hand ... μέν ..., δέ ... (3)

one εἷς, μία, ἕν (numerical adj.) (9)

one another ——, ἀλλήλων (reciprocal pronoun) (8)

only μόνος, μόνη, μόνον (2); μόνον (adv.) (2)

openly εἰς/ἐς κοινόν (3[†])

opinion γνώμη, γνώμης, ἡ (1); δόξα, δόξης, ἡ (2)

opposing ἐναντίος, ἐναντίᾱ, ἐναντίον (+ gen. or dat.) (8)

opposite ἐναντίος, ἐναντίᾱ, ἐναντίον (+ gen. or dat.) (8)

or ἤ (conj.) (2)

orator ῥήτωρ, ῥήτορος, ὁ (5)

other ἄλλος, ἄλλη, ἄλλο (5)

ought χρή, χρῆσται, ——, ——, ——, —— (impersonal verb) (8)

our ἡμέτερος, ἡμετέρᾱ, ἡμέτερον (6)

(out) from ἐκ, ἐξ (prep. + gen.) (1)

out of ἐκ, ἐξ (prep. + gen.) (1)

over ὑπέρ (prep. + gen.) (6)

pain λύπη, λύπης, ἡ (8)

passion ἔρως, ἔρωτος, ὁ (5); πάθος, πάθους, τό (7)

path ὁδός, ὁδοῦ, ἡ (1)
to pay attention νοῦν/γνώμην προσέχειν (7)
peace εἰρήνη, εἰρήνης, ἡ (1)
  in (time of) peace ἐπὶ εἰρήνης (4†)
(the) people δῆμος, δήμου, ὁ (2)
perhaps ἴσως (adv.) (8)
persuade πείθω, πείσω, ἔπεισα, πέπεικα, πέπεισμαι, ἐπείσθην (3)
Phoebus Φοῖβος, Φοίβου, ὁ (§59)
plain σαφής, σαφές (7)
plan βουλή, βουλῆς, ἡ (1)
  to plan βουλὴν ποιεῖσθαι (4†)
pleasure ἡδονή, ἡδονῆς, ἡ (8)
poet ποιητής, ποιητοῦ, ὁ (2)
political office ἀρχή, ἀρχῆς, ἡ (2†)
Polymnia Πολύμνια, Πολυμνίᾱς, ἡ (§59)
Poseidon Ποσειδῶν, Ποσειδῶνος, ὁ (voc. = Πόσειδον) (§59)
power δύναμις, δυνάμεως, ἡ (7); τέλος, τέλους, τό (9)
(supreme) power ἀρχή, ἀρχῆς, ἡ (2)
practically ὡς ἔπος εἰπεῖν (7)
practice trans., πρᾱ́ττω, πρᾱ́ξω, ἔπρᾱξα, πέπρᾱχα (trans.)/πέπρᾱγα (intrans.), πέπρᾱγμαι, ἐπρᾱ́χθην (7)
be present ἥκω, ἥξω, ——, ——, ——, —— (5); πάρειμι, παρέσομαι, ——, ——, ——, —— (7)
presently (τὸ)(τά) νῦν (9†)
prevail (over) νῑκάω, νῑκήσω, ἐνῑ́κησα, νενῑ́κηκα, νενῑ́κημαι, ἐνῑκήθην (4)
Priam Πρίαμος, Πριάμου, ὁ (1)
property χρήματα, χρημάτων, τά (5)
prudent σώφρων, σῶφρον (9)
public κοινός, κοινή, κοινόν (3)
public affairs κοινά, κοινῶν, τά (3)
public speaker ῥήτωρ, ῥήτορος, ὁ (5)
public treasury κοινά, κοινῶν, τά (3)
publicly εἰς/ἐς κοινόν (3†)
to exact punishment δίκην λαμβάνειν (9)
purpose τέλος, τέλους, τό (9)

quarrel πολεμέω, πολεμήσω, ἐπολέμησα, πεπολέμηκα, ——, ἐπολεμήθην (4)
(quite) all ἅπᾱς, ἅπᾱσα, ἅπαν (6)

race γένος, γένους, τό (7)
be ready πάρειμι, παρέσομαι, ——, ——, ——, —— (7)
real ἀληθής, ἀληθές (7)
really ὄντως (adv.) (7); ὡς ἀληθῶς (7†)
receive δέχομαι, δέξομαι, ἐδεξάμην, ——, δέδεγμαι, —— (6); λαμβάνω, λήψομαι, ἔλαβον, εἴληφα, εἴλημμαι, ἐλήφθην (9)
recount λέγω, λέξω, ἔλεξα/εἶπον, ——, λέλεγμαι, ἐλέχθην (3)
regarding εἰς, ἐς (prep. + acc.) (1)
rejoice (in) χαίρω, χαιρήσω, ——, κεχάρηκα, ——, ἐχάρην (7)
remain μένω, μενῶ, ἔμεινα, μεμένηκα, ——, —— (9)
reply ὑπολαμβάνω, ὑπολήψομαι, ὑπέλαβον, ὑπείληφα, ὑπείλημμαι, ὑπελήφθην (9)
reputation δόξα, δόξης, ἡ (2)
require ἀξιόω, ἀξιώσω, ἠξίωσα, ἠξίωκα, ἠξίωμαι, ἠξιώθην (4)
responsibility αἰτίᾱ, αἰτίᾱς, ἡ (2)
(the) rest (of) in the attributive position, ἄλλος, ἄλλη, ἄλλο (5)
resulting from ἐκ, ἐξ (prep. + gen.) (1)
reveal δηλόω, δηλώσω, ἐδήλωσα, δεδήλωκα, δεδήλωμαι, ἐδηλώθην (4)
rhetor ῥήτωρ, ῥήτορος, ὁ (5)
right δίκαιος, δικαίᾱ, δίκαιον (2)
road ὁδός, ὁδοῦ, ἡ (1)
ruin διαφθείρω, διαφθερῶ, διέφθειρα, διέφθαρκα/διέφθορα, διέφθαρμαι, διεφθάρην (9)
rule ἀρχή, ἀρχῆς, ἡ (2); ἄρχω, ἄρξω, ἦρξα, ἦρχα, ἦργμαι, ἤρχθην (+ gen.) (3)
ruler ἄρχων, ἄρχοντος, ὁ (5)

safety σωτηρίᾱ, σωτηρίᾱς, ἡ (8)
same αὐτός, αὐτή, αὐτό (6)

say λέγω, λέξω, ἔλεξα/εἶπον, ——,
λέλεγμαι, ἐλέχθην (3); ——, ἐρῶ,
——, εἴρηκα, εἴρημαι, ἐρρήθην (8);
*φάσκω, ——, ——, ——, ——,
—— (8); φημί, φήσω, ἔφησα, ——,
——, —— (8)

sea θάλαττα, θαλάττης, ἡ (2)

see ὁράω, ὄψομαι, εἶδον, ἑώρᾱκα/ἑόρᾱκα,
ἑώρᾱμαι/ὦμμαι, ὤφθην (6)

seize λαμβάνω, λήψομαι, ἔλαβον, εἴληφα,
εἴλημμαι, ἐλήφθην (9)

-self αὐτός, αὐτή, αὐτό (6)

send πέμπω, πέμψω, ἔπεμψα, πέπομφα,
πέπεμμαι, ἐπέμφθην (3)

send away ἀποπέμπω, ἀποπέμψω, ἀπέπεμψα,
ἀποπέπομφα, ἀποπέπεμμαι, ἀπεπέμφθην
(7)

send away from oneself *middle,* ἀποπέμπω,
ἀποπέμψω, ἀπέπεμψα, ἀποπέπομφα,
ἀποπέπεμμαι, ἀπεπέμφθην (7)

sense νοῦς, νοῦ, ὁ (7)

severe χαλεπός, χαλεπή, χαλεπόν (4)

shameful αἰσχρός, αἰσχρά, αἰσχρόν (3)

shared (with) κοινός, κοινή, κοινόν (+ gen.
or dat.) (3)

show δηλόω, δηλώσω, ἐδήλωσα, δεδήλωκα,
δεδήλωμαι, ἐδηλώθην (4)

skill τέχνη, τέχνης, ἡ (5)

sky οὐρανός, οὐρανοῦ, ὁ (3)

slave παῖς, παιδός, ὁ or ἡ (5); δοῦλος,
δούλου, ὁ (6)

small ὀλίγος, ὀλίγη, ὀλίγον (4); (σ)μῑκρός,
(σ)μῑκρά, (σ)μῑκρόν (8)

so οὕτω(ς) (adv.) (4); ὧδε (adv.) (4)

so then *in transitions to a new subject,* μὲν
οὖν (particle combination) (6[†]); ἄρα
(postpositive particle) (9)

so to speak ὡς ἔπος εἰπεῖν (7)

Socrates Σωκράτης, Σωκράτους, ὁ (7)

soldier στρατιώτης, στρατιώτου, ὁ (8)

some τις, τι (indef. adj.) (9)

somehow πως (enclitic adv.) (5)

someone τις, τι (indef. pron.) (9)

something τις, τι (indef. pron.) (9)

sometimes . . . , sometimes . . . ποτέ . . . ,
ποτέ . . . (5)

somewhere που (enclitic adv.) (7)

son υἱός, υἱοῦ, ὁ (4)

son of Atreus Ἀτρείδης, Ἀτρείδου, ὁ (2)

sort γένος, γένους, τό (7)

soul ψῡχή, ψῡχῆς, ἡ (1)

Spartan Λακεδαιμόνιος, Λακεδαιμονίᾱ,
Λακεδαιμόνιον (2)

Spartans Λακεδαιμόνιοι, Λακεδαιμονίων,
οἱ (2)

speak (of) λέγω, λέξω, ἔλεξα/εἶπον, ——,
λέλεγμαι, ἐλέχθην (3); ——, ἐρῶ, ——,
εἴρηκα, εἴρημαι, ἐρρήθην (8);
to speak λόγους ποιεῖσθαι (4[†])

speech λόγος, λόγου, ὁ (1)

spirit γνώμη, γνώμης, ἡ (1); δαίμων,
δαίμονος, ὁ or ἡ (5)

state κοινόν, κοινοῦ, τό (3[†])

stay μένω, μενῶ, ἔμεινα, μεμένηκα, ——,
—— (9)

still ἔτι (adv.) (8)

stop (intrans.) *middle,* παύω, παύσω, ἔπαυσα,
πέπαυκα, πέπαυμαι, ἐπαύθην (3)

stop (trans.) παύω, παύσω, ἔπαυσα, πέπαυκα,
πέπαυμαι, ἐπαύθην (3)

straight ὀρθός, ὀρθή, ὀρθόν (6)

strange δεινός, δεινή, δεινόν (2)

stranger ξένος, ξένου, ὁ (3)

struggle ἀγών, ἀγῶνος, ὁ (6)

student μαθητής, μαθητοῦ, ὁ (5)

stupidity ἀμαθίᾱ, ἀμαθίᾱς, ἡ (9)

suffer πάσχω, πείσομαι, ἔπαθον, πέπονθα,
——, —— (7)

suffering πόνος, πόνου, ὁ (3); πάθος,
πάθους, τό (7)

suppose οἴομαι/οἶμαι, οἰήσομαι, ——, ——,
——, ᾠήθην (8); ὑπολαμβάνω,
ὑπολήψομαι, ὑπέλαβον, ὑπείληφα,
ὑπείλημμαι, ὑπελήφθην (9)

supreme power ἀρχή, ἀρχῆς, ἡ (2)
sure σαφής, σαφές (7)
surely τοι (enclitic particle) (5)

take λαμβάνω, λήψομαι, ἔλαβον, εἴληφα,
    εἴλημμαι, ἐλήφθην (9)
take hold (of) *middle,* λαμβάνω, λήψομαι,
    ἔλαβον, εἴληφα, εἴλημμαι, ἐλήφθην
    (+ gen.) (9)
take up ὑπολαμβάνω, ὑπολήψομαι,
    ὑπέλαβον, ὑπείληφα, ὑπείλημμαι,
    ὑπελήφθην (9)
talk (with) διαλέγομαι, διαλέξομαι, ——,
    ——, διείλεγμαι, διελέχθην (+ dat.) (7)
tall μακρός, μακρά, μακρόν (8)
task ἔργον, ἔργου, τό (1)
teach διδάσκω, διδάξω, ἐδίδαξα, δεδίδαχα,
    δεδίδαγμαι, ἐδιδάχθην (3)
    cause to be taught *middle,* διδάσκω,
    διδάξω, ἐδίδαξα, δεδίδαχα, δεδίδαγμαι,
    ἐδιδάχθην (3)
teacher διδάσκαλος, διδασκάλου, ὁ (5)
tell (of) λέγω, λέξω, ἔλεξα/εἶπον, ——,
    λέλεγμαι, ἐλέχθην (3); ——, ἐρῶ, ——,
    εἴρηκα, εἴρημαι, ἐρρήθην (8)
Terpsichore Τερψιχόρᾱ, Τερψιχόρᾱς, ἡ
    (§59)
terrible δεινός, δεινή, δεινόν (2)
Thalia Θάλεια, Θαλείᾱς, ἡ (§59)
that ἐκεῖνος, ἐκείνη, ἐκεῖνο (demonstr. adj./
    pron.) (4); ὅς, ἥ, ὅ (rel. pron.) (5); ὅτι
    (conj.) (6); ὡς (proclitic conj.) (6)
the ὁ, ἡ, τό (article) (1)
them αὐτοῦ, αὐτῆς, αὐτοῦ (6)
then οὖν (postpositive conj.) (6);
    τότε (adv.) (7)
    (so) then ἄρα (postpositive particle)
    (9)
    so then *in transitions to a new subject,*
    μὲν οὖν (particle combination) (6[†])
there ἐκεῖ (adv.) (9)

there is need δεῖ, δεήσει, ἐδέησε(ν), ——,
    ——, —— (impersonal verb) (+ gen.)
    (5)
therefore οὖν (postpositive conj.) (6); *in
    transitions to a new subject,* μὲν οὖν
    (particle combination) (6); ἄρα
    (postpositive particle) (9)
these οὗτοι, αὗται, ταῦτα (demonstr. adj./
    pron.) (2); οἵδε, αἵδε, τάδε (demonstr.
    adj./pron.) (4)
thing χρῆμα, χρήματος, τό (5); πρᾶγμα,
    πράγματος, τό (7)
think οἴομαι/οἶμαι, οἰήσομαι, ——, ——,
    ——, ᾠήθην (8)
think (it) right ἀξιόω, ἀξιώσω, ἠξίωσα,
    ἠξίωκα, ἠξίωμαι, ἠξιώθην (4)
think worthy ἀξιόω, ἀξιώσω, ἠξίωσα,
    ἠξίωκα, ἠξίωμαι, ἠξιώθην (4)
this οὗτος, αὕτη, τοῦτο (demonstr. adj./
    pron.) (2); ὅδε, ἥδε, τόδε (demonstr.
    adj./pron.) (4)
those ἐκεῖνοι, ἐκεῖναι, ἐκεῖνα (demonstr.
    adj./pron.) (4)
thought νοῦς, νοῦ, ὁ (7)
through διά (prep. + gen.) (2)
through to the end, διὰ τέλους (9)
throughout κατά (prep. + acc.) (5)
thus οὕτω(ς) (adv.) (4)
in time of peace ἐπὶ εἰρήνης (4[†])
to εἰς, ἐς (prep. + acc.) (1); ἐπί (prep. + acc.)
    (4)
to (the side of) παρά (prep. + acc.) (5)
to a great extent ἐπὶ (τὸ) πολύ (4[†]);
    μέγα (9[†])
to somewhere ποι (enclitic adv.) (7)
to the end ἐς τέλος (9[†])
to where ποῖ (interrog. adv.) (6)
toil πόνος, πόνου, ὁ (3)
tool ὅπλον, ὅπλου, τό (1)
toward εἰς, ἐς (prep. + acc.) (1); πρός
    (prep. + acc.) (3)

treat ποιέω, ποιήσω, ἐποίησα, πεποίηκα, πεποίημαι, ἐποιήθην (+ adv.) (4[†])
troubles πράγματα, πραγμάτων, τά (7)
true ἀληθής, ἀληθές (7)
truly ὡς ἀληθῶς (7[†])
truth ἀλήθεια, ἀληθείᾱς, ἡ (2)
truthful ἀληθής, ἀληθές (7)
turn to προσέχω, προσέξω, προσέσχον, προσέσχηκα, ——, —— (7)

ugly αἰσχρός, αἰσχρά, αἰσχρόν (3)
unclear ἄδηλος, ἄδηλον (6)
under ὑπό (prep. + gen.) (3); ὑπό (prep. + dat.) (3); ὑπό (prep. + acc.) (3)
under the power of ὑπό (prep. + dat.) (3)
understand μανθάνω, μαθήσομαι, ἔμαθον, μεμάθηκα, ——, —— (5); λαμβάνω, λήψομαι, ἔλαβον, εἴληφα, εἴλημμαι, ἐλήφθην (9)
understanding φρόνησις, φρονήσεως, ἡ (9)
unjust ἄδικος, ἄδικον (2)
upon ἐπί (prep. + gen.) (4)
Urania Οὐρανίᾱ, Οὐρανίᾱς, ἡ (§59)
us ἡμεῖς, ἡμῶν (6)

valor ἀρετή, ἀρετῆς, ἡ (4)
value *middle*, τῑμάω, τῑμήσω, ἐτίμησα, τετίμηκα, τετίμημαι, ἐτῑμήθην (4)
very περ (enclitic particle) (5); αὐτός, αὐτή, αὐτό (6)
very (much) πάνυ (adv.) (8)
victory νίκη, νίκης, ἡ (4)
(wanton) violence ὕβρις, ὕβρεως, ἡ (7)
virtue ἀρετή, ἀρετῆς, ἡ (4)

wall τεῖχος, τείχους, τό (8)
want βούλομαι, βουλήσομαι, ——, ——, βεβούλημαι, ἐβουλήθην (6)
wanton violence ὕβρις, ὕβρεως, ἡ (7)

war πόλεμος, πολέμου, ὁ (1)
be at war (with) πολεμέω, πολεμήσω, ἐπολέμησα, πεπολέμηκα, ——, ἐπολεμήθην (+ dat.) (4)
(engaged) in war ἐπὶ πολέμου (4[†])
have war made upon one *passive*, πολεμέω, πολεμήσω, ἐπολέμησα, πεπολέμηκα, ——, ἐπολεμήθην (4)
make war (upon) πολεμέω, πολεμήσω, ἐπολέμησα, πεπολέμηκα, ——, ἐπολεμήθην (+ dat.) (4)
way ὁδός, ὁδοῦ, ἡ (1); τρόπος, τρόπου, ὁ (9)
we ἡμεῖς, ἡμῶν (6)
wealth πλοῦτος, πλούτου, ὁ (7)
weapons ὅπλα, ὅπλων, τά (1)
welcome δέχομαι, δέξομαι, ἐδεξάμην, ——, δέδεγμαι, —— (6)
well εὖ (adv.) (3)
well, . . . *in narrative transitions and responses in dialogue,* ἀλλά (conj.) (2[†])
what τίς, τί (interrog. pron./adj.) (9)
when πότε (interrog. adv.) (3)
where ποῦ (interrog. adv.) (6)
which ὅς, ἥ, ὅ (rel. pron.) (5); τίς, τί (interrog. adj.) (9)
who ὅς, ἥ, ὅ (rel. pron.) (5); τίς, τί (interrog. pron.) (9)
whole πᾶς, πᾶσα, πᾶν (6); ἅπᾱς, ἅπᾱσα, ἅπαν (6)
whom ὅς, ἥ, ὅ (rel. pron.) (5)
whose ὅς, ἥ, ὅ (rel. pron.) (5)
why τί (9[†])
wicked πονηρός, πονηρά, πονηρόν (4)
wife γυνή, γυναικός, ἡ (7)
will βουλή, βουλῆς, ἡ (1)
be willing ἐθέλω/θέλω, ἐθελήσω, ἠθέλησα, ἠθέληκα, ——, —— (3)
win νῑκάω, νῑκήσω, ἐνίκησα, νενίκηκα, νενίκημαι, ἐνῑκήθην (4); *middle*, φέρω, οἴσω, ἤνεγκα/ἤνεγκον, ἐνήνοχα, ἐνήνεγμαι, ἠνέχθην (9)

wisdom σοφίᾱ, σοφίᾱς, ἡ (1)
wise σοφός, σοφή, σοφόν (2)
wish ἐθέλω/θέλω, ἐθελήσω, ἠθέλησα,
    ἠθέληκα, ——, —— (3); βούλομαι,
    βουλήσομαι, ——, ——, βεβούλημαι,
    ἐβουλήθην (6)
(along) with σύν/ξύν (prep. + dat.) (1);
    μετά (prep. + gen.) (4)
with a view to εἰς, ἐς (prep. + acc.) (1)
with difficulty χαλεπῶς (adv.) (4)
with the aid of σύν/ξύν (prep. + dat.) (1);
    μετά (prep. + gen.) (4)
without ἄνευ (prep. + gen.) (6)
wits *sing. or pl.,* φρήν, φρενός, ἡ (5)
woman γυνή, γυναικός, ἡ (7)
word λόγος, λόγου, ὁ (1); ἔπος, ἔπους,
    τό (7)
work ἔργον, ἔργου, τό (1)

worthless πονηρός, πονηρά, πονηρόν
    (4)
wretched ἄθλιος, ἀθλίᾱ, ἄθλιον (9)
wrong ἀδικέω, ἀδικήσω, ἠδίκησα, ἠδίκηκα,
    ἠδίκημαι, ἠδικήθην (4)

(yes,) by *expresses strong affirmation,* νή
    (particle + acc.) (5)
yet ἔτι (adv.) (8); πω (enclitic adv.) (9)
you (sing.) σύ, σοῦ/σου (6)
you (pl.) ὑμεῖς, ὑμῶν (6)
you know τοι (enclitic particle) (5)
young νέος, νέᾱ, νέον (4)
young man νεᾱνίᾱς, νεᾱνίου, ὁ (2)
your (sing.) σός, σή, σόν (6)
your (pl.) ὑμέτερος, ὑμετέρᾱ, ὑμέτερον (6)

Zeus Ζεύς, Διός, ὁ (5)

PRINCIPAL PARTS OF VERBS

When no meanings are offered for a voice of a verb, the verb *never* appears in that voice. An R indicates that a verb *rarely* appears in that voice. Only commonly occurring forms should be included in a synopsis.

Verb	Active	Middle	Passive
ἄγω, ἄξω, ἤγαγον, ἦχα, ἦγμαι, ἤχθην (5)	lead, bring; keep	carry away with oneself; marry	be led, be brought
ἀδικέω, ἀδικήσω, ἠδίκησα, ἠδίκηκα, ἠδίκημαι, ἠδικήθην (4)	(do) wrong (to); injure		be wronged; be injured
ἀκούω, ἀκούσομαι, ἤκουσα, ἀκήκοα, ——, ἠκούσθην (5)	listen (to), hear (of)	*(future only)* listen (to), hear (of)	be listened to, be heard
ἀξιόω, ἀξιώσω, ἠξίωσα, ἠξίωκα, ἠξίωμαι, ἠξιώθην (4)	think worthy; think (it) right; expect, require	R	be thought worthy
ἀποθνῄσκω, ἀποθανοῦμαι, ἀπέθανον, τέθνηκα, ——, —— (8)	die; *perfect,* be dead	*(future only)* die	
ἀποκτείνω, ἀποκτενῶ, ἀπέκτεινα, ἀπέκτονα, ——, —— (8)	kill		
ἀποπέμπω, ἀποπέμψω, ἀπέπεμψα, ἀποπέπομφα, ἀποπέπεμμαι, ἀπεπέμφθην (7)	send away	send away from oneself	be sent away
ἄρχω, ἄρξω, ἦρξα, ἦρχα, ἦργμαι, ἤρχθην (3)	rule (+ gen.)	begin (+ gen.)	be ruled
βούλομαι, βουλήσομαι, ——, ——, βεβούλημαι, ἐβουλήθην (6)		want, wish	*(aorist only)* want, wish
γίγνομαι, γενήσομαι, ἐγενόμην, γέγονα, γεγένημαι, —— (6)	*(perfect only)* become; happen; arise, be born	become; happen; arise, be born	
δεῖ, δεήσει, ἐδέησε(ν), ——, ——, —— (5)	it is necessary, must; there is a need (+ gen.)		

Verb	Active	Middle	Passive
δέχομαι, δέξομαι, ἐδεξάμην, ——, δέδεγμαι, —— (6)		accept, receive; welcome	
δηλόω, δηλώσω, ἐδήλωσα, δεδήλωκα, δεδήλωμαι, ἐδηλώθην (4)	show, make clear, reveal		R
διαλέγομαι, διαλέξομαι, ——, ——, διείλεγμαι, διελέχθην (7)		talk (with), converse (with), discuss (with) (+ dat.)	(*aorist only*) talk (with), converse (with), discuss (with) (+ dat.)
διαφθείρω, διαφθερῶ, διέφθειρα, διέφθαρκα/διέφθορα, διέφθαρμαι, διεφθάρην (9)	destroy (utterly); corrupt, ruin		be destroyed (utterly); be corrupted, be ruined
διδάσκω, διδάξω, ἐδίδαξα, δεδίδαχα, δεδίδαγμαι, ἐδιδάχθην (3)	teach; explain	cause to be taught	be taught; be explained
ἐθέλω/θέλω, ἐθελήσω, ἠθέλησα, ἠθέληκα, ——, —— (3)	be willing, wish		
εἰμί, ἔσομαι, ——, ——, ——, —— (5)	be; exist; *impers.*, it is possible	(*future only*) be; exist; *impers.*, it is possible	
ἕπομαι, ἕψομαι, ἑσπόμην, ——, ——, —— (9)		follow (+ dat.)	
ἔρχομαι, ἐλεύσομαι, ἦλθον, ἐλήλυθα, ——, —— (6)	go, come	go, come	
——, ἐρῶ, ——, εἴρηκα, εἴρημαι, ἐρρήθην (8)	say, tell (of), speak (of)		be said, be spoken
ἔχω, ἕξω/σχήσω, ἔσχον, ἔσχηκα, -ἔσχημαι, —— (4)	have, hold; inhabit, occupy; *intrans.*, be able (+inf.); be (+ adv.)	hold on to, cling to	be held; be inhabited, be occupied
ζάω, ζήσω, ——, ——, ——, —— (8)	be alive, live		
ζηλόω, ζηλώσω, ἐζήλωσα, ἐζήλωκα, ——, —— (7)	emulate; envy		be deemed fortunate
ἥκω, ἥξω, ——, ——, ——, —— (5)	have come; be present		

Verb	Active	Middle (future only)	Passive
θνῄσκω, θανοῦμαι, ἔθανον, τέθνηκα, ——, (8)	die / *perfect*, be dead	die	
κτείνω, κτενῶ, ἔκτεινα, ——, ——, (8)	kill		
λαμβάνω, λήψομαι, ἔλαβον, εἴληφα, εἴλημμαι, ἐλήφθην (9)	take, seize; understand; receive	take hold (of) (+ gen.)	be taken, be seized; be understood; be received
λέγω, λέξω, ἔλεξα/εἶπον, ——, λέλεγμαι, ἐλέχθην (3)	say; speak (of), tell (of), recount; call	R	be said; be spoken, be recounted; be called
μανθάνω, μαθήσομαι, ἔμαθον, μεμάθηκα, ——, —— (5)	learn; understand	*(future only)* learn; understand	R
μάχομαι, μαχοῦμαι, ἐμαχεσάμην, ——, μεμάχημαι, —— (8)		fight (against) (+ dat.)	
μέλλω, μελλήσω, ἐμέλλησα, ——, ——, —— (3)	intend, be about, be likely		
μένω, μενῶ, ἔμεινα, μεμένηκα, ——, —— (9)	remain, stay; *trans.*, await		
νικάω, νικήσω, ἐνίκησα, νενίκηκα, νενίκημαι, ἐνικήθην (4)	conquer, defeat; prevail (over), win	R	be conquered, be defeated
οἶδα, εἴσομαι, ——, ——, ——, —— (9)	know	*(future only)* know	
οἴομαι/οἶμαι, οἰήσομαι, ——, ——, ——, ᾠήθην (8)		think, suppose, believe	*(aorist only)* think, suppose, believe
ὁράω, ὄψομαι, εἶδον, ἑόρακα/ἑώρακα, ἑόραμαι/ὦμμαι, ὤφθην (6)	see	R *(except in future)* see	be seen
πάρειμι, παρέσομαι, ——, ——, ——, —— (7)	be present, be near; be ready	*(future only)* be present, be near; be ready	

Verb	Active	Middle (future only)	Passive
πάσχω, πείσομαι, ἔπαθον, πέπονθα, ——— (7)	suffer; experience	suffer; experience	
παύω, παύσω, ἔπαυσα, πέπαυκα, πέπαυμαι, ἐπαύθην (3)	stop (trans.)	stop (intrans.), cease	be stopped
πείθω, πείσω, ἔπεισα, πέπεικα, πέπεισμαι, ἐπείσθην (3)	persuade	obey; heed; believe (+ dat.)	be persuaded
πέμπω, πέμψω, ἔπεμψα, πέπομφα, πέπεμμαι, ἐπέμφθην (3)	send		be sent
ποιέω, ποιήσω, ἐποίησα, πεποίηκα, πεποίημαι, ἐποιήθην (4)	make; do	make; do; deem, consider	be made; be done
πολεμέω, πολεμήσω, ἐπολέμησα, πεπολέμηκα, ———, ἐπολεμήθην (4)	make war (upon), be at war (with) (+ dat.); quarrel; fight		have war made on (oneself), be treated as an enemy
πράττω, πράξω, ἔπραξα, πέπρᾱχα (trans.)/πέπρᾱγα (intrans.), πέπρᾱγμαι, ἐπρᾱχθην (7)	do; bring about; practice; manage; intrans., fare	R	be done; be brought about; be practiced; be managed
προσέχω, προσέξω, προσέσχον, προσέσχηκα, ———, ——— (7)	hold to; turn to, apply	R	R
τελευτάω, τελευτήσω, ἐτελεύτησα, τετελεύτηκα, ———, ἐτελευτήθην (4)	accomplish, end, finish; die		R
τῑμάω, τῑμήσω, ἐτίμησα, τετίμηκα, τετίμημαι, ἐτῑμήθην (4)	honor	value, deem worthy	be honored; be deemed worthy
ὑπολαμβάνω, ὑπολήψομαι, ὑπέλαβον, ὑπείληφα, ὑπείλημμαι, ὑπελήφθην (9)	take up, reply; suppose	(future only) take up, reply; suppose	be taken up; be supposed
*φάσκω, ———, ———, ———, ———, ——— (8)	say, assert	R	
φέρω, οἴσω, ἤνεγκα/ἤνεγκον, ἐνήνοχα, ἐνήνεγμαι, ἠνέχθην (9)	bring, bear, carry; endure	carry away with oneself; win	be borne, be brought, be carried; be endured

Verb	Active	Middle	Passive
		(*future only*)	
φεύγω, φεύξομαι, ἔφυγον, πέφευγα, —— , —— (9)	flee, avoid, escape	flee, avoid, escape	
φημί, φήσω, ἔφησα, —— , —— , —— (8)	say, assert	R	
φιλέω, φιλήσω, ἐφίλησα, πεφίληκα, πεφίλημαι, ἐφιλήθην (4)	love, like; be accustomed, be fond of (+ inf.)	R	be loved, be liked
χαίρω, χαιρήσω, —— , κεχάρηκα, —— , ἐχάρην (7)	rejoice (in), enjoy		(*aorist only*) rejoice (in), enjoy
χρή, χρῆσται, —— , —— , —— , —— (8)	it is necessary, ought		

VERBS INTRODUCING
INDIRECT STATEMENT

	ὅτι/ὡς with a Finite Verb	Subject Accusative with an Infinitive	Subject Accusative with a Supplementary Participle
ἀκούω	x	x	x
δῆλόν ἐστι(ν)	x		
δηλόω	x	x	x
——, ἐρῶ	x	x	
λέγω	x	x	
μανθάνω	x		x
οἶδα	x	x	x
οἴομαι/οἶμαι		x	
ὁράω	x		x
πείθω	x	x	x
ὑπολαμβάνω	x	x	
φάσκω		x	
φημί		x	

GENERAL INDEX

English Index

Greek Index